DISPATCHES FROM THE ARAB SPRING

Paul Amar and Vijay Prashad
Editors

Dispatches from the Arab Spring

Understanding the New Middle East

University of Minnesota Press
Minneapolis
London

First published in the United States in 2013 by the University of Minnesota Press

Published by the University of Minnesota Press
111 Third Avenue South, Suite 290
Minneapolis, MN 55401-2520
http://www.upress.umn.edu

Library of Congress Cataloging-in-Publication Data
Dispatches from the Arab spring : understanding the new Middle East / Paul Amar and Vijay Prashad, Editors.
    Includes bibliographical references and index.
    ISBN 978-0-8166-8998-9 (hc)   ISBN 978-0-8166-9012-1 (pb)
    1. Arab Spring, 2010– 2. Arab countries—Politics and government—21st century. 3. Middle East—Politics and government—21st century. I. Amar, Paul (Paul Edouard), 1968– II. Prashad, Vijay.
    JQ1850.A91D58 2013
    909'.097492708312—dc23

                                                                    2013018884

20 19 18 17 16 15 14 13   10 9 8 7 6 5 4 3 2 1

Contents

Introduction

Revolutionizing the Middle East

PAUL AMAR AND VIJAY PRASHAD

> Imperious despot, insolent in strife,
> Lover of ruin, enemy of life!
> You mock the anguish of an impotent land
> Whose people's blood has stained your tyrant hand,
> And desecrate the magic of this earth,
> Sowing your thorns, to bring despair to birth.
>
> —Abul-Qasim al-Shabbi, *Ila Tughat al-Alam*

IT IS TIME TO RETHINK how we all apprehend the Arab world. The myriad revolts and revolutions of the so-called Arab Spring unleashed forces of emancipation and spirits of social justice that swept across the region with unprecedented speed, ferocity, and joy. As these epochal movements faced violent devolutions and frustrating detours, horizons of transformation remained in question. But there is no doubt that the ways we in the region and around the world learn about, report on, and appreciate Arab peoples and politics were definitively revolutionized. In this light, this volume reintroduces global publics to the Arab world and dispenses with old paradigms of understanding. We set aside "authoritarianism studies" that depicted governments as impermeable monoliths. We dispose of the "political sociology of the Arab Street" that represented popular movements as mindless, reactive mobs. And we dismiss the "Arab exceptionalism" that for decades conceived of the region as culturally unfit for the cultivation of democratic politics or social justice claims. Like the dictators of so many Arab countries, these regimes of perception have been toppled, and in their places we offer fresh starts. We offer modes of engagement and analysis inspired by the methodology of revolt, and our chapters are authored by activist scholars whose writings pulse with the rhythms of revolt. We provide a comprehensive reintroduction to the entire region, not just those countries and spectacles that most captivated the media. Our aim is to weave comprehension of new forms of domination and resistance into the whole cloth of social history, political geography, cultural creativity, global political economy, and power politics. We insist that the study of the Arab world is no longer limited to grasping the intractability of imperial or colonial or bellicose pasts: it is turning to recognize the exciting imminence of global futures.

After the match of revolt was first lit in Tunisia in December 2010, flames moved rapidly across North Africa to the Gulf states and onward into West Asia. Urban centers and rural enclaves of Egypt, Bahrain, Yemen, Libya, and Syria filled with everyday people who were willing to sacrifice their lives for a new dispensation. The guns of the regimes came out rapidly, unwilling to let go of the way things were and, to their minds, should always be. Every ruling elite believes itself eternal and, even if secular, in its place by divine right. Every ruling elite believes, as well, that those who rise up are either deluded or drugged, proxies for some global chess game that they do not understand. But the self-immolation of Mohamed Bouazizi set the dial to Courage, and, despite the gunfire and the tear gas, the crowds paralyzed their rulers and opened a new historical time for the region.

This remarkable set of events has been called the Arab Spring, in honor of the annual rebirth of nature after the winter thaw. But there is nothing cyclical about these protests, nor is there anything natural. These are the products of a set of unique events, based on local political grievances and global structural forces, and they are the products of human bravery and ingenuity. Our book recognizes the currency of the expression *Arab Spring* but styles these transformations more in terms of a new Arab Revolt, al-Thawra al-Arabiyya, a nod certainly to the great uprisings of 1916–18 and 1936–39, and in terms of a new Arab Revolution, as it is referred to by peoples and parties within the region today. This term hearkens back to the Nasserite phase of 1952–67, but it also reflects the fact that various mobilizations in the Arab world today are referencing, in contentious and contradictory ways, the Iranian Revolution of 1979, Eastern Europe's civic revolutions of 1989–92, South America's antimilitary uprisings of the 1980s, "Pink Tide" new left populisms of the 1990s, and Bolivarian revolutions of the 2000s.

Each term—*spring, revolt, revolution*—has its advocates and its detractors. The term *Arab* also has its limitations, particularly when the Revolt settled into Libya and across the Maghreb. There non-Arab Imazighen/Amazigh people (known derogatorily as the Berber) forced a crucial part of the uprising, and one of their grievances is that they were discriminated against by the Arabs.

Arab Spring, nonetheless, has become a shorthand term for the exhilarating show of force of suppressed social classes against the despotic regimes that governed from the Maghreb to the Mashriq, from one end of the geography that holds Arabic-speaking peoples to the other. But what is it that galvanized them, and why did their revolt happen as if in a tidal wave? How do we understand the initial moment of 2010–11, and the time that follows? How do we grasp the local dynamics, the hasty removal of such long-standing leaders (Qaddafi, forty-two years; Mubarak, thirty years; Ben Ali, twenty-three years), their security states willing to dispense with them when confronted by largely nonviolent protesters? How do we make sense of the imperial retreat in the face of these protests, an imperial power bloc from the Atlantic world and its Gulf Arab emirs, whose tentacles suffocated the dreams of the Arabs with maniacal intensity? How do we make sense of the restoration of the older imperial power bloc, the Atlantic world with its Gulf Arab clients and Israel, using the Trojan horses of the International Monetary Fund and humanitarian intervention to make inroads into North Africa and West Asia?

The retreat came momentarily in the early part of 2011, and then counterrevolution found ways to reassert itself (only provisionally, we sense) in the Arabian Peninsula and then in Libya and Syria. In Egypt and across the region, newly legitimated Islamist leaders surprised many observers by tucking themselves in swiftly and comfortably with

Western diplomats, Israeli security officials, Gulf investors, and IMF bankers. But the Arab Spring, for us, is a dynamic for freedom and justice that transcends these significant moments of retrenchment. It always has been a process not just of toppling headmen but also of revealing repressive structures and making power blocs show their cards. The Revolt's adversaries were not simply the exiled or killed leaders (Ben Ali, Mubarak, Qaddafi) but also the members of a power bloc that had been consolidated over the course of the past six decades: the United States and the Europeans, the Gulf Arab monarchies, and, of course, Israel. They could not protect their friends (Ben Ali and Mubarak), so they had to accede to their departure. Nevertheless, they did not give in. The IMF swooped in, and Washington allowed Riyadh and Doha to act as brokers for its outreach to the political Islamists: tentative nods and smiles reassured the old power elites that the old ways might be able to continue. The Arab Spring did thaw the frozen soil of politics by making adversaries apparent and alternatives tangible, unleashing processes of solidarity, organization, consciousness-raising, and institutional transformation that will have long-term impacts.

Regional actors also inserted themselves. Turkey and Iran sought to claim the mantle of the revolts for their own ambitions, as did the Gulf Arabs and a resurgent Egypt. Initially their goal was to propose themselves as the models for the new social forces, with the Turks offering their modern Islamism as an example, the Iranians their own historical breakthrough from 1979 as the spur, and the Gulf Arabs their money and their fealty to modes of more conservative Islamism (with the range running from the less accommodative Saudis to the less harsh Qataris). Egypt, the self-identified center of the Arab world, had its own aspirations, and when the Syrian conflict seemed irresolvable, it tried to offer its leadership over the disparate regional actors (including such adversaries as Iran and Saudi Arabia). The Arab Revolt and its spring thaw were, then, not just the emergence of new social forces within nation-states but also the catalytic arrival of the regional entities who wanted to act in their neighborhood absent the older Great Powers of the United States, Europe, and Russia.

To us, the larger arc of the Arab Spring has at least three moments. These are not chronologically distinct stages, going from the first to the third, but moments with different temporalities, with one moment in advance and another in retreat, and then the order changed. These moments indicate the political flux that continues in the region, with no one set of social forces yet in a position of dominance. The Revolution, therefore, continues.

Moment 1: the Arab Spring, the jubilant rise of the people of Tunisia and Egypt, with expectations of a rapid collapse of the despotic regimes from the Atlas to the Qandil Mountains. The departure of Ben Ali and Mubarak are emblematic, but so too is the resignation of Yemen's Saleh. Few expected that these authoritarian leaders and their families would be forced out. The regimes did not depart, but the apex of the kleptocracy was certainly removed. That Arab Spring continues, unfurling banners of hope among the demonstrators in Amman, Jordan, and in the Occupied Territories of the Palestinians—unfinished endeavors linked to the hopefulness of the spring of 2011.

Moment 2: the Arab Winter, the entry of the Gulf Cooperation Council (primarily Saudi troops) into Bahrain and NATO missions (primarily funded by Qatar) over the skies of Libya, with the irrepressible repression in Syria and the Israeli bombardment of Gaza, with its land grab in the West Bank. Expectations of the renaissance withered, even after the fall of the Qaddafi regime in Libya. Fears of civil war and retribution lurked at every turn, sentiments that were not present after the fall of Ben Ali and Mubarak. Older animosities took advantage of the stalled social development: sectarianism reared its head and threatened to eclipse the forward motion of the Arab Spring. The bloodletting in Syria and Israel's wars on the Palestinians menaced the reinvigoration of the ancien régime.

Moment 3: the Arab Resurgence, the new regimes' efforts with the creation of democracy (in the form of halting and tightly circumscribed elections) and the holding off of the policies of neoliberal consumerism foisted on them by a relentless IMF and the Atlantic powers (now emboldened by their Libyan adventure and by their rhetorical flourish over the bloodbath in Syria). Strikes and demonstrations returned with a vengeance to become commonplace in Egypt and Tunisia, in Yemen and Bahrain. Political Islamists began to substitute their antagonistic relationship to the regime with disputed programs for governance.

Absent an alternative agenda and a robust political policy, these new Islamist regimes floundered. Liberal formations made their slow strides, although many of these came to terms with the fact that they would not be able to create a mass base and would have to hope for populist figures to carry their standards forward. A nascent Left emerged, buoyed by the working-class strikes and by the gestures of anti-imperialism that made their appearance as well as by the presence of new social forces that bespoke a new social environment on such issues as family and sexuality. What we saw in this moment were political forces trying at record speed to create spaces in their societies for active and energetic political debate and practice, something suspended during the bureaucratic despotisms that these forces were trying to break down.

Dispatches from the Arab Spring: Understanding the New Middle East lays out a tentative map for the future, hewed of a rough comparative agenda for introducing the region to students, the public, and researchers, for tracking new actors, structural economic formations, and political possibilities. The book collects writings by some of the world's most respected intellectuals who have turned their attention to the region. They are deeply aware of the national and local dynamics, schooled in the world of detail—where the devil lurks but so do optimism and hope. Their analytical gaze zeros in not just on protest spectacles in capital cities but also on the brave uprisings in Sidi Bouzid and Mahalla, in Karzakan and Misrata, looking for the clashes between different social classes and at the emergence of new social identities in the midst of these inspiring struggles. The scholars and journalists who contribute chapters here are fully aware of the debates in the halls of Paris and London, and of course in Washington and Moscow, aware too of the imperial logics that constrain the horizon in the towns of North Africa and West Asia. The essays are written in national terms because we are of the view that the nation remains a fundamental container for the aspirations of the many, who seek justice in their constitutions and in their legacies of national unity. Somewhere between democracy and equality lies the path to the future, for it is the thrust for political rights and socioeconomic rights that envisions a new culture, a new radical imagination.

Dispatches from the Arab Spring takes its word *from* very seriously. Much has been made of the trigger role of social media (Facebook,

Twitter) and of President Obama's 2009 Cairo speech. But this is trivial when one considers the long history of rebellion in the region and the much more recent history of unrest against the policies of neoliberal consumerism. These are revolts that come *from* the region and are consequently not revolts that are plucked by outsiders, even as the impact of these alien forces (IMF pressure for neoliberal policies, U.S. pressure to prosecute the War on Terror) tried to smother the lives of the many. Our authors offer us the stories from below that give us a sense of where these revolts came from, nudged on in the conjuncture by each other but driven by the structural forces that affect each society and each nation differently. To articulate these differences, our authors take us on a tour of the history of the nations to help us better understand the sociology of the revolts.

The Arab Spring was an opening, a stage in a long-term struggle. The agreement in the states that have thrown off their despots is to create a liberal democracy: neither a religious state nor a military state. The intelligence apparatus has not been dismantled, nor have the commitments to neoliberal economic policy been challenged yet. The political Islamists who have taken charge do not have an adequate economic program and have largely adopted the neoliberal economic agenda for lack of anything else. Apart from modest populist transfer payments to the poor (and even that seems improbable), it is not likely that the Islamists or the liberals will be willing to challenge the IMF and the banks for a different policy direction, toward the creation, for instance, of a more robust social wage and inclusive health and education system; to create a social order and security regime committed to freedom and justice; to make democracy substantive and participatory, not just a game of electoral manipulation; to assure gender, ethnic, and cultural justice beyond the divide-and-rule models of identity politics and religious cantonization; and to ensure the right to a dignified life.

This time bore witness to brave advances and explosive new formations, as well as to enormous structural challenges and forces of backlash. It is in the gap between these that new mobilizations, solidarities, resistances, revived histories, and state-transforming processes emerged, promising that the spirits and structures of the Arab Spring would continue to animate revolt and revolution.

Tunisia

NOURI GANA

ON FEBRUARY 4, 2011, British television personality and journalist Piers Morgan interviewed the former prime minister of Tunisia, Mohamed Ghannouchi, on his CNN show *Piers Morgan Tonight*.[1] Here is an excerpt of the short interview:

> PIERS MORGAN: Mr. Prime Minister, can I ask you, have you been surprised by the events in Egypt and do you believe that President Mubarak should now go immediately?
>
> MOHAMED GHANNOUCHI: We are worrying about our own country. Our revolution is unique. It was caused by the young. Facebook and Twitter were the levers. It's been held in a peaceful way. Today we were able to break with the past thanks to what we have in our DNA. Tunisia, as you know, is an exporting country, but we do not pretend that we export revolutions. We have friendly relationships with all peoples, regardless of the region where they live.

Ghannouchi might have tactfully, and not without a touch of humor, avoided commenting on Egypt's internal affairs at a time when Tunisia was caught in the midst of its own mass revolt as millions of protesters in Egypt's Tahrir Square raged against then president Mubarak. Diplomacy obliges, of course. What he could have possibly said, however, as a proud Tunisian and first prime minister after the ouster of Zine El Abidine Ben Ali on January 14, 2011, was the following: "Tunisia is known for exporting olive oil and *degletnour* dates but is pleased to add *revolution* as one of its principal items of export." It could have been argued, of course, that revolution had become in the year 2011 Tunisia's only around-the-clock, never-out-of-stock, and free-of-charge export item par excellence. It may without exaggeration have been equally argued that the Tunisian revolution offered a promissory exemplar of nonviolent democratization—really, nothing less than a Marshall Plan for fostering homegrown democracy across the Arab world.

Never before in the history of the modern Arab world had a grass-roots uprising toppled an entrenched dictator of Ben Ali's caliber and longevity without recourse to any established ideology, social movement, or political party or to foreign intervention, which has continued to be bandied about as the only midwife to real democracy in the Arab world. Never before had the will of the Tunisian people, for so long expropriated or trodden upon and denigrated, lived up to its latent potential of courting the impossible and led the way to revolutionary change not only in Tunisia but also across the entire region. The deposition of Hosni Mubarak, for instance, did not start on January 25, 2011, as is commonly documented, but rather on December 17, 2010, when a young street vendor, Mohamed Bouazizi, immolated himself in front of the municipality headquarters in Sidi Bouzid, Tunisia, and sparked a series of protests against Ben Ali's regime that soon reached the capital, Tunis, and from there spread across the Arab world.

This is not to say that Tunisia was by any means riper for a popular revolution than Egypt, Libya, Yemen, Syria, or any other Arab country, for that matter. But since most of the popular uprisings that followed elsewhere in the Arab world are in one way or another indebted to the pioneering role of Tunisia, it is perhaps worthwhile to inquire about the origins of the Tunisian revolution. After all, the fact that Tunisia has played a leading role in the revolutionary and democratizing current that is sweeping the Arab world should not be taken lightly given the extent to which Tunisia was marginalized in Arab affairs, particularly because of the unbendingly secularist and gradualist philosophy of its first president, Habib Bourguiba, whose injunction that Arabs accept the 1947 United Nations partition plan for Palestine (which handed most of historic Palestine to European Jewish settlers) earned him, among other things, many enemies and unpleasant insults. So marginal was Tunisia's role in Arab affairs that the nation became in the Arab imagination the equivalent of a strange land folded in the bosom of Francophonie. No wonder, then, that when the Palestinian Liberation Organization (PLO) headquarters relocated to Tunisia in 1982, in the wake of the Sabra and Shatila massacres, the whole episode was perceived as a severe punishment of the PLO, given that Tunisia had by then become a stable symbol of a land of banishment par excellence.

It will perhaps go down as one of the ironies of history that a small nation such as Tunisia, at the margins of Arab affairs, would—from its very position of marginality—so profoundly transform Arab contemporaneity. For the former prime minister and Ben Ali's man, Mohamed Ghannouchi, Tunisians had it in their DNA to rise up against tyranny. Yet, was Tunisia indeed meant to happen? What inspired and incited Tunisians to take to the streets in protest against the massive level of youth unemployment, high food and fuel prices, state coercion and corruption—in short, all the by-products of the neoliberal policies of Ben Ali and his cronies? Tunisia submitted to a foreign form of protectorship for seventy-five years and then to an internal or indigenous form of dictatorship for fifty-five years. It was a French protectorate from 1881 to 1956. Unlike Algeria—which was under direct French control and was indeed settled by more than a million French colons (the so-called *pieds-noirs,* or Black Legs) and annexed administratively to France—Tunisia was mainly ruled by France through the Beys, the representatives of the Ottoman Empire or what was left of it since 1917 (when it collapsed after almost five centuries of uninterrupted rule over the Arab world with the exception of Morocco). This double colonization, so to speak, is important because it would pave the way to proxy colonialism, or neocolonialism proper, after Tunisia's independence in 1956.

In the very same period when the United States had no fewer than ten successive presidents, Tunisia was ruled by Habib Bourguiba, a self-professed nationalist and francophone secularist who sought to hitch the wagon of the young nation to the train of European modernity both socially and economically. While his era was marked by laudable developments in the areas of education and women's rights, unmatched by any other Arab nation, his reign was unbendingly autocratic. He established a strict one-party rule and gradually but steadily tightened his grip on power, becoming president for life in 1975, a position he held until he was suddenly deposed in a bloodless palace coup led by then prime minister Ben Ali in 1987. After serving in various positions—as director of military security, secretary of state of national security, minister of national security, and minister of the interior, among others—Ben Ali was prime minister for only five weeks before he invoked Article 57 of the Tunisian constitution, which stipulates that the prime minister should succeed the president in the event of the president's death, resignation, or (as was the case with Bourguiba, based on a medical report signed by seven doctors) physical and mental inability to carry out the duties of the office of the presidency.

Since November 7, 1987, Ben Ali had amended and re-amended the constitution in such a way as to enable himself to remain in power, and this is partly why some commentators referred to his twenty-three-year rule over Tunisia as "Bourguibism without Bourguiba." As U.S. ambassador to Tunisia William J. Hudson reported in a cable dated September 1, 2006, "One of the standard jokes about President Zine el Abidine Ben Ali (usually delivered only half in jest) is that he has three goals for his presidency: to stay in power; to stay in power; and to stay in power" (*Guardian* 2011). On January 14, 2011, however, massive popular protests forced Ben Ali to flee to Saudi Arabia. At the very same time that Ben Ali was suspended in the air looking for asylum, his prime minister, Mohamed Ghannouchi, declared himself acting president based on Article 56 of the constitution, which stipulates that a sitting president may delegate his powers to the prime minister in case of temporary disability. But because Ben Ali had never actually delegated his powers to Ghannouchi before his unceremonious exit, the constitutional assembly met on the following day, January 15, and adopted Article 57 of the constitution, which stipulates that the president of the Chamber of Deputies becomes president of the nation should there be a vacancy in the office of the president. Fouad Mebazaa then served as acting president and ordered Ghannouchi and then Béji Caïd Essebsi to form successive interim governments.

There is no need here to go into more details from a constitution that had been heavily amended by Ben Ali and then became officially obsolete; it is depressingly ironic to note, however, that a country that had only two presidents in a period of fifty-five years should switch from one president to another in a matter of hours and from one prime minister to another in a month and a half. Not only that, but the interim government was shuffled and reshuffled more than once following two sit-in protests in the Qasbah Government Square that called for the banning of Ben Ali's ruling party and the eviction of all its members from the transitional government. Above all, the protests called for the dissolution of the formidable state security apparatus ("RCD dégage" ["RCD out"], protesters shouted) and the formation of a National Constituent Assembly to write a new constitution for the country (see Gana 2011).

The National Constituent Assembly elections took place on October 23, 2011, and an interim coalition government was formed, with Mustapha Ben Jafar (from Ettakatol, or the Democratic Forum for Labour and Liberties) as president of the National Constituent Assembly, Moncef Marzouki (from CPR, or the Congress for the Republic) as president of the republic, and Hamadi Jebali (from Al-Nahda, or the Renaissance Party) as prime minister. While the left-leaning Ettakatol and center-left CPR were widely viewed as variably moderate secular parties, Al-Nahda was predominantly viewed as an Islamist party despite its insistence on moderation in its overall religious and civic dispositions and policies. Apart from writing a new constitution instituting the second republic, the tripartite coalition government (aka troika) had been assigned the task of governing as well as that of holding new elections, either presidential or parliamentary (or a bit of both), depending on what the new constitution would stipulate.

The question that I would like to ask and try to answer, however schematically, henceforth is as follows: If Tunisians were this impatient with the interim government of Mohamed Ghannouchi and then with that of Béji Caïd Essebsi, not to mention their impatience with the troika, why did they wait for fifty-five years before they rose up against the successive authoritarian regimes of Bourguiba and Ben Ali? In other words, from where did the popular uprising that forced Ben Ali to flee the country on January 14 emerge?

As Mohamed Ghannouchi mentioned to Piers Morgan in the aforementioned interview, the revolution was instigated by the youth—"Facebook and Twitter were the levers." Little wonder, then, that the Tunisian revolution was referred to early on as the "Internet Revolution," the "Facebook Revolution," and the "Twitter Revolution" before it was extended a host of other names, including the "WikiLeaks Revolution," the "Al Jazeera Revolution," the "Jasmine Revolution," the "Dignity Revolution," the "Sidi Bouzid Revolution," and the "Bouazizi Revolution." Obviously, there is no gainsaying the fact that social media and Al Jazeera played a pivotal role in relaying reports of dispersed protests and agitations in the southwestern regions of Tunisia at a time when mainstream media were deliberately oblivious to what was going on in Sidi Bouzid, Talla, and Gasserine. Moreover, the crucial importance of the combined effort of social media and Al Jazeera in finding and circulating the news lay in channeling—or actually *channelizing*—them toward a single affective disposition to civil disobedience. The emergent sense of discontent, in other words, had become—thanks to the mediating role of Facebook, Twitter, and Al Jazeera—nothing less than an incitement to revolt. What was more important by far was that once the sociopolitical grievances at the origin of the revolt in Sidi Bouzid started to unravel and travel to neighboring cities, and from there to major cities such as Sfax and Sousse before reaching Tunis by the end of December 2010, the role of social media, cell phone technology, and Al Jazeera became key to the sustenance and continuation of the protests, which led to Ben Ali's deposition.

In the weeks that followed, Facebook became de facto the gathering space par excellence for *mobilizing* Tunisians and for organizing and coordinating sit-in protests in the Qasbah Government Square and elsewhere across the country. The Facebook community became in the postrevolutionary moment markedly divided and polarized, not to say stigmatized, especially for sharing false information, using foul language, and disseminating baseless allegations while it continued to gather full-fledged oppositional forces, coming together in virtual space to oppose the status quo. This space was dynamic at times in the ways its different participants tirelessly pointed out and critiqued the actions of the interim government and the opposition parties alike. But many Tunisians eventually felt dismayed and disenchanted with Facebook and social media writ large. The same could be said about Al Jazeera, which became very much associated in the imagination of a large segment of Tunisians (especially from the opposition parties) with the role Qatar was increasingly playing in Tunisia (and elsewhere in the Arab world) as a proxy for American hegemony.[2] Be that as it may, the fact of the matter was that social media and Al Jazeera, however important a role they might have played in the Tunisian revolution, could have by no means replaced the actors on the ground, the actual demonstrators and protesters who stormed the streets and braved live ammunition to rid themselves and all Tunisians of Ben Ali and his mafia ring. After all, both Facebook and Al Jazeera had been around for quite some time by 2010 and must have had ample opportunities to start a revolution in Tunisia long before if they were indeed capable of doing so.

This might not be the case with Julian Assange's subsequent whistle-blowing Web site, WikiLeaks, which publicized diplomatic cables that exposed the opulent lifestyle and widespread web of corruption of Ben Ali and his wife and their extended families (the Trabelsis). For instance, one cable dating back to November 17, 2007, chronicles Ben Ali's decision to revoke Suha Arafat's Tunisian citizenship after she had a falling-out with his wife, Leila Trabelsi. The cable includes Suha Arafat's perspective on her ouster from Tunisia and details the criminal and illegal means whereby all her properties in the country had been "confiscated, even by falsifying documents transferring ownership."[3] The cable concludes with Mrs. Arafat pointing out to the U.S. ambassador, Robert F. Godec, that while Ben Ali was totally absorbed in battling cancer, his wife and her family were stealing everything of value in the country with impunity. Elsewhere, Arafat claimed that she was one of the first victims of the dictatorship and that "Leila Ben Ali was the real President of Tunisia for twenty-three years" (Ben Ghazi 2011).

Notwithstanding the crucial importance of the likes of this leaked cable in stirring the outrage of Tunisians and their contempt for the Trabelsis, WikiLeaks can be said to have added in the end no more than mere details to what every Tunisian already knew about the president and his wife and the Trabelsi mafiosi clans in particular, who were the worst offenders. What I want to suggest here is that there is no master narrative of the Tunisian revolution and certainly not a theory of its origins that might explain adequately, let alone justifiably, what happened on January 14, 2011. Neither social media and Al Jazeera nor WikiLeaks can fully account for the Tunisian people's grassroots revolt. So what else could have started this popular uprising?

Most retrospective narratives of the events that led to Ben Ali's deposition have stressed the catalyzing role of Mohamed Bouazizi's self-immolation. There are conflicting reports of Bouazizi's story, but the majority agree that he was a fruit and vegetable street vendor who had to drop out of high school to go to work to provide for his family. He was constantly harassed by the local police because he did not have a vendor's permit and, allegedly, because he did not make enough money to offer bribes to the officers. On December 16, 2010, the police confiscated Bouazizi's cart and electronic scale, and, what is worse, they insulted and mistreated him. A municipality worker allegedly slapped him across the face, although the worker, Fedia Hamdi, denied having done so on multiple occasions after her release from prison (Totten 2012). The following day, Bouazizi went to the governor's office to complain, but when the latter refused to see or listen to him, he bought a can of gasoline, doused himself in front of the municipal headquarters of Sidi Bouzid, and set himself ablaze.

In the wake of Bouazizi's self-immolation, protesters started gathering regularly in downtown Sidi Bouzid and in front of local government buildings. Although these early protesters initially shouted slogans making social demands for "shughl, hurriya, karāma wataniyya" (work, freedom, and national dignity), they soon started to be more daring and called upon the "yā Trabelsī yā haqīr, khellīil-khubza lil-faqīr" (mean Trabelsis [to] spare some bread for the poor) before they took on a more openly political bent and asked for the ouster of Ben Ali altogether: "Khubz wa-ma' wa-Ben Ali lā" (We can live on bread and water, but no more Ben Ali). The gradual evolution of the slogans from generic ones about work, liberty, and dignity to more specific ones that not only targeted individuals such as the Trabelsis but also pointed toward the way out (i.e., the ouster of Ben Ali) had proven of crucial importance to the process of mobilizing protesters and inciting revolt; not infrequently, protesters would be more inclined to join protests against specific individuals (such as Leila Trabelsi, who was denounced as "Leila al-hajjama, sarraqit flous leitama" [Leila the hairdresser, the thief of orphans' money]) than elitist protests against neoliberalism, authoritarianism, cronyism, abuses of human rights, and so on.

Initially, local activists and syndicalists in Sidi Bouzid deliberately promoted an adapted version of Bouazizi's story that portrayed him as an unemployed university graduate in an attempt, first, to capitalize on and mobilize a new disgruntled majority of unemployed university graduates (accounting for 250,000 of the 750,000 job seekers in the country), and second, to counter the disparaging campaign of pro–Ben Ali pundits who had left no stone unturned to psychologize, privatize, and discredit the sociopolitical grievances at the origin of Bouazizi's act.[4] Besides, this tactical lie (in a stockpile of lies circulated during the revolution) proved of crucial importance for the early protesters, as it helped them win the sympathy and solidarity of Tunisians and simultaneously of the international public at large. The intelligibility of the slogans—their accessible content and clear target—encouraged more and more people to take to the streets. When the news of Bouazizi's self-immolation and ensuing protests in Sidi Bouzid was downloaded on Facebook and on YouTube by field bloggers, the reports went viral; no sooner were they picked up by urban bloggers and Facebookers, and then by Al Jazeera, than the wave of protests quickly reached the major cities in Tunisia and eventually hit the capital, Tunis. What Bouazizi committed was not so much a suicidal act as a suicidal protest: the difference cannot be overemphasized, as the former pertains to despair and resignation and the latter to defiance and hope. It is important to note here that Bouazizi could have killed himself in the privacy of his room if his goal had indeed been suicide for suicide's sake, as pro-government pontificators have argued in an attempt to privatize and discredit the sociopolitical grievances at the origin of his act. He could also have chosen a less painful means of suicide. However, he chose to set himself alight in the public square and in front of those who treated him with indignity and injustice.

While both symbolic and tragic, even Bouazizi's self-immolation could not by itself have triggered a revolution of this magnitude, which not only sent shockwaves throughout Tunisia but also swiftly spread to other countries in the Arab world. The fact that the many copycat burnings that followed Bouazizi's act in such countries as Algeria, Mauritania, and Morocco—and that continued for days to come—had not so far resulted in revolutions in those places made it less likely that Bouazizi's act per se should be located retrospectively at the very origin of the Tunisian revolution. Moreover, Bouazizi's self-immolation could have been thrust into oblivion as had that of another street vendor before him, Abdesslem Trimech, who set himself ablaze inside the city hall in Monastir on March 3, 2010, after his fruit cart was confiscated by the police and his demand to meet with the city mayor was rebuffed. This is not to say that Bouazizi's self-immolation was not inspiring and empowering, much less to say it was not an incitement to action, but rather to maintain that the protests that followed his action must have capitalized on long-standing rebellious instincts that Ben Ali's police state repressed but could not fully eradicate. Otherwise, how could Bouazizi's death have mobilized so many, so quickly?

I am pointing here toward a genealogical and polydirectional approach to the Tunisian revolution, one that can take stock of both the long-term and the short-term factors at its origin. The short-term factors would, of course, include such aforementioned immediate triggers as social media and Al Jazeera as well as WikiLeaks and Bouazizi's self-immolation. The long-term factors include not only the neoliberal economic restructuring of Tunisia in the mid-1990s and the culture of corruption it fostered but also the long-standing U.S. and French foreign policies and their deliberate support for autocratic regimes for the sake of stability. Above all, if the Tunisian nonviolent revolution attested to anything, it attested to the longevity of the traditions of political dissent and civil disobedience in decolonial and postcolonial Tunisia despite Ben Ali's transformation (or rather disfiguration) of the country into a gigantic surveillance camp.

The question here becomes not so much how Bouazizi's suicide protest sparked a popular revolution (which at this point has been the most-traveled road of inquiry about the Tunisian and Arab revolutions), but how a popular revolution sparked by Bouazizi's suicide protest was indeed the materialization of a cultural and critical capital that had largely been determined by a collective tradition of dissenting practices. The tradition of cultural critique dates back at least to the decolonial struggle against French colonialism in the 1930s and 1940s and to the formation of the intellectual Against the Wall Group (Jamā' ittahta al-sūr), which brought together a heterogeneous collection of intellectuals and helped raise awareness about the colonial condition through regular meetings and debates organized in popular cafés. From among the most important intellectual figures of this preindependence period, I should name at least Tunisia's foremost national poet, Abul-Qasim al-Shabbi, as well as Tunisia's foremost national playwright, Mahmoud al-Messadi. Both al-Shabbi and al-Messadi wrote about the human will to freedom and to a life worthy of its name. They are known for their ability, in their works, to transform existential and political paralysis into a basis for elaborating strategies of survival and defiance of French colonialism (euphemistically termed "protectorship").

It was not for nothing that the early protesters both in Tunisia and in Egypt reiterated al-Shabbi's most compelling and influential couplet from his poem "'Irā'dit al-hayāt" (The Will to Life):

'Idhā' al-sha'bu yawman 'arāda al-hayāt / fa-lā budda 'an yastajība-l-qadar
Wa-lā budda lil-layli 'an yanjalī / wa-lā budda lil-qaidi 'an yankasir

Once a people reclaim their will to life / Gods must answer their call
Their Night will have to vanish / and their chains to break and fall

The resurrection of al-Shabbi's memorable lines—and their reverberations across the Arab world during and after the Tunisian revolution—should be understood not as a mere form of facile sloganeering but as an evocation of the inextricable relationship between foreign and indigenous forms of oppression, and the need to fight both. As journalist and activist Fahem Boukadous (2011) has observed: "We all must pull together, overcoming sectarianism, to reclaim this minimum common denominator: not only the struggle against the local dictatorship, but against imperialism."

The timelessness of al-Shabbi's couplet matches only its timeliness: not only did it inspire the one slogan—"Al-sha'b yurīd 'isqāt al-nizām"

(The people want to topple the regime)—that would animate all of the Arab uprisings from Tunisia to Syria through Egypt, Libya, Bahrain, and Yemen, but it also gave rise to other forms of expression, such as speeches, chants, and graffiti. I believe there was a repository of critical dissent that was sustained and consolidated by the insurgency of various cultural practices in modern Tunisia, not to mention the robust educational system that was put in place since independence by Mahmoud al-Messadi himself, the playwright who also acted as minister of national education in postcolonial Tunisia for a decade from 1958 to 1968 and minister of cultural affairs from 1973 to 1976. Thanks to al-Messadi's vision, which survived even Ben Ali's onslaughts on public education, Tunisia has always boasted a high literacy rate, estimated at almost 90 percent, one of the highest in the region. Yet, what bears mentioning here is that the level of literacy that most Tunisians had acquired remained for decades at variance with the repressive policies of the successive regimes of Bourguiba and Ben Ali, a fact that made the popular uprising inevitable, if long overdue.

Critique has not always been manifest or explicit, however, even though some critics have quite explicitly opposed Bourguiba's and Ben Ali's regimes and paid a high price for doing so. I am not here speaking merely about historical political opponents and opposition leaders such as Rachid al-Ghannouchi, Hamma al-Hammami, and Moncef Marzouki, among others, but about everyday Tunisians, journalists, novelists, playwrights, filmmakers, intellectuals, lawyers, high school teachers, as well as school and university professors. Even soccer players, singers, and other popular figures have at times embraced and passed on the tradition of dissent in the Tunisian public sphere, whether through explicit or encoded means and intents. Sociopolitical and cultural critique is there in cinema and in theater as well as in poetry and music. Anyone who studies Tunisian literature and culture since independence cannot miss the latent or indirect critique it carried and disseminated.

Take, for instance, the cinematic careers of Nouri Bouzid, Moufida Tlatli, and Mohamed Zran, among others: throughout their films, they have been preoccupied with the staging of broken and defeated individuals (both men and women, from leftist intellectuals and hip-hop artists to housekeepers, prostitutes, and misguided terrorists). By depicting defeat for Tunisian audiences, Bouzid, Tlatli, and Zran not only have made it possible for viewers to identify with and distance themselves from the defeated individuals on the screen but also—simultaneously—have offered them an opportunity to immunize themselves against the psychology of defeat and the state apparatuses that perpetuate it. In the final analysis, the cinematic tendency to grapple with and visualize the experience of defeat becomes indirectly the basis for fostering strategies of empowerment. Shakespeare's metadramatic injunction to his readers to "by indirections find directions out" serves to describe one of the tactics that artists make use of to evade censorship and simultaneously keep alive the culture of critique and dissidence. Since independence, Tunisian cinema had gradually developed a singular reputation for its audacious treatment of controversial and taboo subjects (even for an allegedly progressive Muslim country such as Tunisia). Yet the treatment of such wide-ranging and contentious topics as Islam, imperialism, and secular modernity—or variations on such topics—is almost always infused, directly or indirectly, by a penetrating critique of the postcolonial regimes of Bourguiba and Ben Ali, their midterm or long-term policies and their social, economic, and political ramifications.

Férid Boughedir's *Halfaouine* (1990) and Jilani Saadi's *Tender Is the Wolf* (2006)—along with Moufida Tlatli's *The Silences of the Palace* (1994), Mohamed Zran's *Essaïda* (1996), and Moncef Dhouib's *The TV's Coming* (2006)—chart a subtle genealogy of dissent from normative representations of Tunisianness in mainstream media, history, and state rhetoric, as do the half dozen films of Nouri Bouzid, including the 1986 *Man of Ashes,* the 1988 *Golden Horseshoes,* and the 2006 *Making Of.* The crucial importance of these films lies in their ability to challenge the sociocultural status quo and form the basis for challenging the governmental and political state apparatus itself. The obsession with the body in Tunisian cinema bespeaks an allegorical obsession with the body politic. Dissidence is contagious: once you practice it somewhere, chances are you will be able to practice it elsewhere, even in the realm of everyday or grand politics, which had been something practically unheard of in Ben Ali's Tunisia until December 17, 2010. It bears mentioning here that Zran's 1996 *Essaïda* can arguably be said to have anticipated Bouazizi's suicide protest insofar as the character of Nidal (Chadli Bouzayen), a wretched youngster living in a popular neighborhood (Essaïda, part of the *bidonville,* or shantytown, around Tunis), is driven at the end of the film to commit suicide. When chased by the police for murdering a cabdriver, Nidal deserts his motorbike and climbs up a tall, high-voltage steel tower before he accidently falls or deliberately jumps to certain death. Zran's *Essaïda* paints a bleak vision of Ben Ali's Tunisia, which, needless to say, was proven prophetic in the wake of Mohamed Bouazizi's self-immolation in Sidi Bouzid.

The same can be said about Jalila Baccar's most important and compelling play to date, *Khamsoun* (aka *Captive Bodies*). The starting point of *Khamsoun* is a suicidal act committed by Jouda, a young veiled physics and chemistry teacher, on Friday, November 11, 2005, in the courtyard of her own school and, significantly enough, at the foot of a pole carrying the Tunisian flag. The play unfolds in a sequence of scenes organized along three major parts that move forward and simultaneously as far back as the early years of Bourguiba's presidency of the free republic of Tunisia. *Khamsoun,* which means fifty in English, was produced in 2006, fifty years after Tunisia's independence from France in 1956. Baccar wants us therefore to understand her play literally, not metaphorically, as an allegory of the postcolonial Tunisia. This is a play in which the many individual stories Baccar weaves together are situated firmly in the canvas of national history. As a female playwright, actress, and filmmaker, Baccar has consistently been interested in the margins of the rhetoric of nationhood from Bourguiba to Ben Ali. Her consistent reactivation of the unassimilated histories of injustice and victimhood in postindependence Tunisia bespeaks a pedagogical and methodological investment in the psychoaffective valences of artistic and creative reckoning, and thus bears deep similarities to Nouri Bouzid's and Moufida Tlatli's early work in cinema. *Khamsoun*'s contestatory wherewithal is not the exception here but the exemplar.

In the months leading up to the revolution, critique had become, surprisingly enough, more and more adventurous, vocal, and direct, particularly on YouTube and Facebook, which circulated, among other things, explosive hip-hop videos that produced instantaneous effects. Indeed, the role of hip-hop and rap music in particular as a vehicle of popular discontent against Ben Ali's regime before and after the revolution became so vital that many could no longer imagine the cultural scene in Tunisia without it (despite the fact that this genre is so novel in Tunisia and the Arab world in general). Take, for instance, the case of rapper El Général (whose real name is Hamada Ben Amor). He was hardly known before the autumn of 2010, even in Tunisia's rap scene, which was dominated by artists such as Psyco M, Balti, and Lak3y, among a few others. On November 7, 2010 (the very same day that Tunisia was celebrating the twenty-third anniversary of Ben Ali's seizure of power, infamously known as the Blessed Change, or al-Tahawal al-Mubarak), El Général uploaded a rap song called "Rais lebled" (Head of state) onto Facebook. The raw fury and politically combustible rhymes of the song cannot be overstated. The refrain of the song paints an apocalyptic picture of Tunisia and became the rallying cry of protests from Avenue Bourguiba to Tahrir Square:

Rais lebled, sha'bik met
Barsha 'bed miziblaklet
Hek etshouf eshqā'id sāyirfil-bled
Ma'āsi partout we'bed mal-qātish wīn tbet
Hānī nihkī bi'sm eshsha'b illī tzalmū willī 'indāsū bissubbāt

Mr. President, your people are dead
Many, today, on garbage fed
As you can obviously see what's going on nationwide
Miseries everywhere and people find nowhere to sleep
I speak on behalf of those who were wronged and ground under feet

El Général dares the president to come down to the streets and see for himself how people lead their everyday lives and how the political police are clubbing and harassing Tunisians wherever they show any resistance to the regime's whims and wills. El Général dares the president to offer evidence of the stark contrast between the rhetoric of democracy he embraces, simulates, and dissimulates and the culture of corruption that prevails in the country and in Palace Carthage. El Général's plea became prophetic, given that in his third and last speech on January 13, 2011 (one day before he fled to Saudi Arabia), Ben Ali avowed that he was "misled" by his advisers who apparently kept him deliberately out of touch with the Tunisian people (out of a concern for his health). Ben Ali was a dying man both physically and politically. At any rate, the song galvanized young men and women, sending shock waves across the country before it was banned and El Général was arrested on January 6, 2011. By then, however, the revolution had reached a stage of no return, and Ben Ali was living on borrowed time.

One of the reasons the song resonated with every Tunisian is that it exposed the widespread governmental corruption, nepotism, and ineptitude—in effect, all the detriments of Ben Ali's neoliberal restructuring of the country that started in the late 1980s and intensified in the wake of Tunisia's association with the European Union in the mid-1990s through a drastic process of widespread privatizations. Indeed, privatization spared nothing, not even the educational sector on the brink of being completely marginalized by the emphasis placed on the private sector of education, particularly since Leila Trabelsi, infamously nicknamed "the regent of Carthage," started her own private and for-profit-only school, the Carthage International School (Beau and Graciet 2009).

Tunisia's economic reform program seemed to work quite well at first, and the country had been able to privatize 140 state-owned enterprises since 1987. Georgie Anne Geyer wrote an article in the mid-1990s that was then turned into a book titled *Tunisia: A Journey through a Country That Works* (2003). During the period between 1970 and 2000, the World Bank was confident enough about Tunisia's success that it gave the country more loans than any other Arab or African country. Whoever was misled by statistics seemed to believe that Tunisia was a success story. That was not necessarily the case, however, much to the surprise and bewilderment of both Arab and non-Arab observers.

What Ben Ali did was to create a "Tunisian entrepreneurial class eager to engage in globalized patterns of economic activity" and to "[locate] himself (and his family) firmly within that class" (Murphy 2002, 255). In other words, under Bourguiba the state controlled the bulk of the resources, and the private sector assisted it in negotiating the rules of the game. Under Ben Ali, by contrast, private operators acted as catalysts of progress and were assisted by the state in determining its political and economic priorities (Erdle 2010). As a result, Ben Ali and his wife and their extended families put their hands on more than 40 percent of the economy at a time when the national unemployment rate reached 13 percent and went as high as 40 percent in the southern and interior parts of the country. Economic growth was mostly confined to Ben Ali's entrepreneurial class in the greater Tunis area and along the coastal urban areas, to the detriment of the interior regions, which trailed behind.

While more than a third of the country's youth were unemployed, Ben Ali's entrepreneurial class continued to prosper by legal and illegal means. The State Department cables released by WikiLeaks exposed the extent to which the clan composed of the extended families of Ben Ali and his wife formed the nexus of corruption in the country. This "quasi-mafia" or "owning family" (as they are called by Tunisians) put their hands on more than a third of Tunisia's economy; they had no scruples whatsoever about coveting more assets under any form of shady dealings, be it cash, services, theft, property expropriation, extortion of bribes, money laundering or drug trafficking, or illegal privatizing of national assets and companies.

The U.S. ambassador to Tunis (2006–9), Robert F. Godec, was right to conclude that corruption was the "elephant in the room" in Tunisia: every Tunisian knew about it, but no one dared to address it. Until the revolution started, this state of affairs seemed to beggar the imagination; indeed, whoever visited, studied, and appreciated Tunisia could not fail to notice the striking disconnect between the will and dignity of its people and the corrupt and oppressive regime to which they almost readily submitted. Ben Ali's neoliberal adventure deliberately marginalized the southern and interior parts of the country, where protests erupted in the mining area of Gafsa in 2008 and lasted for six months before they were brutally repressed by the security forces (who ended up killing a number of workers).

The Tunisian revolution could very well have started in 2008 (in the manner in which the bread riots of 1984 against Bourguiba's economic policies prepared the ground for Ben Ali's palace coup in 1987), but neither Facebook nor Al Jazeera saved the day then. The six-months-long demonstrations were contained within a media wall of silence and never gained national and international attention until months afterward, when they had completely died out. What I am trying to suggest here is that, in addition to the wide-ranging repository of cultural dissent, there was also a tradition of spontaneous workers' movements that kept alive the spirit of rebelliousness, particularly at a time when the UGTT (the General Union of Tunisian Workers) was officially co-opted by the successive regimes of Bourguiba and Ben Ali after its last effective general strike in 1978.

Ultimately, cultural and political dissent became synonymous with doing what comes naturally. Note, for instance, that following the deposition of Ben Ali on January 14, 2011, countless demonstrations and sit-in protests took place in the Qasbah Government Square and elsewhere in Tunis. The first sit-in came right after the formation of the interim government and lasted for six days, January 23–28. It forced a major cabinet reshuffle even though it was forcefully dispersed by riot police. The second sit-in protest in the same place (Qasbah Government Square) went on around the clock for a dozen days and nights from February 20 to March 3 and achieved almost all its goals; unlike the first one, it ended peacefully with protesters rejoicing, cleaning the Government Square, and preparing for their journey to the border with Libya, where a humanitarian crisis was unfolding.

What bears mentioning here is that collective and civic action continued after the revolution, and in fact were it not for the successive sit-in protests in the Qasbah Government Square, there would not have been a National Constituent Assembly election on October 23. It was the February 20–March 3 sit-in protest in the Qasbah Government Square that asked for a new constitution and for Constituent Assembly elections. As protest coordinator Mohamed Fadhel insisted on February 28, 2011, "We will continue our sit-in until the formation of a constituent assembly and the recognition of the Council for the Protection of the Revolution" (quoted in Harrison 2011). The sit-in protest, composed mostly of young and marginalized Tunisians, refused to become a movement or to endorse a specific party. Eventually, however, most of these young activists were absorbed by political parties. The success of this sit-in has since achieved mythical status; in addition to the fulfillment of its central demand for Constituent Assembly elections, it forced not only the resignation of then prime minister Mohamed Ghannouchi and the appointment of Béji Caïd Essebsi as a new prime minister but also the dissolution of Ben Ali's state security apparatus and former party, the Constitutional Democratic Rally, on March 7 and 9, respectively. The National Constituent Assembly elections eventually took place on October 23, 2011 (initially, on March 3, 2011, Fouad Mebazaa announced that they would take place on July 24, 2011). Regarding the elections themselves, let me say at the outset that everyone in Tunisia and elsewhere was hopeful but apprehensive because interim prime minister Béji Caïd Essebsi had confessed to Ahmed Mansour on Al Jazeera that, under Bourguiba, he had consistently rigged the elections. Not that it was not obvious to most Tunisians that elections had always been rigged, but for him to own up to it further cast doubt on his honesty. Not many Tunisians trusted that he would actually keep to his promise and not interfere with the electoral process, which was overseen by an autonomous body called the Independent High Authority for the Elections (ISIE). However, the elections did deliver, indeed.

What is interesting is that despite the more than one hundred parties and hundreds of independents that took part in the elections, Tunisians voted in great numbers for the parties and political leaders who had established credentials and long histories of resisting and opposing Bourguiba and Ben Ali. Again, this was not much of a surprise. It was inevitable. This explains, for instance, why Al-Nahda, founded in the early 1980s in opposition to Bourguiba's Destour party, was the biggest winner in these elections. It earned 89 seats out of the total 217 in the National Constituent Assembly. The runner-up party was the Congress for the Republic (CPR), which won 29 seats. Together with Ettakatol (the Democratic Forum for Labour and Liberties), Al-Nahda and CPR formed a coalition government. Ettakatol was an opposition party to Ben Ali, but Al-Nahda and CPR were what might be called resistant parties. Moncef Marzouki, the leader of CPR, believed that Ben Ali's regime was incorrigible and that normal political opposition to it would lead to nothing. Unlike the leader of Ettakatol, Mustapha Ben Jafar, Marzouki chose therefore to resist Ben Ali. Hence, he called his party Congress for the Republic out of a sense that the Republic of Tunisia was yet to come.

Tunisians dealt a sobering blow to the remnants of Ben Ali's regime and to the old and new parties that based their entire electoral campaigns on the denigration of the Islamic party, Al-Nahda. By voting for the three parties that now formed the coalition government, Tunisians wanted also, in part, to correct the incalculable wrongs (such as exile, imprisonment, and torture) that were inflicted on the militants of these parties under both Bourguiba and Ben Ali. In an analysis of the election, Karem Yehia (2011) notes the views of Al-Hadi Bulleid, a professor of constitutional law at the University of Tunis:

> In Bulleid's opinion, one of the chief reasons why Al-Nahda received such a large vote was because the Ben Ali regime had cast it as the primary target for repression in his police state. At the same time, the movement recast itself and presented itself to Tunisians as consistent with the Bourguiba legacy and the modernist reform movement. It did not oppose women's right to sue for divorce, the ban on polygamy or other such advances that were introduced in the 1959 personal status law.

Yehia also quotes syndicate activist Al-Zein Hamami, however, who believed that the success of Al-Nahda "stems from the lack of political culture, from poverty and from their philanthropic activities. But, more importantly, they created a massive smokescreen that deceived the public into believing that they were moderate and modernist, and they spent huge sums of money that reeked of petrodollars from conservative Arab regimes."

With the rise of Salafism, however, and its ongoing duel with laicism, there continued to be some security threats and fears that Tunisia ran the risk of sliding into a theocracy, but these fears remained largely unrealistic given the liveliness of the public sphere and the irrevocable rights of speech and protest that Tunisians had earned.[5] Besides, Salafism in Tunisia has been more than a rising phenomenon that needs to be dealt with at the level of social policy; it has been at the heart of the political race for hegemony between the so-called Islamists and secularists or modernists—the former exploiting it to position themselves against it and create an image of moderation, and the latter conjuring it up to attack Al-Nahda, which for them supports Salafism (with some commentators going as far as calling Salafists the military wing of Al-Nahda). The challenge for postrevolutionary Tunisia has been not the fear of

"Talibanization," "Iranization," or "Wahabbization," all of which might allegedly transform the country into "Tunistan" or a caliphate-to-come; Tunisia's challenge has been to stay clear of interest- and identity-based politics, which has continued to fuel debate and appropriate attention away from the more urgent issues of creating jobs, offering reparations to the families of the martyrs, and bringing the members of the old regime to justice.

Despite the continuing entrenchments of the counterrevolutionary forces, the Tunisian revolution did seem to be heading in the right direction: the National Constituent Assembly had drafted the new constitution, and the prime minister announced that the next elections, parliamentary or presidential or both, would take place sometime in the spring or summer of 2013. It was very hard to speculate on the future, however, partly because the policies of the interim coalition government had proven unproductive and partly because the alternatives (or lack of them) of the opposition parties had proven counterproductive. Not unlike its predecessors, the coalition government was quite reluctant to bring to justice the major players in the old regime along with the riot policemen and snipers who killed more than three hundred protesters; what is worse, it even allowed former Ben Ali men to reassemble and form political parties and prepare for the next elections.

Reassuringly, throughout the year 2012 and beyond, the Tunisian people and particularly the cyberspace community remained very vigilant. Elections alone could not attest to the health of democracy as much as the everyday practice of democracy by the people themselves. Pedagogy played and continued to play an important role in the long process of eradicating and overcoming the "culture of corruption" that was promoted by Ben Ali's regime. By 2012, the whole process of unlearning the corrupted and corrupting habits of mind had just begun. Tunisians proved worthy of the challenge they set for themselves—that "the impossible is not Tunisian." It would take time and more sacrifice for Tunisians to reap the fruits of their exemplary revolt. Nevertheless, as this process of learning and culture of opposition deepened, democracy became a historical inevitability. As one of the most enduring postrevolutionary slogans states, "Notre 14 ne sera jamais 7x2" (Our January 14 will never be seven multiplied by two), which is to say that Ben Ali's dictatorship (as symbolized by the iconic number seven, commemorating his access to power on November 7, 1987) would never again return to Tunisia. The Tunisian revolution changed the course of history.

Notes

1. See "Interview with Mohamed Ghannouchi Tunisian Prime Minister," YouTube video, February 4, 2011, http://www.youtube.com/watch?v=bW3Tcq2l3Y4 (accessed November 14, 2012).

2. See "Tunisian Man Lashes Out Qatar and Al Jazeera," YouTube video, January 14, 2012, http://www.youtube.com/watch?v=QUEGUqjZu_Q (accessed November 14, 2012). Hundreds of demonstrators protested in front of the Tunisian parliament building during the opening session of the Constituent Assembly on November 22, 2011. "No to foreign interference in Tunisia's affairs," one banner read, while protesters shouted, "No Jazeera, no Qatar, the Tunisian people are free." Some of the protesters attacked an Al Jazeera camera crew and called them "mercenaries" and spy "agents."

3. See "The Png'ing of Suha Arafat: Many Rumors, Few Facts," TuniLeaks, December 14, 2010, https://tunileaks.appspot.com (accessed November 14, 2012).

4. Listen, for example, to the remarks of Lamine Bouazizi (no relation to Mohamed) on the radio show "Les Vrais Blogueurs de la révolution" [The true bloggers of the Tunisian revolution], Express FM podcast, December 18, 2011, http://www.radioexpressfm.com/podcast/show/les-vrais-blogueurs-de-la-revolution (accessed July 13, 2012).

5. Alarmist discourses about an Islamist takeover, the death of secularism, and myriad threats to women's rights were vulgarized in social media as well as in the old media in Tunisia, which became antistate media at large, as well as in books and research articles. See, for instance, Bradley (2012) and Tchaicha and Arfaoui (2012).

References

Al-Shabbi, Abul-Qasim. 1966. *Aghani al-hayat* [Songs of life]. Tunis: al-Dar al-tunisiya li-l-Nashar.

Beau, Nicolas, and Catherine Graciet. 2009. *La Régente de Carthage: Main basse sur la Tunisie.* Paris: La Decouverte.

Ben Ghazi, Myriam. 2011. "Suha Arafat: I Am the First Victim of Leila Ben Ali." Tunisia Live, November 1. http://www.tunisia-live.net (accessed November 14, 2012).

Boukadous, Fahem. 2011. "Tunisia: Interview with Fahem Boukadous, Member of the Communist Workers Party of Tunisia." By Alma Allende, translated by John Catalinotto. Links: International Journal of Socialist Renewal, February 7. http://links.org.au/node/2151 (accessed November 14, 2012).

Bradley, John R. 2012. *After the Arab Uprising: How Islamists Hijacked the Middle East Revolts*. New York: Palgrave Macmillan.

El Général (Hamada Ben Amor). 2010. "Rais le bled." YouTube video, November 7. http://www.youtube.com/watch?v=TbMEYNnXCC4 (accessed March 1, 2013).

Erdle, Steffen. 2010. *Ben Ali's "New Tunisia" (1987–2009): A Case Study of Authoritarian Modernization in the Arab World*. Berlin: Klaus Schwarz.

Gana, Nouri. 2011. "Let's Not Forget about Tunisia." Jadaliyya, January 30. http://www.jadaliyya.com (accessed February 28, 2013).

Geyer, Georgie Anne. 2003. *Tunisia: A Journey through a Country That Works*. London: Stacey International Publishers.

Guardian. 2011. "US Embassy Cables: Finding a Successor to Ben Ali in Tunisia." January 27. http://www.guardian.co.uk (accessed November 14, 2011).

Harrison, Patrick. 2011. "Tunisia: PM Forced Out, Constituent Assembly Elections Called." Green Left, March 6. http://www.greenleft.org.au (accessed November 14, 2012).

Murphy, Emma C. 2002. "The Foreign Policy of Tunisia." In *The Foreign Policies of Middle Eastern States*, edited by Raymond Hinnebusch and Anoushiravan Ehteshami, 235–56. Boulder, Colo.: Lynne Rienner.

Tchaicha, Jane D., and Khedija Arfaoui. 2012. "Tunisian Women in the Twenty-First Century: Past Achievements and Present Uncertainties in the Wake of the Jasmine Revolution." *Journal of North African Studies* 17 (2): 215–38.

Totten, Michael J. 2012. "The Woman Who Blew up the Arab World." *World Affairs*, Dispatches blog, May 17. http://www.worldaffairsjournal.org/blog (accessed November 14, 2012).

Yehia, Karem. 2011. "News Analysis: Al-Nahda Victory." Al-Ahram Weekly Online, October 27–November 2. http://weekly.ahram.org.eg/2011/1070/re5.htm (accessed November 14, 2012).

Egypt

PAUL AMAR

WHAT KIND OF LARGE-SCALE political and social changes were initiated by the mass uprisings in Tahrir Square and throughout Egypt in 2011 and by the continuing waves of protests and mobilizations during the two years that followed? Given the persistence of forms of repression, exclusion, and sociopolitical paralysis that characterized the aftermath of the uprisings, should we call this a failed revolution, or a stolen revolution, or a revolution in progress? Or perhaps it never was a revolution at all?

With its large population and its cultural and geographic centrality, Egypt is likely to make or break Arab regional trends toward democracy and social justice. So Egypt may be considered the fulcrum of the "Arab Spring" and of future transitions to democracy in the region. But what does the future hold for this cradle of innovative, fearless popular activism that captivated the world's imagination so vividly in 2011?

In this chapter I offer some tentative answers to these questions. First, I briefly profile the country's political economic history of development, its experience of forced "reverse development," and its modern history of successive revolutions and pseudorevolutions. I define four different types of revolution and identify which terms can be accurately applied to the Egyptian experience. Then I offer a time line of critical moments of uprising and repression since 2011, grouping them into three phases: first, the era of Tahrir Square protests and the successful toppling of President Mubarak in January and February 2011; second, the time of military rule by the Supreme Council of the Armed forces from February 2011 until June 2012; and third, the government of Muslim Brotherhood officials and of elected president Mohammad Morsi that followed, lasting twelve months.

In order to provide more substantive insights into the political events and forms of power embodied in each of these three stages, in the second part of this essay I present an analysis that distinguishes particular substructures of persistent domination in the country. I identify splits between these substructures that allowed for the most exciting moments of progress. And I draw attention to dispiriting forms of accommodation and deal making among dominant groupings that ensured that progressive movements faced severe headwinds at critical junctures. I conclude by exploring the most promising indications of revolutionary deepening: new forms of self-rule and community-generated models of participatory governance, progressive labor and student mobilizations, exciting forms of dynamic political party organization, and visionary new kinds of class and gender solidarity. I argue that, taken together, these deepening processes ensure that Egypt's uprisings, over the long term, will be seen to constitute a revolutionary dynamic.

Tahrir and Emancipation

In 2011 Egypt held the world spellbound. Millions of citizens flooded Cairo's central Tahrir Square starting on January 25, battling the police forces that had tortured them and facing down the brutal Central Security Forces (a massive paramilitary antiriot force) that had crushed their hopes and movements for more than two generations. Inspired by Tunisia's revolt the month before—but also driven by Egypt's own homegrown wave of mass-scale labor, civic, feminist, and antipolice mobilizations, which had begun to emerge around the year 2000[1]— demonstrators came together in unprecedented force, crying, "The people want the regime to fall" and "Bread, freedom, and social justice." Had the long-awaited revolution led by and for the people been accomplished at last?

Fifty-nine years before, Egypt's 1952 "Free Officers" military coup had expelled the British colonial "protectorate." After 1954, the pan-Arab nationalist vision and Third World socialist policies of President Gamal Abdel Nasser, a lieutenant colonel from among the Free Officers, attempted to shatter the prison of Cold War containment and uproot the legacies of centuries of imperial rule by the Ottomans and the British (Shokr 2012b). But the economic austerity plans and exclusionary politics of President Anwar Sadat (in office 1970–81) and his *infitah* (open-door) policies, and the corruption and elitism of Mohammad Hosni Mubarak's regime (1981–2011) turned that generation's revolutionary efforts back.

The country that Arabs call "the Mother of the World," Egypt, had reigned for much of the long span of human history as the world's richest and most developed territory, flourishing at the center of the planet's prime ocean-, desert-, and river-based trade routes, endowed with rich energy and agricultural resources, and serving as a timeless crossroads of peoples, cultures, creativities, and spiritualities. Indeed, Egypt by the mid-nineteenth century enjoyed more developed infrastructure, institutions, and civil societies than, by some estimates, Spain or Italy. But then a process of peripheralization (Abul-Magd 2010), underdevelopment, or forced "reverse development" began, as international financial and military interventions, often in partnership with large landowners and commercial interests within Egypt, converged to reduce the country's economic diversity, transforming Egypt basically into one big cotton plantation (Wallerstein 1979). During that period, Egypt's economy became almost wholly dependent on unstable global markets for cotton, and this vulnerability eventually trapped the country in debt and led to political narrowing as well. In the 1950s and 1960s, Nasser's revolutionary pan-Arab socialist state launched attempts to lead Egypt out of this dependent status, to foster a more expansive and independent development profile, and to broaden the participation of workers and peasants in social and economic life, but all while maintaining exclusion from participation on the political front. This political repression, combined with the failure of land reform and redistribution policies, contributed to "making the army movement of 23 July not a revolution, but an anti-democratic military coup that established a corporatist regime with populist social policies . . . similar to Peronism in Argentina or Mexico under Cardenas and the PRI" (Beinin 2013a).

In the Sadat and Mubarak eras, these initial socioeconomic advances made by Nasser's state were reversed. By the start of the twenty-first century, Egypt's human capital, industrial infrastructure, and extensive resources had been dismantled or drained by vampiric national rulers and international exploiters, and the nation was left to languish not just behind Europe but behind nearly all of Latin America and Asia as well, forced to wallow in inequality, illiteracy, degradation, and futureless-ness. By the arrival of the year 2010, Egypt remained the most populous country in the Middle East, with a population of ninety-one million, mostly speaking Arabic. Approximately 6–10 percent of the population was made up of Coptic Christians (the Coptic Church is the historic indigenous Orthodox Church in Egypt). And as the twenty-first century began, Egypt still featured a multicultural society comprising a variety of other religious groupings, ethnic identities, and sects, including Nubians, Baha'is, Armenians, Sudanese, Somalians, Bedouins, Roma ("Gypsies"), Amazigh ("Berbers" in Siwa), and hundreds of thousands of international residents from China, Korea, India, Russia, Central Asia, sub-Saharan Africa, the Persian Gulf, the United States, and the Levant. But during the last generation, Egypt's rich cultural fabric had been torn apart by dramatic declines in industrial services, health, and social infrastructure. To take the educational sphere as representative, even as late as the early 1990s, Egypt's schools were still providing a decent education. Schools had served as key spaces for forging the social universe of the modern nation, where distinct religious communities, and both girls and boys, had met and commingled for generations. But since the mid-1990s, catastrophic cuts to education mandated by international financial institutions (and the desire by authoritarian rulers to keep the poor from communicating and organizing among themselves) had forced the country back to a pitiable state of 66 percent adult illiteracy (UNICEF 2003). The cuts encouraged even the lower middle classes to flee the public schools, which had in past eras served as the common ground for class and cultural conviviality. By 2010, Egypt had dropped far down on the U.N. Human Development Index, to be ranked 101st among countries, with poverty rates growing fast and with an additional 10 percent of the pupil population dropping out of schools in the period 2006–8 alone (U.N. Development Programme and Institute of National Planning, Egypt 2010).

However, the revolutionary spirit of Egypt that had been building momentum, especially since the start of the new millennium, crested with a righteous vengeance in 2011. Protesters in Tahrir Square—surviving attacks by security forces in tanks and on motorbikes and camels, absorbing sniper fire and tear gas volleys, and enduring systematic sexual violence by plainclothes thugs unleashed by the state—held their ground and forged a remarkable living community of courage and solidarity (Amar 2011c). Coming together were women and men, young and old, working class and upper class, Christians and Muslims, leftists and liberals, radicals and the previously apolitical, labor unions and syndicates, university student organizations, community committees who had tossed out the police in their neighborhoods and declared self-rule, masses of young soccer fans (who provided powerful pushback against the police), and a new generation of younger Islamists who refused to heed the orders of prominent Islamist leaders that they stay home and respect the government. After eighteen days of courage and rage, the "Republic of Tahrir Square" succeeded in deposing President Mohammad Hosni Mubarak, the headman of a thirty-year regime of institutional paralysis, religio-moral hypocrisy, crony capitalism, and police atrocity.

The world was electrified. Stereotypical depictions of the public sphere of the Middle East as choked by the irrational mobs of the so-called Arab Street or strangled by cultural values inimical to democratic aspiration or civic participation vanished overnight as Egypt and its people suddenly became sexy, fearless, and powerful—the model for young activists worldwide and the embodiment of surging popular sovereignty. Worldwide, protesters and social movements took this popular uprising in Egypt as their inspiration, including the UK Uncut movement, ATTAC in Germany, the Indignados in Spain, participants in the Wisconsin labor uprisings in the United States, the Occupy Wall Street movement and other Occupy movements, as well as pro-democracy and antipolice state demonstrators in East Africa and in the increasingly repressive and unequal cities of China (Gerbaudo 2011; Horowitz 2011; Liang 2011). "Going full Egyptian" became a global slogan (Urban Dictionary 2011): Let's go the full Egyptian. Let's go all the way to justice and freedom. Let's abandon fear, unleash solidarity, and reoccupy public space. Let's refuse to give ground until the regime falls.

Worldwide activists would have been even more awed and inspired had they been able to watch the other radical mobilizations that erupted in other parts of Egypt that were not witnessed by those cameras strapped to balconies overlooking Tahrir Square. Labor organizers had finalized the formation of a national independent workers' federation, uniting millions of workers in the public and private sectors in coordinated action.[2] As prominent Egyptian activist Hossam Hamalawy (2011) stated:

> We might ask, where were the workers at the beginning of the revolution? The workers participated in the revolution from the beginning. In areas of Suez, in areas like Mahallah, areas like Kafr el-Dawwar . . . these areas are working-class areas. So when you hear that tens of thousands—and at times there were hundreds of thousands—of people protesting in these cities, I think it's understood that the vast majority of them were workers. But the workers were taking part in these demonstrations as *demonstrators,* not as workers. They were not acting as a separate force.

University student groups, as well, had created a national organization of movements and student governments up and down the country to facilitate coordinated strikes and protests and to ensure the freedom of key student-government elections, which serve as bellwethers for democracy nationwide (Amar 2011a). (Imagine what the United States would look like if all university student governments and assembly organizations across the entire country, from the huge state schools to the private colleges, acted together and in coordination to push for progressive education, youth, and social policies.) Also, new kinds of antifundamentalist religious movements came to the foreground in Egypt during the 2011 uprisings. Progressive break-off groups of youth from the Muslim Brotherhood, activist Coptic Christians struggling against the oppressive rule of their own church hierarchy as well as against the state, and the new Youth Congress of Sufi Guilds (personal interview 2012) (representing in theory four million progressive, working-class, and antiorthodox Muslims versus the five hundred thousand to eight hundred thousand members of the Brotherhood) emerged. These groups all shared a common goal: a "civil state" (one not dominated by either religious or military doctrines or institutions), opposing army tribunals and emergency decrees as well as the politicization of faith by the Muslim Brotherhood and other conservative church-led and puritan (Salafist) Islamic movements.[3]

Not all the popular movements during the initial days of uprising in 2011 limited themselves to peaceful protest. Some of the most critical interventions were forceful, action-oriented popular sovereignty movements that did not stop merely at demonstrating in public squares; they moved to violently tear down the system's structures of repression and manifest new forms of authority in their place. Community organizations across the megacities of Cairo and Alexandria and in the villages and smaller towns of Egypt rose up against the security state, emptied prisons, burned police stations, and then set up "popular committees for security" and myriad other forms of local collectives. These grassroots groups experimented with new concepts and practices of self-rule, public safety, service provision, and conflict resolution that often became long-term organizations of governance facilitating participation at the local level (Bremer 2011; El-Meehy 2012). Women's movements and feminist organizations exposed and challenged the sexual brutality of the state and security apparatus, refusing to pull back as they faced "virginity tests" by the military and the continuation of practices of traumatic sexual harassment from police and hired thugs (Amar 2012b). And a spectrum of youth movements and sports-fan clubs mobilized brave battalions of resistance against repressive police and military troops and then against Muslim Brotherhood militias (Dorsey 2012); these youth movements became the force behind a popular cultural explosion of inspiring murals, captivating graffiti artworks, and uninhibited songs and chants that came to define a generation of angry, joyful solidarity uniting social classes and sensibilities that urban segregation during the 1980s and 1990s had sundered (El-Sherif 2012b; Abaza 2013).

Repressors and Reactionaries

Yet as the revolutionary clock of 2011 and 2012 spun forward in Egypt, a dark storm of violence began to gather against the would-be revolutionaries. First to unleash repression were the armed forces that had stood by the revolutionary youth and social movements in February 2011, protecting the people from the vicious police and thugs, eventually ushering their own colleague, former air force commander Mubarak, out of power. But once the military leadership, in the form of the Supreme Council of the Armed Forces (SCAF), assumed total control, it revealed its true face and utter disinterest in pursuing even the narrowest social justice, empowerment, or inclusion agenda (Abul-Magd 2012). By the autumn of 2011, the SCAF had become its own ruthless dictatorship, not just preserving Mubarak's hated emergency decree but actually extending the use of military courts, torture, and evidence-free convictions for political detainees (Eskandar 2011). And the SCAF became infamous for utilizing distinctive forms of brute force. The council deployed sexual molestation and "virginity tests" in order to somehow distinguish between "civil" protesters and "Whores of the Revolution," who would be detained and would face military tribunals and prison (Shafy 2011).

The hated police forces of the Ministry of the Interior by February 2011 had become identified with the worst brutalities and corruption of Mubarak's regime and its hired thugs. That February, the military had countered the police, standing protectively as guardians of the people, holding at bay the bloody threats offered by the police's paramilitary branch, the Central Security Forces. But soon afterward, by the autumn of 2011, the military had stopped protecting the people from the police and Central Security Forces. And the SCAF allowed the worst police atrocities in Egypt's modern history to be unleashed on the youth and democratic movements. Interior Ministry officials ordered sniper fire that targeted the eyeballs of protesters. And they ordered endless overdeployments of tear gas, not as crowd control but in quantities and intensities that qualify as lethal gas poisoning and as chemical warfare against civilians, literally suffocating dozens of protesters to death, including female doctors and nurses treating injured protesters. These aid workers went on to join the ranks of martyrs. And meanwhile, the army blamed the victims, identifying protesters with criminals and outside agitators.

On October 9, 2011, Christian Egyptians came together at the Maspero Building (the national television broadcasting headquarters next to Tahrir Square). They came to protest a perverse verdict absolving arsonists in Aswan for destroying a church and to protest the state media's propagandistic treatment of religion (Iskandar 2012) and sectarian issues that "fanned the flames of hatred" (BBC News 2011). In what became known as the Maspero Massacre, more than twenty-five Christian demonstrators and their Muslim supporters were killed by the military—that is, under direct command from the SCAF, not at the hands of Central Security or the Interior Ministry's police. Protesters were murdered by the army in the most stupidly brutal ways; young demonstrators were rolled over by tank treads or crushed against the walls of buildings by army vehicles.

Then, during the period November 19–24, 2011, Interior Ministry troops, with the SCAF's full complicity, gassed and crushed demonstrators on Mohammad Mahmoud Street, which connects Tahrir Square to the area where the police headquarters of the Interior Ministry is located, killing more than forty people. On December 16, 2011, demonstrators at sit-ins held in the vicinity of government buildings demanded a "civil state" (that is, a state not dominated by religious or military institutions) and an end to SCAF rule. In an attempt to dislodge the protesters, military and police troops leveled particularly gender-selective forms of vicious punishment. Security forces were filmed beating and nearly lynching a woman protester in what became known as the "blue bra scandal"; five soldiers shoved the woman's face-and-body-covering *'abeya* upward, revealing her underclothes, while they clubbed her prone body.

Violence continued to escalate as the repressive apparatus of the state attracted new forms of collaboration. From December 16 through December 19, 2011, during confrontations in the vicinity of the government's cabinet building, Muslim Brotherhood members stood against protesters, "protecting" the military and state institutions from the people, providing evidence that the Brotherhood and the military establishment had established broad pacts for mutual accommodation and collaboration, to preserve each others' institutional and political interests (Eskandar 2013). In the "battles of the cabinet building," the military beat to death more than ten demonstrators who were among a group of hundreds staging a sit-in at the Cabinet of Ministries. Then on February 1, 2012, police forces and possibly military leaders were complicit in a shockingly grim massacre in Port Said: security troops sealed off a packed football (soccer) stadium and turned off all the lights before sending in thugs who used machetes to hack to death no fewer than seventy-five youth and preteen soccer fans associated with protest movements.

By the time elections for president came on May 23 and June 16, 2012, the horrified public had lost its faith in the armed forces that had stood by the people and evicted Mubarak. As the elections approached, the traumatized public was exhausted but nevertheless thrilled by the possibility of bringing in new civil leadership and, at last, installing a democratically elected president. When the Muslim Brotherhood's Mohammad Morsi launched his administration in June 2012, he gave exhilarating speeches in Tahrir Square; soon afterward he spoke at the meeting of the Non-Aligned Movement in Tehran and at the Arab League headquarters in Cairo, promising to fulfill the aspirations of the 2011 Egyptian Revolution and the popular will of the Arab Spring, and to bring democratic inclusion and social justice to a region crushed by inequality, war, and international interference. But hardly before his words had stopped echoing, Morsi's policies and actions began dragging the country in exactly the opposite direction, pushing back against the revolutionary current. By July, just one month into his term, Morsi had redeployed troops in the Sinai and had begun talking directly with Israeli military officials and coordinating security operations with them in order to stop small militant actions in the Sinai and along the border with Gaza (Dekel and Perlov 2012), cooperating openly with U.S. and Israeli military and intelligence officials—actions that neither Mubarak nor the SCAF would ever have taken so explicitly.

This cooperative security profile earned Morsi accolades from the United States and Israel, which then appointed him to broker the end of Hamas hostilities and the Israeli bombardment of Gaza's civilians on

November 21, 2012. Could a conservative Islamist engineering professor and business-friendly free market advocate such as Morsi become the reassuring face of a "moderate" Arab Spring? Could an Islamist populist legitimized by an election end up serving the status quo of U.S. and Israeli security interests in the region rather than challenging them? These speculations led to exuberance in the Western media, which proclaimed Morsi "the most important man in the Middle East" (Ghosh 2012). Flooded with pride and overconfidence from Western praise, Morsi made a sudden grab for power (Sallam 2012); on November 22, he drafted an extraordinary constitutional declaration granting himself dictatorial powers in Egypt until a new parliament could be elected (and this parliament itself would be elected according to an illegitimate and narrow constitution that he forced into ratification). With this move, Morsi pushed aggressively against the long-established independence and legitimacy of the judiciary in Egypt, a judiciary whose autonomy had managed to survive even the Mubarak years.

But the capitulations of Morsi's Brotherhood presidency were not limited only to the realms of geopolitics and law. On the economic front, Morsi veered to the right of Mubarak. In 1991, President Mubarak did sign an accord with the International Monetary Fund and began to usher the country through what would be a twenty-year phase marked by the most irrational and corrupt forms of privatization, crony capitalist favoritism, and wealth hoarding by a Persian Gulf–linked privileged class (Soliman 2011). But since 1991, Mubarak had signed no new agreements, and the SCAF government of 2011 that followed Mubarak and preceded Morsi refused to sign a deal with the IMF—not because of any animosity toward capitalism, but because the budget deal of which the IMF loan was a part would have raised capital gains taxes, raised the minimum wage, and instituted more oversight over the wealth of the nation's richest businessmen (Reuters 2011). Also, the SCAF generals wanted to protect their own monopoly over touristic and residential properties and their control over certain markets and factories whose terrible quality, inefficiency, and horrific labor practices would never survive exposure to market competition or oversight by accountants. But Morsi went where Mubarak for the previous twenty years and the SCAF in 2011 refused to go, meeting with IMF officials and coming to rough agreement on a draft accord on November 20, 2012 (Salem and Rogers 2013; Shokr 2012a), that was negotiated behind closed doors, with no transparency, and without the engagement of stakeholders or the public. Through this agreement, Egypt gave up some of its sovereignty over its labor practices, its environmental protections, and its public patrimony, all for a promise of a paltry US$4 billion loan—a handful of beans in a world of multitrillion-dollar economic stimulus packages. In December 2012, the state acted to make sure labor and social justice activists would be punished if they resisted the IMF accords and new pro-business regime. Morsi decreed a "Revolution Protection Law" that created new extraordinary tribunals that would try persons accused of certain crimes, including inciting strikes (Fahmy 2012). Further, Morsi hosted regular forums with visiting Saudi and Gulf investors, promising them that Egypt would provide them with a yielding and disciplined climate for new investment.

On the security and human rights front at home, Morsi also revealed the Brotherhood's preference for pursuing its own party's hegemony rather than seeking justice. Attempts to reform the brutal police were halted or reversed (Egyptian Initiative for Personal Rights 2013). Prisons were filled once again. Instead of banning Guantánamo-style military courts and military tribunals, as the Brotherhood had demanded for decades and Morsi had promised, the government reaffirmed these tribunals and enshrined them in the new constitution. The government also drafted a law banning any public protests that "insult" the state or president or at which protesters "rudely shout." Apparently, the state anticipated that a new wave of protests would come with the new parliamentary elections or the future anniversaries of the January 25 launch of the Tahrir Square uprising.

A particularly revealing set of protests and conflicts that took place December 5–9, 2012, came to be known as the Battles of Ittihadiya— Ittihadiya being the name of the presidential palace where Morsi worked in Heliopolis, an elite northeastern suburb of Cairo. Starting on December 5, hundreds of thousands of protesters marched from their home neighborhoods or from miles away in Tahrir Square to the grounds of the presidential palace in Heliopolis to protest Morsi's power grab and the fact that a constitution had been slapped together exclusively by Islamists, without the mandated participation of any other political parties, or to protest the fact that sword-wielding thugs from the Muslim Brotherhood had forced the December 2 closure of the Constitutional Court, which thus could not judge the legitimacy of the constitution-writing process (the proud judges' syndicate has called December 2, 2012, the "blackest day on record" in the history of the Egyptian judiciary; Associated Press 2012). Other protesters who converged on Ittihadiya were there to demonstrate against the new restrictions on labor organizing and journalism, others to protest the drafting of new sharia laws overseeing women's personal status and behavior, and still others to protest Morsi's uncomfortable closeness to U.S. security officials or the IMF.

The demonstrators had aimed to protest peacefully in front of the palace and possibly hold a sit-in there. Instead, they were met by a new and terrifying phenomenon: armed Muslim Brotherhood militias, acting as did El Salvadoran paramilitaries in the 1980s, brandishing swords and rifles, attacking the crowds, lynching protesters, capturing progressive women leaders and dragging them through the streets into tents for interrogation and molestation (Associated Press 2012; Sukarieh 2012). And these attackers were not just nameless thugs or "rabble for hire." The men whom citizen journalists witnessed and photographed beating and dragging protesters included prominent Brotherhood leaders (Hussein 2012), including some in Morsi's inner circle as well as the editor in chief of the Brotherhood's moderate and modern media face, Islam Online. The nation watched the attacks live on television and on the Internet in horror.

The result of the Battles of Ittihadiya was that Morsi's last claim to be "president for all Egypt," rather than just a Brotherhood man, evaporated and public support for the constitution collapsed, along with public support for Islamist political parties, which had peaked when Islamist parties were voted into parliament in December 2011. So when Morsi insisted a week later on forcing a vote on the constitution that the Brotherhood had drafted by breaking every procedural propriety and legal norm imaginable, 70 percent of the Egyptian electorate refused to participate in the referendum. And although the Brotherhood's electoral machine managed to turn out enough people in the countryside to pass the measure, the vote was split nearly fifty-fifty in Alexandria

(Egypt's city most populated by Islamist Salafi and Brotherhood organizations and supporters). And the capital, Cairo (where 25 percent of the country's population lives and where the Brotherhood supposedly had a very strong base), voted strongly against the constitution. So did Gharbiya, the home of Mahalla, Egypt's capital of labor organizing. Also voting in the no column was Menoufiya, an agricultural province in what is often thought of as a conservative, rural region of the Nile delta.[4]

Another result of the Battles of Ittihadiya was that the armed forces began to pull back from Morsi. In July 2012 the military had established a tenuous agreement to support Morsi and the Brotherhood's government in exchange for promises to protect their profitable economic interests and their legal impunity for responsibility for the massacres of 2011 and 2012. But in the wake of the violence at Ittihadiya, the armed forces made it clear that they were neutral in these conflicts and would not necessarily side with Morsi (GlobalPost 2012). The Republican Guard, the army's wing specifically charged with protecting the presidency, signaled this change of heart by letting youth protesters enter the grounds of Ittihadiya on December 8 to dance and chant against the president and spray-paint rude slogans. And then between June 30 and July 3, 2013, the largest popular protest in human history, in which twenty to thirty million Egyptions took to the streets, triggered the military to remove Morsi from office.

Revolution in Question

As described above, new processes of mass uprising and mobilization in Egypt in 2011–12 met wave after wave of crushing repression and disappointment, first during the period of the military junta in 2011–12 and then in the initial year of Mohammad Morsi's Brotherhood-led presidency in 2012–13. Does this mean that a revolution did not happen or that it had been lost, turned back, or stolen? The fact that many old-regime officials, discredited economic policies, and military emergency dictates remained in vigor by the start of 2013 in Egypt, even after twenty-four months of constant, grueling, increasingly mortal struggle—and after cycle after cycle of elections and referenda—led many to say that there had been no revolution at all since January 25, 2011 (Agha and Malley 2012; Bremmer 2011; Bayat 2011; Beinin 2013a).

Many Egyptians began to feel that they were moving backward, not forward, and that maybe what they had experienced had all been one big conspiracy by the United States to put its new best frenemies—the business-friendly Muslim Brotherhood—in power.

Here it may be useful for us to step back for a moment to define the terms around which the success or failure of a revolution can be assessed. One can distinguish among at least four kinds of revolutions: political, civic, and social revolutions (Carapico, cited in Mock 2012), and then revolutions in consciousness. A *political revolution* is marked by the overthrow of the leadership and some of the main institutions of a state and the institution of new leadership in political society. Certainly Egypt achieved a political revolution, with the Muslim Brotherhood, long a dissident organization, taking the presidency and a new constitution pushed through. A *civic revolution* is one in which public life, public space, and public participation change. Egypt, too, achieved many of the benchmarks of such a civic revolution, with the occupation of city centers, the banishment of the state from some local neighborhoods and villages, and the invention of new practices of self-rule, conviviality, collective action, and public morality. A *social revolution* takes place when social class hierarchies are overthrown or dramatically equalized; when rights to jobs, housing, health, and education are secured; and when substantive democratic inclusion (not just the occasional vote) replaces systematic exclusion. A social revolution had not yet occurred in Egypt by 2013, two years after Tahrir. Two or three corrupt businessmen had been jailed, but the country's superrich were still superrich, and the socioeconomic domination embedded in the military's control over real estate, shopping malls, and factories producing essential commodities remained unchallenged. Moreover, Brotherhood businessmen had extended their monopoly control over supermarkets, retail shops, and communications businesses. So a social revolution overthrowing class hierarchies and exclusions had not happened. But another kind of revolution, a *revolution in consciousness* (thawra dhihniya) had certainly taken place, as new cultures of criticism and irony—and new forms of knowledge distribution and awareness spreading—had taken root among all classes and groupings. A whole universe of new popular cultures, slang languages, political analyses, vernacular theories of power, and genres of political music, art, theater, blogs, and chants had created an utterly new set of public spheres, popular sovereignty claims, and mobilizing languages.

Focusing on Egypt's particular achievements in the realms of civic revolution and revolution in consciousness, in the rest of this chapter I will trace aspects of an ever-deepening process of politicization in Egypt, identifying the groups and forces mobilized around them. And I will insist that this process has indeed been revolutionary, since it has exposed three invisible substructures of power in Egypt (or regimes within the regime):

1. *Structures of cronyism:* These are social systems that assure that privileged, corrupt business elites retain power over national wealth, that they are granted huge development concessions and below-market rates for privatized public-sector assets, and that they are allowed to enforce their economic power through coercive means, including by contracting with street thugs and private security forces to provide protection and enforcement.

2. *Military political economies:* These structures of law and complicity assure that certain generals from the armed forces maintain monopolistic power over useful land and productive factories.

3. *Religionized commercial cartels:* These social organizations and clientelist networks (which under Morsi penetrated state institutions) assure that the elite inner circles of the Muslim Brotherhood maintain power over investment markets and certain merchant sectors. The organizations' political party and policies act to displace any critique of these cartels' economic power by generating panics around public morality, Islamic legality, and gendered piety.

These three formations remained misunderstood, politically imperceptible, or misrecognized for the three decades of the Mubarak era. The broader public in Egypt and abroad, including even most journalists, activists, and social scientists, was not aware of how these formations operated, who most benefited from them, or to what degree they operated in consonance or dissonance with the others. Since 2011, however, Egypt's mass movements and popular efforts have exposed, one by one, these three sets of coercive and dispossessive institutions and cultures of power. These movements gradually forced an exciting deepening and broadening of social mobilization and political consciousness among an increasingly widening set of class, gender, and cultural groupings. Revolutionaries also discovered, as they exposed and confronted these three substructures of domination, that each of these three spheres tends to disagree with, distrust, and yearn for the destruction of the others. Although the processes of revolution and counterrevolution since 2010 have pushed these three forms of structural domination to seek modes of accommodation and alliance among themselves, because they have shared interests in socioeconomic exclusion, profit maximization, and political demobilization, essential differences among these clusters of power have continued to offer distinct strategic opportunities for those organizing for change. Thus mobilizations have been able to wedge themselves into the spaces between these spheres—the realms of cronies, generals, and merchants—to split them apart from each other, at times turning them against each other in useful ways. This revolutionary process thus has continued not only to spread new forms of consciousness but also to portend possibilities for triggering structural changes to social class structures and institutional power relations.

However, by the start of 2013 these civic revolutions and revolutions in consciousness had not yet transformed the essential orderings of economic and institutional power or the moralistic politics that brutally repressed efforts to raise questions of justice around gender, class, and sexuality that formed the common infrastructure of these three formations of patriarchal, moralistic, and brutally coercive governance. Nevertheless, the initiation of possibilities for transformation was exhilarating. I will argue below that in order to succeed in establishing the foundations for a more substantive democratization process, popular movements in Egypt have generated specific kinds of action to broaden consciousness of alternatives to these three formations and to deepen solidarity among social groupings.

These processes of deepening, which will eventually help Egypt's revolution win back the future, have taken the following four forms:

1. *Alternative movements for local self-rule:* These include community collectives, popular security committees, and urban improvement organizations that have invented new practices and concepts of self-policing, citizenship, and local problem solving.

2. *Innovative electoral mobilizations:* These include new parties, campaign strategies, and forms of outreach that by the first round of presidential elections demonstrated the maturation of new coalitions and the popularity of social justice discourses.

3. *Imaginative labor actions:* These consist of nationwide organizations of workers' groups, marked by the declaration of the "Independent Workers' Republic of Mahalla" and other bold efforts that have spread political consciousness and militancy among workers and other social sectors.

4. *Boundary-challenging gender solidarities:* These forms of alliance have brought feminist groups together, more and more, with very important mass youth movements, which are led by rowdy boys often identified by the media as the "hypermasculine" adversaries of women. These different kinds of groups have forged alliances and modes of sociability that have brought classes and gender identities together, countering moralistic hypocrisy and class and gender segregation.

Even as the three formations of domination have struggled to accommodate each other and join forces against these processes of surging mobilization, each of these forms of opposition has acted to deepen and extend Egypt's revolutionary social transformations. I will discuss each in turn below.

Alternative Movements for Local Self-Rule

January 25, 2011, marked the "Day of Rage" and the start of eighteen days of mass occupations and demonstrations in Tahrir Square. But it was January 28, 2011, that marked the day that "the people" of Egypt, in the broadest and bravest sense, took up the banner not just of protest but of revolution. On that day, while the international media and national security apparatuses were focused on Tahrir Square, neighborhoods, towns, and villages far from the glare of the spotlight erupted into uncontainable revolt against the security state and its coercive and economic infrastructures (Kirkpatrick 2011).

Communities rose up against the police who had long squeezed them with "protection rackets" that would close down businesses if the owners did not bribe the corrupt cops to provide "security." Police beat young Khaled Saeed to death, either because he had videotaped police involved in shaking down hashish dealers or because he had refused to pay off the policemen who burst into his "Spacenet" Internet café. As neighbors watched the police shatter his skull on the public street, young Saeed cried out, "God, I am dying!" The police replied, "We are not leaving you until you are dead" (Ali 2012). The martyred Khaled, and the pictures of his smashed visage, quickly gained mythic status. "We are all Khaled Saeed," the Facebook groups and human rights campaigns chanted, sparking a mass outpouring of mourning and outrage (Herrera 2011).

But the working classes that were largely untouched by online networks and human rights politics also identified passionately with these victims of state violence and police brutality. On January 28, rage exploded collectively throughout the country as literally millions rose up on the same day—with information traveling between individuals and groups by every means of communication or signal imaginable— to attack and burn down police stations, chasing every officer out of neighborhoods and communities, and to overwhelm the country's prisons, releasing hundreds of thousands of detainees. Police stations and security bureaus burned in coastal Alexandria, in the working-class neighborhoods of Cairo, down in Aswan, up in the villages of the Nile delta, and across the country.

This act of national rebellion resembled the landmark assault by the French people, on July 14, 1789, on the Bastille (a prison that, at the time, held only two inmates). Yet the Egyptians went quite a bit further than the French. They did not just attack one prison; they routed dozens of penitentiaries and police stations across the land, not only making a symbolic gesture but also literally crippling the security state and seizing control of local governance. And they did not just seize the nodes of police repression; they also assaulted the sites of economic oppression, with workers' unions and Robin Hood–style bandit groups detonating the pipelines through which Mubarak's family and the military elite siphoned profits by selling natural gas to Israel. And popular militants and Bedouin tribesmen came close to overtaking Suez Canal port facilities, declaring that the people, not just the elites, would decide how Egypt would insert itself into the flows of international trade (Avitabile 2011).

This remarkably revolutionary day of collective action, January 28, 2011, was led not by the "Facebook generation" of middle-class activists fawned over by the press but by the popular classes on their home turf. And these working-class groupings then launched new experiments in self-policing, societal security, conflict resolution, and self-government. Popular committees for security (al-ligaan al-sha'abiya) cropped up spontaneously in remarkably parallel forms across the urban fabric and in smaller towns, keeping the police out. These committees acted to protect neighborhoods from petty criminals and looters and from the bands of thugs unleashed by trafficker headmen or wealthy businessmen wreaking havoc on the insurgent neighborhoods. The popular commit-tees, of course, were not made up of angels. Some of these groups of men acted just as brutally as the police had before them, capturing their enemies and torturing them underground in subway stations or in back alleys, harassing women or banishing them from public space in order to "protect" them. But, remarkably, many of these committees did begin to experiment with new models and concepts of security that were far more legitimate than those of the police and were welcomed by local societies. These alternative models included informal dispute resolu-tion mechanisms (Ezzedine 2012), women-run mutual finance associa-tions that offered collective economic rather than coercive means for providing security, and participatory forms of urban problem-solving and street-securing organizations that supplanted the paralyzed roles of local urban administration. The people involved in these grassroots efforts began to negotiate and innovate, developing means to safeguard businesses, reduce crime, develop new public spaces and means of access to services and transportation, end intimidation by police and police-linked thugs, and ensure openness in terms of participation and communication among members and subgroups within communities (Amar and Roushdy 2012).

But it was not just these popular committees that expanded to fill the void after the people evicted the hated police. Labor unions stepped into the breach in some towns and neighborhoods to provide economic and social forms of security, in place of the old punitive and coercive notions of security. And as Mubarak's business cronies pulled out their investments or fled, women-led financing collectives (gama'iyaat tamwiliyya) expanded their purview to provide employment supplements and spread community resources to those most traumatized by unemployment. These were not bank-linked "microcredit" projects but local, self-generated mortgage- and rent-paying cooperatives that did not charge interest. Their financial and economic efforts to stabilize certain hard-hit working-class and lower-middle-class communities helped to reduce violence and crime, in some cases much more successfully than did the committees of self-declared protectors and vigilantes.

Likewise, Salafist *da'wa* campaigns ("born again"–type appeals by puritan Muslim preachers) and Muslim Brotherhood charity initiatives extended themselves to offer spiritual and material assistance in communities that were paying an economic price for standing up against the state. At first these were welcomed by many communities, but when the Islamic groups insisted that aid recipients comply strictly with ideological and behavioral commands while also providing votes and support in exchange for bits of aid, their supposed benevolence began to backfire and breed resentment. Communities began to regard these forms of charity as another kind of coercive protection racket, not as routes to true participatory citizenship or community empowerment. The campaigns came to be perceived as heavily moralistic versions of Mubarak's old police state.

By the end of 2012, some of the dissident communities that had burned down police stations and chased out law enforcers had come full circle. Some were now asking the state to reintroduce the police, but on terms the community would dictate, in accordance with new concepts of participatory security and societal safety that the experiments of the past two years had generated. The genius of these nationally patterned but locally unique experiments in redefining and reenacting policing, social security, and protection practices provided glimpses of the deepening of substantive democratization in the country.

Innovative Electoral Mobilizations

The initial round of Egypt's first open presidential elections, on May 23 and 24, 2012, was indeed a high point that revealed the exciting pluralism, dynamism, and productivity of a long-latent democratic political culture in Egypt, one that the uprisings and violence of 2011 had brought to the surface and emboldened. However, it first seemed that the older Islamist parties would be best positioned to take advantage of the democratic opening. In the hastily organized and clumsily executed two-stage parliamentary elections of November 2011 and January 2012 that predated the presidential election, the Muslim Brotherhood drew upon previous electoral organizations and patron-client networks in urban neighborhoods and villages. Counter to the assumptions of most international observers, the members of the Brotherhood had not merely been languishing in prison during the past two decades, but had in fact been permitted as independents to participate in the rump parliamentary elections held under Mubarak since the mid-1980s (in coalition with the Labor Party) and on their own as independent Brotherhood-backed candidates since the late 1990s. Before that, Sadat's state in the 1970s had helped the Muslim Brotherhood establish electoral experience and social power by facilitating the election of its members into prominent civil society positions at the heads of professional syndicates and student unions. The state backed this Brotherhood ascendancy in civil society and electoral processees in an explicit attempt to crush the organized power of progressives and leftists in these spheres. Through this process, the Brotherhood had developed significant organizational and campaign experience, as much in support of the regime as in opposition. The organization's members had grown accustomed to working with the officials and within the norms of Mubarak's regime and, in fact, the Brotherhood had come to dominate the semiofficial moral policy and cultural censorship programs of the state during the last decade of Mubarak's rule. During that period the Brotherhood had also grabbed control of many professional syndicates and businessmen's organizations. Parliamentary debates in the last decade or so of Mubarak's rule had often been dominated by Brotherhood members of the People's Assembly who advocated neoconservative economic and moralistic cultural policies, not regime-critical or revolutionary ones.

During the 2011–12 parliamentary elections, during a time of food crisis and political crisis, the Brotherhood's distribution of gas, cooking oil, and foodstuffs to citizens, as well as the organization's well-honed constituent lists and get-out-the-vote operations on the ground, brought many votes to the polls (BBC News 2012b; Jadaliyya 2012). So it was no surprise when the Brotherhood was able to win 37 percent of the popular vote in the first elections to the People's Assembly, which translated into 47 percent of the seats. At the time of that vote in autumn 2011, the leftist, progressive religious groupings, youth, labor, and liberal groups that Mubarak's state had more rigidly excluded from politics, had only just begun to organize on the ground. What was surprising was how many Egyptians lodged protest votes not just against the old regime but against the Brotherhood as well, often choosing to vote for Salafist candidates, who won 24 percent of the vote. The Salafists' anticorruption and antiregime credentials may have seemed, at the time, to be much more solid than the Brotherhood's, or maybe the Salafist candidates achieved such a high percentage of the vote because their campaigns were flush with a flood of illegal funds coming from Saudi Arabia and other Persian Gulf sources. In the end, liberal and revolutionary parties gained 25 percent of seats, an impressive share given the organizational hurdles and the mountains of negative media propaganda the state had deployed against them and their inability to benefit from illicit campaign funds from the Gulf. A surprising number of truly revolutionary candidates did get elected to the first People's Assembly, including Mona Khalil, a bold woman leftist from the Upper Egyptian and partially Nubian-populated city of Aswan, whose strong popular base allowed her to lead the charge against old-regime policies as well as the hypocrisies of the conservative businessmen of the Brotherhood who were newly elected.

By the first round of the presidential elections in May 2012, just four months later, the spectacle of self-righteous, hypermoralistic grandstanding and sermonizing Salafi and Brotherhood parliamentarians in the newly elected People's Assembly had already disappointed or offended huge swaths of the Egyptian electorate. Meanwhile, progressive, populist, and leftist groupings were improving their ground organization and media profiles. These progressive groups identified positively with the revolution and also drew upon Egypt's proud nationalist past. They began to organize throughout the smaller cities and countryside in Egypt and to gain favorable coverage in the media. In the first round of the presidential elections, the changed attitudes of the voting public reflected the deepening of revolutionary consciousness, the expansion of progressive organization, and registered the rapid decline of public interest in or toleration for the Brotherhood's condescending moralism and Salafist sermonizing.

In a surprise victory, Hamdeen Sabahy, a young-spirited, charismatic, and articulate leader who identifies with the populism of the Nasser era, polled incredibly well. Sabahy had been a leader in social justice mobilizations since the time of the first anti-IMF protests and "Bread Riots" of the late 1970s. And while other older opposition leaders had hesitated, he had immediately stood with the revolutionaries in January 2011. In the May 2012 vote, he won the largest number of popular votes in all the cities of Egypt (BBC News 2012a; Kirkpatrick 2012). This victory disproved the misconception so common among international observers—and even among many Egyptian political analysts—that working-class and poor people would somehow "naturally" vote for Islamists in a democratic environment. To the contrary, Egypt's urban popular classes shifted wholesale against the Brotherhood and Salafis and into the progressive camp. Alexandria, which many had regarded as the strongest base for Islamist candidates and where their influence over civil society had been strongest for the longest period, voted in small numbers for the Brotherhood presidential candidate, placing Mohammad Morsi fourth in vote totals and Sabahy first.

But outside the cities, in the villages and countryside where open television media, youth journalism, and progressive organizations were tenuous or nonexistent, the old Brotherhood patron-client networks and political machines did pull in votes, and Morsi managed to move slightly ahead (25 percent of the vote went to Morsi, 24 percent to Ahmed Shafiq, and 22 percent to Sabahy). But the tidal shift in popular voting preferences between the parliamentary and presidential polls— with 70 percent of voters choosing Islamist parties in the parliamentary election and only 25 percent voting for a Brotherhood candidate four months later in the first round of the presidential race—signaled to many that the early parliamentary vote had been a vote *against* the old regime rather than *for* the Islamists. In the May election, only seven hundred thousand votes (out of fifty million) separated progressive-left candidate Sabahy from military man Shafiq. But because of these splits among the voting blocs of the opposition candidates, it was Morsi who entered the second round of presidential elections, standing against Mubarak-era aviation minister and former prime minister Shafiq, who was also a prominent military general and big-business contractor. In the second round in June (in which the top two vote-getters from the first round square off against each other to make sure that one person enters office with a 50 percent-plus mandate to rule), the Brotherhood mobilized reluctant voters through an "Anyone but Shafiq" campaign, promising to create access for all revolutionary and progressive forces (a promise Morsi would betray). So in that second round, Morsi eked out a narrow victory of less than 1 percent and became Egypt's first democratically elected president.

As this complex process revealed, however, Morsi was elected in the context not of uncontested Brotherhood popularity but during a period of cataclysmically fast Brotherhood decline and public dissatisfaction with conservative religious political groupings. And the paralysis, repression, secretive behavior, and animosity toward consensus that became the hallmarks of Morsi's governing style as president did not reverse but in fact accelerated this process of decline and dissatisfaction with Islamists among the Egyptian public and accelerated the formation or revival of popular non-Islamist political parties.

These newly formed and reinvigorated parties that came to constitute the visibly more pluralistic public sphere in Egypt included the Socialist Popular Alliance, the European-style Social Democrats, and the charismatic, Nasserist-leaning Popular Current (headed by the above-mentioned Hamdeen Sabahy). In the liberal center, parties that gained popularity included the Constitution Party (headed by Nobel Peace Prize laureate Mohamed ElBaradei) and Strong Egypt (the party of liberal Brotherhood dissident Abdel-Monem Abdel Fottouh). And on the pro-business but anti-Islamist center-right side of the political spectrum, the public sphere included the Free Egyptians Party (founded by Coptic billionaire Naguib Sawiris), the Conference Party (of former Arab League chief Amr Moussa), and the New Wafd Party (the historic party of the conservative nationalist establishment). All these parties came to be familiar fixtures in the media, with their leaders and essential policies creating a flourishing spectrum of debate. And all of these non-Brotherhood, non-Salafist parties came together by the end of 2012 to form the National Salvation Front to support a civil state and democratic pluralism and to challenge the exclusionary dynamic that Morsi's regime had pursued.

Imaginative Labor Actions

The spirit of revolution in Egypt had upended the once calcified political party system but also reinvigorated Egypt's professional syndicates, which from February through April 2011 overthrew many of their leaders who were tied either to Mubarak's party or to the conservative wing of the Muslim Brotherhood. In other countries, professional syndicates are often status-based organizations protecting the privileged, but in Egypt they tend to operate more like public-sector unions in the West, as vigilant protectors of the middle class.[5] As feminist leader and human rights specialist Mozn Hassan noted, "The March [2011] elections in the doctors' syndicate, where they threw out the old guard Muslim Brothers as well as Mubarak-linked leaders and where women captured some leadership roles, represented the end of an era when professionals had leaned toward social conservatism" (Amar 2011a). The doctors' syndicate also voted to give three thousand Egyptian pounds to the family of each person killed in the Tahrir demonstrations. In the same period, the Supreme Constitutional Court declared the state's attempts to freeze syndicate elections unconstitutional, the journalists' syndicate dumped its old-regime leader and mobilized to end state control and corruption of television and the press, and the lawyers' syndicate sent its Mubarak-linked leader on a "permanent holiday" and organized new elections.

The state was also forced to draw up a new independent syndicate for public-sector pensioners (which then got stuck awaiting parliamentary ratification). This giant organization, representing more than 8.5 million people and asserting control over 435 billion Egyptian pounds in pension funds, immediately became a huge player in revolutionary politics. Moreover, the other professional syndicates came together in late February to form a unified coalition to mobilize an additional 8 million professionals.

While the middle-class syndicates were on the march, the working class was not slowing down either. In the spring of 2011, *Al-Masry Al-Youm*, a progressive Arabic newspaper in Egypt, published a survey of the strikes happening on a typical midweek workday up and down the Nile in small towns and factory outposts: 350 butane gas distributors demonstrating against the Ministry of Social Solidarity in the town of Takhla; 1,200 bank employees on strike, demanding better wages in Gharbiya; 350 potato chip factory workers striking in Monufiya; 100 nursing students holding a sit-in to take over the medical syndicate in Beheira; 1,500 villagers in Mahsama protesting the city council's decision to close a subsidized bread bakery; workers at a spinning and weaving factory on strike in Assiut; 30 teachers blocking the education ministry in Alexandria to demand tenure; and 200 tax authority employees occupying the collector's office in Cairo and demanding better wages and benefits.

In late 2012, another wave of labor mobilizations began cresting, in cigarette factories, in weaving mills, and at port facilities and container shipment units. National coordination of the workers' actions was somewhat hampered by splits between the Independent Trade Union Federation and the Egyptian Democratic Labor Congress, but these organizations continued to collaborate on supporting pro-labor policies and opposing Morsi's repressive rule (Beinin 2013b). Despite these tensions, in 2012 all evidence pointed to the intensification rather than the exhaustion of workers' militancy. The revolution deepened as anger against Brotherhood antilabor policies unleashed another round of labor mobilization. In November 2012, President Morsi issued a labor law decree that forced all labor leaders over the age of sixty into retirement; Brotherhood figures were put in their place. This move reversed the independence of labor movements, a decades-long struggle that had achieved its hard-won goal finally in December 2010. In response, thousands of workers from the Misr Spinning and Weaving Company, both women and men, marched on the central square of Mahalla, a factory town in a northern province that has a proud history of setting trends for social justice and worker organizing and that has been a hub of popular uprising at the forefront of Egypt's three revolutions—in 1919, 1952, and then 2011. On December 7, 2012, residents of Mahalla declared themselves the "Independent Republic of Greater Mahalla," a "Brotherhood-free zone," and stated that they would not support the new slapdash constitution or reactionary labor laws (Charbel 2012). Notably, the

"Republic of Mahalla" also stood firmly against the rollback of women's rights that the new constitution and Morsi's policies represented. The Mahalla labor leadership, which includes many women, viewed workers' rights and women's rights as two sides of the same struggle. These labor movements want to push the more middle-class-leaning National Salvation Front opposition leaders to focus on economic, social, and workers' rights issues, and gender within this intersection, rather than exclusively on questions of secularism and civil/political liberties.

In response to the militancy of Mahalla, the Brotherhood sent in plainclothes militias who used birdshot, rocks, Molotov cocktails, rifles, and even fireworks against the demonstrators, injuring more than seven hundred, as evidenced by the many videos shot by witnesses. The "Republic of Mahalla," which came to be supported by liberal, leftist, popular groupings in the province, pensioners' associations, and popular committees, as well as by many religious youth who broke off from Brotherhood and Salafi parties, did not define itself as a separatist movement. Rather, it presented itself as the embodiment of opposition to Morsi's return to Mubarak-era repression, and its supporters dedicated themselves to preserving and extending the aims and momentum of the January 25 revolution at the popular level. The "Republic of Mahalla" represented one more instance of revolutionary deepening in Egypt, showing that popular consciousness, grassroots organizing, and collective and community power were growing and becoming more articulate, hollowing out the repressive structures of power that at the top of the state seemed, deceptively, to be stable and unchanged.

Boundary-Challenging Gender Solidarities

Perhaps one of the most surprising and groundbreaking processes that demonstrated the deepening of revolutionary culture and consciousness in Egypt during the first two years of transformation was the creation of new kinds of alliances, interactions, and common forms of radical conviviality between disparate gender and class-identified groups. These groups had at first embodied starkly opposed understandings of the social character of public space and resistance action. In the first waves of protests and demonstrations that rocked Tahrir Square in 2011, the front lines of the revolution included feminist groups and other masses of women aiming for empowerment and emancipation. These groups, at first, drew largely from the middle classes and utilized an insistently respectable and peace-oriented human rights discourse. On the other hand, the same demonstrations were also energized by phalanxes of young men organized into sports-fan clubs, called Ultras (El-Sherif 2012b), who identified in hypermasculine ways as ruthless and fearless vanguards unafraid to use violence (Amar 2011b). These groups saw human rights discourse as effete and tended to regard women as passive, to be protected or excluded from public space while battles with the state were launched. These Ultras deployed intentionally vulgar, mocking discourse and used aggressive means, not just passive resistance, to push back the police and army and to occupy public spaces.

The two sets of groups resented the same adversaries—police officers and military troops—who had systematically harassed and molested women protesters with intensifying regularity since 2003 and had beaten, detained, and killed boys and young men from the sports clubs, branding them thugs and hooligans, in a series of incidents since the 1990s. But when the initial occupation of Tahrir Square began in 2011, suspicion and tension characterized the relationship between these two sets of revolutionaries. Were the boys of the Ultras just another mass of sexual harassers, too similar to Mubarak's plainclothes thugs who infiltrated the square to humiliate and torture protesters? Were their lower-middle-class and working-class norms of masculinity and aggressiveness a threat to the women's movements' commitments to peaceful protest and human rights discourse?

In the first months of uprisings, women had asked men's organizations, even the Muslim Brotherhood, to protect them not just from thugs but from some of these aggressive popular youth clubs that had become the shock troops of the revolution. But by October 2011 new forms of co-understanding had begun to develop, reflecting a will to remake gender relations, challenge discourses of protection and violation, and bridge the class divide that Mubarak's segregationist urban housing policies and public morality campaigns had produced (Amar 2013) and that would be revived and extended by the Muslim Brotherhood's proposals for gender segregation on buses and other public transport and at public facilities. In the autumn of 2011, during the battles of

Mohammad Mahmoud Street, and after the notorious blue bra scandal described above, women's groups and Ultras began to mobilize shoulder to shoulder. Women began protecting themselves and taking physically assertive action rather than asking for police or Brotherhood protection. During their long encampment around the parliament building, in February 2012, the Ultras allowed women and girls to join them, altering their doctrines whereby women were not allowed to participate in neighborhood sit-ins overnight or to join in explicitly vulgar chants and marches. Younger girls and women began to be seen merging into the front lines of these kinds of exuberant campaigns, which had abandoned middle-class notions of respectability and had faced the coercive apparatuses of the state physically and fearlessly (Sharafeldin 2012).

These new gender and class mergings were also reflected in the explosions of new graffiti and public murals, often painted and repainted by artists from Upper Egypt as well as countless artists from among the Ultras. These wall paintings, particularly in downtown around Tahrir Square and government ministries, were often vulgar cartoons of police, state, military, or Brotherhood officials, or angelic portraits of boys martyred during the revolution and its massacres. But as revolutionary time advanced, the dominance of masculinist imagery receded and this radical art culture began to take on feminist themes as well, with women martyrs and mothers of martyrs depicted as iconic and courageous (Schielke and Winegar 2012). *Graffiti harimi,* women's murals painted by both feminist activists and Ultras, memorialized female militants as physically assertive, sometimes heroically violent superheroes (Fecteau 2012). And as 2012 began, haunting images of veiled women martyrs, stenciled in black spray paint on trees, under bridges, and at street crossings, became the specters of the revolution, taking the place of the predictable Che Guevara and V-for-Vendetta iconographies that had been the more common fixtures of youth graffiti art in the first month of the uprising.

This process of creating cultural and social bridges between radical feminists and young male militants reflected the reterritorialization of certain urban spaces by the revolution. Huge swaths of downtown Cairo were abandoned by "respectable" classes and reoccupied by open-air political cultures, debate cafés, and new music scenes that brought class and gender groups together regularly in ways that would have been considered perverse or risky in the Mubarak age (Abaza 2013). Of course, this intermingling was not seamless. Sexual harassment of women persisted, but some members of working-class Ultra groups stood against this and designated themselves antiharassment vigilantes (Elkamel 2012).

By the time of the Ittihadiya protests in front of Morsi's presidential palace in December 2012, remarkable forms of commingling were becoming commonplace. Ultras wearing gas masks and carrying rocks and shields mixed more or less comfortably with members of elite women's community groups who had streamed into the plaza from the chic villas of neighboring Heliopolis (Long 2012). Of course, women's groups were not composed only of middle-class individuals. On the occasion of the Ittihadiya protests, thousands of working-class women labor activists from the newly declared "Independent Republic of Greater Mahalla" also traveled into town to join the demonstrations. And women leaders of *gama'iyaat,* social security collectives from the slum areas of urban Cairo, also joined en masse. In these reterritorialized spaces of public cultures and mingled protest actions, a new nation of cross-class solidarity and gender justice began to be performed. With this, decades of intentional efforts by the state and ruling classes to create mutual suspicion and deploy sexualized violence to divide and rule Egypt were countered by a deepening revolutionary dynamic of radical sociability and gendered conviviality.

Conclusion

The appeal of Egypt's January 25, 2011, revolution—for social justice, a civil state, gender parity, economic equalization, the end of police brutality and security forces' impunity, the strengthening of worker and welfare rights, and the establishment of a newly independent foreign policy—has been described by many as constituting a "third way" between Islamic conservatism and military-secular authoritarianism. This terminology resembles how political activists in the Global South used to talk of a Third World in a good way, as a progressive alternative to both communism and capitalism, or, in a very different sense, how Bill Clinton or Tony Blair used to declare support for a "third way" between neoliberal trickle-down economics and social-democratic welfare statism. But this chapter's analysis of the struggles and advances in Egypt has demonstrated that these third-way metaphors may be inaccurate and anachronistic.

There is only one road to substantive democracy in Egypt, and it is paved with mobilizations such as those described above, mobilizations that improve social movement capacities, generate new forms of political consciousness and policy options, and invent new everyday ways for Egyptians to identify with each other across class, gender, and cultural divides. These deepening practices and processes advocated by the demonstrators and activists identified with the January 25 revolution spread, by 2013, across diverse classes and evolved into modes of participation and autonomy in local contexts. The other two "alternatives," Islamic conservatism and military-secular authoritarianism, by the start of 2013 had proven in fact to be two-thirds of the old triangle of domination—cronies, generals, and religionizing merchants—that characterized Mubarak's regime for thirty years and that persistently maintained that "no alternative was possible."

As demonstrators, organizers, and new nationwide political party coalitions insisted, military-authoritarians and the Brotherhood were not distinct regimes vying with each other to provide alternative futures. Instead, each constituted an essential element of the old three-part structure of the ancien régime, that is, the triangle of *cronyism* (Mubarak's "Barons of Privatization") (Amar 2011c), *militarism* (the SCAF generals and their economic and coercive monopolies) (Abul-Magd 2011; Amar 2012a), and hypocritical *moralism* (conservative Brotherhood businessmen who mask their profit interests and security alliances behind patriarchal and moralistic religious agendas of protection).

These new waves of political assertions and cultural creations, described above, demonstrated that democratization in Egypt would move forward by decentering and removing from hegemony these three aspects of the old regime, not by choosing one of these "three paths": Not the pseudosecular liberalism that preserves Mubarak's crony authoritarianism. Not the path of militarist populism that shoots and incarcerates citizens in order to save the nation from itself. Not the route of Brotherhood moralism, which was not part of the revolution at all but an old strategy, used since the 1980s, for producing economic dependence and merchant wealth for a few corrupt, conservative businessmen. Of course, the revolution would not aim to eliminate any one or all three of these centers of power; rather, it would aim to split them apart from each other and shatter their repressive hegemonic bloc, so as to allow popular aspirations to rise to the surface.

Egypt's forms of uprising, creativity, bravery, and resistance, beginning at the start of 2011 and barreling forward into 2013, accomplished the phenomenally transformative work of exposing these three invisible aspects of domination that made up the triangle of authoritarian rule. The new revolutionary movements succeeded in raising consciousness, creating new political organizations, enabling previously impossible coalitions and solidarities, and mobilizing new passions, visions, and identities. This was a wholly necessary process of struggle, to bring these relations of power and domination into the light. Their actions cannot be summarized in merely the toppling of a dictator or measured by the results of any one election or referendum. By 2013 a deeply exhausted, but deeply changed, wiser public sphere and popular consciousness had emerged. And bold alternatives could start to be imagined.

Even if it had not yet arrived, the future had been unleashed. This, we can see, is the reality in Egypt that deserves the name Revolution.

Notes

1. In the year 2000, huge protests, hundreds of thousands strong, began to appear, at first in struggle with the Palestinian Intifada, the uprising against the Israeli occupation, and then in 2003 against what was perceived as an illegal U.S. invasion and occupation of Iraq. By 2006, these movements had turned away from regional issues and turned their attention toward social injustice, political repression, and entrenched authoritarianism within Egypt itself.

2. As analyzed by prominent labor analyst Joel Beinin (2012): "Workers were quick to mobilize in the early stages of the groundswell that eventually unseated Hosni Mubarak, and they deserve more credit for his ouster than they typically receive. Soon after the uprising began, workers violated ETUF's legal monopoly on trade union organization and formed the Egyptian Federation of Independent Trade Unions (EFITU)—the first new institution to emerge from the revolt. Labor

mobilization continued at an unprecedented level during 2011 and early 2012, and workers established hundreds of new, independent enterprise-level unions. They also secured a substantially higher minimum wage. Yet, though the labor movement has made headway, problems persist. New unions face funding difficulties and the independent labor movement is internally divided."

3. The Muslim Brotherhood, a worldwide movement today, was founded in Ismailia, Egypt, in 1928 by Hassan El-Banna. The organization has long mixed economic and merchant business activities, nationalistic agendas, conservative moralistic religious ideologies, and clientelistic support-building charity organizations. In the past it supported violence, strongly resisting the British colonial occupation of the country and then attempting to assassinate Egyptian president Nasser in 1954. Nasser's government repressed the Brotherhood, but the organization was rehabilitated and partially co-opted by the Egyptian state during the administration of Anwar Sadat in the 1970s. In 2011, the Muslim Brotherhood became a legal organization and founded a political party, the Freedom and Justice Party, that successfully contested elections (Mitchell [1969] 1993).

The Salafist movement (or Salafis or, in Arabic, *al-Salafiya*) is made up of charismatic preachers and grassroots piety movements that have long roots in Egypt but that gained momentum and popularity when infused with funding and leadership imported from Pakistan in the 1980s and Saudi Arabia in the 1990s. Distinct from the Brotherhood, Salafists are not unified into one political organization or doctrine, and they range from anticapitalists to Persian Gulf plutocrats, from populists to hierarchists. Their doctrines often focus on the need to return to an originalist Islam and sharia jurisprudence, which in their interpretations orbit intensively around the control of women's bodies and of public moralities. They also proclaim against the corruption brought on by wealth, power, and vanity, so they often formerly spoke against participation in politics—that is, until 2011, when they jumped at the opportunity to form several political parties, including the Party of Light, Hizb anNour (El-Sherif 2012a; Brown 2011).

4. Menoufiya is the hometown of presidents Sadat and Mubarak and benefited from their patronage, so some of the anti-Brotherhood and anticonstitution vote there may have been more pro–old regime than pro-revolution.

5. The following two paragraphs on labor movement activity appeared in slightly different form in Amar (2011a).

References

Abaza, Mona. 2013. "Walls, Segregating Downtown Cairo and the Mohammed Mahmud Street Graffiti." *Theory, Culture & Society* 30 (1): 122–39.

Abul-Magd, Zeinab. 2010. "Rebellion in the Time of Cholera: Failed Empire, Unfinished Nation in Egypt 1840–1920." *Journal of World History* 21 (4): 691–719.

———. 2011. "The Army and the Economy in Egypt." Jadaliyya, December 23. http://www.jadaliyya.com (accessed January 21, 2013).

———. 2012. "Understanding SCAF: The Long Reign of Egypt's Generals." *Cairo Review of Global Affairs* (Summer): 11–159.

Agha, Hussain, and Robert Malley. 2012. "This Is Not a Revolution." *New York Review of Books,* November 8. http://www.nybooks.com (accessed January 20, 2013).

Ali, Amro. 2012. "Saeeds of Revolution: De-mythologizing Khaled Saeed." Jadaliyya, June 5. http://www.jadaliyya.com (accessed January 27, 2013).

Amar, Paul. 2011a. "Egypt after Mubarak." *The Nation,* May 23. http://www.thenation.com (accessed January 19, 2013).

———. 2011b. "Turning the Gendered Politics of the Security State Inside Out?" *International Feminist Journal of Politics* 13 (3): 299–328.

———. 2011c. "Why Mubarak Is Out." Jadaliyya, February 1. http://www.jadaliyya.com (accessed January 21, 2013).

———. 2012a. "Egypt as a Globalist Power: Mapping Military Participation in Decolonizing Internationalism, Repressive Entrepreneurialism, and Humanitarian Globalization between the Revolutions of 1952 and 2011." In *Global South to the Rescue: Emerging Humanitarian Superpowers and Globalizing Rescue Industries,* edited by Paul Amar, 179–94. New York: Routledge.

———. 2012b. "The Revolution Continues." *International Feminist Journal of Politics,* December 24.

———. 2013. *The Security Archipelago: Human-Security States, Sexuality Politics, and the End of Neoliberalism.* Durham, N.C.: Duke University Press.

Amar, Paul, and Noha Roushdy. 2012. "Concept Paper: Societal Violence and Alternative Security Practices." Nazra for Feminist Studies, October 22. http://nazra.org/en/2012/10/concept-paper-societal-violence-and-alternative-security-practices (accessed January 27, 2013).

Associated Press. 2012. "Egypt's Top Court Suspends Work Indefinitely Amid Protest." Fox News, December 2. http://www.foxnews.com (accessed January 20, 2013).

Avitabile, Matthew. 2011. "Tribes Threaten to Attack Suez Canal if Mubarak Does Not Step Down." The Total Collapse, January 30. http://www.thetotalcollapse.com (accessed January 27, 2013).

Bayat, Asef. 2011. "Paradoxes of Arab Refo-lutions." Jadaliyya, March 3. http://www.jadaliyya.com (accessed January 20, 2013).

BBC News. 2011. "Cairo Clashes Leave 24 Dead after Coptic Church Protest." October 9. http://www.bbc.co.uk/news/world-middle-east-15235212 (accessed January 27, 2013).

———. 2012a. "Egypt Election: Hamdin Sabbahi Seeks Recount." May 27. http://www.bbc.co.uk/news/world-middle-east-18223551 (accessed January 20, 2013).

———. 2012b. "Egypt's Islamist Parties Win Elections to Parliament." January 21. http://www.bbc.co.uk/news/world-middle-east-16665748 (accessed January 20, 2013).

Beinin, Joel. 2012. *The Rise of Egypt's Workers.* Washington, D.C.: Carnegie Endowment for International Peace. http://carnegieendowment.org/files/egypt_labor. pdf (accessed January 27, 2013).

———. 2013a. "Was There a January 25 Revolution?" Jadaliyya, January 25. http:// www.jadaliyya.com (accessed January 27, 2013).

———. 2013b. "Workers, Trade Unions and Egypt's Future." Middle East Research and Information Project, January 18. http://merip.org/mero/mero011813 (accessed January 25, 2013).

Bremer, Jennifer Ann. 2011. "Leadership and Collective Action in Egypt's Popular Committees: Emergence of Authentic Civic Activism in the Absence of the State." *International Journal of Not-for-Profit Law* 13 (4): 70–92.

Bremmer, Ian. 2011. "Why Egypt Was Not a Successful Revolution." Big Think, video, April 11. http://bigthink.com/ideas/37829 (accessed January 20, 2013).

Brown, Jonathan. 2011. *Salafis and Sufis in Egypt.* Washington, D.C.: Carnegie Endowment for International Peace. http://carnegieendowment.org/files/ salafis_sufis.pdf (accessed January 27, 2013).

Charbel, Jano. 2012. "In Opposition to Morsy, Mahalla Declares Autonomy." Egypt Independent, December 12. http://www.egyptindependent.com (accessed January 21, 2013).

Dekel, Udi, and Orit Perlov. 2012. *President Morsi and Israel-Egypt Relations: Egyptian Discourse of the Social Network, July 2012.* INSS [Institute for National Security Studies] Insight, no. 357, July 25. http://www.inss.org.il/upload/ (FILE)1343217753.pdf (accessed January 19, 2013).

Dorsey, James M. 2012. "Egyptian Ultras Emerge as Powerful Political Force— Analysis." Eurasia Review, September 10. http://www.eurasiareview.com (accessed January 19, 2013).

Egyptian Initiative for Personal Rights. 2013. "25 January 2013: The Revolution Two Years On . . . Injustice Continues State Crimes Remain Unpunished: The Interior Ministry Is above the Law and the Public Prosecution Is Missing in Action." http://eipr.org/en/print/report/2013/01/22/1602 (accessed January 27, 2013).

Elkamel, Sara. 2012. "The Protester: Mariam Kirollos. Special Report: The Voice of the Veil." GlobalPost, August 1. http://www.globalpost.com (accessed January 27, 2013).

El-Meehy, Asya. 2012. "Egypt's Popular Committees: From Moments of Madness to NGO Dilemmas." *Middle East Report* 42 (265, Winter). http://www.merip. org/mer/mer265 (accessed January 19, 2013).

El-Sherif, Ashraf. 2012a. "The Salafi Movement: Competing Visions (Part I)." Egypt

Independent, January 11. http://www.egyptindependent.com (accessed January 27, 2013).

———. 2012b. "The Ultras' Politics of Fun Confront Tyranny." Jadaliyya, February 5. http://www.jadaliyya.com (accessed January 27, 2013).

Eskandar, Wael. 2011. "SCAF: A Brief History of Injustice." Al-Ahram Weekly, November 10. http://english.ahram.org.eg (accessed January 27, 2013).

———. 2013. "Brothers and Officers: A History of Pacts." Jadaliyya, January 25. http://www.jadaliyya.com (accessed January 27, 2013).

Ezzedine, Mohamed Saeed. 2012. Research report for project "Societal Violence and Alternative Security Practices." Nazra for Feminist Studies, November 25. http://nazra.org/en/2012/11/introducing-societal-violence-and-alternative-security-practices-research-projects (accessed January 27, 2013).

Fahmy, Heba. 2012. "The Pitfalls and Limitations of the Revolution Protection Plan." Egypt Independent, November 27. http://www.egyptindependent.com (accessed January 27, 2013).

Fecteau, Andre. 2012. "A Graffiti Campaign Brings Strong Female Votes to the Streets." Egypt Independent, March 10. http://www.egyptindependent.com (accessed January 21, 2013).

Gerbaudo, Paulo. 2011. "Los Indignados: The Emerging Politics of Outrage." Red Pepper, August 2011. http://www.redpepper.org.uk/los-indignados (accessed January 19, 2013).

Ghosh, Bobby. 2012. "The Most Important Man in the Middle East: Morsi's Moment." Time, November 28. http://world.time.com (accessed January 19, 2013).

GlobalPost. 2012. "Egypt: President Mohammed Morsi 'Annuls' Decree." Video from Ahram Online, December 5. http://www.globalpost.com (accessed January 20, 2013).

Hamalawy, Hossam. 2011. "English Translation of Interview with Hossam El-Hamalawy on the Role of Labor/Unions in the Egyptian Revolution." By Bassam Haddad. Jadaliyya, April 30. http://www.jadaliyya.com (accessed January 20, 2013).

Herrera, Linda. 2011. "Two Young Men Who Sparked Egypt's Revolt." The Tyee, February 1. http://thetyee.ca (accessed January 20, 2013).

Horowitz, Adam. 2011. "Ready for a Tahrir Moment? — Occupy Wall Street, the 'Arab Spring' and Israel/Palestine." Mondoweiss, October 4. http://mondoweiss.net (accessed January 19, 2013).

Hussein, Abdel-Rahman. 2012. "Egyptian Protesters Claim They Were Tortured by Muslim Brotherhood." Guardian, December 12. http://www.guardian.co.uk (accessed January 27, 2013).

Iskandar, Adel. 2012. "A Year in the Life of Egypt's Media: A 2001 Timeline [Updated]." Jadaliyya, January 26. http://www.jadaliyya.com (accessed January 27, 2013).

Jadaliyya. 2012. "Egyptian Elections: Preliminary Results." January 9. http://www.jadaliyya.com (accessed January 20, 2013).

Kirkpatrick, David D. 2011. "Mubarak Orders Crackdown, with Revolt Sweeping Egypt." *New York Times,* January 28. http://www.nytimes.com (accessed January 20, 2013).

———. 2012. "First Fighting Islamists, Now the Free Market." *New York Times,* December 25. http://www.nytimes.com (accessed January 20, 2013).

Liang, Sidney. 2011. "Riots in China: The Arab Spring Has Encouraged Workers to Fight." Socialist Worker Online, July 2. http://www.socialistworker.co.uk (accessed January 19, 2013).

Long, Scott. 2012. "Cairo Diary, December 2012: Walls, Women, Rape, Fear." A Paper Bird blog, December 4. http://paper-bird.net (accessed January 21, 2012).

Mitchell, Richard P. (1969) 1993. *The Society of the Muslim Brothers.* Oxford: Oxford University Press.

Mock, Geoffrey. 2012. Keeping Alive the Hope of the Arab Uprisings. Duke Today, February 20. http://today.duke.edu/2012/02/arabspringconference (accessed January 20, 2013).

Reuters. 2011. "Egypt Budget Targets Poor, Introduces Capital Gains Tax." June 1. http://www.reuters.com (accessed January 27, 2013).

Salem, Sara, and Amanda Rogers. 2013. "Neo-liberal Islamism and the Effects of Egypt's IMF Loan." Muftah, January 6. http://muftah.org (accessed January 20, 2013).

Sallam, Hesham. 2012. "Morsy and the 'Nationalization' of the Revolution: Some Initial Reflections." Jadaliyya, November 22. http://www.jadaliyya.com (accessed January 19, 2013).

Schielke, Samuli, and Jessica Winegar. 2012. "The Writing on the Walls of Egypt." *Middle East Report* 42 (265, Winter). http://www.merip.org/mer/mer265 (accessed January 21, 2013).

Shafy, Samiha 2011. "'Horribly Humiliating': Egyptian Woman Tells of 'Virginity Tests.'" Spiegel Online International, June 10. http://www.spiegel.de/international (accessed January 27, 2013).

Sharafeldin, Marwa. 2012. "'The Revolution Continues': A Conversation." Paper presented at the conference "The Egyptian Revolution, One Year On: Causes, Characteristics and Fortunes," Oxford University, May 18–19. http://oxford egyptconference.wordpress.com/programme (accessed January 21, 2013).

Shokr, Ahmad. 2012a. "Back to the Table, Egypt and the IMF." Egypt Independent, August 23. http://www.egyptindependent.com (accessed January 20, 2013).

———. 2012b. "Reflection on Two Revolutions." *Middle East Report* 42 (265, Winter). http://www.merip.org/mer/mer265 (accessed January 19, 2013).

Soliman, Samer. 2011. *The Autumn of the Dictatorship: Fiscal Crisis and Political Change in Egypt under Mubarak.* Stanford, Calif.: Stanford University Press.

Sukarieh, Mayssoun. 2012. "The Sounds of Cairo." *CounterPunch Newsletter,* December 5. http://www.counterpunch.org (accessed January 20, 2013).

UNICEF. 2003. "Egypt, Statistics." Updated February 21. http://www.unicef.org/infobycountry/egypt_statistics.html (accessed January 27, 2013).

United Nations Development Programme and Institute of National Planning, Egypt. 2010. *Human Development Report 2010: Youth in Egypt—Building Our Future.* Cairo: U.N. Development Programme. http://hdr.undp.org/en/reports (accessed January 19, 2013).

Urban Dictionary. 2011. "Going Egyptian." http://www.urbandictionary.com (accessed January 19, 2013).

Wallerstein, Immanuel. 1979. "The Ottoman Empire and the Capitalist World-Economy: Some Questions for Research." *Review* 2 (3): 389–98.

Personal Interview

Personal interview. 2012. Osama al-Mahdy, journalist and Sufi political organizer. Cairo, June 12.

Bahrain

ADAM HANIEH

IN A *WASHINGTON TIMES* OPINION PIECE published on April 19, 2011, Bahrain's ruling monarch, King Hamad, proudly recounted his government's response to the demonstrations that had spread throughout the country in February (Khalifa 2011). Noting that the people's "grievances about civil and political rights for all Bahrainis are legitimate," the king claimed that "demands for well-paying jobs, transparency in economic affairs and access to better social services were received with good will." In answer to these demands, the king stated that he had "offered an unconditional dialogue with the opposition so as to maintain the stability of our country and address the demands for reform." Even though "extremist elements" had attempted to undermine this process, the king insisted that he was optimistic and had "faith in our people. We all realize that now is the time to strike a balance between stability and gradual reform, always adhering to the universal values of human rights, free expression and religious tolerance."

Reading these words, a casual observer might be forgiven for thinking that Bahrain's leadership had averted a replay of the popular uprisings that had struck North Africa and many of the country's neighbors throughout the first half of 2011. Yet reality—as is so often the case with the claims of Middle East regimes—was entirely at odds with the seductive language of the monarch. In the single week leading up to the op-ed, four Bahraini political prisoners had died in custody. One of those killed was Karim Fakhrawi, a founder of *Al-Wasat,* the country's only independent newspaper, whose corpse was released to his family covered in cuts and bruises. A BBC reporter was to describe the body of another of those killed in detention as "beaten black and blue, his lacerated back resembled a bloody zebra; he appeared to have been whipped with heavy cables, his ankles and wrists manacled" (Gardner 2011). As the king spoke of his regime's "good will," a twenty-seven-year-old Bahraini woman, Zainab al-Khawaja, was entering the second week of a hunger strike in protest of the arrest, torture, and attempted rape of her father—the renowned human rights activist Abdulhadi al-Khawaja. Khawaja, who required a four-hour operation after his jawbone had been smashed by his interrogators, was later sentenced to life imprisonment by a military court. In addition to these high-profile cases, hundreds more Bahrainis were being detained and tortured as the king penned his article.

In comparison to the uprisings elsewhere in the Middle East, this repression received scant coverage in the Western media. Informed discussion of Bahrain's history and its recent protests was conspicuously absent from the wider popular discourse, and any mention of the events in Bahrain usually formed a simple addendum to the other, higher-profile struggles of 2011. Bahrain's uprising, however, was no less significant than the revolts elsewhere. The popular movement that emerged in early 2011 was the latest manifestation of a decades-long struggle for political and socioeconomic rights in the country. Media silence and the lack of international criticism confirm a long-standing pattern of open backing of Bahrain's rulers by U.S. and European leaders. This support indicates the fundamental importance of the country to Western interests in the Middle East. It also means that any full assessment of the 2011 uprisings across the Arab world needs to recover Bahrain's story from the back pages of international news.

The central argument of this chapter runs against a dominant narrative that portrays Bahraini politics through the lens of superficial and largely erroneous depictions of religious conflicts between Sunni and Shia sects. In contrast, this chapter aims to situate Bahrain within a two-pronged analytical frame: (1) the wider context of a U.S.-led regional order in the Middle East, and (2) the particular characteristics of the country's political economy as it has developed historically. Within this perspective, the first part of the chapter presents a brief account of Bahraini history, covering the country's long experience of colonialism, the imprint that this left on its social structure, and the labor and political struggles that emerged during the postcolonial oil era. The second part turns to the key features of Bahrain's political economy and the country's significance for patterns of foreign domination in the Middle East. The final section presents an account of the uprising itself—drawn from interviews with participants, news reports, and other analyses—and concludes with an assessment of possible future trajectories that the country may witness.

Bahrain: The Colonial Imprint

For centuries, successive colonial and regional powers have viewed Bahrain as a key node in a wider matrix of control extending across the Gulf and the broader Middle East. This geopolitical significance has been an important factor in constituting the country's own distinctive socioeconomic structure. In the early 1500s, the thirty-three-island archipelago had become a focal point of Portuguese, Iranian, and Ottoman struggles to dominate trade networks in the Gulf. By 1602, Iran had won this conflict, but with the decline of the Safavid Dynasty in the early 1700s, its grip on Bahrain weakened. Soon after, the current ruling family of Bahrain, the al-Khalifa, arrived in the area from Kuwait (Crystal 1995). In 1783, following several years of rivalry with Arab tribes that owed fealty to Iran, the al-Khalifa conquered Bahrain and moved their prosperous pearling and trading operations there.

Despite its political instability during the eighteenth century, Bahrain was a key location for trade and merchant activities in the Gulf. It formed the major port in the trade of Indian goods between Basra (in modern-day Iraq) and Muscat (Oman) and was one of the most important pearling centers in the Gulf. The coming of the al-Khalifa instigated a series of profound social changes that continue to shape the country today. Unlike the people living in Qatar, Kuwait, or the sheikhdoms of the Southern Gulf, the majority of Bahrain's population adhered to a version of Shia Islam, while the al-Khalifa joined an existing, much smaller, Sunni community (Cole 2002; Fuccaro 2009). These sectarian differences were reflected in social divisions—the Sunni constituted the bulk of the merchant and ruling elite, dominating the lucrative pearl trade that was the socioeconomic base of al-Khalifa rule. Distinct from the pearling trade, the Shia majority was concentrated in rural date farming and fishing. Shia farmers were required to pay a poll and water tax to the al-Khalifa—similar taxes were not placed on the Sunni population (Khuri 1991, 48). Politically, these divisions were reflected, as Fuccaro (2009, 17) notes, in the "different sociopolitical organisations and built environments of towns and villages, and in the strictly compartmentalised religious and political life of their Sunni and Shi'i residents." The imprint of this early history on the country's class and sectarian makeup remains vitally important to this day.

Contemporaneous with the consolidation of al-Khalifa rule, the end of the nineteenth century saw British dominance extend across all the Gulf Arab states (with the exception of the areas known as Najd and Hijaz—the future Saudi Arabia—and some recalcitrant Arab and Iranian tribes along the coastal areas). Throughout the region, Britain encouraged the concentration of power within the hands of individual rulers who were connected to wider ruling families and could trace their origins back to one of the Arabian Peninsula tribes. Britain's major concern was to exclude other colonial and regional powers from the Gulf region so that it could continue its own profitable engagement with pearling and other trade. These interests in the Gulf were subordinate to a broader colonial framework centered on enduring control over India. Under the pretense of fighting "piracy," the British negotiated treaties with the ruling families across the Gulf, forbidding them from entering negotiations with any other foreign powers and preventing a buildup of any rival naval power. British control was so extensive that no foreigner could enter any of the Southern Gulf states without explicit British permission (Zahlan 1998, 21).

In addition to the ruling families, a network of influential Arab, Persian, and Indian merchant families helped the British maintain control over the Gulf, serving as "native agents" who supplied the British with information, petty rumors, and other intelligence about the goings-on within Gulf society (Onley 2004). As had the rulers of other Gulf states, the al-Khalifa had signed a series of treaties with the British between 1861 and 1914, and a native agent was stationed in the country's capital, Manama. In 1946, the headquarters of Britain's chief colonial officer in the Gulf, the political resident, was moved to Manama, where it remained until Bahrain's independence in 1971. From the vantage point of Bahrain, Britain thus coordinated its control over the entire Gulf.

The Oil Era

The discovery of oil in the Gulf region in the early 1930s both disrupted the social relations that had developed under colonialism and reinforced the position of the Gulf rulers who were so central to British rule in the region. U.S., British, and French oil companies were granted exploration concessions from 1923 onward, but it took until 1931 before oil was first discovered in Bahrain. Oil production expanded immediately after World War II, following the consolidation of oil as the world's most important "strategic commodity" (Bromley 1991)—a critical source of energy and essential raw material for global production chains. Oil's status meant that the Gulf had become a focal point for the geostrategic rivalries that emerged following the end of the war. Consequently, processes of state and class formation in the region became firmly tied to U.S.–British rivalries, as well as to those nations' shared interest in avoiding any popular control of oil resources by the people of the Middle East.

The significance of the Gulf meant that both the United States and Britain looked to the region's rulers as major pillars of support. The 1950s corresponded, however, with the rise of a range of nationalist and left-wing movements across the Middle East. These movements profoundly affected Bahrain, with workers agitating for national rights and opposing the servile attitude of the al-Khalifa monarchy toward Britain. In 1954, Bahrain was the site of the founding of the Gulf's first political party, the Higher Executive Committee, which demanded the expulsion of the British political resident, Charles Belgrave. Demonstrators responded to a visit by the British foreign secretary, Selwyn Lloyd, in

1956 by stoning his car and chanting anticolonial slogans (Smith 2004, 9). Later that year, workers at the Bahrain Petroleum Company agitated for the right to form unions. Britain aided the al-Khalifa monarchy in suppressing these protests by, among other actions, supplying helicopters to drop tear gas and identify demonstrators (ibid., 22).

Militant labor struggles took place through the 1960s, most significantly a three-month uprising in March 1965 following the firing of hundreds of workers at the Bahrain Petroleum Company. These struggles were led by communist and nationalist leaders who fused agitation against British rule in the Gulf with demands around worker and social issues. The strikes drew support from wide layers of society—including high school students who walked out in solidarity with the workers (Nakhleh 1976, 79). Several protesters were killed during the uprising, and the government instituted the 1965 Law of Public Security, which essentially gave it a free hand to issue any order deemed necessary for "security" (Khuri 1991, 216). Notwithstanding the repression, ongoing strikes and demonstrations meant that Bahrain was the site of the most sustained and powerful protests against British rule in the Gulf.

By the late 1960s, Britain's control over the Gulf states had become untenable, and in 1971, Bahrain—along with Qatar and the United Arab Emirates—gained independence from its formal colonial master (Zahlan 1998). Despite the vitality of the country's social movements, the al-Khalifa monarchy retained its position of power after British departure. Bowing to popular sentiment, however, Bahrain's ruler, Sheikh Isa bin Salman bin Hamad al-Khalifa (who reigned from 1961 to 1999) announced that a constitution would be drafted by a constitutional assembly that would consist of twenty-two elected delegates plus twenty additional members appointed by Sheikh Isa (Federal Research Division 2004, 97). Elections for seats in the constitutional assembly were held in December 1972, with the electorate restricted to native-born male citizens aged twenty years and older (ibid.). The constitution, drawn up in 1973, provided for elections for a National Assembly, which had no legislative powers but was authorized to comment upon and consent to laws proposed by the ruler-appointed Council of Ministers. The 1973 constitution was only to last two years, yet its restoration remains a key focus of political mobilization in Bahrain today.

The few years immediately following independence also witnessed a resurgence of nationalist and labor struggles that bear important implications for the contemporary period. Two leftist organizations with considerable popular support—the Popular Front for the Liberation of Bahrain (PFLB) and the National Liberation Front (NLF)—contested elections in December 1973 for the National Assembly. The NLF and PFLB collaborated in the People's Bloc, winning eight out of thirty seats in the National Assembly (Khuri 1991, 220). From their elected positions, they agitated for the repeal of the 1965 Public Security Law and legalization of labor unions. They worked with the so-called Religious Bloc, a grouping of six Shia representatives who also supported greater labor freedoms (although they simultaneously advocated more conservative social measures, such as a ban on the sale of alcohol) (ibid., 226). Arrayed against the People's Bloc and Religious Bloc was a group of sixteen independents that generally worked closely with the monarchy and Council of Ministers.

The new National Assembly provided a platform for public debate despite its limited powers. Labor struggles also continued outside the Assembly—with thirty-six strikes recorded in the first six months of 1974, twenty-four of which lasted more than ten days (Khalaf 1985, 25). In response, the monarchy issued the new State Security Law, which abrogated earlier security measures and opened the way to extremely harsh suppression of any political opponents, including arrest without trial for a period of up to three years. The National Assembly refused to give its consent to the new law and also objected to the renewal of the lease for a massive U.S. naval base located in the country. In response, the regime issued a royal decree that dissolved the Assembly and inaugurated a long period of political repression. State security courts operated without legal oversight, and torture was widespread. Hardest hit were the leftist parties—the NLF and PFLB—with thousands of members exiled, tortured, or killed by the regime.

The 1990s Intifada

The weakening of the left during the 1980s opened the opposition space to political movements based more on religious identity, particularly following the 1979 Iranian Revolution. One of these organizations, the Islamic Front for the Liberation of Bahrain (IFLB), attempted a coup against the al-Khalifa regime in 1981. Another religious group, the Bahrain Freedom Movement, was established in 1982 and drew upon traditional village-based structures in Bahrain while conducting exile-based advocacy against the regime from London. Both these Shia organizations evolved into Bahraini parties that have been prominent in the most recent uprisings.

In June 1994 an uprising began that was to last until 2000. The uprising was sparked following demonstrations by unemployed Bahraini citizens outside the Ministry of Labor and quickly took up other related issues around political freedoms, release of political prisoners, and the return of the hundreds of exiled Bahrainis. The movement was distinguished by its nonsectarian character—bringing together nationalist, leftist, and religious forces from both Shia and Sunni communities. A political front was formed, called al-Haraka al-Disturiyya, or the Constitutional Movement (CM), with thirty representatives. In November of that year, the CM submitted a petition signed by more than twenty thousand people that called on the government to take the following actions: (1) reactivate the constitution and restore the democracy through calling for National Assembly elections, (2) release all political prisoners and repatriate those exiled, (3) grant women civil and political rights, (4) assure that justice would prevail among all citizens, and (5) institute economic reforms (al-Mdaires 2002).

Demonstrations continued, and the regime responded with violence and widespread arrests. Between December 1994 and October 1995, Human Rights Watch (1997, 273) later reported, at least three thousand people were arrested, of whom about eight hundred were formally charged. Hundreds of detainees faced torture, which took place under security forces that were commanded by British nationals, including the Security and Intelligence Service (SIS), which was headed by Ian Henderson, a former British police officer who had been instrumental in suppressing the Mau Mau rebellion in Kenya (Amnesty International 1995, 8). Henderson ran the SIS until 1998 and was widely known as the "Butcher of Bahrain" because of the torture methods employed under his watch (Amnesty International 2000). Named a Commander of the British Empire by Queen Elizabeth II in 1986, Henderson was the subject of a police investigation by Scotland Yard, which was quietly dropped in 2008 (Crichton 2008). At the time of this writing, he is believed to still reside in Bahrain, where he serves as an adviser to King Hamad.

In addition to the violent repression of the 1990s uprising, Bahrain's ruling regime consciously pushed the sectarian card, attempting to foster divisions between Shia and Sunni, and accused regime opponents of being a fifth column backed by Iran. Repeatedly, the regime forced prisoners—denied any legal representation or access to fair courts—to confess that they were agents of Iran or members of previously unknown organizations such as "Hizbullah Bahrain." This repression was met with wide acclaim by Western powers. Alongside direct British involvement in the torture of detainees, the U.S. government gave open support to the Bahraini government and its authoritarian measures. In early 1996, the U.S. assistant secretary of state, Robert Pelletreau, claimed that the uprising was "urged on and promoted by Iran, across the Persian Gulf" and congratulated the Bahraini government for "dealing with it . . . in a responsible way that deserves our support" (quoted in Stork 1997, 93–94). In late May 1996, General John Shalikashvili, chairman of the Joint Chiefs of Staff, reiterated U.S. support for the Bahraini government during a visit to the country, stating, "We support Bahrain's efforts to ensure its stability, and we continue to accuse Iran as a threat to the stability of the region" (quoted in Human Rights Watch 1997, 276). President Bill Clinton sent a letter to Bahrain's ruler that stated, "The U.S. fully supports . . . your government's commitment to economic and social development and political reconciliation" (quoted in ibid.). That same year, former president George H. W. Bush remarked during a visit to Bahrain that the Bahraini government was to be congratulated for "preserving order and for guaranteeing for every Bahraini citizen a secure environment" (quoted in ibid.).

National Action Charter

With the ascension of King Hamad bin Isa al-Khalifa to the throne in 1999, it initially appeared to many Bahrainis that a series of changes would ensue. The new king announced a reform plan called the National Action Charter (al mithaq al-'amal al-watani), which promised the establishment of a bicameral parliament consisting of two councils: an elected forty-member Chamber of Deputies (majlis al-nawwab) and a forty-member Shura chamber appointed by the king (majlis al-shura). The NAC also pledged to restore the 1973 constitution, thus fulfilling a key demand raised by the popular movements. Perhaps most significant, Hamad moved to dismantle aspects of the repressive machinery built up during the preceding decades—dissolving the State Security Courts, canceling the State Security Law, and promulgating an amnesty for political prisoners.[1]

After the political opposition received assurances that the proposed Chamber of Deputies would have full legislative powers and that the Shura Council would play only a consultative role, a referendum on the National Action Charter took place in February 2001. Bahraini citizens over the age of twenty-one (both men and women) were eligible to participate, and a turnout of 90 percent endorsed the NAC with a 98.4 percent vote. Despite the optimism that surrounded the NAC referendum, however, King Hamad soon confirmed that he did not intend a significant break from the practices of his predecessor. In February 2002, on the anniversary of the referendum, he put forward a new constitution that essentially replaced the 1973 document—doing so without any public consultation and breaking a key promise to the opposition. At the same time, he granted the Shura Council equal legislative authority with the Chamber of Deputies and gave himself the deciding vote in case of any deadlock. Any amendment to the constitution required a two-thirds majority of both councils, meaning that change was virtually impossible. Only the royal-appointed cabinet had the power to initiate legislation, and the Shura Council could effectively veto any decision by the elected house. Ultimate power would remain with the king— including the rights to issue decrees, to amend the constitution, and to dissolve the Chamber of Deputies.[2] The ruling family's finances would not be subject to review by any public body. Moreover, the position of the al-Khalifa monarchy could never be challenged, with Article 120, paragraph C, of the 2002 constitution stating, "It is not permissible under any circumstances to propose the amendment of the constitutional monarchy and the principle of inherited rule in Bahrain."

In this context, the key political societies in Bahrain oriented their demands around reform of the parliament. Four main opposition organizations emerged, each of which can trace its lineage to an earlier movement from the 1950–90 period.[3] On the left, the National Democratic Action Society (Waʻad) came out of the earlier PFLB (dissolved in 2000), and the Progressive Democratic Tribune was formed by returning members of the NLF in 2002.[4] Among the Shia community, Al Wefaq National Islamic Society emerged largely out of the Bahrain Freedom Movement and is the largest political society in Bahrain, and the Islamic Action Society is descended from the IFLB. In addition, two Sunni-based organizations gained prominence—Al Menbar National Islamic Society and Al Asalah.

Waʻad, Al Wefaq, and the Islamic Action Society boycotted the 2002 elections but participated in 2006, when Al Wefaq won seventeen out of forty seats (the remaining twenty-three were divided between pro-government Sunni parties and independents). But despite electoral participation, political rights within the country deteriorated on all levels. Press freedom continued to be highly restricted, with laws preventing publication of material deemed to violate "national unity." Opposition activists continued to charge the government with arbitrary arrests and torture in detention.

Bahrain's Significance

Stepping back from this historical narrative for a moment, several points about the broader political economy of Bahrain need emphasis. Central to this is its location within a wider configuration of Gulf states. In 1981, Bahrain was one of six countries—alongside Saudi Arabia, Kuwait, United Arab Emirates, Oman, and Qatar—that came together to form the Gulf Cooperation Council (GCC). The GCC is a regional integration project, similar in many ways to the European Union, which has aimed at promoting economic and political linkages among these six monarchical states. Dominated by Saudi Arabia, the nations of the GCC possess approximately 40 percent of the world's proven oil reserves and 25 percent of the world's natural gas. Ownership of these resources has also brought vast amounts of surplus capital into the region. These "petrodollars," as they were dubbed during the first oil price rise in the 1970s, have been essential to the formation of the global financial system over the past few decades.

For these two reasons—its status as the world's chief supplier of oil and gas and its position as the source of prodigious amounts of surplus capital—the Gulf has become a geographical zone with decisive impacts on the overall development of contemporary capitalism (Hanieh 2011a). This does not mean that the primary concern of the leading capitalist states has been direct ownership of the Gulf's hydrocarbon supplies (although this may certainly be part of the struggles between individual countries); rather, there has been a shared interest to ensure that the GCC remains fully aligned with the interests of the world market. Given these trends, the interdependence of the GCC ruling elites and U.S. interests has been one of the most important relationships in the world today. It has been the overriding consideration in the making of U.S. foreign policy in the Middle East (Hanieh 2011b).

Bahrain has been central to this configuration. Following the formation of the GCC in 1981, the United States began moving expensive weapons systems to the GCC states. In 1983, a regional unified command known as U.S. Central Command (CENTCOM) was permanently stationed on U.S. Navy ships in Bahrain, from which it liaised with U.S. embassies and nations across the Middle East (Stork 1985, 5). Although CENTCOM was moved to Qatar in 2003, Bahrain continued to play a fundamental part in the projection of U.S. power in the region. A sixty-acre U.S. naval base was located in Bahrain's capital, Manama, with 2,250 military and civilian personnel living off the base. The U.S. Navy's Fifth Fleet, responsible for naval forces in the Gulf, the Red Sea, the Arabian Sea, and the coastal waters off East Africa, operated from the base and was key to the U.S.-led invasions of Afghanistan in 2001 and Iraq in 2003.

This is the regional context through which to understand the uprisings in Bahrain. But, as the preceding narrative of Bahrain's history indicates, the country has been distinguished from the rest of the GCC states in important respects. Like other GCC states, the country continued to rely heavily on migrant labor—in 2005, around 58 percent of the Bahraini population consisted of noncitizen migrant workers (Central Informatics Organisation 2005, 2), yet much of its Shia majority remained poor and faced discrimination from the largely Sunni elite. This more proletarianized character of the Bahraini citizen population, in comparison with the other GCC states, overlapped with the entrenched sectarian discrimination against the majority Shia population and was an important reason labor and left-wing movements had long been such a prominent feature of the country's political makeup. The discrimination against Bahrain's Shia majority, in other words, cannot be understood as separate from the country's class structure.

Another essential characteristic of Bahrain's political economy is its lengthier and more advanced experience of neoliberalism (relative to other GCC states). Bahrain holds the least amount of oil in the GCC (only 0.03 percent of proven GCC reserves), all extracted from one field, Awali. With less revenue from oil, Bahrain has, since the 1970s, consciously decided to promote itself as a financial center modeled on Singapore and the Cayman Islands. In 1975, the Bahraini government introduced regulations to allow banks to operate "offshore banking units" that were exempt from all corporate taxes and were required to pay only a small fee to establish themselves on the island (Wilson 1983). This process coincided with the beginning of restrictions on foreign banks in Saudi Arabia and the decline of Lebanon as the banking capital of the Middle East due to the country's prolonged civil war. For these reasons, Bahrain quickly developed into the key financial intermediary between the Gulf's petrodollar flows and financial markets in Europe and elsewhere.

Over the first decade of this century the government moved to allow foreign companies, particularly those based in other GCC states, to open access to financial and real estate markets through a sustained program of privatization and liberalization. In 2007, the World Trade Organization remarked on the pace of neoliberalism in Bahrain, claiming that the country "has shown significant change in terms of economic transformation, but the next six years are projected to be nothing short of remarkable." It further noted that the state "has been reshaped in order to focus on the private sector as the economic driving force, and consequently has been gradually removing itself from involvement in the productive processes, through the process of privatization and divestiture" (World Trade Organization 2007, 5).

The frontal embrace of neoliberalism in Bahrain deeply accentuated the unevenness of capitalist development—widening gaps between poorer citizens (concentrated among Shia) and the private-sector and state elites that had benefited from Bahrain's position as the "freest economy in the Middle East" (according to the Heritage Foundation 2010). One indication of this was the very high unemployment levels, with unofficial estimates ranging from 15 to 30 percent among Bahraini nationals (Wright 2008, 10). Unemployment had a disproportionate impact on Shia citizens, and many Shia villages resembled "suburban shanty towns from which residents have little hope of escape" (International Crisis Group 2011, 5). In 2004, the Bahrain Center for Human Rights estimated that more than half of Bahraini citizens were living in poverty and yet, simultaneously, the richest 5,200 Bahrainis had a combined wealth greater than $20 billion.

These statistics are a striking confirmation that the results of neoliberalism in Bahrain included not just the increased impoverishment of large layers of the society but also the widening of gaps within the society as a whole. A very significant aspect of these outcomes was the question of real estate. The government refused to regulate the distribution of state-owned land, which meant that privatized land ended up being subject to speculation and extraordinary price rises, with high-end real estate projects out of the reach of most Bahrainis (Wright 2008, 7). In 2008, the U.S. embassy in Manama noted in a cable to the U.S. secretary of state that rental and purchase prices of real estate had risen by about 30 percent annually since 2006.[5] By 2011, real estate companies were reporting that poorer Bahrainis faced a wait of up to seventeen years for social housing, with a waiting list exceeding well over fifty thousand units (CB Richard Ellis 2011, 3). These problems were compounded by a rapidly growing population, with more than one-quarter of Bahrainis under the age of fourteen (Wright 2008, 10).

Bahraini activists explicitly linked the issue of housing and land inequality to the recent uprisings. This issue first hit the popular consciousness in 2006, when Google Earth began publishing satellite images of Bahrain. Thousands of Bahraini citizens were outraged when they compared their squalid, overcrowded living conditions to the large tracts of land owned by the royal family and the rich. Although the government subsequently banned access to Google Earth, activists have reproduced these images in "revolutionary newspapers" linked to the uprising. Indeed, one such newspaper, *Bahrain Revolution News* (2011,

7), has pointed out that the coastal line of Bahrain is 161 kilometers long and yet more than 90 percent of the beaches are privately owned with no access to the public—making Bahrain an "island with no beaches." In this context, the liberalization of real estate markets in Bahrain generated a polarization of wealth that further fueled the discontent of the poorer layers of society.

The 2011 Uprising

Bahrain's history shows that the 2011 uprising was merely the latest in alternating cycles of struggles and repression. Indeed, just six months earlier, youth demonstrations had erupted across Bahrain, taking aim at the issues of poverty, discrimination, and political freedoms. Hundreds of Bahrainis had faced detention and torture in a wave of arrests that occurred in August–September 2010. Web sites were shut down and media outlets closed, and twenty-two individuals were charged under 2006 antiterrorism legislation with incitement and plotting to overthrow the government. Those arrested—including two high-profile Shia clerics and a prominent blogger—were tortured.

This repression was largely aimed at weakening opposition in the October 2010 elections. Despite the arrests and restrictions on freedoms—and the gerrymandered political system—the largest Shia organization, Al Wefaq, was able to win a plurality of seats (eighteen out of forty). These results, however, did little to reassure the Bahraini population that real political and economic changes were possible. High levels of unemployment, skyrocketing prices, and political repression continued. Shia were denied access to government jobs and barred from serving in the security forces. In a long-standing grievance that indicates the way the regime has used migrant workers as part of its sectarian divide-and-rule policy, Shia also raised complaints that the government was bringing in Sunni Arabs and Pakistanis to work as police and security forces in the suppression of protests. Opposition politicians claimed these Sunni workers were being granted citizenship in order to alter the sectarian balance of country.[6]

This is the context in which demonstrations were first called for February 14, 2011. As one participant noted:

There was a general sense that the political process was going nowhere—the failure of the "half-democratic" political model, and the generally bankrupt economic policies that came with it in which private development (often of once public areas) was given free reign, but did not reap much for the majority. Major "national" initiatives to decrease unemployment followed the mantra of the "free" market—privatize, liberalize, franchise, internationalize. . . . Bahrain is too small a country for such inequality to exist—literally face-to-face with the glass towers of the financial harbor you have the decaying old souk. (personal interview 2011a)

February 14 itself was a highly symbolic date, the tenth anniversary of the referendum for the National Action Charter. So was the location, the Pearl Roundabout, at the center of which was a monument built in 1982 to symbolize the unity of the six GCC states. The "day of rage," as it was called, saw tens of thousands of Bahrainis come out in protest. The large crowd called for political reform but did not criticize King Hamad directly.

The initial organizing for the demonstrations relied heavily on social networking sites such as Facebook and online forums, most notably, Bahrainonline.org. One blogger noted, "In terms of planning, much of it happens online through quite a fascinating open census mechanism on forums (now it's pretty much only Bahrainonline). . . . people throw out ideas back and forth and they are critiqued and amended until there is a critical mass of support for the idea." He went on to say that ideas would be raised "on Bahrainonline, with someone saying something like 'I have an idea what we should do next.' It [would be] discussed and debated, and then the Feb 14 youth alliance [decide] to endorse. There are many ideas that didn't receive much support on the forums so they were never realized."[7]

This use of online forums is not new. The Bahrain Freedom Movement has had an online presence since the mid-1990s, but the emergence of Bahrainonline in the early 2000s acted to challenge the regime's monopoly on information. One activist noted in 2010 that "the number of users on Bahrain Online . . . is in the hundreds, and at peak hours it is in the thousands. That is significant for a country of less than 600,000 nationals" (Desmukh 2010).

With the occupation of the Pearl Roundabout, however, the physical space "took on a life of its own and became a center of organization" (personal interview 2011b). There would be "daily (morning) press conferences, a media center, and a multitude of groups running different programs (including ad hoc classes for kids, an arts corner, seminars on politics and economics at the political parties' tents, and of course the program of speeches and events onstage)" (personal interview 2011c).[8] For this reason, the regime made a determined effort to remove demonstrators from the area. Over the first three days, security forces killed seven protesters, igniting demonstrations throughout the country (often linked to the funeral marches for those killed in earlier protests). On February 17, government troops attacked protesters camped at the roundabout, killing five and injuring hundreds more (Al Jazeera 2011b). News reports spoke of police targeting doctors and medics, and also preventing ambulances from reaching the area. Although the clampdown managed to clear the roundabout, it acted to radicalize demonstrators throughout the country. Demands for an end to the rule of the al-Khalifa dynasty began to be expressed openly (Associated Press 2011). In response to the suppression and killings, the legal Shia opposition, most notably Al Wefaq, joined the protests, and its eighteen deputies resigned from parliament. Labor strikes also spread across the country.

The regime's reaction to the protests mirrored its reactions to every previous uprising in the country in its combination of violence, divide-and-rule tactics, and promises of financial aid and political reform. On February 17, Bahraini TV broadcast pictures of weapons that were allegedly taken from protesters at the roundabout in an attempt to cast blame for the deaths that had occurred (*Guardian* 2011). Foreign Minister Khalid al-Khalifa stated that the attack on protesters, and the clearing of the Pearl Roundabout, was necessary because the demonstrations were "polarising the country" and pushing it to the "brink of the sectarian abyss" (quoted in Al Jazeera 2011a). A pro-government demonstration held on February 21 reportedly involved the coerced participation of migrant workers as a means to increase numbers.

Despite the government's attempts to portray the movement as a sectarian revolt, the demands at the root of the uprising resonated throughout all layers of Bahraini society. From the first demonstrations in mid-February, both Sunni and Shia participated in the mobilizations and endured the subsequent government repression. One participant noted:

> Protesters, perhaps wise to the government's age-old strategy of pitting Bahrain's various ethnic/religious groups against each other, made a very deliberate point of avoiding sectarian overtones at rallies—many banners, leaflets, stickers, and flags bore the slogan "No Shia, No Sunni, Just Bahraini," and a popular chant was "ikhwa sunna wa shia, hadhal watan ma nbeey'a" (brothers Sunni and Shia, we won't sell this country). (personal interview 2011d)

The Pearl Roundabout became a relatively nonsectarian space, with the Bahraini flag seen as a symbol of the movement. A clear illustration of this unity was the regime's persecution of the secular left organization Wa'ad, which traces its origins to the Popular Front for the Liberation of Bahrain. Wa'ad was the first political group to support the February 14 actions and consequently had its offices raided and members harassed. Its general secretary, Ebrahim Sharif, was arrested and tortured on March 17 (Amnesty USA 2011). Sharif is Sunni, and he remarked that the government's stirring up of sectarianism "is not about the Shia versus Sunni; it is about conserving the status quo" (quoted in Hamilton 2011). Wa'ad was subsequently banned by the Bahraini government.

Through early March, demonstrators continued to occupy the Pearl Roundabout, and others protested across the country. On March 1, demonstrators blocked the parliament building, and teachers also stopped work in many schools (Katzman 2011, 5). Significantly, a new group, the Coalition of the Republic, emerged among the Shia opposition, bringing together smaller groups that had split from Al Wefaq and were focused on mobilizing youth at a grassroots level through the Shia mourning houses *(maatam)* rather than relying on traditional elite-based politics. The coalition distanced itself from the conciliatory tone of Al Wefaq and openly called for "bringing down the existing regime in Bahrain and the establishment of a democratic republican system" (Noueihed 2011).[9] Indicative of the combative mood among some protesters was the call for a march on the royal palace on March 11.

Despite the fact that the mainstream opposition parties condemned the action as too divisive, thousands gathered and called for an end to al-Khalifa rule. The protest mood continued to deepen, and demonstrations spread to the financial district over subsequent days—thus openly challenging the "financial stability" that the regime had carefully marketed to outside investors.

At this conjuncture, however, the government began to exploit the political differences in the ranks of the opposition. One participant stated: "There was never really any coherent list of demands that unified the opposition. The established 'opposition groups' focused mainly on creating a constituent assembly for a new constitution, while the 'Coalition of the Republic' wanted an end to the monarchy. Generally though, there wasn't a very developed unified front of demands" (personal interview 2011b). Various youth groups that had initiated the demonstrations and were central to organizing the Pearl Roundabout encampment were excluded from elite-led political negotiations with the regime. This further reinforced a palpable split between the "street" and the "official opposition" (personal interview 2011d). Moreover, the regime once again employed the divide-and-rule tactic, with King Hamad linking the protesters to Iran-backed conspiracies and telling a meeting of the GCC joint armed forces, the Peninsula Shield Command, that "an external plot has been fomented for twenty to thirty years" (quoted in Bahrain News Agency 2011). Sectarian clashes began to emerge at this time between Sunni and Shia communities (personal interview 2011b).[10]

This developing sectarian discourse helped to legitimate one of the key moments in the regime's response to the protests—its support for the military intervention of other GCC states on March 14. The Bahraini government had long been conferring with the other Gulf Arab states about the course of the uprising; the intervention of one thousand Saudi army and national guard troops, five hundred police from the United Arab Emirates, and some Qatari soldiers indicated that other GCC states felt that action needed to be taken quickly to prevent any further spread, both within the country and regionally.[11] A three-month emergency law was declared on March 15, and security forces raided the Pearl Roundabout the next day, tearing down the Pearl Monument on March 18.

In the weeks following the GCC intervention, hundreds of protesters, bloggers, and medical personnel were arrested. Shia villages were raided, and hospitals were invaded by security forces. In mid-May, the human rights group Médecins Sans Frontières (2011) gave a chilling account of the situation based on testimony from its offices in Bahrain:

> Our team has seen patients in villages across the country who were severely beaten or tortured in jail; schoolgirls who have been both physically abused and threatened with rape; and patients in urgent need of hospitalization who still refuse to be referred due to the high risk of their arrest. . . . Doctors and nurses also continue to be arrested during raids on health facilities, or on their homes at night.

The deputy director of the U.S.-based Physicians for Human Rights confirmed this assessment, noting that the Bahraini authorities were engaged in "the most extreme violations of medical neutrality in the past half century, and history will remember them as such" (Sollom 2011).

Throughout this period of repression, the government kept a tight reign on the local media. Government-aligned stations broadcast a steady diet of pro-regime material while the only independent newspaper in Bahrain, *Al-Wasat,* had its offices ransacked and its editor, Mansour Al-Jamri, and three other journalists were arrested and charged with deliberately targeting the security and stability of the country (Krauss 2011). Al-Jamri remarked to the *New York Times* that the attack on *Al-Wasat* was "a message to everybody that there is a new Bahrain. They are re-engineering the country" (quoted in ibid.).

In the wake of the crackdown, thousands of Bahrainis lost their jobs and had their unemployment insurance revoked for alleged participation in the demonstrations (Human Rights Watch 2011). University students and employees of state-owned firms were required to sign "loyalty oaths." Further afield, the government informed the families of Bahraini students studying abroad that they would have their scholarships and financial support revoked for attending solidarity protests three thousand miles away. In July 2011, the king announced he would be holding a "national dialogue," a development U.S. president Barack Obama described as "an important moment of promise for the people of

Bahrain" (White House 2011). Despite this praise, hundreds of opposition activists remained in prison and Al Wefaq, the largest opposition party, boycotted the process. By mid-August, according to the Bahrain Center for Human Rights, more than one thousand people had been detained or had disappeared since February, forty had been killed, and close to two hundred had been sentenced by military courts. Authorities had destroyed dozens of mosques and Shia mourning houses (Fisk 2011).

Demonstrations continued on a daily basis throughout July and August, however, mostly concentrated in the poorer Shia villages throughout the country.

By September 2011, Bahrain's uprising and the regime's ongoing repression showed no sign of abating. A by-election held in September to fill the seats vacated by Al Wefaq garnered a turnout of only about 17 percent, and all opposition groups united in boycott of the process. In October, the key opposition groups—including Al Wefaq and Wa'ad—issued a joint statement, known as the Manama Document, in which they described Bahrain as a police state akin to Mubarak-era Egypt and called for the al-Khalifa to "govern without powers" in a constitutional monarchy. It was the first joint statement to be issued by the opposition since the uprising began and is perhaps indicative of an increased political unity in their ranks (Al Wefaq National Islamic Society 2011).

The issues that brought all sectors of Bahraini society onto the streets in February had in no way been addressed by the regime. High levels of unemployment and inequality, sectarian discrimination against the Shia majority, and the concentration of wealth in the hands of the ruling clique and a handful of Sunni tribes around it all continued to characterize Bahraini society. This polarization of wealth and power was necessarily backed up by the regime's repressive apparatus and its decades-long persecution of popular movements and political opposition. The calls for democracy heard at the Pearl Roundabout and throughout the country in 2011 were thus not simply a question of representation; they struck at the heart of a system in which politics and economics are interwoven and inseparable.

Likewise, the unwavering support extended to the Bahraini regime by the United States, Britain, and the other Gulf Arab states confirmed the centrality of Bahrain to the nature of imperial power in the Middle East. It is in this sense that the revolutionary movement that swept the Middle East during 2011 formed a single thread that tied North Africa to the Gulf. Although there was considerable variation in the nature of the regimes across the Middle East and in the political issues that stirred the popular mobilizations, imperial domination continued to be articulated through an assortment of despotic rulers of which the al-Khalifa was archetype. The great fear of all these regimes, and of the Western powers that supported them, was that a successful revolutionary movement in Bahrain would quickly detonate similar struggles in Saudi Arabia and the other Gulf states. This explains the furious repression that was unleashed on the Bahraini people in 2011. But precisely because the issues that underlay the 2011 intifada went far beyond any that could be solved simply through regime-led cosmetic changes, we can be sure that the story of Bahrain's uprisings is far from over.

Notes

1. Other reforms included the return of exiles, increased space for political expression and the operation of nongovernmental organizations (NGOs), permission for the formation of trade unions, and the provision of economic support for the unemployed.

2. Early decrees from King Hamad included a new press law, decree 47/2002, which authorized the confiscation and banning of publications that criticized the king or published reports that adversely affected the "value of the national currency." Another decree, 56/2002, granted amnesty for human rights abuses committed by any government officials prior to 2001.

3. Political parties remain banned, so these groups organize themselves as "societies."

4. A third secular party is the Nationalist Democratic Rally Society, a Baathist party.

5. This information comes from a cable dated September 29, 2008, and carrying the subject line "Construction Shortages Drive Real Estate Market Faster than Overall Inflation." The text of the cable is available on WikiLeaks, http://wikileaks .org/cable/2008/09/08MANAMA673.html (accessed August 23, 2011).

6. This issue had been particularly prominent following allegations made in 2006 by Salah Al Bander, a British Sudanese consultant to the government. Bander produced documents that indicated government officials were deliberately stoking

sectarian tensions by supporting pro-government NGOs, gerrymandering elections, and supporting families that "converted" from Shia to Sunni. The allegations became known as "Bandergate," and despite an initial promise to investigate, the government subsequently banned all discussion of the accusations.

7. E-mail correspondence with CB, Bahraini blogger, October 19, 2011. CB pointed to the thread http://bahrainonline.org/showthread.php?t=258985 as the origin of the idea for the February 14 demonstration.

8. This participant went on to note that this also shifted the role of online forums to be more places for information dissemination rather than places for organizing (personal interview 2011c).

9. The call for a republic was not necessarily supported by all those active in the demonstrations. One participant noted: "It certainly annoyed a lot of people in the opposition for the further splintering . . . when a lot of diverse groups were trying to coalesce around some demands they could present as a united front and take advantage of the historic moment. Others said it was 'feeding' the ruling regime's mythology about the opposition wanting an Islamic republic—and there definitely was some 'the mask falls' talk among pro-government/anti-protester groups" (personal interview 2011d).

10. One participant commented, "Although protesters frequently used national slogans 'No Shia, No Sunni, Bahraini brotherhood' in the first weeks of protests, the fact that most of the notable figures were somehow religiously inclined, and also due to the underlying sectarian tensions, the government effectively used its fearmongering campaign to widen the sectarian divide" (personal interview 2011b).

11. On March 10, protests had occurred among the Shia populations in Saudi Arabia, just across the causeway that connects the country with Bahrain. Protests are banned in that country. Likewise, in Oman protests had taken place in the industrial city of Sohar throughout February and March. Protests were also called in Kuwait on March 8. Another side to shutting down the protests was financial inducement. In early March, the GCC announced a $20 billion aid package for Bahrain and Oman (Laessing and Johnston 2011).

References

Al Jazeera. 2011a. "Bahrain Deploys Army after Raid." February 17. http://english. aljazeera.net/news/middleeast (accessed August 19, 2011).

———. 2011b. "Clashes Rock Bahraini Capital." February 17. http://english.aljazeera .net/news/middleeast (accessed April 15, 2011).

al-Mdaires, Falah. 2002. "Shi'ism and Political Protest in Bahrain." *DOMES: Digest of Middle East Studies* 11 (1): 20–44.

Al Wefaq National Islamic Society. 2011. "Jam'iyyat al-siyasiyya ta'lan al-watheeqa al-manama" [Political associations announce Manama declaration]. October

12. http://alwefaq.net/index.php?show=news&action=article&id=5933 (accessed October 18, 2011).

Amnesty International. 1995. *Bahrain: Human Rights Crisis.* AI Index: MDE 11/16/9. London: Amnesty International.

———. 2000. *Amnesty International Welcomes Investigation into Henderson's Role in Torture in Bahrain.* AI Index: EUR 45/03/0. London: Amnesty International.

Amnesty USA. 2011. "Fair Trial Urged for Bahraini Opposition Activists." May 11, 2011. http://www.amnesty.org/en/news-and-updates (accessed September 15, 2011).

Associated Press. 2011. "Bahrain Mourners Call for End to Monarchy." *Guardian,* February 18. http://www.guardian.co.uk/world/2011 (accessed August 29, 2011).

Bahrain Center for Human Rights. 2004. "Half of Bahraini Citizens Are Suffering from Poverty and Poor Living Conditions." http://www.bahrainrights.org/node/199 (accessed September 9, 2011).

Bahrain News Agency. 2011. "HM King Hamad Visits Peninsula Desert Shield." March 20. http://bna.bh/portal/en/news/450362 (accessed September 9, 2011).

Bahrain Revolution News. 2011. "The Pearl Revolution." February 14. http://bahrain14feb.wordpress.com (accessed September 9, 2011).

Bromley, Simon. 1991. *American Hegemony and World Oil.* Cambridge: Polity Press.

CB Richard Ellis. 2011. *MarketView: Kingdom Bahrain* (Q1 2010). Manama: CB Richard Ellis. http://www.cbreresidential.com (accessed March 4, 2013).

Central Informatics Organisation, Kingdom of Bahrain. 2005. *Bahrain in Figures.* Manama: Central Informatics Organisation.

Cole, Juan. 2002. *Sacred Space and Holy War: The Politics, Culture and History of Shi'ite Islam.* New York: I. B. Taurus.

Crichton, Torcuil. 2008. "Police Stop Investigation of the 'Butcher of Bahrain.'" *Sunday Herald,* February 10, 19.

Crystal, Jill. 1995. *Oil and Politics in the Gulf: Rulers and Merchants in Kuwait and Qatar.* Glasgow: Cambridge University Press.

Desmukh, Fahad. 2010. "The Internet in Bahrain: Breaking the Monopoly of Information." *Foreign Policy,* September 21. http://mideast.foreignpolicy.com (accessed October 19, 2011).

Federal Research Division. 2004. *Bahrain: A Country Study.* Whitefish, Mont.: Kessinger.

Fisk, Robert. 2011. "Why No Outcry over These Torturing Tyrants?" *Independent,* May 14. http://www.independent.co.uk (accessed October 5, 2011).

Fuccaro, Nelida. 2009. *Histories of City and State in the Persian Gulf: Manama since 1800.* Cambridge: Cambridge University Press.

Gardner, Frank. 2011. "Bahrain's Security Clampdown Divides Kingdom." BBC News, April 14. http://www.bbc.co.uk/news (accessed November 17, 2012).

Guardian. 2011. "Bahrain in Crisis and Middle East Protests." Live blog, February 17. http://www.guardian.co.uk/world/middle-east-live/2011/feb/14/week (accessed August 23, 2011).

Hamilton, Adrian. 2011. "Bahrain's Uprising Is about Power Not Religion." *Independent,* March 17. http://www.independent.co.uk (accessed August 23, 2011).

Hanieh, Adam. 2011a. *Capitalism and Class in the Gulf Arab States.* New York: Palgrave Macmillan.

———. 2011b. "Finance, Oil, and the Arab Uprisings: The Global Crisis and the Gulf States." *Socialist Register* 48: 176–99.

Heritage Foundation. 2010. "Index of Economic Freedom." http://www.heritage.org/index/Ranking (accessed September 20, 2011).

Human Rights Watch. 1997. *World Report.* New York: Human Rights Watch.

———. 2011. "Bahrain: Revoke Summary Firings Linked to Protests." http://www.hrw.org/news (accessed September 23, 2011).

International Crisis Group. 2011. *Popular Protests in North Africa and the Middle East (III): The Bahrain Revolt.* Middle East/North Africa Report No. 105, April 6. Brussels: International Crisis Group.

Katzman, Kenneth. 2011. *Bahrain: Reform, Security, and U.S. Policy.* Washington, D.C.: Congressional Research Service.

Khalaf, 'Abd ul-Hadi. 1985. "Labor Movements in Bahrain." *MERIP [Middle East Research and Information Project] Reports* 132: 24–29.

Khalifa, Hamad. 2011. "Stability Is Prerequisite for Progress." *Washington Times,* April 19. http://www.washingtontimes.com/news (accessed August 23, 2011).

Khuri, Fuad. 1991. *Tribe and State in Bahrain: The Transformation of Social and Political Authority in an Arab State.* Berkeley: University of California Press.

Krauss, Clifford. 2011. "Editor Silenced, with the Help of Unreliable Sources." *New York Times,* April 8. http://www.nytimes.com (accessed August 24, 2011).

Laessing, Ulf, and Cynthia Johnston. 2011. "Gulf States Launch $20 Billion Fund for Oman and Bahrain." Reuters, March 10. http://www.reuters.com (accessed September 8, 2011).

Médecins Sans Frontières. 2011. "From Hospital to Prison: Medical Aid in Bahrain." http://www.msf.org (accessed August 23, 2011).

Nakhleh, Emile. 1976. *Bahrain: Political Development in a Modernizing Society.* Lexington, Mass.: Lexington Books.

Noueihed, Lin. 2011. "Hardline Shi'ite Groups Demand Republic in Bahrain." Reuters, March 8. http://uk.reuters.com (accessed September 23, 2001).

Onley, James. 2004. "Britain's Native Agents in Arabia and Persia in the Nineteenth Century." *Comparative Studies of South Asia, Africa and the Middle East* 24 (1): 130–37.

Smith, Simon. 2004. *Britain's Revival and Fall in the Gulf: Kuwait, Bahrain, Qatar, and the Trucial States, 1950–71.* London: Routledge.

Sollom, Richard. 2011. Testimony given before the Tom Lantos Human Rights

Commission hearing "Human Rights in Bahrain." May 13. http://tlhrc.house
.gov (accessed September 21, 2011).

Stork, Joe. 1985. "Prospects for the Gulf." *Middle East Research and Information Reports* 132: 3–6.

———. 1997. *Routine Abuse, Routine Denial: Civil Rights and the Political Crisis in Bahrain.* New York: Human Rights Watch.

White House. 2011. "Statement by the Press Secretary on Bahrain." July 2. http:// www.whitehouse.gov (accessed August 3, 2011).

Wilson, Rodney. 1983. *Banking and Finance in the Arab Middle East.* New York: St. Martin's Press.

World Trade Organization. 2007. *Bahrain Trade Policy Review.* June 13. Geneva: World Trade Organization.

Wright, Steven. 2008. *Fixing the Kingdom: Political Evolution and Socio-economic Challenges in Bahrain.* Occasional Paper No. 3. Doha, Qatar: Center for International and Regional Studies, Georgetown University School of Foreign Service in Qatar. http://cirs.georgetown.edu/publications/papers/100764 (accessed August 12, 2011).

Zahlan, Rosemary. 1998. *The Making of the Modern Gulf States.* London: Ithaca Press.

Personal Interviews (e-mail interviews with Bahraini residents)

Personal interview. 2011a. IA (name has been altered). October 4.

Personal interview. 2011b. OF (name has been altered). September 28.

Personal interview. 2011c. IH. October 19.

Personal interview. 2011d. IA. October 19.

Saudi Arabia

TOBY C. JONES

SAUDI ARABIA'S AGING LEADERS were deeply shaken by the revolutionary ferment that swept through the Middle East in early 2011. They watched in frustration as Egyptian and Tunisian publics threw their longtime dictators from power. Anxiety turned to horror as opposition movements mobilized closer to home, especially in the small kingdom of Bahrain. There, just off Saudi Arabia's eastern shore, tens of thousands of pro-democracy protesters launched an ill-fated campaign to end authoritarian rule in one of the Al Saud's longtime vassal states in February. Riyadh's sense of urgency regarding the regional upheaval was on full display by mid-March, when the kingdom dispatched military forces to Manama, Bahrain's capital, to provide cover for a brutal crackdown on the demonstrators.

This military intervention was the most visible sign that the political elites in Saudi Arabia sought to contain the regional fallout of the Arab Spring. Over the course of the year, Saudi Arabia clearly emerged as the region's most powerful and determined counterrevolutionary force (Jones 2011b).[1] While the kingdom's leaders supported the overthrow of Muammar Qaddafi in Libya and, only after months of killing and fence-sitting, came out in August in favor of the fall of Syria's Bashar al-Assad, the reality was that they did not support the forces of democracy in those places (Jones 2011c). Rather, they hoped for outcomes that would serve their interests, preserve some semblance of the political status quo, and, most important, help them in their struggle to check the ambition of their primary rival, Iran. However, for all their anxieties about regional politics and the geopolitical consequences of democratic change in the Arab Middle East, the kingdom's elites were also unnerved by the specter of political change at home. Indeed, with autocrats falling or under pressure across the region, they had good reason for concern.

Although the kingdom was flush with oil revenues and redistributed some of its considerable oil wealth in order to placate its citizens, it shared many of the social and political characteristics that helped mobilize revolutionaries elsewhere. In the land of oil opulence — Saudi Arabia had brought in more than $500 billion in oil revenues since 2009 — many suffered from grinding poverty, with several million people living below the kingdom's own standard for what counts as poor.

Crackdown

Riyadh was well aware of the social despair and the kinds of frustration it generated. Authorities took extreme measures to keep citizens from shedding light on such problems, however. In October 2011 Saudi authorities arrested Firas Buqnah, a filmmaker, and his crew for producing and broadcasting a documentary on poverty in Riyadh (Hill 2011). There were other engines of potential dissent as well. Saudi Arabia is home to a large, restless, and underemployed generation of young men and women who are educated and savvy and who harbor expectations of not only greater economic opportunity but also greater political opportunity. The previous decade had seen repeated calls from this generation for political reform and for the expansion of social and political rights. Perhaps the most visible were women activists, who demanded not only the right to drive but also real political rights, an end to draconian restrictions on their movement in the public sphere, and the abolishment of an oppressive guardianship system (Al Nafjan 2011).

Disillusioned youth were proving to be a potent force of change in the first years of the new century across the Arab world. Up to the events of 2011, while there had been rumblings for political reform in

Saudi Arabia, a popular uprising was yet to materialize. There had been small indications that powerful tensions and the forces of rebellion simmered beneath the surface. The most notable had been in Saudi Arabia's Eastern Province, home to all of the kingdom's oil wealth as well as a large restive Shiite community, the members of which had long been victims of discrimination, persecution, and oppression. Small groups of Shiites in villages across the Eastern Province took to the streets in February and March 2011, partly in support of the uprising in Bahrain but also partly to demand amelioration of their frustrations at home. Another round of unrest took shape in October, with Shiites again taking to the streets demanding political reform, the release of political prisoners, and an end to their second-class status (Abul-Samh 2011).

The kingdom's leaders were fully aware of the potential for challenges to their domestic authority. Rather than entertain the options of sharing power with their citizens or engaging in much-needed political reform, they instead undertook dramatic measures that they hoped would prevent any real domestic challenge to their rule from materializing. In doing so, the kingdom's hard-liners, as was increasingly clear, gained the political edge. Most important was the apparent rise of the kingdom's mercurial and flamboyant chief cop, Naif bin Abd al-Aziz, the country's long-standing minister of the interior and, after the recent death of Crown Prince Sultan, heir to the throne.

Led by Naif, the Saudi royals eschewed political accommodation and instead looked for ways to outmaneuver domestic critics. It might have been tempting for observers to think otherwise. In September Saudi Arabia held its first elections for local municipal councils since 2005. Most Saudis greeted the elections with indifference, choosing not to vote (Al Arabiya News 2011). Women were excluded from the polls again in 2011, although King Abdullah announced in September that the women would be able to cast ballots during the next scheduled municipal council elections in 2015. He also announced that women would be able to serve in the country's consultative council, the Majlis al-Shura. The reality is that the expansion of political opportunities for women, and for all Saudis, was quite limited. Only half the members of the municipal councils are elected, and the councils have no real authority. The inclusion of women in the political process was welcome, but it was cautious and calculated to concede minimal political ground. It is noteworthy that almost immediately after the king's announcement, a Saudi court sentenced Shaima Jastaina to a public flogging for violating the ban on women driving. Abdullah overturned the sentence, most likely out of embarrassment, but the court's decision reflects the absurd contradictions that Saudi women face in the kingdom (*Telegraph* 2011). Limited political empowerment promises them very little when they are confronted with the entrenched power of reactionary religious elites.

The kingdom's minor concessions on elections and women's rights were a sideshow to more important political maneuvering in 2011. More than anything, the ruling elites took dramatic measures to shore up their power, further consolidate control, and crush any possible domestic criticism. The consequences have been and will almost certainly continue to be considerable.

The Saudi Security State

The first sign that the kingdom's leaders would pursue a hard-nosed strategy at home emerged in late February and early March. Caught up in the regional momentum, Saudi activists at home and abroad began a Facebook campaign calling for a "Day of Rage" modeled on and inspired by those taking place in neighboring countries. While it was always uncertain how popular the calls for mobilization would prove to be, Saudi authorities responded as though the planned protests marked a significant threat to their authority. In an effort to preempt even the remotest possibility of public dissent, the Saudi leadership's initial impulse was to threaten violence, imprisonment, and heavy fines for would-be protesters.

While Saudi Arabia had rarely been compelled to flex its security muscle against its own citizens, it did possess tremendous coercive power. Riyadh had spent billions of dollars on the best Western weapons and military training that oil revenues could buy. These weapons of war had not been put to use on the battlefield with any frequency, but they helped bolster the kingdom's counterrevolutionary power. Saudi citizens feared the regime's capacity for violence. It was widely believed that the country's domestic intelligence and security networks were omnipresent. Many suspected that if push came to shove, the Al Saud would happily engage in a Syrian-style crackdown on their own subjects in order to preserve their primacy.

In the few places where citizens took to the streets or spoke out in the public sphere against the regime or against corruption, or dared otherwise to cross unspoken red lines of dissent, they faced stern responses from police or simply disappeared. The latter was the case with Khaled Mohammed, a Saudi teacher who spoke out critically to foreign reporters in March. He was subsequently imprisoned and has not been heard from since his arrest (Jadaliyya 2011). Where Saudis protested, the cost was high. This was especially true for Shiites who took to the streets in the Eastern Province. Demonstrators there suffered injury and arrest. Security forces flooded Shiite-majority communities and made it virtually impossible for citizens to rally in public (Rasid 2011). And further, while most Saudis had not sympathized with the demands of the mostly Shiite pro-democracy protesters inside the kingdom or in Bahrain, the Saudi leadership's support for the violent crackdown in the Eastern Province sent a clear message about the government's capacity and willingness to inflict physical harm. Even Saudi Arabia's Sunni citizens harbored no illusion that they would be spared a violent response if they challenged Riyadh.

While the kingdom's coercive power was considerable, its potential for violence was matched by its ability to use its tremendous wealth to buy off would-be dissenters. At the same time, authorities unleashed a heavy security presence at home and in Bahrain, and in a demonstration of Saudi soft power, King Abdullah announced a $130 billion financial aid program that aimed to preempt danger. The move reflected a well-worn political instinct and represented an effort on the part of the ruling elite to buy their way out of potential trouble. It was announced on Saudi television that a considerable part of the financial package would be used to provide support for the unemployed, housing support, loan guarantees, and various other kinds of social assistance targeting those who faced the most pressing social challenges.

Fundamentally, the turn to financial inducement marked the continuation of politics and business as usual. Riyadh had long used financial incentives and extensive state-provided social services made possible by oil wealth as means to check the political ambitions of the kingdom's citizens. From the late 1960s, and especially after the boom years of the 1970s, Saudi Arabia built an elaborate social welfare state that provided a range of entitlements and cradle-to-grave services. These were all part of a grand political bargain in which the government redistributed oil wealth, which still at that time constituted about 85 percent of the country's gross domestic product, with the expectation that its subjects would remain politically obedient. They possessed limited political rights and no opportunity to participate in political decision making, but their wants and needs would be provided for. It was a bargain that had worked for the most part. Although Saudi Arabia had endured several episodes of domestic unrest in the previous thirty years, most notably in the aftermath of the 1991 Gulf War, when oil prices collapsed and social services were reduced, it had been mostly stable. And although Saudi citizens had long hoped that they would come to enjoy more political rights, they had also been slow to challenge a system that cared for most of their needs. Indeed, in addition to fearing the iron fist of the regime, they feared the creation of a political vacuum, one that might upend the networks of social and financial support upon which they depended.

Along with a heavy security presence, the financial package appeared to yield results. There were no significant demonstrations in March, and there have been none since. The kingdom's rulers appear to have come through the Arab Spring mostly unscathed. It is the country's citizens who have paid a high price.

Manipulating Clergy and Civil Society

Riyadh's financial calculus and its efforts to use cash to buy off those who suffered socially were the least worrisome aspects of the Saudi rulers' response to the political crisis confronting them. In the process of doling out cash, they were also empowering some of the country's most contentious religious figures, hoping to pit them and potential dissenters against one another as well as to deflect attention from themselves. While the expansion of social welfare made up one part of the financial package, a large part of the money was earmarked for various elements of the country's religious establishment. The turn to Islamists in an effort to snuff out dissent also signaled the ascent of the hard-line royal faction dominated by Prince Naif.

Both anticipating and eventually responding to the incentives that they correctly believed would be put before them, some of the members of the country's most senior religious institution, including the Higher Council of Ulama, ruled demonstrations un-Islamic, a clear signal of support for the royal family. It may not be surprising that a place known for its religious orthodoxy and for a clerical establishment that is prostrate before the heads of state would do such a thing. Since the eighteenth century, the Al Saud have worked closely with religious scholars in expanding and protecting their hegemony. In exchange for bestowing upon them the veneer of religious legitimacy, Saudi leaders have historically provided the clergy a free hand to control the religious, cultural, and social lives of the country's citizens. But the relationship between the royal family and the clerics has not always been harmonious.

The modern Saudi-clerical relationship does not date to the eighteenth century or even to the restoration of Saudi political power on the Arabian Peninsula in 1902. In its late twentieth-century form, in which the clergy exercised tremendous social and quasi-political influence, the Saudi-clerical compact was the result of a political crisis that roiled the kingdom in 1979. That year, religious radicals led by Juhayman al-Utaybi stormed and captured the Mecca mosque.[2] It took several weeks and the help of French special forces to root them out. Saudi Arabia's leaders were caught off guard by the rebellious upstarts and even more by the religiously inflected nature of their political discourse, which claimed that the Al Saud had forsaken their political legitimacy by selling the kingdom out to the powers of material and crass consumerism. Riyadh responded by executing those rebels they captured alive. More important, the country's leaders also responded by pouring billions of dollars into Islamic causes and institutions. While the clergy had always enjoyed prominence, their powers expanded in the decade after the 1979 uprising. While they still took their orders from the royal family, their influence was considerable and periodically a source of frustration and concern for the Al Saud.

In the last years of the twentieth century, King Abdullah took significant measures to check the power of the clergy and roll back some of the influence religious scholars had gained after 1979. This was especially true for the most radical members of the religious establishment, which had become an irritant and an embarrassment for the king. Observers both inside and outside Saudi Arabia often described Abdullah as a political reformer, a moderate committed to shepherding the kingdom along a more liberal political path. These claims were always exaggerated, but Abdullah had demonstrated a willingness to strip the religious establishment of some of its most cherished powers. He overturned court rulings, fired controversial religious leaders from prominent posts, allowed for public criticism of the clergy, restrained the power of the country's feared religious police, and even initiated reform of the judiciary, one of the most important centers of clerical authority. Abdullah's interest in curbing the clergy had less to do with opening the kingdom up politically than it had to do with undermining alternative centers of power to the royal family. In essence, Abdullah was seeking to reconsolidate his family's grip on power.

Much of Abdullah's careful and deliberate work to check the power of the clergy quickly came undone in the first months of 2011. In addition to the subsidies provided for a range of Islamic institutions in the financial package announced in March, state officials made clear that criticism of the religious establishment would no longer be tolerated. Public scorn for scholars and some 'ulama had been criminalized. This was a significant reversal. While Abdullah had been slow to usher in meaningful political and institutional reforms, his reign had seen an opening of the public sphere for greater debate and commentary. The press was far from free, but until then it had been a vehicle for criticism of religious excess and for women's and even minority rights. Not only were the kingdom's clergy back in favor, but also enjoying renewed privilege were some the religious establishment's most controversial elements; this included significant new levels of support for the religious police. Moreover, the ability of Saudis to express themselves and to criticize the clergy had been limited.

The reempowerment of the worst of the kingdom's religious authorities suggested there was a new balance of power in Riyadh. Abdullah remained nominally in control of the country's affairs, but it was increasingly clear that he alone was not calling the shots. His preference for inducements had not been enough to soothe the anxieties of those around him in the royal family. Renewed support not just for the clergy but also for particularly powerful and draconian religious authorities, such as the religious police, suggested that hard-liners or a hard-line faction had emerged as the key power brokers inside the kingdom. It was a matter of speculation as to whose personal influence was reflected in the new balance of power. It was likely that Abdullah had conceded authority to his younger half brother Naif, the minister of the interior and, with the passing of Crown Prince Sultan in October 2011, the presumptive heir to the throne. Naif was close to the country's religious establishment and saw it as his most loyal base of power. And as head of the country's police and intelligence services, Naif already exercised a disciplinary and iron-fisted impulse. He had a hard-earned reputation as a tough cop and little patience for reform or the expansion of political rights.

Naif single-handedly destroyed Saudi Arabia's nascent reform lobby in early 2004. In 2003 a small group of Saudi academics, religious figures, and intellectuals had pressed Abdullah, then crown prince, to undertake meaningful political reform. They signed petitions and sent several delegations to meet with Abdullah, who proved agreeable to some of their more substantive suggestions. Over the course of the year he facilitated a dialogue among divergent social and religious networks—even bringing together rival Shiite and Sunni clerics. But Naif was less amenable to reform efforts. As demands for change mounted late in the year and in early 2004, he sent dire warnings that reform activism must be stopped. When prominent figures such as Abdullah al-Hamed pressed ahead, Naif had them tossed in prison, where they remained until 2005. The message was clear: while some might entertain discussion of reform, Naif would have none of it, and the costs of continuously challenging the royal family would be high.

Anti-Shiism and Iran

Aside from his antireform credentials, which might be attributable to a practical streak that simply prioritized the privileges of royal family power, Naif was also believed to be more ideological than his brother in at least one respect: his anti-Shiism. While it is entirely speculative as to whether or not Naif had led the charge against the kingdom's Shiite community or those Shiites demanding democracy in Bahrain, the crystallization of a Saudi hard line had a clear sectarian hue. Perhaps the most dangerous aspect of the kingdom's new balance of power was its anti-Shiite sectarianism. Anti-Shiite sentiment has long been widespread in Saudi Arabia; it has often been directed at the country's sizable Shiite minority community, which makes up between 10 and 15 percent of the kingdom's native population. It has been arguable that the geopolitical dimensions of Saudi sectarianism, most notably the kingdom's cold war with Shiite Iran, trump the nation's domestic concerns. After all, Saudi military forces entered Bahrain to assist that country's crackdown in part to send a message that Riyadh would not allow Shiite empowerment and any potential political advantage for Iran so close to home. Moreover, both Bahraini and Saudi authorities justified the harshness of their response by claiming, without evidence, that Iran was fomenting unrest and encouraging Bahrain's Shiite majority to take to the streets and toss the country's Sunni ruling family from power (Obaid 2011).

It mattered little that there had been no evidence of Iranian meddling or influence. The decision to play the sectarian card enabled both Manama and Riyadh to ignore the substantive claims of the protesters and to reframe the struggle for power in Bahrain as a cosmic struggle between Shiites and Sunnis. These claims also worked to bring Riyadh and Washington closer together. In October 2011, the U.S. Department of Justice unsealed an indictment alleging that elements of Iran's Revolutionary Guard had sought to assassinate Adel al-Jubeir, Saudi Arabia's ambassador to the United States. There was a great deal of skepticism about the claim and little real evidence to suggest the plot was real.[3] Whatever the veracity of the indictment, however, the political result was that the United States and Saudi Arabia agreed that Iran's potential to cause harm in the Middle East was more important than the trampling of human rights in places such as Bahrain, where activists had been brutalized and tortured (see Jones 2011a).

Saudi Arabia's leaders had long claimed to be seeking security and stability, and there was a time when this may have been true. While the

Arab Spring was a source of anxiety, it also created political opportunities for the kingdom, both in the region and at home. And it turned out, in the end, that regional crisis may have been useful for the expansion of Saudi Arabia's power. In the months following the nation's military intervention in Bahrain, Riyadh engaged in an escalating war of words with Tehran. Iran had already cut diplomatic ties with Bahrain. It was mired in claims of espionage with Kuwait. A protracted Iranian-Saudi cold war, and potentially a more significant regional conflict, was now assured. Those tensions also led Riyadh to support the overthrow of Syria's Assad, who depended on Iran for much of his power. But in attempting to deflect the democratic and reform-minded forces sweeping across the region and at the same time check Iranian ambition, Saudi Arabia's rulers unleashed something far worse. Sectarianism and the more reactionary political Islamist instincts that had provided some parts of the royal family credibility at home were being strengthened in the region as well.

Ultimately, however, the toll of Saudi counterrevolution was most keenly felt at home. Saudis were confronted with a political future that was more uncertain than at any time in the previous decade. The kingdom's rulers had turned back the clock. They were banking that by doing so they would gain the time and the political cover they needed to survive the Arab Spring. It remained to be seen how long their efforts would prove successful.

Notes

1. See also Bradley (2011). For an alternative view, see Gause (2011).
2. For more on al-Utaybi, see Lacroix (2011) and Trofimov (2008).
3. For more on this subject, see Ostovar (2011).

References

Abul-Samh, Rashid. 2011. "Saudi Shias Riot Yet Again for Better Conditions." *Al-Ahram Weekly,* October 13–19. http://weekly.ahram.org.eg/2011/1068/re9.htm (accessed October 31, 2011).

Al Arabiya News. 2011. "All-Male Saudi Polls; Candidates Compete for 1,056 Seats." September 29. http://www.alarabiya.net (accessed October 31, 2011).

Al Nafjan, Eman. 2011. "Life for Saudi Women Is a Constant State of Contradiction." *Guardian,* September 29. http://www.guardian.co.uk (accessed October 31, 2011).

Bradley, John R. 2011. "Saudi Arabia's Invisible Hand in the Arab Spring." *Foreign Affairs,* October 13. http://www.foreignaffairs.com (accessed March 6, 2013).

Gause, F. Gregory. 2011. "Is Saudi Arabia Really Counterrevolutionary?" *Foreign Policy,* August 9. http://mideast.foreignpolicy.com (accessed March 6, 2013).

Hill, Amelia. 2011. "Saudi Film-Makers Enter Second Week of Detention." *Guardian,* October 23. http://www.guardian.co.uk (accessed October 31, 2011).

Jadaliyya. 2011. "Where Is Khaled? The Story of a Disappeared Critic." May 29. http://www.jadaliyya.com (accessed October 31, 2011).

Jones, Toby C. 2011a. "Bahrain, Kingdom of Silence." *Arab Reform Bulletin,* May 4. http://carnegieendowment.org/sada (accessed March 6, 2013).

——. 2011b. *Counterrevolution in the Gulf.* Peace Brief 89, April 15. Washington, D.C.: United States Institute of Peace. http://www.usip.org/publications/counterrevolution-in-the-gulf (accessed October 31, 2011).

——. 2011c. "Saudi Arabia's Regional Reaction." *The Nation,* September 12. http://www.thenation.com (accessed October 31, 2011).

Lacroix, Stéphane. 2011. *Awakening Islam: The Politics of Religious Dissent in Contemporary Saudi Arabia.* Translated by George Holoch. Cambridge, Mass.: Harvard University Press.

Obaid, Nawaf. 2011. "A Saudi Perspective on the Alleged Iranian Plot." CNN World, October 25. http://globalpublicsquare.blogs.cnn.com (accessed March 6, 2013).

Ostovar, Afshon. 2011. "Worst. Plot. Ever." *Foreign Policy,* October 13. http://www.foreignpolicy.com (accessed March 6, 2013).

Rasid. 2011. "Isāba khamsa shubbān fī itlāq al-nār li-'anāsir al-amn wasta al-Qatīf" [Five youth fired on by security forces in the center of Qatif]. October 23. http://rasid.com (accessed October 30, 2011).

Telegraph. 2011. "Saudi King Saves Woman Driver from 10 Lashes." October 29. http://www.telegraph.co.uk (accessed October 29, 2011).

Trofimov, Yaroslav. 2008. *The Siege of Mecca: The 1979 Uprising at Islam's Holiest Shrine.* New York: Anchor Books.

Yemen

SHEILA CARAPICO

IN FEBRUARY 2011, Tawakkol Karman stood on a stage outside Sanaa University. A microphone in one hand and the other clenched defiantly above her head, reading from a list of demands, she led tens of thousands of cheering, flag-waving demonstrators in calls for peaceful political change. She was to become not so much the leader as the figurehead of Yemen's uprising. On other days and in other cities, other citizens led the chants: men and women and sometimes, for effect, little children. These mass public performances enacted a veritable civic revolution in a poverty-stricken country where previous activist surges never produced democratic transitions but nonetheless did shape national history. Drawing on the Tunisian and Egyptian inspirations as well as homegrown protest legacies, in 2011 Yemenis occupied the national commons as never before. Whether or not their aspirations would be met, the country's youth—who are the demographic majority—had animated a public civic renaissance. Women's very public participation was one powerful signifier of seismic sociocultural change.

Youthful pro-democracy activists, gray-haired socialists, YouTube videos, gun-toting cowboys, Northern carpetbaggers, mutinous army officers, Shia insurgents, kids wearing face paint, tear gas canisters, WikiLeaks cables, performance arts, foreign-born jihadists, dissident tribal sheikhs, and a female Nobel Peace Prize laureate: Yemen's uprising combined slogans and motifs from the Egyptian and Tunisian revolts with elements of repression emulating Libya and Syria and quintessentially colloquial practices in a gaudy, fast-paced, multilayered revolutionary theater verging on the macabre. The most important trajectory was that day after day, with special energy on Sabbath Fridays, in cities and towns across the land, men, women, and children agitated against dictatorship and the politics of violence. Whether this popular intifada—wracked by intra-elite street battles and complicated by American operations against the local branch of al-Qaeda—would end in glory or tragedy, its social, psychological, and political significance was inestimable. Regardless of the near-term outcome, as in Tunisia and Egypt, the experience of collective contentious mobilization "from below" in solidarity with fellow Yemenis and other Arabs had been transformative for young women and men. They had tasted the power of social mobilization.

The 2011 Nobel Peace Prize was awarded jointly to two Liberian women who helped pull their country out of the abyss of cruel and brutal civil war and to a Yemeni spokesperson for her country's human rights constituency. Nominated in January 2011 shortly after her release from temporary detention and honored by the committee in Oslo for representing the popular outcry for liberty and justice across the whole Arab region, Tawakkol Karman dedicated her prize to all Arab demonstrators and martyrs during the year's revolutionary upheavals. "I am so happy," she told the *New York Times,* "and I give this award to all of the youth and all of the women across the Arab world, in Egypt, in Tunisia" (quoted in Cowell, Kasinof, and Nossiter 2011).

When the prize was announced October 7, Yemen's "peaceful youth" (shabab al-silmiyya) had been in the streets daily for eight months demanding an end to a three-decades-old dictatorship. With their turnout multiplied by their endurance, Yemenis had clocked more demonstrator-days in 2011 than more populous countries such as Egypt. They had practiced novel public modes of expression, combining indigenous arts such as oral poetry recitation, local dances, and public prayer with novel technological applications that allowed them to blog and post and tweet. They rejoiced and uploaded celebratory messages to the Internet upon hearing the news from Oslo. Defying the return volley of rockets and tear gas, protesters called for an international tribunal to bring President Ali Abdullah Saleh and his cronies to justice.

The uprising that began in January in "Change Square," Midan al-Taghayr, near Sanaa University was part of the broader Arab revolution yet also organically associated with Yemeni culture and political history. Yemenis adopted North African slogans, "Irhal" and "Isqat al-nizam," calling for the departure of the president and the rest of his regime (Rosen 2001). As in Egypt, there was advance planning for a first day of protests, but the outpouring and momentum from below soon surpassed the wildest dreams of would-be organizers. Bypassing the organized formal elite partisan opposition of the Joint Meeting Parties, youth congregated in ever-increasing numbers to air their frustrations. In contrast with metropolitan Cairo's central Liberation Square—Midan al-Tahrir—where fantastically photogenic multitudes were filmed from nearby balconies of high-rise hotels by international television crews, Yemen's marches, like its twenty-some million inhabitants, were relatively more dispersed among a half dozen major cities and several smaller towns. Millions strong, they drew much less worldwide media attention than any of the other major upheavals of the "Arab Spring": those in Tunisia, Egypt, Libya, and Syria.

Yet via phone, Arabic-language satellite television, and the World Wide Web they were very much in touch with what was going on elsewhere in the region. Interestingly, unlike in Egypt where to some it seemed that Facebook and the Internet sparked the revolution, in Yemen Facebook membership, blogs, and YouTube posts proliferated from mere handfuls of elites with friends abroad in late 2010 to major means of communications a year later. It was a cyberexplosion. Thousands of Yemenis joined Facebook during the spring of 2011, others created Facebook pages, still more blogged in Arabic or English or other languages, hundreds practiced guerrilla photojournalism. Virtual participants among Yemeni emigrant communities overseas passed images on, and some were picked up by Al Jazeera or analyzed from abroad. As in Egypt, however, for all the talk of a digital revolution, mobile phones were by far the most salient form of technology for domestic communication, and word of mouth spread news within and between neighborhoods.

Discontent in the poorest Arab country had been simmering for years on a number of fronts and levels. Patronage was rampant (Alley 2010), and restlessness stirred around the president's clear intention to ordain his son, already commander of the nation's Republican Guard, as his successor. Added to this were the postponement of parliamentary elections; widespread unemployment, especially among the youth; deteriorating standards of living for all but the upper echelons of the ruling kleptocracy; ecological depredations to a formerly self-sufficient farm economy; a consequentially decimated ecology and acute water shortages; abysmal educational and medical facilities, sanitation, and physical infrastructure; crude resort to censorship, harassment, arbitrary detention, and brutality against journalists, dissidents, and regime opponents; and profound, widespread malaise.

By late 2010 regional demonstrations or uprisings had cropped up in different parts of the country with seemingly different complaints. Most dramatically, governorates in what had been the South Yemeni territory known as the People's Democratic Republic of Yemen until 1990 formed a movement (known simply as al-Hirak) for secession. Agitators had been marching and staging displays in the Indian Ocean port city of Aden and outlying provinces such as Hadramawt and Abyan for several years.

Although Southerners rightly felt particular discrimination, things were not well either in the former North Yemen, where Saleh had ruled since the assassination of his predecessor in 1978. There was a more openly armed rebellion rooted in complicated, sometimes counterintuitive sectarian and tribal frictions around villages and valleys in the far northern province of Sa'adah, seemingly exacerbated by proximity to the Saudi border (Weir 1997).

In cities and provinces between these geographical extremes, people were disheartened by high-level corruption, graft, nepotism, and favoritism toward the president's Hashid tribal confederation, including high-ranking military officers. Often, resentments were highly localized: as we will see below, rival tribes and inhabitants of the Red Sea coast and merchants and farmers from the "middle regions" all expressed particular regional and communal concerns.

Yet, remarkably, over the course of 2011, protests coalesced around a national, pro-democracy, reformist consciousness. To grasp this astonishing episode of mass civic engagement, it is useful to review earlier waves of activism and the ways they constituted national and local public civic realms. From the mid-twentieth century onward, each generation enjoyed a moment of civic efflorescence: the independence movement in the Crown Colony of Aden and the South Arabian Protectorates in the 1950s and 1960s, self-help community betterment projects primarily in North Yemen in the 1970s and 1980s, and a vibrant if short-lived democratic opening after unification of the two parts of the country in the 1990s. The civic outburst of 2011, the fourth such opening, drew on earlier experiences but also shared many elements with what became known in English as the Arab Spring.

Activist Surges and Public Spheres

Civil society is usually thought of as a zone of voluntarism, philanthropy, and public-spirited discourse beyond the affective bonds of family, distinguishable from entrepreneurial ventures and outside the formal apparatus of the state. Most theories of peaceful democratic transitions hold that a vibrant civic associational network and a lively public intellectual sphere of civility are the sine qua non for the development of liberal democracy. It is sometimes argued that formal, modern, liberal, intellectually informed associations often dubbed NGOs (for "nongovernmental organizations") are the necessary precondition for meaningful political reform, or, on the other hand, that civil society cannot exist except under constitutional, elected governments. By these criteria many scholars and pundits, Arab as well as Western, often doubted whether it was possible to speak of civil society anywhere in the region, much less in quaint and colorful but underdeveloped Yemen. Certainly the government of Ali Abdullah Saleh, like other Arab dictatorships, had worked nonstop to curtail, co-opt, and contain civil society within government-dominated institutions or ruling-party bureaucracies. Yet looking at Egypt, Yemen, and other countries' subaltern social movements even before these uprisings, we had recognized that when circumstances demand, civil society can enable communities to cope with physical or political adversity, to navigate bureaucratic obstacles, and even to challenge authoritarianism. Moreover, although successful mass movements had been rare, we knew that in the Arab region as a whole and in Yemen in particular, when legal avenues for complaint and lobbying are exhausted and conditions become intolerable, there are exceptional, take-to-the-streets civic moments of mass engagement, whether organized or spontaneous (Carapico 2010).

Civic activism is a variable, then, not a cultural constant. It consists not only of formal organizations but also of various ways people exercise collective agency. Shaped by sociocultural, economic, and political-legal circumstances as well as trends in the Arab and international arenas, civil society in Yemen has expanded and contracted and varied in shape and content in radically context-dependent ways during the past half century or so. Prior to the 2011 upheaval, the older generation recalled three distinct and distinctive expansions of civic activity in different times, places, and circumstances. Note in advance that none of them had a democratic outcome. Actually, they all ended with a kind of dialectical boomerang effect: closure of public civic space by "states" that drew legitimacy from the same popular energies they subsequently sought to repress. While progress toward democracy or even modernity was halting and faltering, each time people took matters into their own hands, they left an indelible legacy on national politics, governance, and society.

The first great Yemeni civic opening occurred in what were then Aden Colony and the Protectorates of South Arabia during the late colonial era in the 1950s and 1960s. The South Yemeni independence movement, in its civilian manifestations as well as in the armed resistance, was part of a larger Third World struggle for national self-determination and an Arabian flowering of political, artistic, and civic expression, much of it class based (Halliday 1974). Unionized labor stoppages, mass street marches, the distribution of political pamphlets and newspapers, hunger strikes, the founding of Yemen's first feminist organizations, and other arguably imported actions, especially among the polyglot workers in Aden port, combined with creative political performances drawing on religious or tribal traditions in small towns in the Hadramawt and Lahj.

This remarkable populist outburst, culminating under complicated circumstances in the departure of British administrators from Aden and points east in late 1967, did not survive the independence era. A brief Thermidor was followed by a reign of terror. As in so many other countries, from Cuba to Algeria to Vietnam, hard-fought postcolonial independence enabled a revolutionary ruling party, the Yemeni Socialist Party (YSP), to nationalize and centralize all forms of participation into national federations for labor, women, journalists, intellectuals, and other corporate groups. Under the People's Democratic Republic of Yemen (PDRY), women enjoyed rights unparalleled in the Arabian Peninsula if not the whole Arab world: polygamy was outlawed, for instance. Other progressive social policies were pursued. Yet postrevolutionary fervor amalgamated mass mobilization to the party-state project. Civil society retreated underground or fled into North Yemen. The last vestiges of the populist movement that brought it to power were eviscerated in a bloody two-week shoot-out among the Socialist Party elite in 1986.

The second civic renaissance occurred mostly in North Yemen after the downfall of the thousand-year-old Zaydi imamate in 1962 and the establishment of a weak republican government, when communities undertook their own modernization with only minimal assistance from the ostensibly central state. Unlike the South, the Republic of Yemen had no colonial history to speak of and was extraordinarily backward (Halliday 1974). There were hardly any paved roads, public schools, or municipal power and water supplies. Combining a forward-looking urge with native urban management and communal practices including tribal customs, cities and regions built thousands of kilometers of roads and hundreds of primary and middle schools, and rigged up scores of water delivery and electrical power stations. Most of these activities were ad hoc; committees organized around a project often dissolved after its completion. On the other hand, in some localities, especially the Ta'izz region, elections were held for local development boards to manage these projects.

Ironically, decentralized grassroots community betterment projects laid the infrastructural ground for the relative centralization of state power that took place when Ali Abdullah Saleh came to office in the late 1970s, as transportation access and educational curricula connected other urban areas and even remote provinces more tightly to Sanaa. Roads brought goods, strangers, and officials into the provinces, for instance, while schools utilized texts from the embryonic Ministry of Education and taught the national anthem. Ultimately the fledgling military government was able to centralize social capital through bureaucratic controls and to claim credit for every classroom constructed with local resources. The national confederation of local development associations morphed into the Ministry of Local Administration (Carapico 1998). Entirely different in style and substance from the South's struggle for independence, the services-oriented direct-action "cooperative movement" also left its mark on Yemeni political history and socioeconomic development.

Yemen's third major civic opening heralded unification between the PDRY and North Yemen in 1990 according to a deal between Saleh and the remaining Socialist leaders of the PDRY. Stuck at the very end of the Cold War, this arrangement coincided with German unification. Unity introduced a panoply of political parties, including the YSP; Saleh's General People's Congress (GPC); a conservative Northern party called al-Islah, close to the GPC and led by prominent Hashid and Islamist figures; and several smaller Nasserist, Baathist, and Shia parties. All had their own newspapers and agendas, and all fielded candidates in reasonably free and fair elections in 1993. When the two former ruling parties that still commanded the respective armed forces of the two Yemens refused to abide by the power-sharing mandate of the elections, however, armed conflict seemed imminent. The two armies squared off. The Aden-based leadership of the Socialist Party and former PDRY army launched a bid for secession.

Intellectual elites and ordinary people swung into action with mass public conferences in urban and tribal areas alike, with small but significant nationwide peace protests, and with a National Dialogue of Political Forces that produced a constitution-like "contract of accord" to resolve the impasse short of armed combat (Carapico 1998). The forces of peace and reconciliation lost. In the two-month, army-to-army military campaign that followed, Saleh's forces, buttressed by self-declared antisocialist jihadis, conquered the old South and chased the YSP leaders into exile.

Over the next decade and more, the victorious Saleh administration gradually tightened the vise on public civic expression. Elections were increasingly engineered to ensure victory for the president and his party faithful. Aspiring to but never quite mastering the absolute security control achieved in Syria or Libya, Saleh's administration left some room for an impotent opposition coalition comprising the unlikely bedfellows of al-Islah, the Socialists, the assorted Arab nationalists, and small indigenous parties. Known as the Joint Meeting Parties (JMP), this opposition coalition was able to register a modicum of minority parliamentary dissent. Popular social forces were nearly, but never entirely, quelled.

Under these circumstances of only a ceremonial facade of democracy, people were still able to claim pieces of the public civic sphere in quotidian ways independent of state-sponsored spectacles of nationhood. In Yemen one of these is the ubiquitous practice of gathering in private homes to chew *qat* and talk politics in the afternoons, as well as participate in oral recitations of poetry. In the more explicitly public national sphere, expensive pageants such as the celebratory fanfare devoted to the bogus reelection of President Saleh were no more constitutive of what it means to be Yemeni than the moral panic surrounding macabre incidents such as a series of murders in the Sanaa morgue (Wedeen 2008). In other words, shared reactions to extraordinary events as well as shared everyday practices can constitute the Yemeni "self" as an explicitly national or even democratic person, and this sense of national identity can be constituted even in the absence of actualization through state institutions (Wedeen 2008, 15). A fairly vibrant if distinctly male-dominated public civic sphere survived.

The antiregime protests of 2011—and to some extent, perhaps counterintuitively, even the pro-Saleh demonstrations staged in the military reviewing stand near his presidential palace throughout the year—echoed these precedents in distinct though varied ways. In particular, major regions and cities drew on local customs in ways that imagined and expressed national aspirations and the collective will of "the people." To explain this point it is necessary to map the social geography of the pro-democracy movement. The protests transcended all the preexisting divisions of North versus South, urban versus tribal, Sanaa versus the hinterland, Shafaʻi Sunni versus Shia Zaydi, uplands versus lowlands, political party loyalties, and conventional gender roles.

Geographies of Protest

A peaceful intifada had already been in motion since the summer of 2007 in the South, the territory known as the People's Democratic Republic of Yemen and ruled by the Yemeni Socialist Party (YSP) from late 1967 to 1990. In 1990, the South unified with the North, already ruled by Saleh; it attempted secession four years later. During the short civil war, the president called in assorted tribal militias and "Afghan Arabs"— puritanical Salafis ostensibly returned from the victorious anti-Soviet jihad in Afghanistan—to assist the regular army under the command of General Ali Muhsin. A beer factory and civil service administration offices in the Southern capital of Aden were torched and looted. Eventually the erstwhile Southern leadership fled by boat to Oman, and Northern military officers and gangs of scalawags installed themselves as governors, administrators, and landowners. Workers deprived of their jobs, pensioners denied their benefits, and women stripped of the rights they had enjoyed under the old Socialist administration seethed under what they regarded as occupation. Oil revenues from wells on what had been Southern soil flowed into the coffers of Saleh and his cronies (Day 2008).

After more than a decade of economic collapse and political repression, the youth and some of the old YSP cadres launched al-Hirak, a movement motivated largely by resurgent Southern nationalism (Dahlgren 2010). It drew on some of the slogans, motifs, and performative elements of the anticolonial movement in Aden, the cities of the Hadramawt, and other communities. Again these included both Socialist elements and locally distinctive traditions of dance, dress, and dialect. The movement also depended on human rights organizations and municipal newspapers established during the opening that followed unification in the early 1990s. By late 2010, Saleh and his official media could successfully portray their distress as treasonous irredentist threats to national unity reminiscent of the 1994 civil war. And indeed throughout 2011 some citizens flew the flag of the old People's Republic, even as others joined the nationalist movement to oust the regime in Sanaa.

Whether or not they harbored genuinely separatist ambitions, residents of the former PDRY had good reason to feel they were punitively targeted and deprived of basic liberties and entitlements. What was not evident to them until after the uprisings in Tunisia and Egypt began was the extent of popular resentments and yearnings in the rest of the country.

It turned out that many of the tribulations in the South resonated in every province of the republic: the grotesque enrichment of regime cronies at the expense of the multitudes, obscenely bad stewardship of the commons, the skyrocketing prices of meat, staples, and even clean water; the lack of jobs for college and high school graduates. Already by 2005 the American ambassador had noted in a WikiLeaked cable that riots prompted by the lifting of fuel subsidies had stimulated the prospects for a revolt, especially—but not only—among the perennially restive tribes of the northeastern provinces of al-Jawf and Marib, where truckers and pump farmers considered cheap fuel their lifeblood (Carapico 2011). Grandiose pageants of presidential power, half-truths in the official media, the indignities of military checkpoints, arbitrary arrests and imprisonments—these and other daily insults fed popular alienation, despair, and frustration, most notably among the youth. While a privileged few cooled off in swimming pools in their luxury compounds, the water table fell, decimating the farm economy that remained the livelihood of the rural majority. Farmers and ranchers facing starvation flocked to the cities, where water supplies and social services were swamped. Misery became the new normal; millions barely survived on the equivalent of a dollar or two a day. The economy was in shambles (Colton 2010).

The breakthrough came in Sanaa, the capital, a metropolitan area on the high central plateau whose population had quadrupled during the previous generation owing to the lures of government jobs, services, and payoffs. It was now a teaming, sprawling, poorly laid out, still picturesque low-rise city of nearly two million inhabitants, more than half of whom were under twenty years of age. Its schools, sewage disposal system, and water supplies were completely overwhelmed. Nominally both home and center to the ruling family and its security apparatus, Sanaa was also most exposed to its excesses and regulations and the prime site for parades of presidential power.

Early in 2011 Saleh loyalists laid claim to Sanaa's central Midan al-Tahrir so that it would not follow Cairo's example of becoming a stage for malcontents. Also the huge presidential, military, and ministerial complexes remained showplaces for Saleh photographs. Drawing from the precedents of the 1993–94 antiwar, pro-democracy demonstrations, therefore, students, faculty, and other activists assembled around the university campus on the western edge of the old part of Sanaa. They named the space they claimed Change Square (Midan al-Taghayr). Proportionately, the occupiers represented the demographic bulge of fifteen- to thirty-year-olds who had never known another leadership: university students, graduates, dropouts, and wannabes grasping for hope for a better future. In Change Square and adjoining spaces, these "peaceful youth" enlivened the experience with music, dancing, poetry readings, posters, street art, and collective gestures of defiance, such as fifty thousand pairs of clasped hands held high. The call to prayer became a call to civic engagement, and mass prayers became a form of civil disobedience.

Inspired by Karman, who headed the NGO Women Journalists Without Chains, women defied a conservative cultural norm about speaking softly in public. They mocked the president's sleazy innuendo about an un-Islamic "mixing of the sexes" in Change Square. Almost all women in Sanaa wear the all-encompassing black *sharshaf,* which is a modern veil. At one point many thousands lined up, covered in the customary black. Some rows wore white baseball caps on top of their veils. Another group sported red baseball caps. Visually, the effect was to create a white, black, and red Yemeni flag stretching more than a kilometer down a wide road in a show of patriotism.

The crowds around Sanaa University swelled as tribesmen—the ranchers, truckers, and farmers from outlying areas—joined the protests. Many of them pitched tents that eventually grew into a sprawling encampment snaking through the neighborhood around the university campus with its own sanitation system, medical services, teach-ins, and food and water supplies. On March 18, plainclothes snipers fired from neighboring rooftops onto Change Square, killing more than fifty mostly youthful and entirely peaceful protesters. In disbelief, fury, and sorrow, a record 150,000 marched in Sanaa's biggest "day of rage" so far (Carapico 2011). An avalanche of top-level and midlevel resignations from the armed forces, the foreign service, the civil service, and even the president's General People's Congress followed in protest of the excessive use of force against unarmed civilians. Among the defectors were General Ali Muhsin, the commander of the First Army Brigade who had dealt mercilessly with Southern secessionists in 1994, and key leaders of the president's own Hashid tribal confederation, including scions of the paramount sheikhship, the al-Ahmar family (for background on this division, see Phillips 2006). These defections from the president's inner circle split the regime and would eventually divide the capital city into pro- and anti-Saleh territory. At the same time, collective rage and moral panic gradually solidified the protests into a nationwide movement. Sentiments crossed party lines: although they belonged to the same conservative political party, al-Islah, Karman and the al-Ahmar brothers were on very different political wavelengths (for background, see Yadav 2010).

In provincial cities where hundreds or thousands had attended rallies, multitudes now laid claim to public spaces. In Ta'izz, a bustling commercial and industrial city of more than half a million people nestled in the verdant southern mountains of the former North, and in the picturesque neighboring city of Ibb, simmering discontent erupted. The populous Ta'izz-Ibb area, known as the "middle regions," a once rich agricultural zone tilled by peasants and sharecroppers, served as a bridge between the Southern al-Hirak and the revolutionary movement centered in Sanaa. People traveled, telephoned, and tweeted with family and compatriots in Aden, Hadramawt, Abyan, and other parts of the former PDRY already in foment. By summer, reporters were calling Ta'izz—a hub for exiled anti-imperialist Southern forces during the 1960s and a center of the cooperative movement in the 1970s—the epicenter of the democratic intifada. The city's relatively educated, cosmopolitan student body choreographed a nearly carnival atmosphere with music, skits, caricatures, graffiti, banners, and other artistic embellishments. Photos showed throngs massed in dozens of thousands. As in Aden and Sanaa, women and girls frequently organized separate marches and displays to underscore the unarmed, modern character of the revolt. On October 30, 2011, for instance, they posted a YouTube video full of flowers, confetti, balloons, music, and ululating commemorating each of their martyrs by name and portrait. Meanwhile, perhaps even more than Sanaa, Taʿizz became a battlefield between pro- and antiregime security forces.

In Hudayda, the steamy, squalid Red Sea port that is the hub of the Tihama coastal plain where Afro-Yemenis suffer the country's highest rates of poverty and political disenfranchisement, youth and parents also filled their own Freedom Square with banners and chants and insurrectionary graffiti. "Irhal!" they yelled in unison: Go! And, referring to the deposed Tunisian leader who sought refuge in Saudi Arabia: "Oh, Ali Abdullah, join Bin Ali in Riyadh!" First they applauded Mubarak's resignation. Many months later, like their compatriots in the highlands, they celebrated the demise of Libya's dictator Muammar Qaddafi and dedicated mass prayers to the martyrs of Syria. New mantras, skits, and cartoons taunted both the Yemeni and the Syrian dictators: "Come on Ali, come on Bashar, it's time for you to go!" ran the refrain.

Raucous demonstrations mixed with familiar acts of civil disobedience such as road blockages and commercial stoppages in the wide-open, semiarid, sparsely populated plateaus and mountains north, northwest, east, and somewhat south of Sanaa, regions analogous to Texas or Wyoming, the avowed tribal heartland where ranchers, cowboys, truck farmers, and hillbillies carry Kalashnikovs or even bazooka launchers and perennially harbor deep mistrust of the central government. These demonstrations were especially prevalent in al-Jawf and Marib governorates, stretches of the north and east populated predominantly by members of the Bakil tribal confederation, the rival to Hashid. More reminiscent of the 1993–94 mass conferences than of the familiar low-grade armed resistance, kidnappings, and sabotage, these protests adopted the *silmiyya* approach. In al-Baydha, the small provincial capital of a heavily armed Bakil territory somewhat north of the former inter-Yemeni border, men who normally do not leave home without a rifle threw down their guns to march peacefully. This was highly significant: in a country known to be awash in personal weapons, the mass uprising avoided guerrilla warfare or military insurrection. To repeat: tens of thousands of tribesmen with the means to launch an armed revolt resisted the temptation to open fire.

Counterrevolutionary Forces

The response to the peaceful protests was wrathful. Divisions loyal to the president, mostly commanded by immediate members of his family, fired on unarmed demonstrators in Sanaa, Aden, Ta'izz, Hudayda, and elsewhere. Hundreds of deaths stoked rather than quelled the protests, however. Grainy, graphic cell phone footage was uploaded to the Internet. In each community, every funeral provoked more angry or grief-stricken dissenters to call for the downfall of the regime.

More explosively, loyalists and dissidents engaged one another in mortal combat, especially in certain neighborhoods of Sanaa. The bloodiest battles pitted Saleh's family commands, including the Republican Guard and special forces, against the renegade brigade led by General Ali Muhsin and the Hashid tribal militia headed by the sons of the late great Sheikh Abdallah al-Ahmar, who had been part of the Saleh regime for three decades. In other words, powerful elements of the president's inner circle representing key military and Hashid constituencies, long considered his base of support, had turned against him. At various times Saleh labeled them bloodthirsty, seditious traitors, coup makers, terrorists, and thugs. General Ali Muhsin placed an armed cordon around the large neighborhood surrounding Change Square to protect the protesters. There were frequent skirmishes around the al-Ahmar family compound on the airport road. The June explosion inside the mosque in the presidential palace compound, which left Saleh disfigured while killing or crippling several of his deputies, was almost certainly some kind of inside job (Phillips 2011). This was an intraregime squabble. The "peaceful youth" emphatically did not line up behind the general or the sons of the old sheikh, al-Ahmar.

The Saleh regime also repeated a tactic from 1994 in deliberately unleashing zealous militants, nowadays associated with al-Qaeda, against dissidents in parts of the old PDRY, especially Abyan and its provincial capital, Zinjibar. Not more than a couple hundred fighters, many of them foreign, took advantage of the precipitous withdrawal of army and security units to overrun civilian officials in several towns. This subplot in the overall story of the Yemeni revolution dovetailed strangely with American counterterrorism operations targeting al-Qaeda figures inside Yemen, including the U.S.-born Anwar al-Awlaqi and his son, killed separately in their tribal homeland farther east in Shabwa province. Close coordination between American and Yemeni security officers in this field of operations allowed President Saleh to present himself as a reliable ally for the United States and Saudi Arabia against militant Islamists.

The hegemon of the Peninsula, Saudi Arabia, played a high-profile yet rather inscrutable and seemingly ambivalent role, coaxing its long-time ally to sign an agreement to transfer power but failing to press for a cease-fire. In May, Saudi Arabia and the other oil monarchies in the Gulf Cooperation Council (GCC), working with the Yemeni opposition in the Joint Meeting Parties, announced a plan whereby Saleh would relinquish presidential power in exchange for immunity from prosecution for himself and his family. Saleh stalled and negotiated, three times promising and then refusing to sign the same document on the grounds, he said, that it was an invitation to hand power to the mutinous factions of the military. The United States and other Western powers joined the GCC in rhetorically supporting this vague agreement (the precise text of which was never released).

The moment for Saleh's departure from office seemed to come in June, when he was airlifted to a top-of-the-line hospital in Saudi Arabia for emergency surgeries and then convalescence following the explosion inside the presidential compound. It was widely assumed that the Saudi government, a major donor to Yemen and specifically to the regime, would be both willing and able to prevent his return (Haykel 2011). In Saleh's absence, however, his son and nephews took aim at their allies turned rivals. Military and civilian deaths mounted, electricity and fuel supplies waned, and life in the cities became even more intolerable. More than three months later, on September 23, suddenly and somewhat mysteriously, the president returned to Sanaa, still insisting that he would relinquish power only after his government had organized transitional elections. Not entirely unlike the bloodletting that took place among Socialist leaders in 1986 in Aden, intra-elite gun battles raged in Sanaa and Ta'izz throughout October and into November.

Yet the international community did not press for a cease-fire or threaten sanctions against the Saleh regime. As another prominent female activist, Hooria Mashhour, tweeted on September 21, "We were expecting a stronger attitude from the GCC countries towards the crimes committed against the Yemeni people, but we get extremely disappointed to see the meeting between [Saudi] king Abdullah and Saleh." A month later, on October 21, the Security Council of the United Nations issued an ambiguous, toothless resolution condemning human rights violations by "the government and other actors" and calling for all sides to commit to a peaceful transition of power in accordance with the GCC formula. If the reactions were any indication, Resolution 2014 favored the incumbent's position over the protesters' demands. Yemen's official press agency, Saba, enthused that Saleh "welcomed" what it phrased as "support for the Presidential decree of 12 September which is designed to find a political agreement acceptable to all parties, and to ensure a peaceful and democratic transition of power, including the holding of early Presidential elections" (Saba News 2011). Writing for the protesters, Tawakkol Karman (2011) opened an op-ed in the *Guardian* on November 1 with the words "Yemenis are ready to pay the ultimate price to take on a brutal dictator. Yet the UN can't even bring itself to condemn him."

With arms raised, multitudes bewailed escalating violence and petitioned the international community to intercede diplomatically. After a series of attacks on female activists by security forces, urban women in Sanaa, still wearing their customary *sharshaf*, staged a particularly Yemeni form of protest drawing on rural traditions: they set fire to a pile of old-fashioned bedspread-like veils called *makrama*, sending a symbolic distress signal to the tribes. Their pamphlets read: "This is a plea from the free women of Yemen; here we burn our *makrama* in front of the world to witness the bloody massacres carried out by the tyrant Saleh." Marchers in al-Baydha, Ibb, and other cities and towns cried for Saleh's prosecution in an international court. Demonstrators in Sanaa and Ta'izz adopted the slogans "Remaining peaceful is our choice" and

"Peaceful, peaceful, no to civil war." "The Yemenis' voice is one," they shouted in November, "we will bring corrupt Saleh to justice."

At a ceremony on November 23 in Riyadh, the Saudi capital, witnessed by Gulf royalty and Western diplomats, a smiling Saleh finally affixed his signature to four copies of the so-called GCC deal. There was no celebration whatsoever, because few Yemenis trusted either the deal or his signature. The following day, back in the presidential palace, still acting as head of state, he declared an "amnesty" for those who had committed "errors" while vowing to prosecute perpetrators of "crimes" against his person and his administration. Karman, who was on a worldwide speaking tour, charmed audiences, but the specifics of her message went unheeded. Blood continued to flow, particularly in the streets of Ta'izz, while the international community scarcely raised an eyebrow.

Conclusions

The 2011 uprising built on the social capital from earlier civic moments in Yemeni history: the Third World cries for independence of the now-aging 1960s generation, the cravings for modern services and education of the 1970s, and the pro-democracy patriotic sentiments of the early 1990s. Just as each of these very different mobilizations left its legacy, so too would this one. Even should it prove to have been relatively short-lived, this fourth civic opening had been the widest and the most inclusive part of an earth-shattering pan-Arab movement for change.

The uprising will have shaped the national civic consciousness of today's youth for decades to come. The new civic awareness of the Yemeni public was fed by much more than electoral pageantry or moral repugnance at murders in the morgue, displays of intraregime violence and excessive force against demonstrators, or the spuriously bizarre policies of Yemen's international patrons. Moreover, anyone who has participated in mass public events—the American civil rights, antiwar, or Occupy Wall Street demonstrations, for instance, or even highly competitive football matches in huge stadiums—knows how electrifying it is to be part of a crowd cheering or booing in unison. The Nobel Prize that enabled one eloquent and forceful, but rather ordinary, spokeswoman to appeal to the United Nations and the world for action

lgeria

ENCE ALGERIA combines a valiant history of revolu-
for national liberation with a militarized authoritar-
lthough established through a war of independence
he promise of political transformation, Algeria under
ame a political failure whose military successes lie in
rnal armed interventions, police actions, and offensive
ted against the nation's own populace. Beginning in
e invaded and incorporated the region as an overseas
on, Algeria inherited and maintained the structure and
French military and colonial rule even after indepen-
; in 1848, the colony was administratively categorized
legally ambiguous part of France such that the major-
lim population remained largely subjects of a French
order in its various guises. After the brutal 1954–62 war
n, which is said to have killed, wounded, or displaced
third of the indigenous population, Algeria threw off
ower to epitomize for the 1960s a successful, radical
olution in which violent armed struggle was deemed
reverse the oppressions of imperialism (Fanon 1967).
ians have continued to live under a succession of mili-
, whether homegrown or colonial imports.

further nurtured patriotic pride and shored up the hopes of protesters
persevering against long odds.

The near-term outcome probably will be neither full-scale revolution nor a smooth transition. Before all this happened, intelligence
analysts considered Yemen unstable and possibly hovering on the edge
of state failure. The next phase might be cruel, messy, or both. The
country could split along North-South lines or other fractures. Communities could resort to armed resistance. Saleh and his sons and nephews
seemed to prefer civil war or anarchy to stepping down; and General
Ali Muhsin, the al-Ahmar brothers, a few other conventional actors,
and small bands of al-Qaeda-type militants had joined in battle. After
the gruesome death of the Libyan dictator heightened public determination for the demise of both Ali Abdullah Saleh and Syria's Bashar
al-Assad, Saleh's gunmen cracked down harder on civilian protesters and
prepared to wage all-out war with military defectors. Jihadist infiltrators
from Saudi Arabia seemed to be provoking conflict in Sa'adah province.
After the American drone strikes that killed the al-Awlaqis, the risk that
either a terrorist attack or counterterrorism operations would ignite
fighting on new fronts could not be discounted. Uncounted dangers lay
on the road ahead, with little sign of diplomatic intervention from the
United Nations, the United States, the Gulf Cooperation Council, or
any other quarters.

Even under the worst-case scenarios, however, there had been a radical change that amounted to a civic revolution for Yemen and the whole
Arab world. Never in the long history of the Arabian Peninsula had citizens acting as such constituted a body politic and assembled en masse to
insist on political reform. For 2011, at least, Southern malcontents and
rebels in Sa'adah found common national cause with college students
in Sanaa and Ta'izz and with tribesmen from the hinterlands around
ideas about social justice, nonviolence, and better governance. However
divided they were between the more widespread and popular movement
for change and the still not-insignificant minority who turned out for
Saleh rallies, "the people" spoke out and claimed the metaphorical and
physical commons.

Yemen's "peaceful youth" activists raised their voices not only as a
nation but also in unison with revolutionaries elsewhere in the Arab

world. This was also a substantial development. It was not impossible in 2010 to imagine Yemen exploding with mass fury, or to foresee a "take to the streets moment" in Cairo, or to recognize the alienation of Tunisians from the Ben Ali regime. What could not be foreseen were the simultaneity, synchronization, and solidarity that arose among essentially leaderless protests from the Mediterranean Sea to the Indian Ocean and beyond. A virtual Arab/Arabic-language public civic sphere expanded through cell phones and the Internet as well as through Al Jazeera and other broadcasters, until customary forms of censorship and intimidation could not contain the flow of information. It was even more remarkable that a religious thirty-two-year-old mother of three in a head scarf from the most remote, poverty-stricken, socially conservative corner of the Arab world would go down in world history as the embodiment of peaceful pro-democracy agitation in the region. Finally, by the end of 2011, a variation of the somewhat anarchic, antisystemic Liberation Square sit-ins and campouts in Arab countries had spread across the globe as young people from Athens to New York and many other cities occupied physical and virtual civic spaces in a worldwide wave of protests. It was quite remarkable that several million young Yemenis, represented by one young mother, were so much in the vanguard of this global movement for local, national, and worldwide change.

References

Alley, April L. 2010. "The Rules of the Game: Unpacking Patronage Politics in Yemen." *Middle East Journal* 64 (3): 385–409.

Carapico, Sheila. 1998. *Civil Society in Yemen: The Political Economy of Activism in Modern Arabia.* London: Cambridge University Press.

———. 2010. "Civil Society." In *Politics and Society in the Contemporary Middle East*, edited by Michele Penner Angrist, 91–110. Boulder, Colo.: Lynne Rienner.

———. 2011. "No Exit: Yemen's Existential Crisis." Middle East Report Online, May 3. http://www.merip.org/mero (accessed November 23, 2011).

Colton, Nora A. 2010. "Yemen: A Collapsed Economy." *Middle East Journal* 64 (3): 410–26.

Cowell, Alan, Laura Kasinof, and Adam Nossiter. 2011. "Nobel Peace Prize Awarded to Three Activist Women." *New York Times,* October 7. http://www.nytimes.com (accessed December 21, 2011).

Dahlgren, Susanne. 2010. "The Sr[...] in Yemen." *Middle East Repor[...]*

Day, Stephen. 2008. "Updating Y[...] Divisions Bring Down the Re[...]

Halliday, Fred. 1974. *Arabia with[...] Arab World.* New York: Vinta[...]

Haykel, Bernard. 2011. "Saudi Ara[...] Client State." *Foreign Affairs,* [...] November 23, 2011).

Karman, Tawakkol. 2011. "The [...] Freedom." *Guardian,* Novem[...] cember 21, 2011).

Phillips, Sarah. 2006. "Forebodi[...] port Online, April 3. http://wv[...]

———. 2011. "Who Tried to Kill [...] Revolution in Yemen." *Forei[...] (accessed November 23, 2011)[...]

Rosen, Nir. 2001. "How It Start[...] March 18. http://www.jadaliyy[...]

Saba News. 2011. "President Sale[...] http://www.freerepublic.com/[...] 22, 2011).

Wedeen, Lisa. 2008. *Peripheral [...] Chicago: University of Chica[...]

Weir, Shelagh. 1997. "A Clash of [...] *East Report* 204: 22–26.

Yadav, Stacey Philbrick. 2010. "Se[...] Rethinking Space and Activis[...] (2): 1–30.

A[...]

SU[...]

POSTINDEPE[...]
tionary strugg[...]
ian structure.[...]
(1954–62) wit[...]
military rule [...]
the realm of i[...]
campaigns di[...]
1830, when Fr[...]
colonial posse[...]
bureaucracies[...]
dence. Begin[...]
as an integra[...]
ity Algerian N[...]
military impe[...]
of decoloniza[...]
no less than [...]
French colon[...]
Third World [...]
the only mea[...]
Since then, A[...]
tary governm[...]

In the 1980s, the "Berber Spring" movement heralded a first wave of popular demonstrations and strikes. While only a minority of Algerians, estimated at 15 percent, were considered to be Berber speakers, a vibrant citizens' movement arose that went beyond recognizing Algeria's Berber/Amazigh identity to encompass a nationwide demand for an end to single-party rule and lack of civil liberties for all Algerians. The Berber Spring movement was violently suppressed by the government's armed forces. By December 1991, then president Chadli Bendjedid held Algeria's first free, multiparty elections. When the Islamic Salvation Front party garnered the most votes in the first round of elections, the military's role as the legitimating power in Algeria accounted for the 1992 coup d'état that removed Bendjedid from office and brought about nineteen years of a declared "state of emergency." Algeria degenerated into a decade of armed conflict and civil war that claimed between 150,000 to 200,000 lives.

Throughout the internal wars of the 1990s, Algeria pursued a limited form of neoliberal economic restructuring that retained public enterprises and public-sector workers as key economic actors. Because the state controlled domestic natural resources and channeled foreign aid and investment, any state-instigated administrative reform was partial, merely strengthening the profile of an autocratic rent-seeking regime without encouraging growth outside the hydrocarbon sector. As the population more than tripled since the nation's 1962 independence, from 11 million to 35 million (of which one-quarter were below the age of fourteen and half were under thirty years old), the regime that historically positioned itself as revolutionary was faced with the challenges of waves of peaceful democratic movements emblematic of the twenty-first-century political revolutions known as the Arab Spring.

Algeria in Movement

By January 21, 2011, a network of Algerian oppositional movements had formed under the organizational umbrella of the National Coordination for Change and Democracy, which was made up of labor unions as well as human rights, feminist, and student associations from civil society. They called for a peaceful demonstration on Saturday, February 12, at May 1 Square in Algiers, the capital, to demand a free and democratic

Algeria. Numerous online videos depict sloganeers who compared the contemporary situation with Algeria's past colonial struggles: "We want a second liberation, a second independence" (McDougall 2006). Demonstrators often reprised Egyptian and Tunisian chants of "Irhal" and "Dégage" to urge leaders to step down. In the city center, some two to three thousand participants met violence at the hands of a force of thirty thousand police. A second peaceful march a week later, on February 19, never reached the square, as the marchers were impeded again by police force; the confrontation was amply documented in videos and images posted on YouTube and Facebook. In Oran, Algeria's second-largest city, organizers had to content themselves with calling for a meeting on Saturday, February 19, in a public hall because they were unable to secure the necessary permits to march or demonstrate in public space.

In response, President Abdelaziz Bouteflika provided vague assurances to the nation through state-controlled television broadcasts that "a new page would be opened toward global reforms," promising full employment and the engagement of state priorities "to respond to the needs of citizens" (*L'Express* 2011). Nonetheless, on several occasions, fearing the power of social media, the regime cracked down on the Internet, Facebook, and Twitter. For the February 12 demonstration, Al Jazeera launched one of its live blogs to cover the events in Algiers and created a visual and text "timeline of discontent."[1] Social media networks played an important but less pervasive role. Due to the high cost of computers and Internet connections, Algeria lagged behind its neighboring Maghreb states of Tunisia and Morocco in terms of the number of users, registered domain names, cheap Internet cafés, and even state institutions with Web sites available to inform the public. As of 2011, approximately eight million Algerians, or 25 percent of the population (versus Morocco's thirteen million, or one-third of the population) used the Internet. At least half of Algeria's online connections were too weak for users to access videos and games, perhaps because a single government provider of telecommunications, Algérie Telecom, was in control of telephones, cell phones, and Internet services. Bloggers could be charged and faced imprisonment under the same criminal defamation laws that were deployed to harass the print press, and police further nurtured patriotic pride and shored up the hopes of protesters persevering against long odds.

The near-term outcome probably will be neither full-scale revolution nor a smooth transition. Before all this happened, intelligence analysts considered Yemen unstable and possibly hovering on the edge of state failure. The next phase might be cruel, messy, or both. The country could split along North-South lines or other fractures. Communities could resort to armed resistance. Saleh and his sons and nephews seemed to prefer civil war or anarchy to stepping down; and General Ali Muhsin, the al-Ahmar brothers, a few other conventional actors, and small bands of al-Qaeda-type militants had joined in battle. After the gruesome death of the Libyan dictator heightened public determination for the demise of both Ali Abdullah Saleh and Syria's Bashar al-Assad, Saleh's gunmen cracked down harder on civilian protesters and prepared to wage all-out war with military defectors. Jihadist infiltrators from Saudi Arabia seemed to be provoking conflict in Sa'adah province. After the American drone strikes that killed the al-Awlaqis, the risk that either a terrorist attack or counterterrorism operations would ignite fighting on new fronts could not be discounted. Uncounted dangers lay on the road ahead, with little sign of diplomatic intervention from the United Nations, the United States, the Gulf Cooperation Council, or any other quarters.

Even under the worst-case scenarios, however, there had been a radical change that amounted to a civic revolution for Yemen and the whole Arab world. Never in the long history of the Arabian Peninsula had citizens acting as such constituted a body politic and assembled en masse to insist on political reform. For 2011, at least, Southern malcontents and rebels in Sa'adah found common national cause with college students in Sanaa and Ta'izz and with tribesmen from the hinterlands around ideas about social justice, nonviolence, and better governance. However divided they were between the more widespread and popular movement for change and the still not-insignificant minority who turned out for Saleh rallies, "the people" spoke out and claimed the metaphorical and physical commons.

Yemen's "peaceful youth" activists raised their voices not only as a nation but also in unison with revolutionaries elsewhere in the Arab world. This was also a substantial development. It was not impossible in 2010 to imagine Yemen exploding with mass fury, or to foresee a "take to the streets moment" in Cairo, or to recognize the alienation of Tunisians from the Ben Ali regime. What could not be foreseen were the simultaneity, synchronization, and solidarity that arose among essentially leaderless protests from the Mediterranean Sea to the Indian Ocean and beyond. A virtual Arab/Arabic-language public civic sphere expanded through cell phones and the Internet as well as through Al Jazeera and other broadcasters, until customary forms of censorship and intimidation could not contain the flow of information. It was even more remarkable that a religious thirty-two-year-old mother of three in a head scarf from the most remote, poverty-stricken, socially conservative corner of the Arab world would go down in world history as the embodiment of peaceful pro-democracy agitation in the region. Finally, by the end of 2011, a variation of the somewhat anarchic, antisystemic Liberation Square sit-ins and campouts in Arab countries had spread across the globe as young people from Athens to New York and many other cities occupied physical and virtual civic spaces in a worldwide wave of protests. It was quite remarkable that several million young Yemenis, represented by one young mother, were so much in the vanguard of this global movement for local, national, and worldwide change.

References

Alley, April L. 2010. "The Rules of the Game: Unpacking Patronage Politics in Yemen." *Middle East Journal* 64 (3): 385–409.

Carapico, Sheila. 1998. *Civil Society in Yemen: The Political Economy of Activism in Modern Arabia.* London: Cambridge University Press.

———. 2010. "Civil Society." In *Politics and Society in the Contemporary Middle East,* edited by Michele Penner Angrist, 91–110. Boulder, Colo.: Lynne Rienner.

———. 2011. "No Exit: Yemen's Existential Crisis." Middle East Report Online, May 3. http://www.merip.org/mero (accessed November 23, 2011).

Colton, Nora A. 2010. "Yemen: A Collapsed Economy." *Middle East Journal* 64 (3): 410–26.

Cowell, Alan, Laura Kasinof, and Adam Nossiter. 2011. "Nobel Peace Prize Awarded to Three Activist Women." *New York Times,* October 7. http://www.nytimes.com (accessed December 21, 2011).

Dahlgren, Susanne. 2010. "The Snake with a Thousand Heads: The Southern Cause in Yemen." *Middle East Report* 256: 28–33.

Day, Stephen. 2008. "Updating Yemeni National Unity: Could Lingering Regional Divisions Bring Down the Regime?" *Middle East Journal* 62 (3): 417–36.

Halliday, Fred. 1974. *Arabia without Sultans: A Political Survey of Instability in the Arab World.* New York: Vintage Books.

Haykel, Bernard. 2011. "Saudi Arabia's Yemen Dilemma: How to Manage an Unruly Client State." *Foreign Affairs,* June 14. http://www.foreignaffairs.com (accessed November 23, 2011).

Karman, Tawakkol. 2011. "The World Must Not Forsake Yemen's Struggle for Freedom." *Guardian,* November 1. http://www.guardian.co.uk (accessed December 21, 2011).

Phillips, Sarah. 2006. "Foreboding about the Future in Yemen." Middle East Report Online, April 3. http://www.merip.org/mero (accessed November 23, 2011).

———. 2011. "Who Tried to Kill Ali Abdallah Saleh? The Hidden Feud behind the Revolution in Yemen." *Foreign Policy,* June 16. http://www.foreignpolicy.com (accessed November 23, 2011).

Rosen, Nir. 2001. "How It Started in Yemen: From Tahrir to Taghyir." Jadaliyya, March 18. http://www.jadaliyya.com (accessed November 23, 2011).

Saba News. 2011. "President Saleh Welcomes UN 2014 Resolution." October 25. http://www.freerepublic.com/focus/f-news/2797471/posts (accessed December 22, 2011).

Wedeen, Lisa. 2008. *Peripheral Visions: Publics, Power, and Performance in Yemen.* Chicago: University of Chicago Press.

Weir, Shelagh. 1997. "A Clash of Fundamentalisms: Wahhabism in Yemen." *Middle East Report* 204: 22–26.

Yadav, Stacey Philbrick. 2010. "Segmented Publics and Islamist Women in Yemen: Rethinking Space and Activism." *Journal of Middle Eastern Women's Studies* 6 (2): 1–30.

Algeria

SUSAN SLYOMOVICS

POSTINDEPENDENCE ALGERIA combines a valiant history of revolutionary struggle for national liberation with a militarized authoritarian structure. Although established through a war of independence (1954–62) with the promise of political transformation, Algeria under military rule became a political failure whose military successes lie in the realm of internal armed interventions, police actions, and offensive campaigns directed against the nation's own populace. Beginning in 1830, when France invaded and incorporated the region as an overseas colonial possession, Algeria inherited and maintained the structure and bureaucracies of French military and colonial rule even after independence. Beginning in 1848, the colony was administratively categorized as an integral yet legally ambiguous part of France such that the majority Algerian Muslim population remained largely subjects of a French military imperial order in its various guises. After the brutal 1954–62 war of decolonization, which is said to have killed, wounded, or displaced no less than one-third of the indigenous population, Algeria threw off French colonial power to epitomize for the 1960s a successful, radical Third World revolution in which violent armed struggle was deemed the only means to reverse the oppressions of imperialism (Fanon 1967). Since then, Algerians have continued to live under a succession of military governments, whether homegrown or colonial imports.

In the 1980s, the "Berber Spring" movement heralded a first wave of popular demonstrations and strikes. While only a minority of Algerians, estimated at 15 percent, were considered to be Berber speakers, a vibrant citizens' movement arose that went beyond recognizing Algeria's Berber/Amazigh identity to encompass a nationwide demand for an end to single-party rule and lack of civil liberties for all Algerians. The Berber Spring movement was violently suppressed by the government's armed forces. By December 1991, then president Chadli Bendjedid held Algeria's first free, multiparty elections. When the Islamic Salvation Front party garnered the most votes in the first round of elections, the military's role as the legitimating power in Algeria accounted for the 1992 coup d'état that removed Bendjedid from office and brought about nineteen years of a declared "state of emergency." Algeria degenerated into a decade of armed conflict and civil war that claimed between 150,000 to 200,000 lives.

Throughout the internal wars of the 1990s, Algeria pursued a limited form of neoliberal economic restructuring that retained public enterprises and public-sector workers as key economic actors. Because the state controlled domestic natural resources and channeled foreign aid and investment, any state-instigated administrative reform was partial, merely strengthening the profile of an autocratic rent-seeking regime without encouraging growth outside the hydrocarbon sector. As the population more than tripled since the nation's 1962 independence, from 11 million to 35 million (of which one-quarter were below the age of fourteen and half were under thirty years old), the regime that historically positioned itself as revolutionary was faced with the challenges of waves of peaceful democratic movements emblematic of the twenty-first-century political revolutions known as the Arab Spring.

Algeria in Movement

By January 21, 2011, a network of Algerian oppositional movements had formed under the organizational umbrella of the National Coordination for Change and Democracy, which was made up of labor unions as well as human rights, feminist, and student associations from civil society. They called for a peaceful demonstration on Saturday, February 12, at May 1 Square in Algiers, the capital, to demand a free and democratic

Algeria. Numerous online videos depict sloganeers who compared the contemporary situation with Algeria's past colonial struggles: "We want a second liberation, a second independence" (McDougall 2006). Demonstrators often reprised Egyptian and Tunisian chants of "Irhal" and "Dégage" to urge leaders to step down. In the city center, some two to three thousand participants met violence at the hands of a force of thirty thousand police. A second peaceful march a week later, on February 19, never reached the square, as the marchers were impeded again by police force; the confrontation was amply documented in videos and images posted on YouTube and Facebook. In Oran, Algeria's second-largest city, organizers had to content themselves with calling for a meeting on Saturday, February 19, in a public hall because they were unable to secure the necessary permits to march or demonstrate in public space.

In response, President Abdelaziz Bouteflika provided vague assurances to the nation through state-controlled television broadcasts that "a new page would be opened toward global reforms," promising full employment and the engagement of state priorities "to respond to the needs of citizens" (*L'Express* 2011). Nonetheless, on several occasions, fearing the power of social media, the regime cracked down on the Internet, Facebook, and Twitter. For the February 12 demonstration, Al Jazeera launched one of its live blogs to cover the events in Algiers and created a visual and text "timeline of discontent."[1] Social media networks played an important but less pervasive role. Due to the high cost of computers and Internet connections, Algeria lagged behind its neighboring Maghreb states of Tunisia and Morocco in terms of the number of users, registered domain names, cheap Internet cafés, and even state institutions with Web sites available to inform the public. As of 2011, approximately eight million Algerians, or 25 percent of the population (versus Morocco's thirteen million, or one-third of the population) used the Internet. At least half of Algeria's online connections were too weak for users to access videos and games, perhaps because a single government provider of telecommunications, Algérie Telecom, was in control of telephones, cell phones, and Internet services. Bloggers could be charged and faced imprisonment under the same criminal defamation laws that were deployed to harass the print press, and police

were permitted to conduct surveillance on and raid Internet cafés that were labeled sites of terrorist activities.

At the same time as smaller, nonviolent attempts at political mobilizations occurred, other patterns of Algerian civil unrest differed from Tunisian and Egyptian versions not only in frequency of protests over the previous few years but also in the composition of participants and the spaces they temporarily and respectively occupied. On one hand, low numbers of intellectuals, political party members, and members of civil society groups turned out for peaceful takeovers of the main squares in Algeria's larger cities or in front of government buildings throughout the country, where they unfurled banners and shouted slogans to make clear their demands. Simultaneously, much larger numbers of youth protests erupted, often concentrated within the youths' own poorer and crowded neighborhoods, such as Algiers' densest urban neighborhood, Bab el Oued. Participants in these protests were primarily the young, who constituted 75 percent of the population under thirty years old and suffered from 75 percent unemployment. They acted against an all-encompassing *hogra* (contempt, oppression, humiliation) in ways that the government termed rampages, looting parties, and bread riots regardless of the diverse precipitating causes—rising prices for basic foodstuffs, bad housing, lack of jobs, infrastructure breakdowns, and government clampdowns on the informal economy.

So-called bread riots and food protests are not mere "rebellions of the belly," argues Edward P. Thompson (1971, 76–78) in a classic study; rather, they are best viewed as a "highly complex form of direct popular action, disciplined and with clear objectives." Thompson's formulations about the eighteenth-century English crowd offer one description that fits Algeria, where years of large-scale urban antigovernment revolts played out his concept of a "moral economy of protest." These latter uprisings are examples of power and resistance in which the strategies and inchoate language of demands for justice articulated by protesters are dynamic evidence of social claims for greater equity. Young male crowds aimed specific acts of destruction and looting at banks, shops, and cars as symbols of economic injustice, evoking widespread fears of a return to the violence of the bloody decade of the 1990s.

Unlike the economies of Tunisia and Egypt, the Algerian economy posted $160 billion in foreign currency reserves. Due to immense natural gas and oil resources, which accounted for two-thirds of the country's revenues, one-third of the gross domestic product, and more than 95 percent of export earnings, Algeria's hydrocarbon sector had assured a low external debt hovering at 1 percent of the GDP. Sporadic government moves toward a market-based economy indicated that state spending and state-created employment had shrunk. Nonetheless, the populace accurately perceived the government as the principal engine for job creation. Fueling the population's demands was the knowledge of growing hydrocarbon revenues that barely trickled down to make a dent in low living standards and high rates of youth unemployment. Instead of constructing a viable national infrastructure that provided employment for his own people, Bouteflika offered the grandiose Dja-maa el-Djazair, his signature presidential project for the ages: a plan to build the Arab world's third-largest mosque, after Mecca and Medina, off the Bay of Algiers. A costly enterprise approximately the size of a football field, the mosque was to be built on a site that apparently rested on an earthquake fault.

"Mubarak chased from power: Egypt one, Algeria zero," reads the tagline of a 2011 cartoon by acerbic Algerian cartoonist Ali Dilem; the drawing depicts a demonstrator waving the Algerian flag and urging Bouteflika to leave so that Algeria may even the score. By 2009, as Bouteflika approached the limit of two presidential mandates, he initiated a third one after swiftly pushing through a constitutional amendment to allow the president to run for office indefinitely. Echoing the Algerian soccer team's elimination of Egypt from the 2010 World Cup matches, in which Algeria scored one and Egypt zero, Dilem's cartoon image acknowledged Algeria's preeminent position in the Arab world as the country with the highest number of political demonstrations and marches, local violent protests, and street riots. In the years 2010–11, estimates of the numbers of discrete, newsworthy incidents of protest ranged up to several thousands. These constant eruptions of turmoil and unrest—both peaceful and violent—were the principal strategy through which sectors of Algerian society aired their grievances vociferously and en masse to their government leaders.

As a means of political transformation, these persistent and imminent Algerian moments of riots, revolts, or revolution (whatever we choose to call them) were filled with uncertainty and promise. Consider that the alternative for many disaffected Algerians had been forced migration to Europe, as thousands each year burned their identity papers *(harraga)* to cross the Mediterranean in small boats. Few succeeded. In contrast, during 2011, each protest, demonstration, and workers' strike was a product of obvious and specific political and economic demands, from medical interns protesting conditions in Oran to Air Algeria flight personnel shutting down the summer airport traffic back home to the *bled,* and including Annaba youth taking to the streets in protest against regular electricity outages. Each event inevitably met with a brutal police response, and government threats to fire the workers' leadership were followed swiftly by the state's ensuring temporary social peace by means of salary raises, price cuts, and even government cash compensations—all forms of financial appeasement by a regime that could afford it.

Money was also the motor for the 2005 voter-approved "Charter for Peace and National Reconciliation," which consisted of government apologies and substantial monthly cash payouts to those who had been victims of violence during the dark decades from 1992 to 2006 and at the same time granted immunity to the perpetrators of that violence. In 2006, going beyond the norms of reparations commissions and the politics of reconciliation, the Algerian state criminalized citizen opposition to impunity as a new offense punishable by imprisonment, targeting anyone who attributed responsibility to those who organized violations of the law or covered up or justified the atrocities (Slyomovics 2009). Despite legal sanctions, civil society groups and the families of those still missing through forcible disappearance contested the state's gag rule of money disbursements traded for silence.

The Military's Hidden Power

> There exists in Algeria an apparent power and a hidden power. . . . All our institutions are fictitious. Only the military institution really exists. . . .

When one talks about the military institution, it is a "handful" of people who, in the name of the army, control the whole of Algeria and not only the institution it represents. . . . [The military] did this with the complicity of the political power in the framework of a contract: we get the power and you, the responsibility. This is to say: we decide, and you are responsible. (Ghozali 2002)

The logic of this ongoing Algerian regime depended on the role of the military as the primary power. Sid Ahmed Ghozali, Algerian prime minister from June 1991 to July 1992, went so far as to designate the military as the country's sole true, albeit hidden, power. Nonetheless, postindependence Algeria retained continuities with the structures, discourses, and functions left by France's administrators to the overseas empire and exemplified by Algerian military rule (Slyomovics 2013). This was a tragic outcome that perpetuated aspects of the French colonial era, especially the reproduction of an autocratic postindependence regime composed of unknown groups of generals in opposition to their own people, who in turn have reached the stage of living in perpetual, if sporadic, revolt. Therefore, Algerian history could be most fully comprehended through the prism of the military, even as the country approached the fiftieth anniversary of independence.

On the surface, for example, the Algerian military's basic tripartite configuration—a national gendarmerie, the police, and the armed forces (army, navy, air force)—mirrored in many ways that of its French counterpart. As with the French national gendarmerie, the Algerian equivalent, made up of 150,000 people, served as a paramilitary force charged with public safety and policing among the civilian population, especially outside urban areas. Additional core tasks pitted the gendarmerie against the population, since included were counterterrorism patrols and searches in the countryside as well as urban crowd- and riot-control units for each of Algeria's forty-eight administrative *wilaya*. Gendarmerie duties overlapped with those of a police force of 200,000, whose specialized antiriot troops controlled entry into and within the capital Algiers, thereby more than doubling the numbers of uniformed personnel deployed in Algerian cities against protests, marches, and popular uprisings.

In contrast, the Algerian standing army (officially the People's National Army) of 350,000 soldiers could at that time draw on a glorious revolutionary, anticolonial past based on the army's presumed association with the armed wing of Algeria's National Liberation Front (Front de Libération Nationale, or FLN), which fought for and won Algeria's independence from France by 1962. Since then, all Algerian male citizens had to complete military service (at that time eighteen months versus Egypt's three years' conscription), which allowed the armed forces to claim millions more as potential or active reservists. Algerians under French colonial rule had been conscripted into the French army; many served heroically in World Wars I and II and in Indochina as French subjects without the rights of citizens. During the Algerian war of independence, French conscripts were sent to Algeria, while those Algerians who were conscripted by France and unable to desert were sent to do their required military service outside Algeria. Links between France and Algeria in terms of soldiers and army service, but not equitable veterans' pensions, were a hallmark of the colonial era and had repercussions for the composition of the postindependence military leadership.

Subsequent to Algeria's victorious armed revolution, the country was headed by a series of military figures drawn from the armed forces: Ahmed Ben Bella, who headed the FLN, which launched the Algerian war of independence, led the country from 1962 to 1965, when he was overthrown by his defense minister, Houari Boumediene (1965–78), who was then succeeded by another officer, Chadli Bendjedid (1978–92). The formation of the Algerian army in 1962 drew on the fifty thousand–strong "Army of the Border," split between Morocco and Tunisia during the war of independence. Boumediene, head of the army and ruler of Algeria until his death in 1978, willingly incorporated Algerian career officers formerly from the French army, such as his protégé Bendjedid. Following Boumediene's death and for many years afterward, members of that same generation of sclerotic generals and officers were the actual rulers of Algeria. Many belonged to the "Lacoste promotion," a class of men who earned officer rank in the 1950s under Robert Lacoste, resident minister of French Algeria. Certainly, one indication of a major shift by the 1980s in the way in which the population viewed the Algerian army was the insulting name given to this cohort of generals based on their prior, shifting allegiances: *daf*, from a French acronym, "deserters from the army of France."

An analysis of the Algerian army's organization reveals a mix of administrative and logistical elements. Historically, the army was not based on the administrative divisions of Algeria but retained the pre-independence, clandestine-era division into six regions. While its officer corps was French formed, weaponry was Soviet, then Russian and Chinese—purchases that reflected Algeria's alignments with the Soviet bloc countries during the Cold War. Unlike the Egyptian army, which owns and profits from its own hotels, malls, real estate developments, farms, and more, the Algerian army never created a self-supporting, autonomous (or perhaps parallel) economic sector. Given Algeria's hydrocarbon wealth, the army did not need to be entrepreneurial. Algeria's military factories produced only materiel and equipment directly related to the business of soldiering, often through local licensing agreements with arms manufacturers from countries such as Russia and China. Nonetheless, decades of formal and de facto military rule resulted in a military establishment that directed the country's resources, with the result that many individual high-ranking officers amassed great wealth.

The army continued to impose its chosen candidates for the Algerian presidency before and after 1992, the watershed overturning of free elections, when Algeria adopted a comprehensive model of counterinsurgency against armed Islamist groups, which was a paradigm of hegemonic control: gendarmerie roadblocks and checkpoints proliferated throughout the country to play a double-edged role as possible deterrents to terrorism but also as an effective means to harass and shake down the population. Through sustained violence at the hands of its multiple security forces and militias (and the reciprocal violent responses of Islamist groups especially in the 1990s), authorities were able to reinforce already powerful police, military, and paramilitary structures.

Democratic and peaceful alternatives were suppressed, both through internal militarized imperatives and through external American foreign policies targeting the "War on Terror" in the Maghreb region. U.S. diplomatic documents released through WikiLeaks had positioned President Bouteflika since 1999 as a crucial American ally against al-Qaeda in the Islamic Maghreb, an organization whose declared aims were to overthrow the Algerian government and establish an Islamist state. Algerian security forces seemed to have confined the reach of armed Islamist groups to the country's south and in pockets of mountainous areas northeast of the capital. This may have accounted for the possible presence of an active U.S. Central Intelligence Agency group on Algerian soil. Indeed, permission was given to U.S. Navy spy planes operating out of the American naval base in Rota, Spain, after January 2011 to fly over the southern Sahel of Algeria, Mauretania, Mali, and Niger, the vast region labeled a haven for armed Islamic militants (Keenan 2006). American sales to Algeria of gas-powered turbines and Boeing aircraft along with U.S. dependence on crude oil imports from Algeria ensured American support for Algerian repression domestically and acquiescence to the generals' push for access to previously denied American military technology. With oil reserves of more than nine billion barrels, Algeria ranked ninth among the top ten petroleum exporters to the United States at 268,000 barrels per day in 2011, with major annual increases in view (U.S. Energy Information Administration 2011).

The overthrow of Tunisian leader Zine El Abidine Ben Ali in January 2011 and Egyptian president Hosni Mubarak on February 11 sparked conjecture that Algeria may be the next country in the Arab world to attempt to rid itself of its authoritarian military leadership. On its lengthy eastern border, Algeria faced new and difficult relations with Libya under that country's National Transitional Council (NTC), the regime in place and recognized for deposing longtime Libyan ruler Muammar Qaddafi by Tunisia, Morocco, and the Arab League but not Algeria. During the Libyan uprising, Algeria alone in the Maghreb strongly denounced NATO intervention and air strikes by the military forces of Britain, France, and the United States in the region. Moreover, after invoking humanitarian reasons to grant asylum requests from Qaddafi's pregnant wife and sons, Algeria faced strong Libyan reactions. NTC spokespersons threatened to break diplomatic relations with Algeria unless the Qaddafi family was returned, as both countries consolidated the recent situation of a closed Algerian–Libyan border. Algeria's western border with Morocco had also been closed since 1994, leaving Tunisia to the east as the main open land crossing for ordinary Algerian citizens to travel outside the country without restrictions.

Beyond external geographical border constraints, Algerians had lived inside their own country under "state of emergency" laws similar to those enacted for Egyptians once Mubarak came to power after Anwar Sadat's assassination in 1981. Algeria's version, also prohibiting any public demonstrations, was enforced in 1992 after the country's first national multiparty elections and runoff set for January 16, 1992, were suspended and a military coup d'état deposed Bendjedid. On February 24, 2011, responding to the pressure of the Arab Spring and events in neighboring states, President Bouteflika lifted the state of emergency in effect throughout the country. Only the capital, Algiers, remained in a state of exception, meaning that the people continued to be prohibited from forming associations or participating in marches and demonstrations absent the requisite official authorizations, which were rarely granted. Gendarmes and police were perceived as the visible face of a corrupt and repressive regime, as in the comic strip by noted cartoonist Slim that depicts a citizen of the capital arrested for "marching" on the street and charged with the infraction of buying bread without a permit (Slim 2011).

Despite internal military struggles during the 1990s, the black decade of Algeria's civil conflict, and despite the military's murky ties to Alge-

"Saturday," excerpt from Slim's weekly comic strip, *Le Soir d'Algérie,* February 24, 2011.

POLICEMAN: Hey, you, over there—in the name of the law, I'm arresting you!
MAN: Me? Why?
POLICEMAN: I saw you walking. You know that it is forbidden to walk on Saturdays.
MAN: But I was going to buy bread!
POLICEMAN: I don't want to know that: the law is the law. Give me your permit to go buy bread and jump to it.

ria's vast hydrocarbon sector and the public's minimal knowledge about individual identities, it is the case that the Algerian military remained a shadowy force—outside any civilian framework and unaccountable to any institution but itself (Lowi 2009). Therefore, voters' rage centered on the current president, Bouteflika, a disappointment unfortunately not reflected in his third mandate election, because polling results were generally believed to be corrupt. Elected in 1999 and 2004 for two mandates, Bouteflika imposed a hitherto unconstitutional third presidential election and mandate that made it clear that, so far, he stubbornly hewed to the path chosen by despised and deposed autocratic leaders such as Algeria's prior military leaders, Tunisia's Ben Ali, and Egypt's Mubarak: a weak, ineffective multiparty parliament; abuses by unsupervised police and security forces; restricted civil liberties; an impotent judiciary; minimal workers' rights; and, above all, stifling and pervasive government corruption (Roberts 2003; Le Sueur 2010). Algerian sociologist Lahouari Addi (1995, 2011) affirmed:

> How it will end, we can't predict the future. For sure we can say . . . this regime has no future. That is why they are trying to introduce some reforms. But the reforms will break the regime. The authoritarian regime cannot handle genuine reforms. The regime has no future.

The countervailing dynamic was created by the oppositional actions of ordinary Algerians who were attempting to usurp government policing and some of its monopoly on violence. They challenged publicly and vociferously the state's definition of the illegality of all public manifestations, whether peaceable or violent, in favor of the right of association and assembly (Liverani 2008). The cumulative and long-term consequences and outcomes of these defiant initiatives would remain unpredictable.

Note

1. Twitter created a hashtag for the demonstration: #Feb12, http://twitter .com/#search?q=feb12. The Al Jazeera blog is available at http://english.aljazeera .net/indepth/spotlight/algeria.

References

Addi, Lahouari. 1995. *L'Algérie et la démocratie: Pouvoir et crise du politique dans l'Algérie contemporaine.* Paris: Découverte.

———. 2011. "What's Next for Algeria?" Interview. YouTube video. July 11. http:// www.youtube.com/watch?v=fUPDK02Ajso (accessed October 31, 2011).

Dilem, Ali. 2011. "Moubarak chassé du pouvoir: Egypte 1, Algérie 0." *Liberté.* http:// www.liberte-algerie.com/dilem.php?id=2640 (accessed February 13, 2011).

Fanon, Frantz. 1967. *A Dying Colonialism.* New York: Grove Press.

Ghozali, Sid Ahmed. 2002. Interview. *El Khabar-Hebdo,* no. 177: 20, 26. Algeria Watch. http://www.algeria-watch.org/farticle/anp_presidence/ghozali_maitres .htm (accessed August 20, 2011).

Keenan, Jeremy. 2006. "Military Bases, Construction Contracts and Hydrocarbons in North Africa." *Review of African Political Economy* 33: 601–8.

Le Sueur, James. 2010. *Algeria since 1989: Between Terror and Democracy.* London: Zed Books.

L'Express. 2011. "Algérie: Bouteflika promet de nouvelles réformes, y compris politiques." March 19. http://www.lexpress.fr (accessed October 31, 2011).

Liverani, Andrea. 2008. *Civil Society in Algeria: The Political Functions of Associational Life.* New York: Routledge.

Lowi, Miriam R. 2009. *Oil Wealth and the Poverty of Politics: Algeria Compared.* Cambridge: Cambridge University Press.

McDougall, James. 2006. *History and the Culture of Nationalism in Algeria.* Cambridge: Cambridge University Press.

Roberts, Hugh. 2003. *The Battlefield: Algeria 1988–2002, Studies in a Broken Polity.* London: Verso.

Slim. 2011. "Samedi." *Le Soir d'Algérie,* February 24. http://www.lesoirdalgerie.com/ articles/2011/02/24 (accessed November 2, 2011).

Slyomovics, Susan. 2009. "Financial Reparations, Blood Money, and Human Rights Witness Testimony: Morocco and Algeria." In *Humanitarianism and Suffering: The Mobilization of Empathy,* edited by Richard Ashby Wilson and Richard D. Brown, 265–84. Cambridge: Cambridge University Press.

———. 2013. "Visual Ethnography, Stereotypes, and Photographing Algeria." In *Orientalism Revisited: Art, Land, and Voyage,* edited by Ian Richard Netton, 128–50. London: Routledge.

Thompson, E. P. 1971. "The Moral Economy of the English Crowd in the Eighteenth Century." *Past and Present* 50: 76–136.

U.S. Energy Information Administration. 2011. "Crude Oil and Total Petroleum Imports Top 15 Countries." http://www.eia.gov (accessed August 20, 2011).

Morocco

MEROUAN MEKOUAR

IN DECEMBER 2011, Kenza, a young Moroccan pro-democracy activist whose family lives in one of the capital's poorest suburbs shared her puzzlement with me: "Look around you," she said. "We Moroccans have every reason to rebel, yet nothing is happening!" (personal interview 2011a). Kenza, a twenty-nine-year-old hospital worker, was referring to the inability of the February 20 movement (a broad coalition of pro-democracy activists calling for more freedom, dignity, and social justice that coalesced in the country following the Tunisian and Egyptian revolutions in early 2011) to exploit widespread popular frustrations and precipitate mass mobilization against the Moroccan regime.[1] In his personal blog, Nowbi (2011), another young Moroccan in his early thirties, also wondered why his fellow countrymen have not been willing to mobilize: "All the ingredients for a scenario à-la-Bouazizi are present. And . . . nothing happens! Moroccans do not follow. . . . It is like in American cartoons when the fuse burns all the way up to the stick of dynamite, and then silence, the expected explosion does not happen." Indeed, Kenza and Nowbi's puzzlement is understandable. While Moroccans shared many of the grievances that led their Tunisian and Egyptian neighbors to overthrow their respective leaders, the general population had seemed so far unwilling to push for meaningful political

135

reform or to question the absolute leadership of the monarchy. This seeming apathy is even more puzzling given the fact that Moroccan economic and social indicators were even poorer than those of pre-revolutionary Tunisia. Despite widespread poverty, a visible increase in economic inequalities, and a growing frustration with the coterie of local cronies who had been cannibalizing the local economy, King Mohammed VI continued to enjoy levels of popularity virtually unseen elsewhere in the region.[2]

This essay will argue that despite the presence of favorable economic and political conditions, the political transformations sweeping the Arab world since the beginning of 2011 had failed to reach Morocco because of the ability of the government to weaken its different historical opponents using a set of tried and tested strategies implemented since the independence of the country. Mohammed VI had updated these strategies, which had been gradually refined by the various kings who had ruled the country since 1956, to bolster his legitimacy and to adjust to the country's changing political, economic, and social conditions. However, this essay will also show that—despite the fact that these gestures allowed the monarchy to weather the turbulent events of 2011—structural economic challenges, an evolving class structure, and an increasing audacity from some segments of the population (nourished in part by the democratization of access to digital means of communications) could soon put the supremacy of the monarchy to the test. The first two sections of this essay will examine the different strategies used by the Palace to maintain its supremacy in the country. This discussion will be followed by a detailed analysis of Morocco's unique trajectory during the Arab Spring, and the final section will highlight the challenges that the country may be facing in the future.

Traditional Strategies of Power Consolidation

Since the independence of Morocco, all three kings who have ruled the country have used a double strategy based on the fragmentation (and gradual co-optation) of the opposition on one hand and constitutional maneuvering on the other.[3] This double strategy, which was initiated early on by the father of Morocco's independence, Mohammed V, proved particularly effective over the following fifty years and continues to represent a major aspect of his grandson's power consolidation strategy.

After the 1912 signing of the Fes treaty, which granted France sovereignty over most of Morocco's territory, the country experienced forty-four years of French and Spanish colonial rule. From 1927 to 1953, France used Mohammed V to rule the country in an indirect fashion. While all decisions were taken by France's general *représentant,* the sultan symbolically approved the decisions of the colonial authorities. After the departure of the French in 1956, Mohammed V quickly resorted to a divide-and-rule strategy in order to weaken the Palace's most serious opponent, the independence party, Istiqlal. To this end, the king encouraged divisions between urban and rural elites while relying heavily on a solid network of French-trained army leaders (Vermeren 2001, 24). By portraying himself as the defender of traditional values, the king deepened the schism between the conservative rural elite and the mostly urban-based reformists from the nationalist movement. The urban/rural rift exploited by the new king later became one of the major characteristics of Moroccan politics since independence and continues to play an important role today, given that the rural population remains massively supportive of the monarchy. Mohammed V also exploited the divisions between nationalists and socialists within the Istiqlal party itself and encouraged the scission of the socialist Union Nationale des Forces Populaires (UNFP) in 1959 (ibid., 28). By isolating the traditionalist base of the independence party from its radical socialist wing led by the popular Mehdi Ben Barka, a confirmed antimonarchist and Third World socialist leader, Mohammed V was able to weaken the party and avoid the establishment of a unified front that could have successfully pushed for a redistribution of political prerogatives in the country (ibid., 31).[4]

However, it was only after the arrival to power of Hassan II in 1961 that the strategy of fragmentation and co-optation of the opposition reached its full speed. As Ellen M. Lust-Okar (2004, 160) shows, in particular, Hassan II used state patronage and police violence to foster a deeply divided political environment, which helped him pit one opposition group against the other and promote his role as a supreme arbitrator above different warring political parties. The king rewarded loyal members of the opposition by allowing them to access state rent while at the same time cracking down on the different groups challenging his authority.[5] Playing not only on the division between the nationalists and socialists within the Istiqlal party but also on the division between moderates and extremist members of the opposition, Hassan II gradually integrated the former while fiercely cracking down on the latter (ibid., 161–62). Although major figures of the opposition were at least nominally included in the government throughout the 1970s and 1980s, hundreds of members of the left and the far left were arrested, tortured, and jailed. Even when the country went through a series of violent street protests in 1981 and 1984, the king agreed to negotiate only with the Moroccan Workers' Union (Union Marocaine du Travail, or UMT), a pro-government union close to the Istiqlal party; he refused to engage in talks with the socialist-led Democratic Confederation of Labour (Confédération Démocratique du Travail, or CDT), which was close to the socialist opposition, for instance (ibid., 162–63).

Strategies of monarchical consolidation proved so successful that by the end of the 1980s, the main opposition movements in the country were unwilling to challenge the Palace even though the social and economic conditions, following the implementation of a severe International Monetary Fund structural adjustment plan, were becoming even more difficult for the majority of the population (ibid., 159). Following the riots in Fes in 1990 and the rise of the Islamist al-Adlwal-Ihsane (Justice and Charity) movement and the Unity and Reform Movement (later renamed the Justice and Development Party, or Parti de la Justice et du Développement, PJD), the king initiated the co-optation of the socialists through a number of negotiations with their main unions, the CDT and the General Union of Moroccan Workers (Union Générale des Travailleurs du Maroc, or UGTM) (ibid., 164–65). The arrival to power of the Union Socialiste des Forces Populaires (USFP), led by longtime leftist militant Abderrahman Youssoufi, in 1997 marked the full co-optation of the moderate left in the country. After decades in the opposition, the USFP accepted the Palace's invitation by muting its criticism of the monarchy in exchange for access to the state's redistribution channels. With the first socialist government firmly under the control of the Palace, the king had more latitude to tackle the new rising Islamic movements in the country. While gradually allowing moderate Islamists to organize into a political party and run for elections, the Palace was physically cracking down on al-Adl wal-Ihsane, a popular Islamic movement never recognized by the authorities.

After the death of his father in 1999, Mohammed VI found himself with virtually no organized opposition. Playing on the rivalries among the Istiqlal party, the socialists, and the moderate Islamists of the PJD, the king appointed largely technocratic governments in 2002 and 2007 (Zaki 2009, 24) that allowed him to appear as the agent of change while sidelining increasingly discredited warring political parties.

Constitutional Maneuvering

The second leg of monarchical consolidation in Morocco was the regular use of constitutional maneuvering to create the illusion of change while preserving the heart of royal prerogatives. Indeed, as of 1962, the Moroccan constitution had gone through countless revisions and amendments specifically designed not to bring about any significant change but simply to rearrange the power distribution in the country in order to preserve the hegemony of the Palace (Marx 2010, 481). As Daniel Marx (2010, 482) emphasizes, the very dynamic process of making constitutional amendments (which closely paralleled the different periods of social tension) allowed the monarchy to portray itself as an agent of change, although these revisions did not bring about any significant transformation. In particular, the regular tweaking of constitutional rules offered the monarchy new opportunities to react and adapt to internal and external pressures (ibid., 483) but without altering the royal prerogatives in any important way.

In 1962, Hassan II took advantage of the boycott of the opposition to write a constitution giving the Palace the upper hand in the country's political game (ibid., 486). With mounting pressure from the opposition and the king having narrowly escaped two coup attempts, the Palace spearheaded two other constitutional projects in the early

1970s designed to provide the monarchy with more legitimacy by incorporating parts of the opposition into the political realm (ibid.). Various constitutional changes were initiated in the early 1980s and the 1990s in response to mounting social pressures (notably the 1990 popular riots in Fes) and a rapidly changing international context marked by the democratization of Eastern Europe and parts of Africa (ibid.). The 1992 constitution, for instance, reintroduced bicameralism. A new house, the House of Counselors, composed of a mix of regional and corporatist representatives, was specifically designed to counterbalance the House of Representatives (the lower house), where the leftist opposition represented by the USFP was increasingly present (ibid., 487).

Clientelism

Finally, it is important to note that the two strategies described above would not have worked without a sophisticated system of patrimonial redistribution. Although the executive power remained heavily rigged in favor of the Palace, access to parliament had been generally open, which meant that the channels for accessing state rent remained open to new actors (Tozy 2008, 36).[6] From this perspective, the parliamentary elections conducted under Mohammed VI were generally fair and transparent, allowing political entrepreneurs to access state distribution channels (Maâti 2011, 15) in exchange for their loyalty. These benefits included monopolies over transportation lines, fishing and mining licenses, and a wide range of advantages linked to proximity to the legislative and executive spheres.

New Strategies of Power Consolidation

By the late 1990s, Hassan II's strategies of power consolidation were so successful that Mohammed VI found himself without any significant political movement threatening his leadership after his arrival to power.[7] Thus the new king had all the latitude he needed to explore new strategies of power consolidation, the most important of which has been his symbolic political and economic dissociation from his late father's heritage.

Merouan Mekouar

Political Dissociation

One of the first decisions the new king made concerned the highly symbolic removal of Driss Basri—the feared minister of the interior under Hassan II and mastermind of state repression throughout the 1980s and 1990s. The unceremonious dismissal of Hassan II's most unpopular operative was the first in a series of gestures that created an impression of reformist change in the country, even if little was actually changing in terms of executive power distribution (Molina 2011, 436).[8] In particular, the removal of a very visible figure such as Driss Basri diverted attention away from the fact that most of the security figures active under Hassan II were still in place. However, Mohammed VI's most spectacular gesture was the establishment of the Equity and Reconciliation Commission in 2004. Less than five years after his arrival to power, the young king created the commission, the goal of which was to turn the page on the various human rights violations committed under Hassan II's "years of lead," during which thousands of opponents to the monarchy were tortured and jailed. Led by Driss Benzekri, a former political prisoner and longtime opponent of the Palace, the commission held public hearings and broadcast its testimony on public television—a highly symbolic gesture unseen elsewhere in the Arab world. By resorting to the language of human rights and symbolically distancing himself from his father's bloody heritage, Mohammed VI was able to boost his popularity; he projected an aura of change even though the commission was never allowed to reveal the identities of human rights offenders or prosecute them as many victims demanded.[9]

Another tool that helped the king bolster his legitimacy (both internally and externally) was the "political instrumentation" (Desrues 2012, 28) of feminism, which again allowed him to portray himself as a modern and reform-minded leader, in tune with the zeitgeist on women's rights. To this end, the king spearheaded the implementation of a series of legal texts strengthening women's rights and forced the imposition of electoral lists guaranteeing the presence of women in parliament and at the municipal level (ibid.). At the same time, he imposed reforms to the Moudawana—Morocco's family code—that raised the age of marriage to eighteen, removed the requirement for a woman to have a male guardian's permission to marry, eased restrictions on divorce, and put severe restrictions on polygamy. While the king's reforms of the Moudawana were welcomed by feminist circles in the country (Latifa Jbabdi, head of the Union Feminist Action, stated that "the project of the family code is a message showing the world the real image of Islam as a religion guaranteeing equality between men and women"; quoted in IMED 2004), Moroccan Islamist movements organized major protests against the reforms, which they perceived as "cultural aggression from the North" (Kravetz 2002).

Economic Dissociation

The cornerstone of Mohammed VI's strategy of symbolic dissociation from Hassan II's heritage, however, was the visible economic transformation that occurred in the country after the new king came to power. Unlike his father, who did little to develop the country's infrastructure, Mohammed VI invested in highly visible (although sometime superfluous) projects. In particular, he initiated an ambitious program of highway building that would shorten travel time between Morocco's most important peripheral cities considerably. The king also spearheaded the creation of Tanger Med, a $1.2 billion deepwater port located near the city of Tangiers (Agoumi and Maghri 2007) complete with a free trade zone and an important French car plant, while using generous donations and loans from Europe and the Gulf countries to boost Morocco's tourism sector. Other projects initiated thanks to the Palace included tramways in Rabat and Casablanca, new coastal developments in the north of the country, and a highly hyped high-speed train between Tangiers and the capital.

Likewise, Mohammed VI presented himself as a "simple" king close to everyday Moroccans by toning down his father's lavish protocol and relaxing some aspects of the royal etiquette, such as the practice of kissing the king's hand. Breaking with his late father's stuffy protocol, he was regularly seen driving his car with little visible protection in major urban centers while making sure to respect traffic laws. Mohammed VI also made regular visits—well covered by the press—to popular neighborhoods, delivered meals personally during the fasting month of Ramadan, and spearheaded a large program of social housing distribution that led to the near-total removal of shantytowns in the country.

Morocco and the Arab Spring

The king's strategies for generating legitimacy were so successful that by 2008, a poll conducted by the Arab-language journal *Nichane* found that 91 percent of Moroccans were supportive of the king (*Libération* 2009). However, the self-immolation of Mohamed Bouazizi, a young Tunisian street vendor harassed by the local authorities, in December 2010 and the ensuing turmoil that engulfed the Arab world were the real test of the king's strategies of power consolidation.

A couple of weeks after the forced departure of Egyptian president Hosni Mubarak, protesters from the February 20 movement started organizing massive weekly demonstrations held simultaneously in dozens of Moroccan cities. Supported in part by the Moroccan Association of Human Rights and the Unified Socialist Party (a far-left party), the movement was made up of a horizontal, leaderless network of activists who relied heavily on technology to communicate and organize the weekly rallies. The movement comprised large segments of Moroccan society, from apolitical jobless urban youth and Berber militants to the youth sections of various political parties (including the influential Justice and Development Party), as well as a number of intellectuals and businessmen from the traditional elite of the country (Molina 2011, 437). A wide international network of activists located in Europe and North America also supported the movement by organizing a series of parallel demonstrations abroad. At the height of the protests, the marches gathered more than three hundred thousand people in more than fifty cities, a level of mobilization unseen in the country since the arrival to power of the current king. The demands of the February 20 movement included radical democratic and social changes, but the activists did not call for the departure of the king. Slogans chanted in various locations around the country summarized the essence of popular demands, notably frustration with economic inequalities:

Why are we here? Why are we protesting?
The cost of living is too high for us!
Why are we here? Why are we protesting?
Water and electricity bills are too expensive for us!
Why are we here? Why are we protesting?
For the change that we want!
Why are we here? Why are we protesting?
The cost of living is too high for us! (Larbi 2011)

Anger against the privileged was expressed:

Your kids, you got educated!
Your kids, you got educated!
The people's kids, you got expelled!
Your kids, you got stuffed [with food]!
Your kids, you got stuffed [with food]!
The people's kids, you got starved!
Your kids, you got employed!
Your kids, you got employed!
The people's kids, you pushed them to leave the country [illegally]. (ibid.)

And even a sense of irony at the practices that surround the royal palace and the king's official activities found voice:

He [the king] is coming, he's coming! Fix the roads!
He's coming, he's coming! Spread the carpets!
He's coming, he's coming! Plant the trees!
He's coming, he's coming! Get the flags ready!
He's coming, he's coming! Kneel in front of him!
He's coming, he's coming! Kiss his [little] hands! (ibid.)

However, it is important to note that, unlike Egypt and Tunisia, where demands by the population were aimed directly at the leaders, Moroccan pro-democracy activists rarely questioned the monarchy itself, focusing instead on its entourage and the new bourgeoisie that had emerged in the preceding fifteen years. Popular chants during rallies targeted Fouad Ali El Himma and Mounir Majidi, two prominent childhood friends of the king whose involvement in the political and economic life of the country angered many Moroccans: "Oh El Himma! Get your act together! This is Morocco, and we are its people! Oh Majidi! Get your act together! This is Morocco, and we are its people!" (ibid.).

As the calls for protest seemed to gain momentum in the first half of 2011, the Palace reacted immediately by initiating work on the new constitution. Thus, less than a month after the start of the first protests, the king announced the writing of a new constitution on March 9, 2011 (Molina 2011, 439). Following a pattern firmly established by his late father, the king monopolized the constitutional project by nominating only his closest associates to the commission responsible for writing the new text. While political parties and members of the civil society were promised that they would participate in the project, they were in effect kept totally in the dark and were presented with the final draft of the constitution only one day before its formal unveiling (ibid.). On July 1, Moroccans were called to vote in a referendum on a new constitution. In a strategy reminiscent of his father's regime, Mohammed VI strictly endorsed the project and called on the population to mobilize in favor of the new constitution. While all the main political actors vigorously endorsed the royal directive, critics of the constitution were harassed and official imams in state-run mosques across the country were mobilized to preach in favor of the constitution (ibid., 440).

The king himself encouraged the population to vote in favor of the project, calling it "a decisive and historical change" (Jamal2ofev, 2011), and the new constitution was approved with more than 98 percent of the popular vote—a higher percentage than that achieved in a similar referendum a few months later in Syria. Not surprisingly, Morocco's latest constitutional project was marketed as an important democratic step (supposedly unseen elsewhere in the Arab world) in which the monarch was finally giving parliament its proper role. In addition to not including a controversial article about the "sacrality" of the king that had been present in the old constitution, the new text gave more powers to the prime minister (to be picked from the largest party in parliament), increased the prerogatives of the elected parliament, and introduced new provisions reinforcing the rights of women and Berber groups. External observers from the European Union and elsewhere called the new project "positive" (*Afriquinfos* 2011), "a model for other countries"

(*L'Opinion* 2011), and even "historical" (Ministère Français des Affaires Étrangères 2011). However, a close reading of the 2011 constitution shows that the new changes were as superficial as the ones implemented by Hassan II throughout his reign and did not curb the extensive powers of the king in any significant way. Instead of being sacred, the person of the king was now "inviolable," and the monarch retained the power to veto all decisions taken by the government, although he could not get rid of the head of the government at will anymore (Brynen and Mekouar 2013, 35). Although Morocco's new constitution had a number of articles strengthening the power of the elected lower house while entrenching the independence of the judiciary, the king remained the ultimate arbitrator and retained absolute authority over matters related to security, religion, and the strategic orientations of the country (Ottaway and Muasher 2011, 5).[10]

In addition to the constitutional reform of 2011, the monarchy increased public servants' salaries and engaged in a close dialogue with the leaders of major political parties and union representatives (Molina 2011, 437–38). By mobilizing most of the country's decision makers, the regime was able to avoid a linkup between the disgruntled masses and members of the political elite, which might have otherwise tried to capitalize on the international political momentum. Using the same strategies developed by his father and grandfather, Mohammed VI mobilized his most loyal supporters: the Sufis and the rural notables. Once the pro-democracy protests started gaining momentum in early 2011, both groups were called upon to show their support for the monarchy. Faithful to the Palace, important symbolic figures such as Sheikh Hamza, the head of the Sufi Boutchichiya order, as well as the vast majority of rural notables all mobilized their followers to vote in favor of the new constitutional project introduced by the king.[11]

This last element is perhaps the most important one. By making sure that prominent political figures were not bandwagoning on the demonstrations, the state had much leeway to delegitimate protesters by having the king's supporters label them pell-mell as extremists, radical Islamists, homosexuals, communists, atheists, and even supporters of the Polisario, the Sahrawi independence movement (Bruguière 2011). A pro-government (and unusually professionally made) video posted on

YouTube showed altered pictures of some alleged leaders of the February 20 movement hugging Polisario leaders, drinking alcohol, and using drugs. The same video accused the pro-democracy activists of "insulting the prophet Muhammad" and promoting "moral corruption" and even "family disintegration" ("February 20 Hoax" 2011).

Another element that helped the Moroccan authorities keep pressure from the street under control was the cautious use of state violence. While both Mohammed V and Hassan II relied on the security apparatus to maintain their hold over the country—and did not hesitate to use violence to repress a series of popular riots (notably in the Rif mountains in 1958, Casablanca in 1981 and 1984, and Fes in 1990)—the international context forced Mohammed VI to use the coercive means at his disposal much more cautiously. Because the authorities were very much aware of the risk that police violence might fuel more protests, which in turn might spiral dangerously out of control, the government allowed protests to occur regularly and used violence selectively. Contrary to the Tunisian and Egyptian cases, where members of the police fired at protesters and infuriated their friends and families as a consequence, the Moroccan government was very careful not to antagonize the general population by shooting protesters or detaining large numbers of citizens. While a number of February 20 movement protesters were physically assaulted,[12] public shows of violence and arrests remained minimal compared to other countries in the Arab world, and the authorities could generally pride themselves on their self-control.

Instead of a violent crackdown on protesters, the government used a series of ad hoc responses ranging from counterprotests organized by pro-Palace committees to cyberattacks and the selective co-optation of a number of visible figures from the February 20 movement. The government also mobilized the country's intellectuals. Major literary figures such as Tahar Ben Jelloun and Fouad Laroui, as well as a number of former leftist militants who were victims of state violence in the 1970s and 1980s, published articles in newspapers and on personal blogs defending the status quo and calling on local protesters to approve the new constitution and join the "official" political game in the country (Ben Jelloun 2011). A case in point is Salah El Ouadie, a human rights leftist militant jailed and tortured under Hassan II, who published a letter criticizing Moulay Hicham (cousin of Mohammed) for his support of the February 20 movement, saying, "I am telling you that you took the wrong path . . . [supporting those] who want to kill our nation, in a time where enemies of all kinds attempt to destroy [Morocco's] territorial integrity, and when it is threatened by internal and external terrorism" (Aboulahab 2011).

Finally, it is also important to note that once the protests started to gain momentum in the first half of 2011 (particularly in a number of cities in the historically marginalized north of the country), the government was able to rely on the indefectible support of large segments of the new Moroccan middle class, which had benefited greatly from the economic changes introduced by Mohammed VI since his arrival to power. Despite their resolve, the youth of the February 20 movement were never able to link up fully with the rest of the population and change the political dynamic of the country. As one preeminent February 20 movement member emphasized: "The new francophone middle class has been the fiercest opponent to the movement. . . . Somehow it was impossible [for the February 20 movement] to convince francophone bloggers or the kids working in call centers to support our demands" (personal interview 2011b). One representative of the pro-Palace bourgeoisie was Fahd Yata, a journalist and son of a major Moroccan political figure who published numerous contemptuous op-eds denigrating the pro-democracy movement in the country, which he described as nothing more than "a micro-movement of a few hundred militants already involved in far left organizations" (Yata 2012).

The attachment of the majority of the population to the relative political and socioeconomic gains of the past decade was reflected in the cultural scene in the country. With a few exceptions, notably rapper el-Haked, who was jailed for his political views favoring change in the country and especially a song critical of the police called "Klab al-dawla" (Dogs of the state), most of the country's cultural elites (including nearly all of Morocco's popular hip-hop artists) firmly coalesced around the monarchy. Not unlike the rest of Morocco's middle class, these artists were extremely attached to defending the improvements achieved during Mohammed VI's reign and were at the forefront of the defense of the "king's constitution" in 2011. Don Bigg, one of the country's most popular and recognizable hip-hop artists, publicly mocked protesters from the February 20 movement, calling them "brats" and "Ramadan eaters" (Bigg 2011).[13]

Challenges

However, despite these very favorable factors, it was likely that the Moroccan Palace would not be immune to more social unrest in the future. Indeed, young Moroccans shared many of the grievances expressed by their Tunisian and Egyptian counterparts, such as a deep frustration with increasingly visible government corruption and widespread poverty. As one young February 20 militant stated:

> Those who rule are not ruled by the law. . . . Wealth is concentrated in the hands of the royal family and those who govern. Of course, this leaves nothing to the people. There is no social security. . . . We have one of the highest illiteracy rates in the world. These are all major social problems: people cannot afford health care. (Bouhmouch 2012)

Although the unemployment rate fell from 13.4 percent in 2000 to 9.1 percent in 2009, the increase in employment in that decade was mostly the result of the development of the informal sector, whose members did not enjoy any kind of social protection; it did not affect youth in urban centers, where two out of three young people remained jobless (Achy 2010, 14). Similarly, economic inequalities had been steadily increasing in the previous few years, with Morocco's Gini coefficient (which measures levels of economic inequalities) being the highest in North Africa (Vision of Humanity 2012).

Moroccans also shared their Arab counterparts' resentment toward contemptuous political elites and growing unwillingness to accept perceived economic inequalities (Desrues 2012, 31). While the country had not witnessed any major riots since Mohammed VI had come to power, peripheral towns in the north and interior of the country continued to be subject to regular periods of social tensions, during which hundreds of young people attacked police stations and destroyed public infrastructure in order to signal their disgruntlement with the state. The historically marginalized north of the country (where the February 20 movement has been particularly popular) remained especially subject to social unrest. Only a few months after the adoption of the new constitution and the election of the new PJD government, various cities in the Rif mountains (notably Beni Bouayach and Taza) witnessed a series of riots that were violently quelled by the authorities.

However, it was possible that the country's biggest challenge might come from the Palace itself. Indeed, many Moroccans were increasingly disgruntled with the shameless show of wealth coming from both the monarchy and the new local bourgeoisie that was enriching itself under Mohammed VI. With a fortune estimated at $2.5 billion (Serafin 2009), the "King of the Poor" (as well as his close associates) could find his wealth hard to justify in a country where significant parts of the population continued to live below the poverty line. Indeed, one of the major challenges facing the Palace was the increasing popular disapproval of the king's entourage, most notably his closest associates and advisers (most of whom had been his friends since childhood). The gap between an increasingly assertive young generation and the traditional economic and political elite was growing, and the contempt shown to the rule of law by the king's family and associates contributed to a rising sense of frustration among young Moroccans (Desrues 2012, 24). While the legitimacy of the king rested on his role as a neutral arbiter above his turbulent subjects, the Palace did not seem to measure the degree of popular frustration vis-à-vis the king's entourage. Indeed, shortly after the election of the new government in 2011, the king dismissed the demands of the population in a very cavalier fashion by nominating his widely hated friend El Himma to serve as a royal adviser, one of Morocco's most important political functions.

Similarly, it is important to note that the relatively peaceful twelve years of rule under Mohammed VI had been made possible by the Palace's strategy of diverting accountability from the monarchy to the elected government. While the king enjoyed the political benefits related to the implementation of large economic projects, the government dealt with the pettiness of day-to-day decisions and bore the largest share of the popular frustrations. By diverting popular frustrations toward the elected government, the Palace was able to avoid paying the political price for unpopular political and economic decisions. Better still, the king could act as a deus ex machina by unexpectedly fixing problems that the government in place had not been able to solve. Forgotten towns were swiftly connected to the electrical grid during royal visits, political prisoners were freed at the king's whim, and flashy cultural festivals with major international music stars, free of charge to the country's youth, were organized under the king's patronage. However, the monarchy's strategy for diverting accountability could work only if the elected government had real powers and therefore real responsibilities. The more the monarchy (or its associates) undermined the work of the elected government, the less the latter could serve as a magnet for popular anger and the more the person of the king himself would run the risk of being singled out as the most to blame for the country's numerous economic and political challenges. From this perspective, it seemed increasingly clear that the Palace was reluctant to let the elected Islamist government take on real responsibilities. Thus, shortly after the new government was elected in November 2011, the king appointed new ambassadors, forcefully keeping some of his close associates in the new government while continuing to appear as the ultimate leader of the country.

It was possible that even the highly mediatized economic projects spearheaded by the king might start having a negative impact on the Palace. Because Mohammed VI was unanimously seen as the ultimate chief executive of the country, unpopular decisions could backfire on the king himself. The controversial purchase of the high-speed TGV train from France for a staggering $2.3 billion (Railway Gazette International 2010) within a context of deep economic troubles irritated parts of the population, who wondered whether those funds might not have been more usefully invested in sectors such as education and health care. Thus it was increasingly clear that the more the monarchy intervened in the country's political and economic spheres, the less credible the new government was and the more the king became subject to direct criticism. By avoiding real institutional transformations and purposefully making some of the elected government's most popular figures look weak, and thus openly demonstrating the irrelevance of the elected government that it had specifically designed to serve as a democratic facade, the Palace is shooting itself in the foot.

The country was also facing mounting structural economic challenges. Since the late 1990s, the government had been using privatization and extensive borrowing (particularly from Europe and the Gulf) to deal with increasing fiscal pressures. While the country was highly dependent on the fluctuations of international commodities prices (both for imports and exports), the health of the balance of payments (at 7 percent in 2011) was worrisome, and the public debt reached 52 percent of the gross domestic product (M.A.B. 2012). Despite the gravity of these indicators, the authorities did not seem to have the ability or the willingness to take the difficult political and economic decisions needed to address these challenges in the long term (Economist Intelligence Unit 2011, 14).

One possible avenue for the democratization of the country was international pressure coming from European countries or the United States. Morocco had signed a free trade agreement with the United States and had advanced status with the European Union, with which it shared 60 percent of its international trade (Dennison, Popescu, and Torreblanca 2011, 8). Indeed, the Moroccan government greatly valued its close relationships with Western countries and may have been very sensitive to international calls for the democratization of the country. However, the kingdom's international patrons by then were showing little interest in the effective democratization of the country (Dennison et al. 2011), and the Palace continued capitalizing on half a century of intimate relationships with various Western leaders—virtually insulating the country from international criticism.

Finally, it is important to note that Morocco's relative stability had been made possible in part by emigration and drug trafficking, two important socioeconomic safety valves that helped diminish social tensions. Revenues from emigration and drug exports to Europe and the rest of the Maghreb allowed large parts of the population to survive independent of the state, particularly in the traditionally restive northern part of the country. With 20 percent of the workforce living abroad and foreign remittances accounting for 8 percent of the GDP

(Economist Intelligence Unit 2011, 8), Morocco remained particularly vulnerable to international economic fluctuations that could affect its citizens both inside and outside its borders. Combined with the structural challenges the country faced, an economic downturn at the international level might prove to have significant consequences for Morocco's domestic politics. By resorting to easy solutions and refusing to engage in meaningful democratic reform, the Palace was letting popular frustrations grow at its own peril.

Notes

1. This person's name has been changed to protect her identity.

2. The popularity of the monarchy is evident in the impressive number of spontaneous messages of support for the monarchy posted in videos on file-sharing sites by ordinary Moroccans.

3. Mohammed V (1927–53 and 1956–61) was succeeded by Hassan II (1961–99), who was succeeded by Mohammed VI (1999–present).

4. For a complete account of the strategies Mohammed V used to consolidate his control of the country, see Pierre Vermeren's excellent monograph *Histoire du Maroc depuis l'indépendance* (2010). See also Leveau (1985).

5. Official favors granted in return for loyalty included privileged access to governmental positions, government licenses for commercial transportation routes and alcohol distribution, deep-sea fishing authorizations, and privileged access to state-owned agricultural land.

6. Favors stemming from proximity to the Palace included privileged access to state commercial licenses, the ability to sidestep the country's heavy bureaucracy and conduct business affairs more easily, and access to generously paid governmental positions.

7. Notable exceptions were the far left and Sheikh Yassin's al-Adlwal-Ihsane Islamic movement.

8. Driss Basri was contemptuously nicknamed the "leprosy sufferer" by some, in reference to the visible skin disease that afflicted him.

9. It is also important to note that as the commission was publishing its final report highlighting the fact that the country had "turned the page" on torture, Morocco's police services were once again torturing Islamic militants suspected of promoting terrorism in the country.

10. The botched writing of the constitution also meant that the new text was particularly subject to differing interpretations (which could allow parliament to

exercise real powers should it decide to do so) and also allowed the king to intervene at will. However, as many analysts have emphasized, the Moroccan parliament's long history of deference vis-à-vis the king does not indicate a willingness to challenge the status quo, especially given the fact that the previous constitution also gave parliament more latitude than it was willing to take (Ottaway and Muasher 2011, 5).

11. The close relationship between the rural parts of the Moroccan population and the monarchy may be explained in part by the low literacy rate in the country, which makes significant segments of the population less receptive to new political brandings.

12. Notably, on May 29, 2011, demonstrators were brutally dispersed by the authorities during protests in the popular neighborhood of Sbata in Casablanca.

13. Calling someone a "Ramadan eater" is a serious insult in Morocco, where the vast majority of the population take the Ramadan fast very seriously.

References

Aboulahab. 2011. "Lettres de Salah El Ouadie." Cercles de Jeunes Débiles Morocains. http://takhouar.wordpress.com/lettres-de-salah-el-ouadie (accessed September 7, 2012).

Achy, Lahcen. 2010. *Morocco's Experience with Poverty Reduction: Lessons for the Arab World.* Washington, D.C.: Carnegie Endowment for International Peace. http://carnegieendowment.org (accessed March 25, 2013).

Afriquinfos. 2011. "L'UE salue le résultat du réferendum sur la constitution marocaine." July 2. http://www.afriquinfos.com/articles/2011/7/2/breves dafrique-181469.asp (accessed May 30, 2012).

Agoumi, Fadel, and Aniss Maghri. 2007. "Tanger-Med arrivera à saturation d'ici 2015, un port plus grand sera construit." *La Vie éco,* January 12. http://www. lavieeco.com (accessed September 8, 2012).

Ben Jelloun, Tahar. 2011. "Maroc: L'Islam droit rester dans les mesquées." *Le Monde,* December 5. http://www.lemonde.fr (accessed May 6, 2012).

Bigg, Don. 2011. "Don Bigg—Mabghitch." YouTube video. June 29. http://www. youtube.com/watch?v=QNrvUmKsG-g&feature=player_embedded (accessed May 5, 2012).

Bouhmouch, Nadir. 2012. "My Makhzen & Me." Video. Comme une bouteille jetée à la mer! February 20. http://www.larbi.org (accessed September 8, 2012).

Bruguière, Peggy. 2011. "La nouvelle Constitution répond-elle aux attentes des Marocains?" France 24, June 21. http://observers.france24.com/fr (accessed May 6, 2012).

Brynen, Rex, and Merouan Mekouar. 2013. "North Africa: Algeria, Egypt, Libya,

Morocco, Tunisia." In *Beyond the Arab Spring: Authoritarianism and Democratization in the Arab World*, edited by Rex Brynen, Pete W. Moore, Bassel F. Salloukh, and Marie-Joëlle Zahar. Boulder, Colo.: Lynne Rienner.

Dennison, Susi, Nicu Popescu, and José Ignacio Torreblanca. 2011. *A Chance to Reform: How the EU Can Support Democratic Evolution in Morocco.* Policy brief, May. London: European Council on Foreign Relations. http://www.ecfr.eu (accessed March 25, 2013).

Desrues, Thierry. 2012. "Moroccan Youth and the Forming of a New Generation: Social Change, Collective Action and Political Activism." *Mediterranean Politics* 17 (1): 23–40.

Economist Intelligence Unit. 2011. "Country Report: Morocco," edited by Keren Uziyel and Edward Bell. http://www.eiu.com (accessed March 25, 2013).

"February 20 Hoax" [Khud'a 20 February, part one]. 2011. http://www.youtube.com/watch?v=cPshHR2rV20&feature=related (accessed September 7, 2012).

IMED. 2004. *Réforme de la Moudawana au Maroc: Revue de Presse (Mars 2003–Novembre 2004).* Rome: Centre de Documentation, IMED.

Jamel2ofev. 2011. "Discours Royal: La nouvelle Constitution 2011." YouTube video. June 17. http://www.youtube.com/watch?v=zKflC18YKFY&noredirect=1 (accessed September 14, 2012).

Kravetz, Marc. 2002. "Le Maroc. La Tolerance comme identité." *Libération*, August 24. http://www.liberation.fr (accessed September 8, 2012).

Larbi. 2011. "Les Slogans du 20 février." Comme une bouteille jetée à la mer! July 9. http://www.larbi.org (accessed September 6, 2012).

Leveau, Rémy. 1985. *Le Fellah Marocain, défenseur du trône.* Paris: Presses de la Fondation Nationale des Sciences Politiques.

Libération. 2009. "Le Maroc interdit un sondage . . . favorable au roi du Maroc." August 3. http://www.liberation.fr (accessed May 5, 2012).

L'Opinion. 2011. "Le Referendum constitutionnel largement salué à l'échelle internationale." July 4. http://www.lopinion.ma (accessed May 30, 2012).

Lust-Okar, Ellen M. 2004. "Divided They Rule: The Management and Manipulation of Political Opposition." *Comparative Politics* 36 (2): 159–79.

Maâti, Monjib. 2011. "The 'Democratization' Process in Morocco: Progress, Obstacles, and the Impact of the Islamist–Secularist Divide." Working Paper 5, Saban Center, Brookings Institution, Washington, D.C. http://www.brookings.edu (accessed September 19, 2012).

M.A.B. 2012. "Budget: BAM place le déficit à 7%." *L'Économiste,* February 20. http://www.leconomiste.com (accessed May 6, 2012).

Marx, Daniel A. 2010. "North Africa's Constitutions at the 50-Year Mark: An Analysis of Their Evolution." *Journal of North African Studies* 15 (4): 481–95.

Ministère des Affaires Étrangères, France. 2011. "Référendum au Maroc—Déclara-

tion d'Alain Juppé." France Diplomatie, July 2. http://www.diplomatie.gouv.fr/
fr (accessed May 30, 2012).

Molina, Irene Fernandez. 2011. "The Monarchy vs. the 20 February Movement:
Who Holds the Reins of Political Change in Morocco?" *Mediterranean Politics*
16 (3): 435–41.

Nowbi. 2011. "Pour comprendre le con-texte du 'Oui.'" J'écris parce que je chante
mal, July 1. http://nowbi.over-blog.com (accessed September 6, 2012).

Ottaway, Marina, and Marwan Muasher. 2011. *Arab Monarchies: Chance for Reform,
Yet Unmet.* December. Washington, D.C.: Carnegie Endowment for International Peace. http://carnegieendowment.org (accessed September 19, 2012).

Railway Gazette International. 2010. "High Speed Funding Package Agreed." February 18. http://www.railwaygazette.com (accessed May 5, 2012).

Serafin, Tatiana. 2009. "The World's Richest Royals." *Forbes,* June 17. http://www.
forbes.com (accessed May 5, 2012).

Tozy, Mohamed. 2008. "Islamists, Technocrats, and the Palace." *Journal of Democracy* 19 (1): 34–41.

Vermeren, Pierre. 2001. *Le Maroc en transition.* Paris: La Découverte.

———. 2010. *Histoire du Maroc depuis l'indépendance.* 3rd ed. Paris: La Découverte.

Vision of Humanity. 2012. "2012 Global Peace Index." http://www.visionofhuman
ity.org/gpi-data/#/2011/gini (accessed May 5, 2012).

Yata, Fahd. 2012. "La Cohésion sociale et ses mécanismes, treize ans après." La
Nouvelle Tribune, August 2. http://www.lnt.ma/actualites (accessed September
6, 2012).

Zaki, Lamia. 2009. "Pour une analyse localisée des élections marocaines: Introduction." In *Terrains de campagne au Maroc: Les Élections législatives de 2007,* edited
by Zaki Lamia, 11–42. Paris: Karthala.

Personal Interviews

Personal interview. 2011a. A. Kenza. Rabat, December 25.

Personal interview. 2011b. AT. Casablanca, December 30.

Libya

ANJALI KAMAT AND AHMAD SHOKR

AFTER NEARLY THREE DECADES, the gates of Abu Salim were wide open. For Libyans, the very name of the prison still evokes nightmares, visions of a purgatory from which one might never return. A symbol of the terror that came to define Muammar Qaddafi's forty-two-year rule, Abu Salim was where even the regime's mildest critics feared they would end up if they aired their grievances too loudly, or to the wrong person. But in September 2011 the grim compound was flooded with visitors: former prisoners showing their families the insides of the small windowless cells where they lost so much of their lives, neighborhood residents curious about this symbol of Qaddafi's terror, and returned exiles searching for traces of the regime's past abuses.

As we wandered through the prison, Khaled Al Agily, a Benghazi-born exile who founded the Geneva-based rights group Libya Human Rights Solidarity, showed us around. His organization has been at the forefront of international efforts to bring to light the country's worst postcolonial massacre. Walking through the open-air courtyards where the killings took place, Khaled told us the story—well-known across Libya—of how it unfolded (personal interview 2011a). On June 28, 1996, a riot broke out in the prison, started by a small group of Islamist prisoners who were agitating for better conditions, increased family visits, and

157

fair trials. Libyan security chief Abdullah Senussi arrived on the scene and promised a fair resolution, but the next morning, armed security forces executed an estimated twelve hundred political prisoners in the space of three hours.[1]

Fifteen years later, an exhaustive investigation was yet to take place. However, it was the families of the victims of this massacre who began the revolt that would transform the country. On February 15, 2011, heavily armed security personnel arrested a Benghazi-based lawyer who represented these families in their efforts to find justice through the courts. Fathy Terbil was no stranger to imprisonment or torture for his defense of the victims of a massacre that the regime had long denied. But when Terbil was detained this time, his supporters began a spontaneous demonstration just after sundown. The angry crowds grew larger and larger and began marching toward government offices. Their chants shifted from demanding Terbil's release to the refrain heard across Egypt and Tunisia: "Ash-sha'ab yurid isqath an-nidham" (The people demand the fall of the regime). Sensing a grave miscalculation, Senussi released Terbil the next morning and urged him to stop the protests.

But it was too late; the spark had been lit. And by then a framework for the nascent uprising was already in place: in early February, an underground network of activists and intellectuals, inspired by the changes sweeping neighboring Egypt and Tunisia, had put out a call for a nationwide protest on February 17. At the time, they had not known what to expect, and Qaddafi's security and intelligence operatives rounded up dozens of well-known writers, artists, and activists across the country in an apparent attempt to suppress a possible uprising. But the demonstrations that were triggered by Terbil's arrest only grew larger. Two days later, on February 17, thousands of people poured onto the streets in Benghazi, Tripoli, Misrata, and cities across the country, braving a brutal crackdown by Qaddafi's security forces. After a week of bloody clashes that killed a few hundred protesters, Misrata, Benghazi, and the eastern towns of Al-Bayda, Dernah, and Tobruq suddenly found themselves free of Qaddafi's iron grip.

The Libyan revolution began as a popular uprising firmly embedded in the spirit of the revolts that were taking place across the Arab world. However, as the uprising was quickly militarized and NATO became

Anjali Kamat and Ahmad Shokr

involved, Libya came to be seen as different. With Libya portrayed as a violent and messy exception to the Arab Spring, the country's political unrest was too often simplified into neat formulations: entrenched tribalism, imperial domination, civil war, or an Islamist takeover. This chapter will address some of these popular misconceptions about the Libyan uprising, chart a narrative of the revolt that looks at the decades of punitive security and socioeconomic policies that bred widespread disaffection with Qaddafi's rule, and examine the postrevolution contestations that have unfolded in the context of the power vacuum left by the near total collapse of Qaddafi's ruling institutions.

Qaddafi's regime finally fell after a long battle waged by rebel forces, with the NATO alliance providing crucial military and financial support. Although international involvement played a critical role in the triumph of the anti-Qaddafi forces, it never undermined the popular aspect of the revolt. The successes in neighboring Tunisia and Egypt had injected a sense of hope and possibility into the pervasive discontent in Libya and galvanized the vast majority of the population to participate in a grueling eight-month struggle to bring down Qaddafi's regime.

Libya under Qaddafi

Forty-two years after his coup against King Idris, Colonel Muammar Qaddafi was captured and killed in his hometown of Sirte on October 20, 2011. After four long decades in power and months of speculation over his fate in postuprising Libya, his end was brutal, swift, and decisive. It came just as the liberation of Sirte from Qaddafi's forces was officially declared by the ruling National Transitional Council (NTC). Attacked by both an American Predator drone and a French warplane, Qaddafi's fleeing convoy scattered. Qaddafi himself was discovered hiding in a drainage pipe by a group of opposition fighters from Misrata, a city hungry for revenge after Qaddafi's forces had destroyed most of it over months of intense fighting. Very shortly after, Qaddafi was officially pronounced dead, and grisly cell phone videos of fighters taunting and dragging the former dictator as he pled for mercy went viral across the Internet. It was a bloody end to a protracted and bloody uprising.

A State of Repression

Although, for most Libyans, Qaddafi had become largely irrelevant once Tripoli fell from his control in late August, his death two months later marked the official close of a long and singular chapter in Libya's history. It was a chapter that began with some promise: dignity and socialism at home and support for anti-imperialism and revolution abroad. Cushioned by the recent discovery of oil in Libya, when he took power, Qaddafi was able not only to fund revolutionaries from Ireland to Palestine to South Africa but also to institute social welfare policies that, combined with high oil prices, quadrupled Libya's per capita income in a decade (St. John 2008, 173). But for many Libyans, the dream began to sour early on. The primary reason for this was Qaddafi's overblown security and paramilitary apparatus, which enforced harsh repression of any form of dissent to his rule. Notwithstanding limited reforms and rhetoric about human rights in the late 1980s and again in the mid-2000s, Qaddafi's repressive security state remained largely untouched.

From the mid-1970s, Qaddafi's security forces targeted anyone who criticized or could potentially oppose his rule, including hundreds of leftists, Islamists, professors, lawyers, doctors, students, and journalists who opposed laws banning political parties or independent unions and restrictions on free speech. It was also during this period that the feared Revolutionary Committees were established—groups of young loyalists who were charged with monitoring and safeguarding the revolution, often by acting as a paramilitary security force. There were public executions, unforgettably broadcast on national television, and those who fled found little respite as the regime openly adopted a policy in the 1980s of assassinating dissidents in exile, whom Qaddafi infamously called "stray dogs" (Anderson 1986). (It was in this period that the Libyan ambassador to India, Mohamed Magarief, defected from the regime and founded, along with other dissidents, the National Front for the Salvation of Libya, or NFSL. He would survive several assassination attempts and lived in exile for three decades before returning to Libya in 2011 and being elected the head of the General National Congress in 2012.)

Meanwhile, Libya's nominally anti-imperialist foreign policy and sponsorship of international political violence put it on a dangerous collision course with successive American presidential administrations. In 1979, the Carter administration blacklisted Libya as a state sponsor of terrorism. The confrontation steadily intensified under the Reagan administration, culminating in the 1986 American bombing of Qaddafi's compound of Bab al-Aziziya and Benghazi, killing one hundred. From the late 1980s onward, rising economic insecurity also played a role in the simmering discontent. Falling global oil prices and harsh American sanctions were straining the Libyan coffers, and the cash-strapped state began to abandon the distributive system that had been in place for more than a decade. After Libya refused to acknowledge its responsibility for the 1988 Pan-Am bombing over Lockerbie, Scotland, that killed 270 people, the United Nations imposed mandatory sanctions on the country, further weakening its domestic welfare programs.

At the same time, armed Islamist groups began to mushroom across cities east of Tripoli, and, on occasion, militant Islamists allied with disaffected members of the armed forces (St. John 2008, 223). In addition to the swift security response, the regime punished local populations for their resistance through a policy of deliberate impoverishment.[2] In early 1996, a group called the Libyan Islamic Fighting Group (LIFG), made up of some former Libyan mujahideen from Afghanistan, attempted to assassinate Qaddafi and engaged in fierce battles with his security forces in the mountains of eastern Libya. Tanks rolled into Dernah, and security forces conducted house-to-house raids looking for LIFG members. The crackdown on Islamists and anyone suspected of Islamist sympathies reached its zenith with the massacre of some twelve hundred political prisoners at Abu Salim that June.

Warming Up to the West

Under the crippling weight of economic sanctions, and having violently stamped out a domestic Islamist insurgency, Libya emerged from the 1990s looking for a political and economic reorientation. Qaddafi sought to reverse Libya's international status as a pariah state by warming up to the West. The rapprochement would be based on counterterrorism, immigration control, and economic liberalization. One of the first signs of the regime's change of course came in 1998, when it agreed to hand over the two Libyan suspects in the Lockerbie bombing case to a court in The Hague. In return the United Nations eased economic sanctions and Europe renewed its diplomatic and business ties with Libya.

The attacks on the United States of September 11, 2001, gave Qaddafi's regime a golden opportunity to end nearly two decades of American isolation. Citing the threat of Islamist extremism against his own power, Qaddafi extended his condolences to the United States and offered full intelligence and counterterrorism cooperation. Within months, British and American intelligence agencies were on talking terms with Libyan intelligence and soon the three governments were working together in capturing, interrogating, torturing, and imprisoning suspects in both the U.S.-led "War on Terror" and Libya's crackdown on its Islamist opponents. One of the many victims of the George W. Bush administration's "extraordinary rendition" program was Abdel Hakim Belhaj, a former leader of the LIFG. He was captured in Malaysia and tortured by CIA agents in Thailand in 2004 before ending up in Abu Salim prison, where he spent the next six years.

During this period Qaddafi also extended his cooperation with the European Union and former colonial ruler Italy in particular in the realm of immigration control. Qaddafi routinely exaggerated the extent of African migration from Libya into Europe, when in fact most of the 1.5–2 million migrants in Libya came for jobs inside Libya, not to make the treacherous journey to Europe (see Paoletta and Pastore 2010; de Haas 2008; Bredeloup and Pliez 2011). Like many oil states in the Arab world, Libya relied on migrant labor to fill the ranks of low-paid jobs in the oil, construction, and service industries. Despite soaring domestic unemployment, Qaddafi actively encouraged migration from sub-Saharan Africa and the Middle East. The demand for migrant labor in the 1990s coincided with the pan-African turn in Qaddafi's policies, Libya's signing of a freedom of movement agreement with Chad, and the end of the Tuareg rebellion, all of which led to a surge in migration from across sub-Saharan Africa. But as domestic discontent over unemployment rose, migrant workers from Africa became convenient scapegoats.[3]

Anjali Kamat and Ahmad Shokr

Notwithstanding Qaddafi's proclaimed pan-Africanism, the "King of Kings of Africa" was incredibly cynical in his treatment of African migrants, actively welcoming them to Libya but also using their presence to leverage billions of dollars in arms, surveillance equipment, and cash from Europe to prevent their migration across the Mediterranean. Qaddafi also periodically deported tens of thousands of migrant workers or detained them in military internment camps.[4] In August 2010, he went so far as to warn Italian prime minister Silvio Berlusconi at a ceremony in Rome that "Europe might no longer be European" if it did not enhance its financial support for Libya's crackdown on irregular migration from sub-Saharan Africa. "We don't know if Europe will remain an advanced and united continent," he added, "or if it will be destroyed, as happened with the barbarian invasions" (quoted in BBC News 2010).

In early 2004, after Qaddafi renounced his weapons of mass destruction programs, U.S. unilateral sanctions on Libya were completely lifted, and American multinationals, following their European counterparts, started to arrive for business. It was at this time that a group of Western-educated reformers, led by Qaddafi's son Saif al-Islam and men such as Libya's then prime minister Shukri Ghanem and free market proponent Mahmoud Jibril, began their ascent within the ranks of Libya's political elite. They championed a program of economic liberalization and private-sector growth and often couched their projects in the language of political reform. Perhaps their biggest success was luring foreign oil companies back into Libya, either by reviving old contracts or by signing new export and production sharing agreements, known as EPSAs. By 2007, more than forty international oil firms were operating in Libya, including many of the world's heavyweights—ConocoPhillips, ChevronTexaco, ExxonMobil, Shell, and British Petroleum—which worked alongside or in partnership with Libya's National Oil Company.[5]

However, the neoliberal reform agenda remained heavily tempered given the continued grip of Qaddafi's old guard on economic and political decision making. In the years that followed, the reformists' failure to gain the upper hand within the power structure of the regime slackened the pace of neoliberal transformation. The reformists' moderate successes served mainly to polish Libya's global image and helped the Qaddafi regime forge better relations with the West, all the while enriching elites in and around the colonel's family who were deepening their involvement in investment activity (Pargeter 2006).[6] Many of the Qaddafi children had business holdings in oil and gas, telecommunications, media, and consumer goods, and they gained financially from lucrative foreign contracts.

The Oil State That Wasn't

For the majority of Libyans, however, little seemed to change as the reformers and hard-liners alike offered few solutions to Libya's intractable economic troubles. Libya was not poor, by any means, but it was poorly managed. The large but moribund public sector continued to be the country's chief source of formal employment for Libyans, providing a struggling middle class with only modest salaries.[7] The economy revolved around the sale of petroleum, but the revenues were scantily invested in the improvement of government jobs or basic services. Instead, much of the money was stored away in foreign exchange coffers or squandered by the ruling elite or used to buy political influence abroad, especially in sub-Saharan Africa, the focus of Qaddafi's proclaimed pan-Africanist policy.[8] Despite relatively good social indicators (adult literacy stood at 89 percent and gross national income per capita reached above $12,000),[9] Libya was still experiencing mounting social distress that resulted from long-standing problems in the way the country was run. The economy offered limited opportunities, oil wealth and economic decision making were concentrated in the hands of a small oligarchy, deliberate policy had led to uneven regional development, and insufficient public funds were being spent on high-quality education, health care, and infrastructure.[10] Consequently, large parts of the country remained underdeveloped and Libya had one of the highest unemployment rates in the region, a staggering 20–30 percent.[11]

There was little that ordinary people could do to advocate for better conditions. Trade unions had long been banned, and all forms of associational politics or community organizing were harshly repressed. Qaddafi had famously said in 2010 that civil society was a bourgeois invention of the West with no place in Libya. Labor unions, he added, were for the weak (Agènce France Presse 2010). Such prohibitions embodied the core of Qaddafi's rule: Libyans were not just punished for opposing their leader, but they were also proscribed from exercising any independent control over their lives. That did not stop people from trying: underground networks of activists, both secular and Islamist, existed under Qaddafi, but they operated with great caution. Web sites and online networks set up by exiled Libyan activists—such as longtime dissident Hassan Al-Amin's Libya Al-Mostakbal—served as crucial forums for writers across the country. Many used pseudonyms to communicate with each other and share their criticisms of the regime, and it was only during the 2011 uprising that their real identities were revealed.

In the final years of Qaddafi's regime there were marginal openings for dissent, primarily owing to the efforts of human rights lawyers who brought to light the case of the Abu Salim massacre. A figure such as Fathy Terbil could therefore organize weekly demonstrations in front of the Benghazi courthouse along with families of the victims. The Benghazi Bar Association openly campaigned for reforms and for a change in the association's corrupt leadership throughout 2010. It was not until February 2011, after the uprisings in Egypt and Tunisia, that Qaddafi finally gave the dissenters an audience—but by then the time for promises of reform had long passed.

The combination of a quasi-totalitarian state, a brutal security apparatus, stifling economic pressures, a hopelessly inflexible political system, and, perhaps above all, an eccentric leader obsessed with self-preservation who publicly derided his own people set in motion a broad-based confrontation with the regime from which there was no turning back. By 2011, Qaddafi had made many enemies: bold young activists, exiled dissidents, despondent reformists and businessmen, frustrated lawyers and journalists, unemployed youth, wearied Islamists and their families, and anyone suspected of belonging to any of these groups. All of them would take part in the popular revolt when it broke out. Invigorated by the mass protests sweeping across the Arab World, a group of activists and professionals led the call for Qaddafi's overthrow. As their appeal was heeded and the uprising began, resentful ex-officials and defectors gradually seized the opportunity to get rid of Qaddafi and stake out a place in the new political order. But, most important, all these groups were strengthened by tens of thousands of ordinary Libyans who may or may not have suffered personally from the regime's savagery but who suddenly felt inspired to mobilize, after decades of repression and humiliation, by the emerging hope of a new Libya. The multitudes who defied Qaddafi's threats and took to the streets did so with a clear vision: democracy, accountability, social and economic development, and, most of all, freedom.

The Revolt of 2011

As in Tunisia and Egypt, the uprising in Libya began largely as an unarmed, leaderless movement involving men and women from all walks of life with the shared aims of toppling a dictator and establishing a democratic political order. But as the uprising transformed into an armed conflict and the chorus for international intervention grew louder, Libya came to be seen as an exception. To understand the turn of events, foreign observers summoned a clutch of familiar tropes—civil war, tribalism, imperial domination, and Islamism—and in some cases used them to cast doubt on the uprising by rendering it anomalous and, in some cases, illegitimate.

Lost in some of these narratives was an understanding of Libyan specificities: the breadth of popular support for the uprising, the grievances that continued to fuel it, the ambivalence many of the revolutionaries maintained toward the Atlantic powers, and the range of political actors who emerged during the course of the uprising. As a counter to some of the simplistic representations that would prevail in public discussions about Libya in the United States, in this section we draw on the experiences we had while reporting from Libya to provide a narrative of what the uprising looked like to people on the ground. We begin by recalling a history that was quickly forgotten: the early rumblings of the revolt.

The Birth of a Popular Uprising

When Libyans first took to the streets in mid-February, no one knew what outcome to expect. But after Qaddafi's security brigades opened fire on the protesters and arrested hundreds, the crowds only grew larger. The Facebook-organized "Day of Rage" on February 17 ended in a bloodbath. Bodies began piling up at the morgues, and hospitals scrambled to treat the injuries inflicted by the high-caliber munitions used by security forces.

Despite the brutal repression, a remarkable sense of fearlessness took hold. After witnessing security forces killing a young man on his street, Mahdi Ziu, a forty-eight-year-old state oil company executive in Benghazi, was moved to act. On the morning of February 20, Ziu loaded up his truck with propane tanks and drove straight into the imposing gates of the *katiba*, Qaddafi's military barracks where his fighters were based. The explosion blew open the gates, and protesters rushed inside. After several hours of bloody clashes, Abdel Fattah Younes, at the time Libya's feared interior minister, arrived with a contingent of special forces. He was supposed to deliver the decisive blow against the protesters, but instead he defected and the rest of Qaddafi's forces at the barracks either fled or joined the revolution. In the space of these four days, the Libyan uprising was born.

After decades of fearing Revolutionary Committees and armed brigades loyal to Qaddafi, Libyans in the eastern part of the country suddenly found themselves in a liberated zone of more than a million people. Qaddafi's apparatus had crumbled, and one by one, Al-Bayda, Benghazi, Dernah, and Tobruk—cities long neglected by Qaddafi—declared their freedom. Protesters established city councils and organized groups of young men to direct traffic and guard against looting. Avuncular college professors and women lawyers overnight became the spokespeople for the revolution. Victorious anti-Qaddafi graffiti was splashed over walls. The promenade in front of the Benghazi courthouse became Libya's version of Tahrir Square: a colorful encampment of dozens of tents representing different towns, workplaces, and newly formed associations supporting the revolution, where crowds of thousands—men, women, and children—gathered every evening. Independent newspapers were set up and a handful of former state radio employees took over the local airwaves, broadcasting news about the unexpected rebellion and urging everyone to join what came to be known as the "February 17 revolution."

Even as eastern Libya was celebrating and transforming, on February 22, Qaddafi gave his now-infamous hour-long speech responding to the uprising. Many had hoped he would show some remorse for the deaths of some three hundred protesters, but he remained stubbornly defiant, and his words served only to temper the euphoria and compound fears of retaliation. Standing in the ruins of the compound bombed by U.S. forces in 1986, Qaddafi called the protesters rats and drug addicts who deserved the death penalty and accused them of pushing a range of foreign agendas—al-Qaeda and American imperialism, as well as revolutionary ideals from the Egyptian and Tunisian revolutions. Ominously, he warned that he had millions of supporters, not just in Libya but from all over the desert, and he vowed to hunt down protesters street by street, house by house, and, most memorably, alleyway by alleyway (zenga zenga).

Some dismissed his words as the inchoate ramblings of a dictator whose days were numbered, but for many others monitoring the continuing crackdown in western Libya, these were not idle threats. In city after city, as Qaddafi's forces fled, scores of young men who had resisted them with Molotov cocktails and rocks rushed to the now-abandoned weapons depots and stocked up on arms and explosives, readying for the next assault. As fears of an aerial bombing campaign escalated, calls for an internationally enforced no-fly zone began to emerge from Libyan activists, defected diplomats, and Mustafa Abdel Jalil, Libya's former minister of justice, who had resigned after the protests were met with force.[12]

Despite—or perhaps because of—the incredible novelty of the rapid transformations and the widespread lack of political experience among the protesters, the Libyan uprising developed a political leadership with astonishing speed. In late February, a group of protest leaders, academics, lawyers, and defected military officials and politicians established the National Transitional Council as the political face of the revolution. The thirty-three-member NTC claimed to have representatives from across Libya, but in light of the crackdown on the rest of the country, only the names of those from the completely liberated eastern zone were made public. By March 5, following a wave of defections by high-level former regime officials and diplomats, the NTC was declared the sole representative of Libya, and Abdel Jalil was named its chairman. Five days later France became the first country to recognize the council's legitimacy.

Even during these early moments, the urge for revenge against Qaddafi and his supporters reared its ugly head. As inflammatory reports began to circulate that Qaddafi was using African mercenaries to attack Libyan protesters, enraged crowds set upon anyone suspected of being such a mercenary—most often, hapless migrant workers from sub-Saharan Africa.[13] The fledgling authorities in the east were unprepared to deal with such race-based attacks, and the lawyers and human rights activists among them tried to temper the public thirst for retribution. But as stories began to spread of African workers being lynched by civilian mobs, the exodus of foreign workers gathered pace.[14] Assembled in camps run by Libyan volunteers, tens of thousands of workers waited in Benghazi for Greek cruise ships to carry them to safety. Workers from China and Eastern Europe found a reasonably quick exit, but for the vast majority—the global underclass from sub-Saharan Africa, the Philippines, and Bangladesh—no ships came. Desperate to leave Libya, they were bused to the borders with Egypt or Tunisia, where they awaited help from their embassies or international agencies. The wait took weeks—sometimes months—often with alarmingly little in the way of shelter, food, and water.

Migrant workers in Qaddafi-controlled areas were no safer: as European condemnation of the regime's use of violence increased, Qaddafi threatened to flood Europe's southern borders with Africans. Once NATO began dropping bombs, Qaddafi spokesman Moussa Ibrahim acknowledged that migrants were being sent to Italy as a reprisal for Italy's support of NATO's bombing campaign: "We cannot be the guards of Europe at this moment" (quoted in CBC News 2011). Between March and August some twenty-eight thousand migrants in Tripoli—mostly black Africans—were forced into leaky fishing boats by Qaddafi's security forces to make the perilous trip across the Mediterranean, sometimes with nothing more than a compass (Meo 2011). Nearly seventeen hundred people died en route, mostly from hunger and thirst.[15]

Whereas the Qaddafi regime used migrant workers in a cynical and desperate ploy to warn Europe against foreign intervention, the fate of migrant workers, particularly once they left Libya, seemed barely to register in the minds of the emerging leaders in Benghazi. Their sights were set on securing Tripoli and winning international legitimacy. By early March protesters in the western cities of Misrata, Zawiya, and Nalut had also succeeded in driving out Qaddafi's forces. Emboldened by the spate of recent victories, NTC members declared somewhat foolhardily that the council would send armed groups of volunteers to help liberate the rest of the country. Legions of men and teenage boys, politicized by the uprising and the possibilities it promised, signed up for the fight. In early March 2011, we spoke to Muhannad Bensadik, a twenty-one-year-old Libyan American medical student fighting on the front lines of the oil towns of Ras Lanuf and Brega. He said most of the volunteers were young men with no prior military training. With Qaddafi's brigades having fled or defected, the nascent "rebel" army had an outdated but massive stockpile of weapons at its disposal. "It's going to be a long, hard fight, but nobody's thinking of turning back," Muhannad said (personal interview 2011b).[16]

Despite a wave of defections from both high-level figures and military forces, Qaddafi's brigades did not ease their assault on the uprisings across the country. Fierce clashes continued in the western towns of Misrata and Zawiya, where Qaddafi's forces used tanks, warships, and warplanes to regain control. As towns fell back into the regime's hands, thousands of residents were rounded up, and anyone suspected of sympathizing with the uprising was arrested (Human Rights Watch 2011c). After rebel fighters in the east had made some initial gains, Qaddafi's better-trained fighters overpowered them and used their military edge to launch a counteroffensive into rebel-held territory. The fall of Tripoli began to seem like a pipe dream, and by mid-March, amid air strikes from Qaddafi's forces, the fighters had retreated closer to Benghazi.

Faced with the imminent possibility of a bloody takeover of the east of the country, calls for a no-fly zone grew even louder. These calls, it should be noted, were accompanied—both on the streets and in public statements by NTC officials—by a clear rejection of what was widely seen as an unacceptable form of foreign intervention: Western boots on the ground.

Enter NATO: Beyond Humanitarianism versus Imperialism

The decision to ask for foreign military support after having taken up arms against Qaddafi was not an easy one, but from the perspective of almost everyone we met in eastern Libya at the time, it was a necessary one. Many believed that had Qaddafi not used lethal force on peaceful demonstrators, the Libyan uprising could have had a very different trajectory.

Led by France and the United Kingdom, backed by the Arab League, and joined, after some hesitation, by the United States, the United Nations Security Council passed a no-fly zone resolution on March 17, invoking the international community's "responsibility to protect" civilians.[17] In Benghazi, the decision was met with relieved celebrations and a sense that it could not have come a moment too soon. What would have happened had Qaddafi's forces retaken the city will remain unknown.[18] But if Qaddafi's response in the first days of the uprising offered a glimpse of what his security forces were capable of, then the signs did not bode well. At the time, the brutality of the crackdown seemed to exceed the response of any other Arab regime facing a revolt; government forces used lethal force to quell protests almost immediately, relying on heavy arms, such as antiaircraft artillery and machine guns, and not just crowd-dispersal weapons.[19] Within days hospitals were strained by a surge of casualties and countless injuries from live ammunition. By March, the rebellion seemed to be losing momentum as Qaddafi's forces recaptured key cities in the west and began to push back in the east. Fears that losing ground to the regime would mean the end of the revolt and the collective punishment of those parts of the country that had dared to rise up were widespread. And the harrowing memories of Qaddafi's treatment of dissidents — the targeted killings, public hangings, and prison massacres, and the lethal suppression of public assemblies — left many Libyans feeling that if given the chance the regime would try to obliterate anyone remotely involved in the uprising. It was in this context that Benghazi residents were certain they faced an impending massacre and wholeheartedly supported France's bombing of Qaddafi's forces on the outskirts of their city on March 19. For months afterward, the stretch of highway west of the city was littered with the remains of Qaddafi's destroyed tanks, serving as a grim reminder of how quickly the revolution could have lost its hard-won gains.

In the United States, NATO's military action took center stage in almost every public discussion as most observers focused their attention on whether the Libya intervention marked a success or a failure for

U.S. foreign policy. On one side were liberals who applauded President Barack Obama's decision to involve the United States as a victory for humanitarian intervention. Libya was a successful military engagement, they claimed, one that wisely avoided the perils of the Iraq war: the action was multilateral, morally sound, and necessary. This triumphalist account conveniently elided the history of Libya's relations with the West since 2003, whereby successive American and European administrations had forged a cynical alliance with Qaddafi, even when it meant silencing his domestic opponents. This rapprochement was based on safeguarding core interests in national security, oil, and migration control. Notwithstanding the stirring rhetoric of Western leaders, the Libyan intervention was not about saving lives—indeed, the violent repression of protests in other Arab countries such as Bahrain and Yemen, although not on the same scale, never elicited such a forceful response—it was about geopolitics.

The Atlantic powers, led by France and the United Kingdom, were likely motivated by reasons beyond the humanitarian: domestic political considerations, a desire to harness the revolutionary momentum of an Arab Spring that had caught them off guard, and, most of all, a determination to avert the troublesome consequences of a prolonged conflict on the coast of North Africa. It was not Qaddafi who was an obstacle to Western interests, as some anti-imperialist critics mistakenly argued, but the prospect of a drawn-out struggle with no end in sight. With half the country out of Qaddafi's control after less than a week of protests and neither side willing to negotiate, the resulting instability could hamper oil production, erode border security, enable the proliferation of weapons, and nurture radical armed groups. Ironically, then, the very same reasons that prompted Western states to embrace Qaddafi in 2003 led them to help unseat him eight years later.

On the other side were naysayers of varying stripes: conservatives who sought to undermine the Obama administration, cynics who warned of a looming quagmire, and leftists who argued that the intervention was a success for imperialism, not humanitarianism.[20] For many anti-imperialist observers abroad, the foreign intervention eclipsed the popular origins of the uprising and came to define the character and fate of the Libyan struggle. Until early March, they had explained the protests across the Arab world in terms of political grievances, socio-economic pressures, and novel forms of popular mobilization. In the Libyan case, these prevailing frameworks were pushed aside as the possibility of a NATO mission loomed. NATO's involvement was seen as the factor that would most profoundly shape Libyan political dynamics in the future, raising questions about the international interests at stake and, in some cases, even about the credibility of the revolutionaries.[21] It evoked the specter of previous imperial misadventures carried out under the cover of humanitarian concerns.[22] Libya in 2011 became no different from Iraq in 2003, Afghanistan in 2001, and Kosovo in 1999.[23] The main politics that mattered were those set in motion by Western powers. Saving Libyans from the inevitable prospect of foreign domination became more important than supporting their ongoing struggle against a loathed dictator.

From the vantage point of Libyans on the ground, the reality was very different. NATO's role was never as all-encompassing as the critics perceived it to be, and the excitement and hope of liberation initiated by the mass uprising in February lived on, undeterred by foreign involvement. Few felt as though outsiders had stolen their revolution. The early days of the uprising had given people a glimpse of liberation, especially in western cities such as Misrata and Zawiya that had briefly broken free of Qaddafi's control before being violently retaken. What mattered most was to complete what they had begun. Almost every Libyan knew someone who had joined the armed struggle, and people dedicated themselves to helping in any way they could. Many expressed how, for the first time in their lives, they felt a sense of dignity and pride. While the main story abroad remained centered on the virtues and pitfalls of Western military action in a foreign country, for a vast segment of Libyan society that debate was superseded by something more important: a unique chance for freedom.

Although most Libyans who supported the uprising welcomed NATO's air cover and military support as a necessary compromise to meet the ultimate goal of defeating Qaddafi, the rhetoric of humanitarian intervention, so prevalent in the United States and Europe, had few takers. The irony of the sudden about-face of countries such as Italy, Britain, France, and the United States was not lost on Libyans. Many recalled how these countries had publicly supported Qaddafi over the past decade and even hailed his regime's alleged steps toward democratic reform. "The West does not pick democrats; it picks winners, even if they are murderers," Terbil joked with us cynically in late February when the possibility of a NATO intervention first appeared on the horizon (personal interview 2011c). For the most part, Libyan attitudes toward NATO were characterized by a cautious pragmatism. The initial gratitude quickly turned to criticism when NATO was seen to be slowing the advance of anti-Qaddafi fighters in order to push for a negotiated settlement with the regime. NATO—or any other international force—was barely present for some of the heaviest fighting in Misrata, only offering what many described as belated assistance on the edges of the battlefield. During the summer, many wondered whether the stalemate at the eastern oil port of Brega could really be blamed on the incompetence and inexperience of what the media routinely described as the "ragtag rebel army," or, as commentators such as Gilbert Achcar (2011) argued, was NATO stalling the revolutionaries' progress to keep all options on the table?

Despite the mounting criticism of NATO, at no point did Libyans who supported the uprising believe that the NATO intervention, hypocritical and self-serving as it may have been, undermined the righteousness of their struggle to topple Qaddafi. Ultimately, Libyans were simply willing to accept the contradiction that their aspirations for freedom and justice might coincide with the cynical motives of empire.

Civil War, Tribalism, or Revolution?

One of the enduring descriptions international observers used in characterizing the Libyan uprising was that of a civil war, a term that caught on once Libyan revolutionaries took up arms against the regime. It was a strange label, since Libya had not been particularly prone to internal strife and was one of the more homogeneous societies in the Middle East. With the exception of the Amazigh community, Libya had no major fissures along lines of religion, sect, or ethnicity.[24] When the armed struggle did begin, fighting very rarely took place between groups of civilians—as in Iraq or Lebanon—and the overarching dynamic was one of untrained volunteer fighters, backed by NATO and Qatar, taking on Qaddafi's trained military and security forces. While it is fair to say that NATO intervened in a popular armed uprising, the characterization that stuck was that of NATO taking sides in a civil war.

Early on, commentators drew on Ottoman-era divisions of the country into Cyrenaica to the east, Tripolitania to the west, and Fezzan to the south to explain what was happening as an uprising of the eastern tribes, historically loyal to the Senussi dynasty and opposed to Qaddafi (see Levinson 2011a). This was at a time when the NTC membership, as well as the discontent, seemed to be concentrated in the east of the country and international reporters were unable to report independently from cities in "Tripolitania."[25] While the east had effectively fallen from Qaddafi's hands and thrown open its borders to international reporters, the only way to report from the areas still controlled by Qaddafi's regime was to join a group of journalists invited and closely monitored by his information minister, Moussa Ibrahim. These journalists offered a fascinating look at the final days of a regime in crisis, but they were restricted to a single luxury hotel in Tripoli and could interview people only in the presence of a minder from the regime (see, for example, Miller 2011; Smith 2011). From late February on, however, there were consistent reports of ongoing clashes between civilian protesters and security forces in the western towns of Zawiya, Misrata, Nalut, and Tripoli.[26]

Some observers predicted imminent warfare between rival tribal groups that lacked any sense of national identity or civic belonging. "Libya is just the front-end of a series of moral and strategic dilemmas we are going to face as these Arab uprisings proceed through the tribes with flags," wrote Thomas L. Friedman (2011b) in the *New York Times*, speculating that Libya, Syria, Yemen, and Bahrain were all "Iraq-like civil-wars-in-waiting." Benjamin Barber (2011b), an American political theorist and longtime adviser to Saif al-Islam, excoriated amateur observers who mistakenly drew comparisons between Libya and Egypt. Instead, he boasted, the apparent stalemate in midspring vindicated his conviction that Libya's was not a democratic revolution but a tribal war costly in human lives (see also Barber 2011a).

Lost on these commentators was the possibility that what was unfolding in Libya was more of a city-based uprising in a highly urbanized country, motivated by a deep sense of injustice and a collective desire to rediscover a feeling of national pride.[27] Clan loyalties, while present and sometimes called upon by both Qaddafi and the rebel leadership, were not the main motivation for political action on Libya's streets and battlefields (see Fitzgerald 2011; Cherstich 2011; Benkato 2011; al-Ameri 2011). Libyan cities were diverse places, where people of all classes, ages, and tribes joined the revolt. Major tribes, even in Qaddafi strongholds such as Bani Walid and Sirte, included both loyalists and rebels, some of whom rose to the highest ranks of the NTC.[28]

This did not mean there were no rifts within the anti-Qaddafi consensus. As the uprising unfolded, one division that did surface was between cities that had developed divergent relationships with the regime. Qaddafi's uneven treatment of different parts of the country—whereby resistance to his regime was punished by deliberate impoverishment and loyalty was rewarded by an infusion of public funds—was largely to blame for this. But the more immediate reason for the rivalry between cities was the fact that the uprising had a distinct history in each town and city in Libya: whereas Benghazi and areas farther east became relatively calm after the initial week of clashes (except for the day before the French bombing on March 19, 2011), other parts of the country had a much longer and bloodier struggle. Thus Benghazians, Misratans, Tripolitans, and Berbers from the Nafusa mountains all developed their own narratives about who was leading the revolt and the unique sacrifices they made to topple the regime. Libyans' perceptions of events were shaped largely by the cities they were from, not by their tribal affiliations.

"Flickers" of al-Qaeda

When Libyans decided, in the face of massive state violence, to take up arms against the regime, one of their first challenges was to find a group of experienced fighters who could take on Qaddafi's well-trained forces. At first the uprising's fighting forces consisted of defected members of Qaddafi's forces, such as Abdel Fattah Younes, but soon another category of battle-hardened trainers and military leaders emerged. To the consternation of Western observers, these were individuals who had cut their teeth in the Afghan jihad against the Soviets and had later gone on to fight American troops in Iraq and Afghanistan. Most were former members of the Libyan Islamic Fighting Group, which had mounted fierce armed opposition to Qaddafi in the early 1990s before the movement was brutally crushed.

In March, a flurry of news reports noted that the eastern town of Dernah had sent the highest number of suicide bombers to Iraq.[29] At a U.S. Senate hearing, Admiral James Stavridis, NATO supreme commander for Europe, said that U.S. intelligence had picked up "flickers" of a potential al-Qaeda or Hezbollah presence among the fighters (Ryan and Cornwell 2011). Indeed, hundreds of LIFG members who survived Qaddafi's crackdown fled to Sudan and Afghanistan in the late 1990s, where some of them reportedly trained in al-Qaeda camps. Their precise affiliation with al-Qaeda, however, remained a matter of dispute.[30] But a key part of the story of "al-Qaeda" in the Libyan uprising was often elided: the role of the United States and the United Kingdom in the troubled trajectory of former LIFG members in the 2000s.

In exchange for post–September 11, 2001, intelligence from the Qaddafi regime on Islamists in Afghanistan in 2003, the Bush administration added the LIFG to its list of foreign terrorist organizations. As was revealed by the stash of documents found in former intelligence chief Moussa Koussa's office in late August, the Bush and Blair administrations relied almost entirely on Libyan intelligence sources to identify, capture, torture, imprison, and ultimately "render" some former LIFG members back to Libya (Human Rights Watch 2011f; see also Nordland 2011). Former LIFG members told Human Rights Watch they had been subjected to waterboarding and other forms of torture in CIA-run detention centers in Afghanistan (Human Rights Watch 2012a).

Some of the most prominent trainers of the rebel forces in 2011 included those who had been imprisoned at Guantánamo Bay, such as Abu Sufian Bin Qumu and others who were victims of the CIA's extraordinary rendition program, including Belhaj. They were all transferred to Libya, where they joined hundreds of other political prisoners in Abu Salim prison. There, Belhaj and other former LIFG members publicly renounced violence. In 2010, many were released following a well-publicized reconciliation initiative with Islamists led by Saif al-Islam.

Just before the protests broke out in February 2011, some former LIFG members had formed a new organization called the Libyan Islamic Movement for Change, which advocated peaceful political opposition to the Qaddafi regime. A week into the revolt, they announced their support for the "February 17 revolution," praising the Libyan air force pilots who had refused to attack protesters and urging them to attack Bab al-Aziziya instead. While lambasting Western nations for silence on Qaddafi's campaign of violence and complicity with his abuses, they also called for international intervention, adding that they would "accept the hand of any who come to their aid at this critical moment in their history" (*Asharq al-Awsat* 2011).

When some Western observers censured the Obama administration and NATO for supporting an uprising led by militant Islamists, many Libyans laughed this off, hearing echoes of Qaddafi blaming al-Qaeda for the popular revolt.[31] During the early months of the uprising, Libyans saw former LIFG members as long-standing opponents of the Qaddafi regime, Islamist nationalists rather than proponents of global jihad or terrorism (Abdurrahman 2011; Pelham 2012). Belhaj, in particular, shot to fame in late August as the military leader who led the assault on Qaddafi's compound of Bab al-Aziziya.

For many Libyans we spoke to in 2011, the danger was not a jihadist takeover of the Libyan struggle but deepening fractures among rebel forces that would, for example, pit Islamists against defected Qaddafi officials such as Abdel Fattah Younes.[32] At the helm of Tripoli's military council after Qaddafi's forces were routed from the Libyan capital, Belhaj spoke out forcefully against attempts to marginalize Islamists in the new order. "It is as though they want to push Islamists towards a nondemocratic option by alienating and marginalizing them," he wrote in an article for the *Guardian* in September. "We will not allow this: all Libyans are partners in this revolution and all should be part of building the future of this country" (Belhaj 2011).

The New Libya

After eight months of violent revolution and countless deaths on all sides, most Libyans entered the post-Qaddafi era trying to rebuild their lives and their battle-scarred country amid the mounting challenges of reconciliation and disarmament. Although the uprising developed a civilian leadership with remarkable speed, the NTC was deeply divided,

Anjali Kamat and Ahmad Shokr

and state institutions remained remarkably weak if not altogether absent. To the alarm of many inside and outside Libya, the country's transitional leadership had little control over the hundreds of armed groups that mushroomed in the wake of the uprising. As the initial elation over the fall of Qaddafi's regime faded, Libyans experienced a growing recognition that the challenges ahead were grave, and that in many senses the real struggle for a new and transformed Libya was only just beginning.

Reconciliation, Revenge, and Militarization

One of the earliest controversies in the new Libya concerned the presence of Qaddafi-era officials and technocrats who became prominent figures on the NTC. The council publicly promised to investigate and try all former Qaddafi-era officials who were involved in murder, torture, and corruption, but the continued presence of individuals from the old regime, many of whom were affiliated with the Western-backed reform efforts led by Saif al-Islam, remained a source of contention for months. These individuals included, most prominently, a key figure who headed the NTC during the course of the uprising—the U.S.-trained neoliberal economist Mahmoud Jibril. (In September 2012, Jibril narrowly lost the newly elected national congress's vote for prime minister to Mustafa Abu Shagour, a U.S.-trained engineer who is close to Mohamed Magarief, the head of the congress and a longtime regime dissident.) Many Libyans initially welcomed Jibril's efforts to win international support, but activists and fighters would soon call into question his political credibility and representativeness. Figures such as Jibril were seen to have jumped ship after the start of the revolt, spending most of the eight months of fighting in Rome, Paris, London, Doha, and Washington, D.C., negotiating a political transition with the same politicians who had become Qaddafi's most powerful friends over the past decade.

Western countries, particularly the United Kingdom, France, and Italy, were seen to have supported the reintegration of select former Qaddafi-era officials—particularly those associated with Saif al-Islam's reform program. The leaked Western-backed NTC draft road map for Libya's future emphasized the need to include former regime officials in the new dispensation to avoid a situation like that seen in postinvasion Iraq in 2003, where the U.S.-promoted de-Baathification program led to civil war.[33] Activists as well as armed groups hotly disputed this characterization, arguing that Libya is not Iraq and that no former officials with blood on their hands should be given positions of power before they had been tried.[34]

With the existing balance of weapons—almost all of which were in the hands of the fighters—these demands for accountability could not be dismissed lightly. Libya had witnessed an unprecedented militarization of its civilian population since the uprising began. When Qaddafi's apparatus crumbled in city after city in the east, the first sites to be abandoned were the warehouses where vast stockpiles of weapons were stored. As opposition fighters closed in on Tripoli and other cities still under his control, Qaddafi distributed arms supplies to civilian volunteers. As the months dragged on, communities amassed as many weapons as they could, fearful of future retribution for their perceived support of or opposition to Qaddafi.

In September 2011, Zahi Mogherbi, a political science professor in Benghazi who advised the NTC, told us the situation was "extremely volatile." "Once the battle against Qaddafi and his forces is officially declared to be over, what will happen to these militias and all these weapons?" he asked, referring to the armed brigades that had been organized in towns across Libya to fight Qaddafi's forces. "We Libyans have to get rid of these militias or organize them immediately; I'm afraid that if we fail to do our job, NATO or others will intervene," he warned (personal interview 2011d). In the months that followed, however, only a handful of militias were successfully disbanded; hundreds of others remained beyond the control of the fragile leadership, whether the NTC or the elected government that followed (Amnesty International 2012). As for the munitions, Human Rights Watch (2011e) estimated that thousands of weapons, including powerful surface-to-air missiles, had gone missing.[35]

The fall of Tripoli unleashed an unsavory wave of retribution that the NTC made little effort to contain. Armed revolutionary brigades that had formed in towns across Libya to counter Qaddafi's forces took it upon themselves to "complete the revolution," drawing up "wanted lists" of people who had been pro-Qaddafi, either during the uprising or in the four decades before it. Ibrahim, a former oil engineer from Misrata turned commander, plainly told us his brigade did not trust the NTC: "We don't want to be ruled by people who worked for Qaddafi for forty-two years and never said anything against him." The fight would be over, he said, only after Qaddafi was killed and "we know for sure that his people can no longer do anything to us" (personal interview 2011e).

In town after town, makeshift detention centers run by bands of rebel fighters filled up with people whom others perceived as having supported or, worse, fought for Qaddafi. To the dismay of the Libyan human rights activists who had struggled for years against Qaddafi's security state and his brutal retaliatory policies toward anyone who opposed him, rebel fighters abused prisoners and summarily executed suspected Qaddafi fighters (Human Rights Watch 2011a, 2011b; Amnesty International 2011b). Among those most victimized in the ugly reprisals were dark-skinned Libyans and sub-Saharan African migrant workers, partly as a result of persistent claims about Qaddafi's use of African mercenaries to attack civilian protesters as well as rebel fighters.[36] "They kept calling me a mercenary and one of Qaddafi's African dogs," said one prisoner we met at a detention center in Misrata, describing what happened when anti-Qaddafi fighters captured him. The slight twenty-five-year-old from the southern Libyan town of Sabha used to play in Qaddafi's military band. "If your skin is black you are not considered Libyan; this is the problem of the revolution. Don't you think this is racism?" he asked bitterly (personal interview 2011f). NTC officials never adequately addressed the racist aspects of the retributive attacks, although they issued a mild rebuke against armed groups taking the law into their own hands. Their words seemed to have little effect, however.

One of the most vicious divides of the uprising, that between the neighboring towns of Tawergha and Misrata, remained smoldering months later. Tawergha, a small town of largely dark-skinned Libyans that had fallen into Qaddafi's favor in recent years, was seen to have actively participated in the brutal siege of Misrata, which suffered attacks from Grad rockets and cluster bombs. Hundreds of Tawerghans joined Qaddafi's army during this period, but when his forces were routed over the summer, fighters from the hundred different armed brigades in Misrata went on a vengeful rampage in Tawergha. The town's thirty thousand residents fled and remained fearful of ever returning (Human Rights Watch 2011d).

Similar retaliatory attacks took place in several flashpoint towns across the country after the fall of Tripoli in August 2011. Brigades from Souq al-Jumaa and Misrata led attacks on Bani Walid and Sirte, which were perceived to be loyalist bastions, and in the Nafusa mountains brigades from Zintan attacked the Mshashiya and Qawalish communities that had allegedly backed Qaddafi. Fierce armed battles were fought between Amazigh militias from Zuwara in northwest Libya and the neighboring Arab towns of Jmail and Rijdalin, fueled by preexisting land disputes, resentment over Qaddafi's patronage system that had marginalized Zuwara, and attempts to control border routes to Tunisia. Fighting in the southern border areas of Sebha and Kufra between the Arab Zway and the black Toubou was also driven by struggles over the lucrative trans-Saharan smuggling routes (Pelham 2012).

Although the NTC tried to bring the myriad revolutionary brigades under its control, it seemed to have subcontracted some security responsibilities to autonomous armed groups that functioned in parallel to the fledgling army and police forces set up in the aftermath of the uprising.[37] This created a climate of impunity for militias and concerns over a breakdown in security. In Benghazi, several military officers and figures associated with the former regime had been assassinated, and armed gangs violently disrupted the elections in July 2012. In Tripoli, Misrata, and Zlitan, police reportedly stood by as armed Salafists attacked Sufi shrines. According to a March 2012 report published by the Congressional Research Service in the United States, "Libya's security remains a function of Libyans' self-restraint rather than the capability of security authorities" (Blanchard 2012, 8).

It was only after the September 2012 armed attack on the U.S. diplomatic mission in Benghazi that the de facto immunity enjoyed by the militias took on the shape of a national emergency. On September 11, 2012, a heavily armed militia with suspected ties to al-Qaeda stormed the U.S. compound, killing Ambassador Christopher Stevens and three other Americans. One of them was a former Navy Seal who had reportedly been sent to Libya by the U.S. State Department to help track down and destroy missing munitions (Ferran 2012). The attack led to the evacuation of nearly a dozen CIA operatives and contractors from Benghazi, where the agency had maintained a covert presence, apparently without the full knowledge of Libya's leaders. One American official called the attack "a catastrophic intelligence loss" (quoted in Schmitt, Cooper, and Schmidt 2012).

Foreign Influence: NATO and Qatar

NATO's military operations ended officially on October 31, 2011, soon after the capture and killing of Qaddafi and the declaration of the complete liberation of the country. The dead remained uncounted, but estimates were staggering, though unverifiable. In April, the NTC estimated that between ten thousand and thirty thousand Libyans had been killed in the fighting. By late August, that figure went up to fifty thousand. According to Human Rights Watch (2012b), NATO air strikes killed at least seventy-two civilians, including women and children, in incidents that the alliance had refused to investigate.[38] There had been growing fears outside Libya about the precedent that NATO's mission would set. In intervening in Libya, NATO did overstep its mandate as defined in a U.N. Security Council resolution of 1973, a fact that had observers worried about the continued use of the "responsibility to protect" as a cover for regime change and prolonged Western military and security actions.

Inside Libya, the discussion had been largely about how foreign players may influence the political process. Hassan Al-Amin explained in September 2011 that activists like him appreciated NATO's support in their moment of need, but they will be vigilant in monitoring continuing foreign influence in Libya: "We have been through too much pain and lost too many lives in this revolution to hand it over to a foreign power—we will not allow our country to be exploited" (personal interview 2011g). Once Libyans were free of Qaddafi's control, the armed presence of foreigners became a controversial matter even among NTC members, who were quick to publicly reject Western and U.N. ground troops, military bases, and private security contractors.[39] Soon after, however, the NTC quietly awarded "no objection" documents to half a dozen British, Canadian, and French security firms, allowing them to operate inside Libya to provide security for foreign embassies and companies (United Press International 2011). In the aftermath of the attack on the U.S. consulate in Benghazi in September 2012, the Obama administration admitted it had been flying drones over eastern Libya for almost a year after the official end of NATO's mission, reportedly for surveillance purposes and with the consent of the Libyan government (Ackerman 2012).[40] Following the attack, the United States rushed fifty marines, more drones, and warships to Libya to assist with the hunt for the attackers.

However, one should be careful not to exaggerate Libya's vulnerability to foreign control post-Qaddafi. Libya was not in the full grip of any single external player as foreign agendas continued to be tempered by local dynamics and contestations. Perhaps the most significant, although controversial, check against the ability of Western and Gulf states to determine the outcome of the revolt had been the heterogeneity of the interim Libyan authorities, the military leadership, and the militias. The West might have had the ear of technocrats such as Mahmoud Jibril, Ali Issawi, and Ali Tarhouni and former CIA asset turned rebel commander Khalifa Heftir, but much harder to win over were the activist lawyers such as Terbil or the Islamists such as Belhaj and some of the powerful local militias (Prashad 2011; Fadel 2011). For some months it seemed as though Heftir's authority had been overshadowed by figures such as Belhaj, whose personal history revealed an uneasy relationship with the West. Far from being compliant with Western demands, Belhaj, among his first public comments after the fall of Tripoli, demanded an apology from the CIA and MI6 for their role in his torture and detention (Chulov 2011).

As for regional powers such as Qatar, they were likely to face the same difficulties. From March 2011 Qatar provided crucial financial, military, and media support to the NTC and anti-Qaddafi fighters (Kerr 2011; Krauss 2011). Qatar helped open credit lines for the NTC, worked around the embargo to market Libyan oil before production largely came to a standstill, supplied diesel to minimize power cuts in eastern Libya, and hosted a "Free Libya" satellite channel. The small and wealthy kingdom not only participated in NATO's air support but also delivered significant amounts of updated arms and communications equipment to the fighters, and, along with the United Arab Emirates and Jordan, sent hundreds of special forces to Libya. Qatar also claims it provided critical training to Libyan fighters in the Nafusa mountains for the advance into Tripoli and acted as a link between NATO and the fighters (Black 2011).

Since the fall of Tripoli, Qatar's popularity with Libyans has waned as it has sought to extend its influence in Libya by supporting key Islamist players. Blogger Ghaidaa Al-Tawati, who spent the early months of the uprising imprisoned at Abu Salim, told us in September 2011 that she did not want Libya's future to be shaped by either former Qaddafi officials or outside powers and wanted limits instituted on the amount of funding Qatar and other foreign countries can channel to Libyan political parties. "I'm nervous about the two competing authoritarian strands — Islamist and liberal — trying to take over. We don't want extremists from either side in charge," she said (personal interview 2011h). In the months that followed, Libyans became more polarized around the question of Qatari influence in domestic politics. Qatar backed figures such as Belhaj and preacher Ali Sallabi, who emerged as two of the most powerful voices opposed to allowing former Qaddafi officials to gain the upper hand within the power structure of the NTC.[41] Briefly, it seemed as though Belhaj and Sallabi had taken a position that resonated with the mass of fighters on the ground who did not want to see their sacrifices hijacked by elite power brokers. But that would soon change.

Anticipating a challenge from their political competitors, and unnerved by Qatar's continued support for some Islamist militias, NTC leaders began to confront the Gulf emirate more openly. In October 2011, then interim prime minister Ali Tarhouni inveighed against any attempts to circumvent the NTC and directly fund and arm rebel militias: "It's time we publicly declare that anyone who wants to come to our house has to knock on our front door first," he said (quoted in Levinson 2011b). In a sign of growing tensions within the NATO–Qatar coalition, an unnamed Western "senior diplomat" questioned Qatar's agenda in Libya: "Qatar is not being respectful, and there is a feeling that it is riding roughshod over the issue of the country's sovereignty" (quoted in Beaumont 2011). The increasingly vocal stance taken by NTC leaders against Qatar seemed to have pervaded the Libyan electorate, which voted against Islamists in the first post-Qaddafi national election in 2012.

While the future of foreign military influence in Libya remained unclear, attempts to expand and consolidate economic influence were likely to intensify. Here the interests of Western and Gulf states may have been aligned quite well. Several NTC officials said that countries that sided against Qaddafi during the revolt would get preferential economic treatment, a pledge that was warmly received in the West. Immediately after the fall of Tripoli, American and European officials wasted no time before coaxing investors to seize the opportunity for lucrative contracts, particularly in oil and reconstruction.[42] After a meeting in September with representatives of 150 American companies, U.S. ambassador to Libya Gene A. Cretz remarked that oil is the "jewel in the crown of Libyan natural resources" and promised his best efforts to bring in American businesses on a "fairly big scale" (quoted in Kirkpatrick 2011).[43] As trade delegations from Western Europe flocked to Libya, China and Russia scrambled to recognize the NTC and salvage billions of dollars in contracts (Saigol and Sanderson 2011; Jian 2011).[44] Qatar had already made one of the first post-Qaddafi foreign investments, purchasing a major stake in Libya's leading private bank (Daragahi 2012).

At the time of this writing only a handful of contracts had been awarded, with very few going to the United States or the United Kingdom (Stephen and Goodley 2012). As a result of the political instability and lingering security concerns, the bonanza that foreign governments and investors anticipated has been slow to materialize. One fear has been that Libya will experience a long period of instability similar to that in Iraq. Eyeing the massive potential for profits in Libya, one of the biggest Emirati investors during the Qaddafi era said, "Iraq was once the great hope, but nothing much has happened. I hope here [in Libya] they speed up decision making and work quickly to sort out their issues — then we will see lots of UAE investors here, otherwise they will look elsewhere" (quoted in Kerr 2012).

In the lucrative oil sector in particular, questions remained about how long Qaddafi-era contracts would be honored and how the new allocation process would work. In October 2011, Libya initiated corruption probes into Qaddafi-era oil contracts, and the Securities and Exchange Commission in the United States was also investigating French and Italian oil deals with Libya that might have violated the U.S. Foreign Corruption Practice Act (Osgood 2012; Donati and Gumuchian 2011). But as the new government took shape, it was hoped that promises to dispense with the old would expand beyond questions of transparency and accountability and spill over into the realm of economic policy. Unlike other Middle Eastern countries where neoliberal reforms had gone into full swing, Libya witnessed only a moderate opening over the previous decade, with many sectors of the economy remaining under extensive state control.[45] A clear economic policy for the coming period was yet to be outlined, but there was a widespread desire in Libya to make a decisive break with the past and provide the language of free market reform some traction. Already, there were signals that some of the power brokers who had been on the NTC—Mahmoud Jibril, Ali Issawi, Ali Tarhouni, Abdallah Shamie—favored greater privatization and foreign investment (Agènce France Presse 2011). If they could retain their influence over Libya's new government, a program of economic liberalization might well be on the horizon.

In the final analysis, Libya's new leaders were not the creation of foreign powers. The men described above emerged to fill the leadership void at a time when no other forces were organized enough to do so. With Qaddafi stymieing the possibility of any homegrown political alternatives, it is no surprise that those who rose to power during the conflict were defected figures from within the reformist wing of the regime or the opposition forces that developed in exile. Just as they did in postuprising Egypt and Tunisia, foreign powers worked with those local figures and groups who seemed most organized, credible, and ready to lead in a manner that was not antagonistic to Western and regional interests. Whatever might happen in Libya in the following years should not be seen simply in terms of the dictates of the NATO alliance. Libya is part of the complex and changing geography of the region, where early signs in the post-Qaddafi era portend the emergence of Islamist players onto the political scene, a more robust role for Gulf countries and capital, a fragmented security landscape, and, lest we forget, more vocal and defiant publics.

Rebuilding from Below

Like its North African neighbors to the east and west, Libya was emerging from dictatorship and revolution to embark on a journey toward a more pluralistic political order. Despite the odds, in July 2012, 65 percent of eligible Libyans voted in their country's first free elections for the two hundred–member General National Congress, which replaced the unelected NTC. Barring a few incidents of violence—most prominently in Benghazi—the elections were largely peaceful (Kirkpatrick 2012). The landslide win for the liberal National Forces Alliance led by Mahmoud Jibril came as a surprise to those expecting an Islamist victory. But Libya's Muslim Brotherhood was never as organized as its counterparts in Egypt; notwithstanding widespread criticism of Jibril, the overt backing the Islamist parties (the Brotherhood and a smaller party headed by Belhaj) received from outside players such as Qatar ultimately worked against them.

The immediate challenges were daunting: reining in the unaccountable militias and bringing a sense of security to the country without compromising on human rights, trying Qaddafi-era officials for their crimes, developing a system to distribute oil revenues equitably, and drafting Libya's first democratic constitution that would ensure fair representation for all parts of the country and enshrine equal civil and political rights for all Libyans. Building more accountable and representative state institutions, with all the political battles that process involves, would have a significant impact on Libya's future. But the bigger challenge of creating a democratic society would require mobilizing the energies of people across the country in the same transformative way that the revolution of 2011 did.

For decades, Qaddafi had denied Libyans the right to assume any independent control over their own lives. By criminalizing freedom of expression and freedom of association, he not only restricted dissent but also, more important, foreclosed the possibility for any kind of democratic politics. More than closure, Qaddafi's demise marked an unprecedented opening: a new Libya where real political struggles could be fought. The future of Libyan democracy would depend not only on politicians' pledges of reform but also on the people's feelings of empowerment in demanding their rights. Perhaps struggle, not transition, would be the appropriate metaphor for coming times.

In the broadest sense, the impending battles would be over constructing an open democratic political culture and a strong independent civil society that is unafraid to hold those in power accountable, regardless of whether their authority is political, military, religious, or corporate. This had not been easy; many of the hundreds of activists who had been at the forefront of the protests when they first broke out had been relegated to the margins. Law professor Hana El-Gallal from Benghazi and imprisoned blogger Ghaidaa Al-Tawati from Tripoli both worried that women's roles—which had been central at the start of the uprising—were being sidelined. In the first months of the uprising, El-Gallal and other lawyers had played advisory roles in the NTC; by the end of the year they had resigned and were publicly protesting the council's lack of transparency. "We need to monitor the actions of the new government, and not just talk about Qaddafi's crimes," said El-Gallal, who has started an independent human rights organization (personal interview 2011i). "We shouldn't be making heroes of our new leaders, or else we will just end up with repeating what happened under Qaddafi," warned Al-Tawati (personal interview 2011h). Another Benghazi-based activist, Mohammad Abu El Naja, who had been imprisoned in Abu Salim for eight years, said he sometimes feared that the NTC could just end up "replacing Qaddafi with another dictatorship" unless there was constant pressure to "replace the whole system with a civil democratic state" (personal interview 2011j).

Yet a stubborn sense of hope permeated the pessimism among even these activists. Indeed, there were several positive signs: dozens of new newspapers were in circulation, cultural activities were flourishing, activists were pressing for public investigations into revenge attacks, feminists were calling for expanded citizenship rights for women, lawyers had set up organizations to monitor the new government and push for transparency in its deals with foreign corporations and governments, civilians had held numerous rallies urging rebel militias to disarm, and workers were organizing themselves and staging strikes.[46]

As in any uprising against an authoritarian regime that employed quasi-progressive rhetoric, a future challenge for Libyan progressives

will be to distinguish clearly between the rejection of Qaddafi's socialist, anti-imperialist, and pan-Africanist posturing and the wholesale
abandonment of liberatory principles in domestic and international
policies. A failure to do so will risk entrenching the most reactionary
aspects of the anti-Qaddafi coalition, threaten the few legal and social
protections that did exist under Qaddafi, and discredit future demands
from women, workers, immigrants, and secular activists as representing
the "old regime."

Conclusion

Unlike the Eastern European revolts of 1989, from which new states
emerged into a world defined by American hegemony and the triumph
of free market principles, the Arab revolts broke out in a changing global
landscape where such certainties may have been eroding. Rather than
celebrate the Libya war as a triumph of humanitarianism or deplore it as
yet another imperial blunder or a protracted civil war, it is best to situate
it within the novel context of the Arab Spring, with all the uncertainties
that development would bring for both the Arab world and the West.

The Arab revolts represented the most serious challenge to U.S.
dominance in the Middle East since America's rise to global superpower
status after World War II. The United States' long-standing calculus in
the region—investing in authoritarian stability to safeguard American
economic and geopolitical interests—had been turned on its head.
Since January 2011, the Obama administration, along with its European
partners, had been scrambling to contain the potential damage caused
by the overthrow of key allies across the region. Washington's immediate response was to voice nominal support for political dialogue and
reform while at the same time closing ranks with the Gulf monarchies
and backing powers across the region that could salvage as much of the
prerevolution status quo as possible. However, it remained unclear what
long-term adjustments these rebellions would impose on U.S. foreign
policy in the Middle East.

As for the European powers and the Gulf Cooperation Council—
Britain, France, and Qatar—their intervention in Libya marked an
aggressive change of course. With the United States recovering from

its debacles in Iraq and Afghanistan and consumed by its own fiscal and economic troubles, Libya offered an opportunity for other players to assert their influence on the global stage.

But in Libya, as in every country across the Middle East, imperial ambitions as well as local and regional reactionary forces were vulnerable to public contestation. The mere fact of NATO's intervention did not necessarily determine the outcome of the Libyan revolt in a manner that served foreign interests at the expense of popular aspirations. Libyan novelist Hisham Matar, whom we met in August 2011, best expressed what seemed to be a widespread sentiment: "Whatever the setbacks may be, this revolution has fundamentally changed Libyans; it has given us a glimpse, for the first time in our lives, of the possibility of an alternate future, of the best versions of ourselves, and it might take years before we can realize this, but no one can take this vision away from us" (personal interview 2011k). Ultimately, it will be up to Libyans to hold their new leaders to account and to continue fighting for the ideals of their revolution. Toward that end, the ouster of Qaddafi was a crucial first step that rid a people of a vicious tyrant and set them free for the many struggles to come. The fate of the Libyan revolution is still far from a fait accompli.

Notes

1. For a more exhaustive account of these events, see Human Rights Watch (2009b).

2. See the U.S. embassy cable dated February 15, 2008, with the subject line "Extremism in Eastern Libya," available on WikiLeaks, http://wikileaks.org/cable/2008/02/08TRIPOLI120.html (accessed September 24, 2012).

3. In September 2000, the simmering anti-immigrant sentiment exploded, and 130 sub-Saharan African workers were killed in race riots in Zawiya and Tripoli. Those found responsible were given harsh sentences, but the regime also described migrants as a fifth column and as criminals and drug traffickers. This is when the language of African migrants being "in transit" to Europe or coming to Libya "illegally" also began to gain traction (see Bredeloup and Pliez 2011).

4. From 2003 through 2006, Libya forcibly expelled some two hundred thousand migrant workers. For more on Libya's detention and abuses of migrant workers, see Human Rights Watch (2009a).

5. See the U.S. embassy cable dated November 21, 2007, with the subject line "Libyan Market Tests International Oil and Gas Companies," available on WikiLeaks, http://wikileaks.org/cable/2007/11/07TRIPOLI979.html (accessed September 25, 2012).

6. See also the U.S. embassy cable dated May 10, 2006, with the subject line "Qadhafi Incorporated," available on WikiLeaks, http://wikileaks.org/cable/2006/05/06TRIPOLI198.html (accessed September 25, 2012).

7. According to the World Bank (2006), an estimated 75 percent of employed Libyans worked in the public sector in 2006. State employees' salaries had been largely frozen since the early 1980s, with a minimum public-sector wage set at 150 Libyan dinars (roughly US$200) per month. For years the Libyan government contemplated public-sector wage reform, but it made little progress. See the U.S. embassy cable dated November 10, 2006, with the subject line "Wage and Pension Reform Unfolding in Libya's Own Style," available on WikiLeaks, http://wikileaks.ch/cable/2006/11/06TRIPOLI647.html, and also the material on Libya on the African Economic Outlook Web site (full country note, "Libya," http://www.africaneconomicoutlook.org/en/countries/north-africa/libya; accessed March 11, 2013).

8. Under Qaddafi, Libya was one of the top five funders of the African Union. Qaddafi also funded infrastructure and development projects, as well as numerous rebel movements across sub-Saharan Africa.

9. Data from the World Bank, http://data.worldbank.org/country/libya, and from the UNESCO Institute for Statistics, http://stats.uis.unesco.org.

10. Although limited in their implementation, the economic reforms and privatization efforts began to have disruptive effects on vulnerable segments of Libyan society. In 2005, the Ghanem government began implementing plans to cut US$5 billion in subsidies for basic goods and services. By 2009, amid soaring global food prices, Libya was suffering from high inflation on consumer goods, especially previously subsidized foodstuffs such as sugar, rice, and flour, with prices nearly doubling over two years. See Wahby (2005) and the U.S. embassy cable dated January 4, 2009, with the subject line "Inflation on the Rise in Libya," available on WikiLeaks, http://wikileaks.org/cable/2009/01/09TRIPOLI1.html (accessed September 25, 2012). As part of its drive to privatize more than 350 state-owned companies, the government adopted a program in 2006 to transfer four hundred thousand government employees out of the public sector. By 2009, less than half of them had successfully transitioned into private-sector jobs. See the country note on Libya on the African Economic Outlook Web site (as cited in note 7 above).

11. Libya's unemployment rate is difficult to measure accurately, but most estimates place it within this range. In April 2011, the World Bank estimated Libya's unemployment rate to be 30 percent (see World Bank 2011).

12. Abdel Jalil was respected among Qaddafi's critics even before the uprising, for his unprecedented public condemnation of Qaddafi's security apparatus when he served as minister of justice and for highlighting the plight of political prisoners (see Human Rights Watch 2009b).

13. Peter Bouckaert, emergencies director of Human Rights Watch, made this observation in an interview with Kamat (2011c).

14. An estimated seven hundred thousand to one million migrants have fled Libya since February 2011, according to numbers from the International Organization for Migration.

15. Italian journalist and activist Gabriele Del Grande tracks these figures on his blog Fortress Europe. See the entry for August 8, 2011, at http://fortresseurope. blogspot.com/2011/08/invasion-that-is-not-there-from-libya.html. See also Shenker (2011).

16. Muhannad Bensadik was killed by Qaddafi's forces a few days after we spoke to him. See Anjali Kamat's (2011a) interview with Muhannad for *Democracy Now!*

17. On the U.S. hesitancy, see Landay (2011). For a later account that gives the United States a more central role, see Warrick (2011).

18. Numerous commentators have questioned the veracity of claims that a massacre would have taken place, arguing that this assertion simply provided a pretext for Western military intervention (see, for example, Miles 2011). Regardless of whether or not a massacre would likely have occurred, from what we observed in eastern Libya we can say that fears of a possible massacre were real.

19. Amnesty International conducted a fact-finding visit to Libya from February 26 to May 28, 2011. The final report accuses Libyan security forces of firing live ammunition into crowds without warning in the first days of the revolt. It also quotes local medical sources who said that in Benghazi alone 109 people died as a result of gunshot wounds sustained during antigovernment protests and clashes with security forces, including peaceful protesters and others who did not pose a threat to the security forces. In Tripoli, security forces fired on protesters in the central Green Square on February 20, 2011, reportedly causing deaths and injuries (Amnesty International 2011a). On February 25, 2011, Amnesty International called on the U.N. Security Council to refer the situation in Libya to the International Criminal Court and to impose an immediate arms embargo (Amnesty International 2011c).

20. For critiques of the Libya intervention by American conservatives and liberals, see Gelb (2011), Cornwell (2011), and Friedman (2011a).

21. Some antiwar critics argued that the Libya war was simply a conflict over natural resources and economic domination (see Dreyfuss 2011; Ratner and Weiss 2011). Others, such as Patrick Cockburn (2011), accused Western powers of selecting Libya's new leaders, in typical colonial fashion, and discredited the NTC as a "Benghazi junta." In March, French philosopher Alain Badiou went so far as to

deny that mass protests of the kind seen in Egypt and Tunisia were taking place in Libya (see "An Open Letter from Alain Badiou to Jean-Luc Nancy," http://www.versobooks.com/blogs/463; accessed March 11, 2013).

22. For critiques of humanitarian intervention, see Falk (2011), Asli Bali and Ziad Abu-Rish (2011), and Mamdani (2011a).

23. On comparisons of Libya with Kosovo/Iraq/Afghanistan, see Johnstone (2011), Bricmont (2011), Rieff (2011), and Ahmad (2011).

24. The Amazigh community (5–10 percent of the population) had long been persecuted by the Qaddafi regime and had been unable to win state recognition for their culture and language. A 2008 U.S. diplomatic cable noted that American diplomats were barred from visiting Amazigh areas and narrated an account of Qaddafi warning Amazigh leaders to "call yourselves whatever you want inside your homes—Berbers, children of Satan, whatever—but you are only Libyans when you leave your homes." The cable, dated July 3, 2008, with the subject line "Libya's Berber Minority Still Out in the Cold," is available on WikiLeaks, http://wikileaks.org/cable/2008/07/08TRIPOLI530.html. Members of the Amazigh community were enthusiastic supporters of the 2011 uprising and formed a strong component of the resistance to Qaddafi's regime (see Thorne 2011).

25. As noted previously, the NTC claimed that the identities of many of its members outside the east had to be kept secret as long as those parts of the country remained under Qaddafi's control.

26. See Robert Mackey's "The Lede" blog on the *New York Times* Web site for multimedia reports of protests across Libya (including the western cities of Tripoli, Misrata, Zawiya, and Sabratha) from February 23, 2011, onward (http://thelede.blogs.nytimes.com).

27. According to the World Bank, 78 percent of Libya's population lived in urban areas in 2010 (see http://data.worldbank.org/indicator/sp.urb.totl.in.zs; accessed November 3, 2011).

28. Mahmoud Jibril, for example, is from the Warfalla tribe in Bani Walid, the second-to-last city to fall to anti-Qaddafi forces.

29. All of these news stories quoted a 2007 study from the Combating Terrorism Center at West Point (Felter and Fishman 2007) that analyzed 600 suicide bombers in Iraq and found that of 440 whose hometowns were known, 52 were from Dernah, the most from any city.

30. LIFG members have consistently claimed that they opposed attacks on civilians and a global jihadist ideology and were never formally associated with al-Qaeda, despite claims to the contrary by Ayman Al-Zawahiri in 2007 (see Pargeter 2011).

31. Examples of commentators who highlighted the rebels' alleged links to al-Qaeda include Pepe Escobar (2011) and Alexander Cockburn (2011) from the left

and contributors to the conservative *American Spectator* from the right (e.g., The Prowler 2011).

32. The tensions reached the boiling point in late July, when rebel military chief Abdel Fattah Younes was killed under mysterious circumstances after being called back from the front lines by the NTC leadership. Before he defected, Younes was Libya's interior minister and had previously been in charge of Qaddafi's special forces. In the mid-1990s, he led the crackdown on the LIFG in eastern Libya, leading many to speculate that Islamist brigades were behind his death in July 2011 (see *Economist* 2011).

33. On the draft road map, see Achcar (2011) and *Telegraph* (2011).

34. For critiques from Libyan activists, see Kamat (2011b).

35. Also, Libyan weapons have poured into parts of the African Sahel through lucrative and illicit arms trading.

36. For an analysis of Qaddafi's use of African mercenaries, see Deycard and Guichaoua (2011).

37. For a comprehensive account, see International Crisis Group (2012).

38. Human Rights Watch (2012b) asserts that its report, based on field investigations in eight different bombing sites before and after the conflict, is the most extensive examination to date of civilian casualties caused by NATO's air campaign.

39. Responding to a leaked U.N. plan for post-Qaddafi Libya in late August 2011, NTC officials rejected the possibility of using armed U.N. or NATO troops to assist with security concerns (see France 24 2011). As for fears that Libya's new leaders could reverse Qaddafi's historic ejection of U.S. bases from Libya and welcome AFRICOM, no public statements indicative of this had been made at the time of this writing. The best check against such a development is perhaps the widespread hostility toward Western troops on Libyan soil. (For discussion of concerns about AFRICOM in Libya, see Mamdani 2011b.)

40. Warning the Obama administration against sending drones into Libyan airspace, Belhaj (2012) wrote in the *Guardian* that Libya's sovereignty must be respected in spite of what he called the "despicable murder" of Ambassador Stevens, which he blamed on small extremist groups and the weakness of the state in Libya.

41. Ali Sallabi called Mahmoud Jibril a "tyrant in waiting" on a television show in September. He told Reuters that "there is an immense mass of revolutionaries that do not want Jibril." His brother Ismail Sallabi, a military commander of the anti-Qaddafi forces, called on the NTC to resign, describing the members of the council as "remnants of the old regime" (quoted in Farge 2011).

42. In late October 2011, British defense secretary Phillip Hammond urged U.K. companies and sales directors to be "packing their suitcases and looking to get out to Libya and take part in the reconstruction of that country as soon as they can"

(quoted in Adetunji 2011). Meanwhile, the French foreign minister, Alain Juppé, denied reports (published in the French daily newspaper *Libération*) of any secret deals between French oil companies and the NTC, but he added that it seemed "fair and logical" that the NTC would "turn in preference to those [countries] who helped it" (quoted in Borger and Macalister 2011).

43. With profit-making opportunities diminishing in Iraq and Afghanistan, Western companies have turned to Libya as a possible destination for lucrative postwar contracts, particularly in construction, security, and infrastructure (see Shane 2011).

44. At the time of the uprising, Chinese investments in Libya were estimated at nearly US$19 billion. On Russia, see RIA Novosti (2011).

45. In their 2011 Index of Economic Freedom, the Heritage Foundation and the *Wall Street Journal* ranked Libya 173 out of 179 countries. The index measures economic liberalization for countries around the world in areas such as property rights, finance, foreign investment, and business (the full index is available at http://www.heritage.org/index/ranking).

46. On labor strikes, see Donati (2011) and Faraj (2011).

References

Abdurrahman, Najla. 2011. "Getting Libya's Rebels Wrong." *Foreign Policy,* March 31. http://www.foreignpolicy.com (accessed September 25, 2012).

Achcar, Gilbert. 2011. "NATO's 'Conspiracy' against the Libyan Revolution." Jadaliyya, August 17. http://www.jadaliyya.com (accessed September 24, 2012).

Ackerman, Spencer. 2012. "U.S. Drones Never Left Libya; Will Hunt Benghazi Thugs." Wired, Danger Room blog, September 12. http://www.wired.com (accessed September 24, 2012).

Adetunji, Jo. 2011. "British Firms Urged to 'Pack Suitcases' in Rush for Libya Business." *Guardian,* October 21. http://www.guardian.co.uk (accessed March 8, 2013).

Agence France Presse. 2010. "Kadhafi Says Libya No Place for 'Civil Society.'" January 28. http://www.google.com/hostednews/afp/article/ALeqM5iHN4BDAS gALw7xKVBgxPDjZKqvjg (accessed September 22, 2012).

———. 2011. "Libya's New Leaders Vow to Remake 'Cocktail Economy.'" Al Arabiya News, September 7. http://english.alarabiya.net (accessed September 24, 2012).

Ahmad, Aijaz. 2011. "Libya Recolonised." *Frontline,* November 5–18. http://www .flonnet.com (accessed March 11, 2013).

al-Ameri, Alaa. 2011. "The Myth of Tribal Libya." *Guardian,* March 30. http://www.guardian.co.uk (accessed March 11, 2013).

Amnesty International. 2011a. *The Battle for Libya: Killings, Disappearances, and Torture*. London: Amnesty International. http://www.amnesty.org (accessed March 11, 2013).

———. 2011b. *Detention Abuses Staining the New Libya*. London: Amnesty International. http://www.amnesty.org (accessed September 24, 2012).

———. 2011c. "Security Council Must Refer Libya to International Criminal Court." February 25. http://www.amnesty.org (accessed March 11, 2013).

———. 2012. *Libya: Rule of Law or Militias?* London: Amnesty International. http://www.amnesty.org (accessed September 24, 2012).

Anderson, Lisa. 1986. "Qadhdhafi and His Opposition." *Middle East Journal* 40 (2): 225–37.

Asharq al-Awsat. 2011. "Libya: Islamists Call on Air Force to Bomb Gaddafi." February 23. http://www.aawsat.net/2011/02/article55247418 (accessed September 24, 2012).

Bali, Asli, and Ziad Abu-Rish. 2011. "Solidarity and Intervention in Libya." Jadaliyya, March 16. http://www.jadaliyya.com (accessed March 11, 2013).

Barber, Benjamin. 2011a. "Why Libya Will Not Be Democratic." Huffington Post, February 22. http://www.huffingtonpost.com (accessed March 11, 2013).

———. 2011b. "Yes, Saif Is a Gaddafi. But There's Still a Real Reformer Inside." *Guardian*, April 13. http://www.guardian.co.uk (accessed September 25, 2012).

BBC News. 2010. "Gaddafi Wants EU Cash to Stop African Migrants." August 31. http://www.bbc.co.uk (accessed September 25, 2012).

Beaumont, Peter. 2011. "Qatar Accused of Interfering in Libyan Affairs." *Guardian*, October 4. http://www.guardian.co.uk (accessed September 24, 2012).

Belhaj, Abdel Hakim. 2011. "The Revolution Belongs to All Libyans, Secular or Not." *Guardian*, September 27. http://www.guardian.co.uk (accessed September 24, 2012).

———. 2012. "Libya Condemns the Embassy Killings, but Its Sovereignty Must Be Respected." *Guardian*, September 21. http://www.guardian.co.uk (accessed March 11, 2013).

Benkato, Jamila. 2011. "Tribes of Libya as the Third Front: Myths and Realities of Non-state Actors in the Long Battle for Misrata." Jadaliyya, May 2. http://www.jadaliyya.com (accessed March 11, 2013).

Black, Ian. 2011. "Qatar Admits Sending Hundreds of Troops to Support Libya's Rebels." *Guardian*, October 26. http://www.guardian.co.uk (accessed September 24, 2012).

Blanchard, Christopher M. 2012. *Libya: Transition and U.S. Policy*. CRS Report for Congress, October 18. Washington, D.C.: Congressional Research Service. http://www.fas.org/sgp/crs/row/RL33142.pdf (accessed March 12, 2013).

Borger, Julian, and Terry Macalister. 2011. "The Race Is on for Libya's Oil, with Britain and France Both Staking Claim." *Guardian,* September 1. http://www.guardian.co.uk (accessed March 11, 2013).

Bredeloup, Sylvie, and Olivier Pliez. 2011. "The Libyan Migration Corridor." EU-US Immigration Systems, Robert Schuman Centre for Advanced Studies, European University Institute, San Domenico di Fiesole, Italy.

Bricmont, Jean. 2011. "Libya and the Return of Humanitarian Imperialism." *CounterPunch,* March 8. http://www.counterpunch.org (accessed March 11, 2013).

CBC News. 2011. "600 Believed Dead in Libya Refugee Boat Sinking." May 10. http://www.cbc.ca (accessed September 24, 2012).

Cherstich, Igor. 2011. "Libya's Revolution: Tribe, Nation, Politics." OpenDemocracy, October 3. http://www.opendemocracy.net (accessed March 11, 2013).

Chulov, Martin. 2011. "Libyan Commander Demands Apology over MI6 and CIA Plot." *Guardian,* September 4. http://www.guardian.co.uk (accessed September 24, 2011).

Cockburn, Alexander. 2011. "Libya Rebels: Gaddafi Could Be Right about al-Qaeda." *The Week,* March 24. http://www.theweek.co.uk (accessed March 8, 2013).

Cockburn, Patrick. 2011. "France Has Clearly Not Learnt Lesson of History." *Independent,* March 11. http://www.independent.co.uk (accessed March 11, 2013).

Cornwell, Susan. 2011. "Senior Republican Ups Criticism of Obama on Libya." Reuters, March 23. http://www.reuters.com (accessed March 11, 2013).

Daragahi, Borzou. 2012. "Qatar Buys into Libyan Bank." *Financial Times,* beyondbrics blog, April 17. http://blogs.ft.com (accessed September 24, 2012).

de Haas, Hein. 2008. "The Myth of Invasion: The Inconvenient Realities of African Migration to Europe." *Third World Quarterly* 29 (7): 1305–22.

Deycard, Frédéric, and Yvan Guichaoua. 2011. "Mali and Niger Tuareg Insurgencies and the War in Libya: 'Whether You Liked Him or Not, Gadaffi Used to Fix a Lot of Holes.'" African Arguments, September 8. http://africanarguments.org (accessed March 11, 2013).

Donati, Jessica. 2011. "US Firms Face Mixed Fate in Libya as Workers Strike." Reuters, October 9. http://www.reuters.com (accessed March 8, 2013).

Donati, Jessica, and Marie-Louise Gumuchian. 2011. "Special Report: The Gaddafi Oil Papers." Reuters, December 23. http://www.reuters.com (accessed September 24, 2012).

Dreyfuss, Robert. 2011. "Obama's NATO War for Oil in Libya." *The Nation,* blog, August 23. http://www.thenation.com (accessed March 11, 2013).

Economist. 2011. "The Rebellion's Leaders: Good Intentions, Fragile Legitimacy." August 27. http://www.economist.com (accessed March 8, 2013).

Escobar, Pepe. 2011. "How al-Qaeda Got to Rule in Tripoli." Asia Times Online, August 30. http://www.atimes.com (accessed March 8, 2013).

Fadel, Leila. 2011. "Rebel Military Commander Wants to Be America's Man on the Ground in Libya." *Washington Post,* April 12. http://www.washingtonpost.com (accessed September 24, 2011).

Falk, Richard. 2011. "Kicking the Intervention Habit." Al Jazeera, March 10. http://english.aljazeera.net (accessed March 11, 2013).

Faraj, Noora. 2011. "Libyan Oil Workers Continue Strike." Al Arabiya News, October 20. http://www.alarabiya.net (accessed March 8, 2013).

Farge, Emma. 2011. "Interview: Libya Islamist Calls for PM Jibril's Exit." Reuters, September 20. http://af.reuters.com (accessed March 8, 2013).

Felter, Joseph, and Brian Fishman. 2007. *Al-Qa'ida's Foreign Fighters in Iraq: A First Look at the Sinjar Records.* West Point, N.Y.: Combating Terrorism Center, U.S. Military Academy. http://www.ctc.usma.edu (accessed March 11, 2013).

Ferran, Lee. 2012. "American Killed in Libya Was on Intel Mission to Track Weapons." ABC News, Blotter, September 13. http://abcnews.go.com/Blotter (accessed September 24, 2012).

Fitzgerald, Mary. 2011. "Tribal Loyalties Have Power to Divide Libya or Help Unite It after Gadafy." *Irish Times,* March 14. http://www.irishtimes.com (accessed March 11, 2013).

France 24. 2011. "NTC Rejects Foreign Military Presence, Says UN Envoy." August 31. http://www.france24.com/en (accessed March 11, 2013).

Friedman, Thomas L. 2011a. "Looking for Luck in Libya." *New York Times,* March 29. http://www.nytimes.com (accessed March 11, 2013).

———. 2011b. "Tribes with Flags." *New York Times,* March 22. http://www.nytimes.com (accessed September 24, 2012).

Gelb, Leslie H. 2011. "Wanted: Humanitarians at Home." Daily Beast, April 6. http://www.thedailybeast.com (accessed March 11, 2013).

Human Rights Watch. 2009a. *Pushed Back, Pushed Around: Italy's Forced Return of Boat Migrants and Asylum Seekers, Libya's Mistreatment of Migrants and Asylum Seekers.* New York: Human Rights Watch. http://www.hrw.org (accessed March 8, 2013).

———. 2009b. *Truth and Justice Can't Wait: Human Rights Developments in Libya amid Institutional Obstacles.* New York: Human Rights Watch. http://www.hrw.org (accessed March 8, 2013).

———. 2011a. "Apparent Execution of 53 Gaddafi Supporters." October 24. http://www.hrw.org (accessed September 24, 2012).

———. 2011b. "Cease Arbitrary Arrests, Abuse of Detainees." September 30. http://www.hrw.org (accessed September 24, 2012).

———. 2011c. "Libya: End Violent Crackdown in Tripoli." March 13. http://www.hrw.org (accessed September 24, 2012).

———. 2011d. "Libya: Militias Terrorizing Residents of 'Loyalist' Town." October 30. http://www.hrw.org (accessed September 24, 2012).

———. 2011e. "Transitional Council Failing to Secure Weapons." October 25. http://www.hrw.org (accessed September 24, 2012).

———. 2011f. "US/UK Documents Reveal Libya Rendition Details." September 8. http://www.hrw.org (accessed September 25, 2012).

———. 2012a. *Delivered into Enemy Hands: US-Led Abuse and Rendition of Opponents to Gaddafi's Libya.* New York: Human Rights Watch. http://www.hrw.org (accessed September 25, 2012).

———. 2012b. "Unacknowledged Deaths: Civilian Casualties in NATO's Air Campaign in Libya." May 14. http://www.hrw.org (accessed September 24, 2012).

International Crisis Group. 2012. *Divided We Stand: Libya's Enduring Crisis.* Middle East/North Africa Report No. 130, September 14. Brussels: International Crisis Group. http://www.crisisgroup.org/en (accessed March 11, 2013).

Jian Junbo. 2011. "China's Second Coming in Libya." Asia Times Online, August 31. http://www.atimes.com (accessed September 24, 2011).

Johnstone, Diana. 2011. "Libya: Is This Kosovo All Over Again?" *CounterPunch,* March 7. http://www.counterpunch.org (accessed March 11, 2013).

Kamat, Anjali. 2011a. "Fate of Libyan-American Student and Rebel Fighter Muhannad Bensadik Unknown after Shooting in Libya." *Democracy Now!,* March 23. http://www.democracynow.org (accessed March 11, 2013).

———. 2011b. "The New Libya: Exclusive Video on Challenges Facing a Nation Emerging from Gaddafi's 42-Year Rule." *Democracy Now!,* October 18. http://www.democracynow.org (accessed March 11, 2013).

———. 2011c. "Thousands of Migrant Workers Stranded at Libyan Borders and Ports as Violent Clashes Spread." *Democracy Now!,* March 7. http://www.democracynow.org (accessed March 11, 2013).

Kerr, Simeon. 2011. "Gamble on Libya Pays Off for Qatar." *Financial Times,* August 28. http://www.ft.com (accessed August 29, 2011).

———. 2012. "Gulf Allies Move to Reap Spoils of War in Libya." *Financial Times,* January 18. http://www.ft.com (accessed March 13, 2013).

Kirkpatrick, David. 2011. "U.S. Reopens Its Embassy in Libya." *New York Times,* September 22. http://www.nytimes.com (accessed September 24, 2012).

———. 2012. "Braving Areas of Violence, Voters Try to Reshape Libya." *New York Times,* July 7. http://www.nytimes.com (accessed September 25, 2012).

Krauss, Clifford. 2011. "For Qatar, Libyan Intervention May Be a Turning Point." *New York Times,* April 3. http://www.nytimes.com (accessed September 24, 2011).

Landay, Jonathan S. 2011. "Despite Reluctance, U.S. Could Be Forced to Act in Libya." McClatchy Newspapers, March 2. http://www.mcclatchydc.com (accessed March 11, 2013).

Levinson, Charles. 2011a. "Behind Libya's Rifts, Tribal Politics." *Wall Street Journal,* March 8.

———. 2011b. "Minister in Tripoli Blasts Qatari Aid to Militia Groups." *Wall Street Journal,* October 12. http://online.wsj.com (accessed September 24, 2012).

Mamdani, Mahmood. 2011a. "Libya: Politics of Humanitarian Intervention." Al Jazeera, March 31. http://english.aljazeera.net (accessed March 8, 2013).

———. 2011b. "What Does Gaddafi's Fall Mean for Africa?" Al Jazeera, October 26. http://english.aljazeera.net (accessed March 8, 2013).

Meo, Nick. 2011. "Libya's Lost Immigrant Souls with Nowhere to Go." *Telegraph,* September 3. http://www.telegraph.co.uk (accessed September 22, 2012).

Miles, Hugh. 2011. "Who Said Gaddafi Had to Go?" *London Review of Books,* November 17.

Miller, Jonathan. 2011. "Reporting Libya's War from Inside Gaddafi's Rixos Hotel." Channel 4 News, April 24. http://www.channel4.com (accessed March 11, 2013).

Nordland, Rod. 2011. "Files Note Close CIA Ties to Qaddafi Spy Unit." *New York Times,* September 2. http://www.nytimes.com (accessed March 11, 2013).

Osgood, Patrick. 2012. "Analysis: Confusion Reigns over Libyan Contracts." Arabian Oil and Gas, April 10. http://www.arabianoilandgas.com (accessed September 25, 2012).

Paoletta, Emanuela, and Ferrucio Pastore. 2010. "Sharing the Dirty Job on the Southern Front? Italian-Libyan Relations on Migration and Their Impact on the European Union." Working Paper 29, International Migration Institute, Oxford University.

Pargeter, Alison. 2006. "Libya: Reforming the Impossible?" *Review of African Political Economy* 33 (108): 219–35.

———. 2011. "Are Islamist Extremists Fighting among Libya's Rebels?" *CTC [Combating Terrorism Center] Sentinel,* April 1. http://www.ctc.usma.edu (accessed March 11, 2013).

Pelham, Nicholas. 2012. "Is Libya Cracking Up?" *New York Review of Books,* June 21. http://www.nybooks.com (accessed September 24, 2012).

Prashad, Vijay. 2011. "Neo-liberal Interventionism: America's Libyans." *CounterPunch,* March 31. http://www.counterpunch.org (accessed September 24, 2012).

The Prowler. 2011. "Obama Arming Al Qaeda?" *American Spectator,* March 28. http://spectator.org (accessed March 8, 2013).

Ratner, Michael, and Phil Weiss. 2011. "This Should Only Happen in Response to Genocide (Two Leftwingers Argue over Libya)." Mondoweiss, March 21. http://mondoweiss.net (accessed March 11, 2013).

RIA Novosti. 2011. "Libya to Honor Russian Contracts—PM." November 1. http://en.rian.ru (accessed March 11, 2013).

Rieff, David. 2011. "The Road to Hell." *New Republic,* March 23. http://www.newrepublic.com (accessed March 11, 2013).

Ryan, Missy, and Susan Cornwell. 2011. "Intelligence on Libya Rebels Shows

'Flickers' of Al Qaeda." Reuters, March 29. http://www.reuters.com (accessed September 25, 2012).

Saigol, Lina, and Rachel Sanderson. 2011. "European Groups Jockey for Libyan Contracts." *Financial Times,* September 15. http://www.ft.com (accessed September 24, 2012).

Schmitt, Eric, Helene Cooper, and Michael S. Schmidt. 2012. "Deadly Attack in Libya Was Major Blow to C.I.A. Efforts." *New York Times,* September 23. http://www.nytimes.com (accessed November 9, 2012).

Shane, Scott. 2011. "Western Companies See Prospect for Business in Libya." *New York Times,* October 28. http://www.nytimes.com (accessed March 8, 2013).

Shenker, Jack. 2011. "Aircraft Carrier Left Us to Die, Say Migrants." *Guardian,* May 8. http://www.guardian.co.uk (accessed March 11, 2013).

Smith, David. 2011. "The Guardian Has Another Reporter Expelled from Tripoli." *Guardian,* July 8. http://www.guardian.co.uk (accessed March 11, 2013).

Stephen, Chris, and Simon Goodley. 2012. "Libya's Promised Reconstruction Bonanza Fails to Materialise." *Guardian/Observer,* August 25. http://www.guardian.co.uk (accessed September 24, 2012).

St. John, Ronald Bruce. 2008. *Libya: From Colony to Independence.* Oxford: Oneworld.

Telegraph. 2011. "Rebel Blueprint for Libya Revealed." August 8. http://www.tele graph.co.uk (accessed March 8, 2013).

Thorne, John. 2011. "Libya's Berbers Seek Their Revenge on Qaddafi." *The National,* May 30. http://www.thenational.ae (accessed March 11, 2013).

United Press International. 2011. "Security Firms Hustle in Lawless Libya." December 9. http://www.upi.com (accessed September 24, 2011).

Wahby, Eman. 2005. "Economic Reforms Anger Libyan Citizens." Arab Reform Bulletin, Carnegie Endowment for International Peace. June 20. http://www.carnegieendowment.org (accessed March 11, 2013).

Warrick, Joby. 2011. "Clinton Credited with Key Role in Success of NATO Airstrikes, Libyan Rebels." *Washington Post,* October 31. http://www.washington post.com (accessed March 11, 2013).

World Bank. 2006. *Socialist People's Libyan Arab Jamahiriya.* Country Economic Report No. 30295/LY. Washington, D.C.: World Bank.

———. 2011. "Libya Country Brief." April 2011. http://web.worldbank.org (accessed November 3, 2011).

Personal Interviews

Personal interview. 2011a. Khaled Al Agily. Abu Salim prison, Tripoli, September 10.

Personal interview. 2011b. Muhannad Bensadik, Libyan-American fighter, killed on the front line in mid-March 2011. Between Ras Lanuf and Brega, March 10.

Personal interview. 2011c. Fathy Terbil. Benghazi courthouse, February 25.

Personal interview. 2011d. Zahi Mogherbi. Benghazi, September 3.

Personal interview. 2011e. Ibrahim. Military checkpoint near Misrata, September 7.

Personal interview. 2011f. Anonymous prisoner. Misrata detention center, September 8.

Personal interview. 2011g. Hassan Al-Amin. Misrata, September 8.

Personal interview. 2011h. Ghaidaa Al-Tawati. Tripoli, September 10.

Personal interview. 2011i. Hana El-Gallal. Benghazi, September 2.

Personal interview. 2011j. Mohammad Abu El Naja. Benghazi, September 4.

Personal interview. 2011k. Hisham Matar. Cairo, August 9.

Syria

PAULO GABRIEL HILU PINTO

Contextualizing the Syrian Uprising

Protests against Bashar al-Assad's rule in Syria started in the aftermath of the ousting of Ben Ali's dictatorship by the Tunisian revolution. In January 2011, civil disobedience and demonstrations of dissatisfaction with the Baathist regime, which included self-immolations, started to occupy the Syrian public arena.[1] Despite these early signs of unrest, Assad affirmed in an interview with the *Wall Street Journal* (2011) that Syria was and would remain unaffected by the wave of revolts and protests spreading throughout the Arab world. Explaining his views on the phenomenon, he described the situation as follows:

> It means if you have stagnant water, you will have pollution and microbes; and because you have had this stagnation for decades, let us say, especially the last decade in spite of the vast changes that are surrounding the world and some areas in the Middle East, including Iraq, Palestine, and Afghanistan, because we had this stagnation we were plagued with microbes. So, what you have been seeing in this region is a kind of disease. That is how we see it. . . . We have more difficult circumstances than most of the Arab countries but in spite of that Syria is stable. Why? Because you have to be very closely linked to the beliefs of the people. This is the core issue. When

there is divergence between your policy and the people's beliefs and interests, you will have this vacuum that creates disturbance.

Nevertheless, by February mass protests had become part of Syria's political landscape, albeit in a pattern much more localized and fragmented than the uprisings of national scale that marked the Tunisian and Egyptian revolutions. Harassment from the police or the security forces, which most Syrians usually endured as a mix of a societal structural problem and individual misfortune, started to create outrage, and people were mobilized into protest. In February 2011 hundreds of people protested in Damascus after traffic police officers assaulted the son of a merchant in the Hariqa district. The protesters chanted "The Syrian people will not be humiliated" while still pledging allegiance to Assad as Syria's president (Al Arabiya News 2011). Ironically, despite Assad's rhetoric of confident calm, it was precisely the reality of overzealous security forces repressing all possible expressions of opposition to his government, or even support for the protesters in other Arab countries, that unleashed the events that ended in an open revolt against Assad's Baathist regime. Throughout February, protests in solidarity with the Egyptian Revolution or with the Libyan rebels were met with violent repression by the Syrian security forces. Some two hundred demonstrators gathered in front of the Libyan embassy in Damascus with placards reading "Freedom for the people" and "Traitors are those who beat their people" before they were violently dispersed by the police, with many demonstrators being beaten or arrested (All4Syria 2011).

The incident that ignited the nationwide revolt against the Baathist regime happened in Der'a, a medium-size town near the Syria–Jordan border. Der'a, the main town of the Hawran, a fertile agricultural region south of Damascus, had been directly affected by years of drought, the negative impacts of which had been enhanced by state underinvestment and mismanagement of resources by state officials. As a result, the town had experienced a sharp rise in poverty and unemployment. Adding to that, the location of Der'a near the border meant that it had a large presence of the security apparatus of the regime, and the town's inhabitants felt strongly the increase in repression and the predatory corruption of government officials that developed during Assad's ruling decade. Der'a's geographic and sociological characteristics constituted the main causal elements behind the Syrian uprising: increasing poverty, decreasing governmental investments and services in rural regions, violent repression, and resource-draining corruption. Thus it was not unsurprising that Der'a became the uprising's early flashpoint.

On March 6, 2011, a group of fifteen kids, between ten and fifteen years old, were arrested for writing the slogan of the Tunisian revolution, "Al-sha'b yurid isqat al-nizam" (The people want the downfall of the regime), on the wall of their school. The kids were interrogated and even tortured under police custody. The arrest was felt as a "moral insult," not only by the families directly related to the kids but also by a large part of the population of Der'a, which had its capacity to protect the honor and safety of the family challenged and denied by the security forces.[2] In a rapid succession of events, local solidarity with the families affected by the arrests transformed personal grievances against the state into political indignation aimed toward the regime. In a matter of days, the population of Der'a took to the streets in protest.

By March 25, the whole central area of the city was under the control of the protesters. Soon, demonstrations spread to other cities and towns, such as Duma, Harasta, Hama, Homs, Baniyas, Latakiya, Qamishli, Dayr al-Zor, and Tal Kalakh. In all these cities protesters chanted "Allah, Suriya, huriyawa bas" (God, Syria, freedom, and that's enough), and held placards reading "Silmiyya" (Peaceful), indicating the early choice of a nonviolent fight against the regime, and "We want freedom for all." While some demonstrations did take place in Damascus and Aleppo, those two cities remained relatively unaffected by the protests. The only exceptions were some working-class neighborhoods, such as the Maydan in Damascus and Saghour in Aleppo, which joined the uprising. The protesters were mainly of working-class and peasant extraction, coming from the regions and social strata that were economically and politically marginalized by Assad's liberal economic reforms. In contrast, the industrial and commercial bourgeoisie of Damascus and Aleppo, who had benefited from these reforms, remained unmoved by the anti-Baathist protests. Both cities have even had enormous pro-government rallies on various occasions, showing that Assad still has some degree of popularity or at least is seen as better than the uncertainty of change by a considerable part of the Damascene and Aleppine populations. At a pro-Assad rally in Damascus people chanted "Allah, Suriya, Bashar wa bas" (God, Syria, Bashar, and that's enough) and denounced foreign "plots" against Syria and the "lies" spread by the foreign media. The demonstrators also held placards reading "Kullna ma'akya Bashar" (We are all with you, Bashar) or "Mnuhibbak" (We love you[, Bashar]).[3]

The Syrian uprising against the Baathist regime was first portrayed in the media as a continuation of the Tunisian and Egyptian revolutions—that is, a widespread revolt against the authoritarian political system. However, as the protests did not manage to launch a general mobilization on a national scale, and the fault lines between religious groups in the Syrian society became deeper and politicized as pro- and antigovernment positions entangled in an increasingly militarized confrontation, a large part of the media started to present the uprising as a prelude to civil war. While these representations do reflect trends that were present in the uprising, they offer a very partial portrait of a larger and complex social and political situation. Therefore, I argue here that in order to understand the dynamics of the Syrian uprising we must look into the reconfiguration of Baathist authoritarianism under Assad and how it reshaped the social basis of the regime, marginalizing peasants and workers while co-opting the industrial and commercial bourgeoisie. This happened in tandem with the constitution of a system of governance that was, in many respects, more repressive as well as ridden by networks of corruption, which became more predatory as the "liberal" economic reforms advanced. In this analysis I will also focus on the social context of adherence or indifference to anti-Baathist protest. Instead of highlighting the political ideologies or interests of the actors, as is typical of analysis in the media, I will deal with the social causes and forces—such as class, regional and local identities, and sectarian mobilization of religious identities and sensibilities—that shaped and organized the mobilization of the Syrians in one or another camp in the political struggle surrounding the uprising.

The protests started with demands for political reform, justice, and combat against government corruption, but they quickly gave way to calls for freedom and the end of the Baathist regime as they grew and, apparently, gained momentum. As a first move, Assad tried to deal with the uprising by making gradual concessions that could indicate his willingness to foster political reform or by addressing the demands of specific social groups, such as the Kurds or pious Sunni Muslims: in March, the mandatory duration of military service was lowered from twenty-one to eighteen months; the fifteen young people arrested in Der'a were freed; the governor of Der'a was removed from office; wages of public-sector employees were increased; plans to allow greater freedom of the press, to combat corruption, and to create new jobs were announced; political prisoners were freed; and the president's cabinet resigned. In April the concessions continued in even more spectacular ways. The law prohibiting teachers from wearing the *niqab* (face veil) was lifted, and Syria's only casino was closed in a move aimed at pleasing pious Muslims (Bayoumy 2011). Syrian citizenship was conceded to thousands of Kurds in the Jazira who were registered as *'ajanib* (foreigners) in the 1962 census and, since then, had been made stateless (Al Jazeera 2011a). Finally, emergency law, which had been in place since 1963, was revoked, and emergency court trials were to stop (BBC News 2011b).

However, in tandem with the concessions, the repression against the protests became more and more brutal and generalized. From April onward, several cities and towns—Der'a, Baniyas, Hama, Homs, Jisr al-Shughur, Rastan—escaped partially or completely from government control, which was reestablished only after their military conquest. Together with the deployment of the Syrian army, in particular the Fourth Armored Division under the command of Maher al-Assad (Bashar's brother),[4] the regime used paramilitary gangs known as *shabiha* (ghosts) to repress the populations of the rebel regions. Therefore, in July 2011, when Bashar al-Assad called for a national "dialogue," or *hiwar,* between the government and the opposition and announced a project of law allowing the creation of political parties, his discourse on political reform had already been emptied of any meaning by the brutal repression to which the protesters and the population in general had been subjected.[5] The contradiction was inscribed in the very speech that announced the dialogue, as Assad denounced "radicals and blasphemous intellectuals who infiltrated the country" and stated that "peaceful demonstrations were used as cover to armed infiltrators" before calling

Paulo Gabriel Hilu Pinto

all Syrians to decide through a national dialogue which reforms were to be done by the government.

The demonstrators throughout Syria rejected Assad's call as an attempt to cover up the ongoing state violence against them. They chanted several slogans expressing their lack of trust in the regime's intentions, such as in 'Amuda, where protesters chanted "Ma fi hiwar; irhal Bashar" (There is no dialogue; leave Bashar). By June 2012, the United Nations estimated that the number of deaths in Syria, which were caused mainly by state repression, had reached fourteen thousand since the beginning of the protests against Bashar; this number has continued to rise since then. The Syrian government claimed that more than four thousand soldiers and members of the security forces had been killed by armed groups of the opposition. Despite the brutality of the repression and the growing violence, demonstrations and protests continued throughout Syria.

In order to understand the dynamics of the uprising and its specificity in relation to previous forms of resistance and opposition against the Baathist regime, it is necessary to look at the transformations that the authoritarian system suffered under the decade of Assad's rule. The transformations in the forms of governance—that is, in the ways that the government produced social consent to its political project—gradually marginalized some sectors of the population, allowing the emergence of new political actors and arenas for opposition to the regime. Unlike previous forms of protest, the uprising was not centered on the urban elite and middle classes of Damascus and Aleppo; rather, it was dispersed across urban and rural populations that had become impoverished and politically marginalized in the Baathist "new order."

Traditions of Protest and the Reconfiguration of Baathist Authoritarianism

A long history of resistance and opposition to the Baathist regime existed in Syria before the uprising that began in 2011. While both secular and religious political movements had tried to counter the control that the regime had imposed on Syrian society since 1963, Islamic groups, such as the Muslim Brotherhood, managed to attract militants from the traditional elites and the urban middle classes into confrontational opposition to the regime. From 1979 to 1982 various Islamic groups under the leadership of the Muslim Brothers had waged an armed struggle against the Baathist regime (Abd-Allah 1983). During the 1970s the grievances of the traditional landowning and industrial elites and of the professional middle class found expression through the idiom of political Islam, as all secular political forces had been disbanded by the Baathist regime.

Several Islamic groups were created, but the Muslim Brotherhood was the largest. The society of the Muslim Brothers in Syria (al-Ikhwan al-Muslimun fi Suriya) was created in the 1940s with the reunion of preexisting Islamic organizations under the leadership of the Syrian sheikh Mustafa al-Siba'i, who had come into contact with the Muslim Brotherhood in Egypt while he was a student in Cairo. Like their Egyptian counterparts, the Syrian Muslim Brothers were committed to the creation of an Islamic state, but unlike the Egyptians, they had a strong presence among the members of the religious establishment, such as Sufi sheikhs and 'ulama (religious specialists), who mobilized their followers into the political project of the movement.[6] The ideology of the Muslim Brothers recruited adepts among the urban middle class of merchants and professionals. The Islamic opposition was particularly active in Aleppo and Hama, where some of the religious leaders had family connections with the traditional urban elites of merchants and landowners, as well as a strong appeal among the middle classes and some popular sectors (Abd-Allah 1983; Batatu 1988; Carré and Seurat [1983] 2001). The conflict with the state culminated in a military confrontation that destroyed a large part of the city of Hama in 1982 and resulted in an enormous number of casualties among the civilian population.[7] After the tragedy of Hama, political Islam declined as a mobilizing force in Syrian society, and Hafiz al-Assad's government adopted a more accommodating stance toward Sunni Islam.

Hence the process of Islamization of Syrian society shifted in focus from the revolutionary conquest of the state to the moral reform of individuals, a tactic that could be said to have been largely successful by 2011 (Pinto 2007b). Efforts to create an "Islamic society" became centered on the production of pious individuals through their engage-

Paulo Gabriel Hilu Pinto

ment in religious education, religious practice, and moral behavior. The traditional religious authorities, such as the *'ulama* and the Sufi sheikhs, were the main promoters of this process, for they already understood the reform of individual behavior as a tool for changing and shaping society within a framework of Islamic values. The accommodation between the Baathist rule and the growing public affirmation of Islam in Syrian society allowed the establishment of governance through negotiation and co-optation of social groups, which translated into a period of relative political stability for the regime. Within the same logic, the mobilization of Islamic vocabulary and symbols during the anti-Baathist uprising reflected the importance of Islam as a cultural idiom for the insertion and positioning of individuals in the public sphere, rather than the presence of organized Islamist movements. Therefore the protesters used religious references in their critique of the regime not because they belonged to Islamic political organizations but rather because Islam had become the major cultural framework for the affirmation of social ideals during the previous three decades in Syria.

The rise of Bashar al-Assad to the Syrian presidency after the death of his father, Hafiz, who ruled Syria from 1970 to 2000, consolidated the grip of the Assad dynasty over Syrian politics. This power transition produced a "dynastic republic" (which its opponents ironically called a *jumlukiyya*), a model that was eagerly copied by other authoritarian regimes in the Arab world.[8] The dynastic succession also signaled the intensification of the concentration and personalization of power within the Baathist regime. This process started under Hafiz al-Assad's rule, as he gradually neutralized the Baath Party and other institutions such as trade unions and peasant organizations, depriving them of any coherent ideological content or political power within the structure of the regime (Le Gac 1991, 135–36; Perthes 1995, 133–202). Already in preparation for the dynastic transition, Hafiz eliminated all centers of power within the regime that could threaten its course. In 1998, Rifaʿat al-Assad, Hafiz's brother, who had been in exile since his frustrated coup in 1984, was stripped of his symbolic position as vice president. In 1999, the network of legal and illegal business in the port of Latakiya that had been controlled by Rifaʿat was dismantled, and groups of his loyalists were disbanded after they took part in armed confrontations with the Syrian army throughout the city. Similarly, 'Ali Duba, chief of the military intelligence services, was dismissed from his post because he was perceived as being a potential threat to Bashar's ascension to the presidency.

The elimination of threatening or potentially bothersome power figures and the dismantling of their networks was an important strategy that Bashar al-Assad often mobilized in his struggle to consolidate his position in the regime. This affected even high-profile figures from Hafiz al-Assad's era, such as Mustafa Tlas, minister of defense, and 'Abd al-Halim Khaddam, former foreign minister and vice president, both of whom were highly instrumental in assuring Bashar's ascension to the presidency. In this way, there was a gradual concentration of power in the hands of the president and his allies, and only the networks of patronage and clientship directly connected to them were allowed to survive (George 2003, 64–81; Donati 2009, 129–60).

Beyond the power disputes within the regime, Bashar al-Assad tried to gain political legitimacy by presenting himself as a leader committed to political reform and the economic modernization of Syria. While in the political realm the reforms were fast and ephemeral, they allowed the emergence of a public debate on democracy and political freedom that had some impact on the political idiom of the current protests. The recognition by Assad, in 2000, of the necessity of social dialogue and debate on political, economic, and social matters unleashed a vast drive toward the organization and institutionalization of a multiplicity of social and political movements. Soon, clubs and circles of debate were organized throughout Syria in what was locally known as the Civil Society Movement (Harakat al-Mujtama' al-Madani) and internationally called the Damascus Spring (George 2003).

However, already in 2001, repressive measures started to be directed against the leaders and participants of the Civil Society Movement. They were, in general, intellectuals from the traditional urban elite and the professional middle classes, mainly from Damascus, who had a very narrow social constituency and few channels of dialogue with other potential forms of opposition to the Baathist regime, such as Islamic or ethnic organizations.[9] By 2002, the movement had already been crushed, although its leaders continued to be active as opponents to the regime (George 2003, 30–63). In the economic realm, while the reforms had a slower pace, they were also more durable. Assad's government launched the idea of a "social market economy" in order to make sense of the adoption of a neoliberal economic model in tandem with the continuity of state intervention in the economy. Therefore, state enterprises were privatized; private banks were allowed to function; new information technologies, such as Internet and mobile phones, became part of everyday life; and various sectors of the economy were opened to foreign investment. In theory, the social market economy, which was inspired by the Chinese model of state-controlled economic liberalization within the boundaries of an authoritarian political order, aimed to develop the commercial and industrial sectors in neoliberal molds without abandoning the Baathist politics of social equality promotion. In practice, it meant the development of capitalist economic sectors controlled by entrepreneurs who had connections to high levels of power in the regime (Aita 2007).

Therefore, the reforms, instead of producing greater economic dynamism, created new networks of corruption and patronage and intensified the predatory grip of those networks on Syrian society. Not that corruption was foreign to the Baathist regime. On the contrary, various forms of corruption constituted a diffuse mechanism of negotiation and co-optation between the state and discrete social groups and agents that was central to the construction of the Baathist governance of Syrian society (Perthes 1995, 181–87). What happened under Assad was the centralization of the networks of corruption and patronage within the circle of the president's allies, so that enormous amounts of resources were channeled into their hands.

Some entrepreneurs who could mobilize *wasta* (influence/mediation) from the inner circles of the regime were able to use state resources and apparatus to get rid of their competition or to enhance their possibilities for profit, which allowed the creation of monopolies and great concentration of wealth. This process enabled the state to keep its power over economic assets and sectors despite their formal privatization. The paradigmatic figure of the new "state bourgeoisie," the entrepreneurial class that rose through its connections with members of the regime, was Rami Makhlouf, Bashar al-Assad's maternal cousin. His economic empire included mobile phone companies, banks, the duty-free shop at Damascus airport, and a real estate business. Makhlouf's connections in the regime were instrumental in guaranteeing his control over the mobile phone business (Aita 2007, 566–67). An ethnographic example shows how this symbiosis between the regime and well-connected entrepreneurs affected the everyday lives of ordinary Syrians. When I was in Syria in 2006, I could see that all public telephones in the country had been removed or destroyed, so that people were forced to acquire mobile phones if they wanted to communicate by telephone outside their homes. It was no coincidence that Makhlouf was the major stockholder of the two mobile phone companies in Syria.[10] Whenever I asked where I could find a public phone, the Syrians would answer that now the only way to make a phone call was to buy a mobile phone. One shopkeeper told me, only half jokingly, "Now we all have to pay for Makhlouf-tel," mixing the names of Rami Makhlouf and Syriatel, the mobile phone company controlled by him.

The emergence of new centers of power and networks of patronage as the result of the reforms fostered by Bashar al-Assad led to a reconfiguration of the Baathist system of governance. Rural regions and urban workers, which were the traditional bases of the regime, were economically and politically marginalized. As result, the public services and social institutions that constituted the core of the Baathist "social pact" and should be protected in the "social market economy" were gradually dismantled or neglected by the state. State farms were privatized, to the benefit of a new class of landowners who acquired the land through personal connections they had established with the state bureaucracy (Ababsa 2007). At the same time, the dismantling of the net of services and Baathist social security increased the social impacts of the successive droughts that, since 2006, had devastated Syria's agricultural areas (Euphrates, Hawran, and Jazira), affecting 1.3 million people (IRIN 2010). The rise in the cost of living also led many *mukhabarat* (security forces) personnel to use extortion and racketeering to supplement their salaries. Therefore, under Bashar al-Assad the Baathist regime not only became a less efficient provider of services but also was transformed, in many respects, into a more repressive and predatory system. As these transformations were felt most acutely in the rural areas and in medium-size and small cities, it was not by chance that these became the centers of the uprising against Assad's rule. A sign of the widespread discontent and shared grievances in these areas was the success that the song "Yallah irahal ya Bashar" (Come on Bashar, leave!) had among the protesters, who chanted loudly the verses "You create new thieves every day / Shalish, Maher, and Rami / they robbed my brothers and uncles / come on Bashar, leave!"

The Dynamics of the Revolt

The 2011 revolt mobilized the regions marginalized and impoverished by the decade of "liberal" economic reforms fostered by Bashar al-Assad: the agricultural regions (Euphrates, Hawran, Idlib, and Hama), the coastal areas (Baniyas, Latakiya), and the industrial city of Homs. While antigovernment protests did happen in Damascus and Aleppo, both cities remained relatively calm, even staging pro-Assad demonstrations.

The Syrian uprising stands apart from the other revolts and revolutions that swept through the Arab world in the local and fragmented character of its protests. Massive protests took place in Der'a, Hama, Homs, Baniyas, Latakiya, Qamishli, and Dayr al-Zor, all of them small or middle-size cities and towns linked to rural hinterlands or industrial and commercial centers where the security apparatus of the state had a strong presence. In general, these protests happened as local revolts succeeding one another, not simultaneously as a national uprising. This pattern shows that there was little or no coordination among the protests' leaders. The creation in May 2011 of coordination committees, which were composed of protesters who pooled their expertise (computer skills, political activism, networking, and so on) to enhance the articulation of their demands, allowed the emergence of a more cohesive dynamic in the uprising. However, as the members of the committees became major targets for state violence, the range of their action was limited, and many committees were dismantled (Abbas 2011).

The relative isolation of the protests made it easier for the Syrian government to repress them through the use of military or paramilitary violence. While the demonstrations and protests did not stop—as soon as one focus of revolt was repressed, another one appeared—they did not manage to occupy in a sustainable way a territory with historical and symbolic significance that could serve as a reference to all protests, such as happened with Bourguiba Avenue in Tunis or Tahrir Square in Cairo. The central squares in Hama and Homs were occupied several times by thousands of protesters, but they were emptied by the army and the *shabiha* soon afterward. Even when peaceful demonstrations were replaced by an armed rebellion guided by the Free Syrian Army, the rebels did not manage to achieve sustained control of any territory with symbolic meaning in national terms. They tried to do so in July 2012, when they undertook an armed offensive in Aleppo, Syria's largest city and economic center. The rebels managed to take control of a large part of the city, but as the population of Aleppo did not join them, the government forces were able to mount a violent counteroffensive and regain control of many neighborhoods. While the battle was still raging in September 2012, there was no evidence that the rebels were likely to take control of the city beyond some popular neighborhoods in which they managed to establish a more permanent presence.

Even Internet-savvy middle-class youth, who had had a central role in the mobilization and articulation of discrete social and political groups during the Tunisian and Egyptian revolutions, seemed to be quite peripheral to the Syrian uprising. The Internet was used more to document and spread images and videos from the protests than to coordinate and organize them. The established opposition figures and groups that were the main advocates of the "Damascus Spring" during the first year of Bashar al-Assad's presidency were also marginal to the protests. Located mainly in Damascus and Aleppo, they were isolated from the arenas of protest in Hama, Homs, and Der'a. In reality, the traditional opposition was deeply divided about the uprising and how to relate to it. While some intellectuals, artists, and political figures joined their voices to those of the demonstrators, others tried to regain their positions of political vanguard by attempting to occupy the role of mediators between the protesters and the government. In July 2012, Aref Dalila, who had pulled out of an early attempt at "dialogue" between the opposition and the government, denounced these initiatives with this statement:

All these procedures which the authorities call political reforms, are being taken by one side only: the authority itself, the security authority, without involving or cooperating with any other side or opinion, and by bluntly ignoring all urgent demands which citizens presented for more than 40 years. (All4Syria 2012)

However, in August 2012, the Syrian National Coordination Committee for Democratic Change, led by Hassan 'Abdulazim, asked for a truce among the battling parties and stated that the only way to solve the current crisis was through "the necessity of dialogue with the government."[11]

The internal divisions of the established opposition had helped the regime to isolate itself even more from the protests. In June some figures of the opposition participated in a meeting sanctioned by the government to discuss the situation in Syria, a move that was condemned by the leaders of the protests (Malas 2011). Other meetings happened without such clear connections to the government, but they did not manage to bridge the differences between the established opposition and the leaders of the protests (BBC News 2011a). The Syrian opposition in exile was still more peripheral to the dynamics of the protests. No group or political leader of the opposition in exile had any significant constituency inside Syria. Even the Muslim Brothers, despite their efforts to capitalize on the potential sympathy of the pious Syrian Sunni Muslims in periods of political crisis, recognized that they did not have any organized group of followers inside Syria. The secretary general of the Syrian Muslim Brothers, Muhammad Riad Shaqfa, declared in an interview in April 2011 that "we do not have an organisation in Syria because of the 1980 law, but we do have a large popular presence" (Oweis 2011a).[12] In this sense, the Syrian National Council, which was formed by the exiled Syrian opposition in Istanbul in September 2011 and became largely dominated by the Muslim Brothers, represented an effort by these groups and individuals to claim a political role in case the uprising succeeded in toppling the Baathist regime; it was not an actual representative body connected with the protests inside Syria (McNaught 2011).

The dynamics of the uprising in Syria were shaped by the expression of local grievances against the government through the political idiom of protest against Assad's rule and the Baathist regime itself. The demands for the fall of the regime and the end of the Assad dynasty's grip on Syria constituted a shared political idiom through which the discrete demands, grievances, and expectations of the protesters could be voiced in the public sphere. This idiom included the performative destruction or subversion of the symbols of the regime. Statues, busts, murals, and posters depicting Hafiz and/or Bashar al-Assad, as well as Bashar's deceased brother, Basil, were destroyed or defaced throughout Syria during the early days of the uprising. The Baath Party's bureaus were burned. Mobile phone shops, symbols of the corruption and nepotism in Assad's economic reforms, were looted and destroyed. In Talbisa, protesters burned Syriatel mobile phone cards while alternating chants of "Allah akbar" (God is great) with vows never to use such cards again; they also denounced Rami Makhlouf and Bashar al-Assad as "Israeli agents" who feared "Syrian nationalism."[13]

The protesters also subverted Baathist slogans praising the president or upholding him as a constitutive part of the Syrian nation. They chanted "Allah, Suriya, huriyawa bas" (God, Syria, freedom, and that's enough), removing the presidential figure as a mandatory reference in the definition of the nation.[14] As the repression increased and the protests continued, shouts of "Kis ukhtak, ya Bashar al-Assad" (Fuck you, Bashar al-Assad; literally, In the vagina of your sister, Bashar al-Assad) and "Yal'an ruhakya Hafiz" (Damn your soul, Hafiz), as well as chants of "The people want to execute the president," could often be heard.[15] Thus the protesters subverted the Baathist tradition of unrestrained praise for the figure of the president and the memory of his father. Also, as time passed the protesters' desire to reimagine the Syrian nation outside the Baathist framework was expressed by the growing presence of the pre-1963 Syrian flag, in a display of political nostalgia for the short-lived democratic period in the 1950s.[16]

While the Syrian protesters appropriated the slogans of the Tunisian and Egyptian revolutions, these were soon articulated with religious codifications of Syrian nationalism. The mobilization of religious symbols and vocabulary in the Syrian protests reflects the importance that religious nationalism acquired under Bashar al-Assad. The Baathist regime had promoted religious nationalism in order to gain the support of pious Muslims as international pressure mounted on Syria after the assassination of the Lebanese prime minister Rafik al-Hariri in 2005 (Pinto 2011).[17] In the Syrian protests, political slogans demanding freedom, justice, or the end of the Baathist regime were combined with the chanting of "Allahu akbar" (God is great) and "La ilahila Allah" (There is no god but God). Furthermore, as the protesters could not take continuous hold of open urban spaces, the mosques became the only spaces were they could gather and start demonstrations away from the vigilant security forces.

The symbolic importance that the Umayyad mosques of Damascus, Aleppo, and Der'a acquired during the protests also reflected their configuration as arenas of dispute and negotiation of religious discourses in Syria during Assad's rule.[18] In March 2011, the Umayyad mosques in Damascus and Aleppo became the sites of antigovernment protests in which people started chanting "hurriya, hurriya" (freedom, freedom) after finishing their prayers. These protests were violently repressed.[19] The 'Umari mosque in Der'a, which also dates from the Umayyad period, became the center of the uprising that took over the city for several weeks in March and April 2011. The government restored its control over the city after a military operation that included the invasion and occupation of the mosque by the army (Al Jazeera 2011b).

From the beginning of the protests, the Syrian government pointed to the importance of mosques and the religious vocabulary used in the demonstrations, accusing the protesters of being Salafi radicals or members of the Muslim Brotherhood. In a speech in January 2012, Assad tried to identify the protesters in Syria and the Muslim Brothers with the terrorists who attacked the United States on September 11, 2001:

> What we are doing now is similar to what the West did against Islam in the wake of 9/11.
> We say that there is a great religion—Islam, and there are terrorists taking cover under Islam. What should we banish: religion or terrorism? Do

we denounce religion or terrorists? Do we fight those who trade in Islam or fight terrorism? The answer is clear: It is not the fault of Islam when there are terrorists who take cover under the mantle of Islam. . . .

If we go back to the 1970s and 1980s, when the devil's brothers, who covered themselves with Islam, carried out their terrorist acts in Syria. In the beginning there were many Syrians who were misguided. . . .

The question is a race between the terrorists and reform. (Syrian Arab News Agency 2012)

The regime aimed to present the protesters as violent Sunni militants, and thus to divide and isolate them from other groups in Syrian society. Notwithstanding the fact that the majority of the protesters were Sunni Muslims and, indeed, used religious references in their demonstrations, they had been careful to make clear that their demands were for greater political freedom and not the Islamization of the state. In this sense, the mobilization of Islamic idioms in the uprising was very different from that of the 1970s and the 1980s, when it was completely linked to the project of creating an Islamic state in Syria.[20]

While the geography of the protests partially overlapped with the regions where the Salafiyya had a stronger presence in Syria—the Hawran, the Euphrates valley, Idlib, and the outskirts of the big cities (Lenfant 2008, 171)—this does not lead to the conclusion that the more radical or politicized versions of Salafism were driving the protests.[21] Even in these regions, the Salafis faced fierce competition from the Sufi-dominated religious establishment. The Salafi milieus in Syria are heavily influenced by Nasir al-Din al-Albani (1914–99), who was opposed to political action (ibid., 169), and they lack the leadership and forms of organization that could allow them to shape the dynamics of the protests. The only Islamist militant organization that has had an organized presence in Syria is Hizb al-Tahrir, which is neither Salafi nor jihadist, with a membership in Homs of an estimated one thousand (ibid., 173).[22] Despite the presence of Salafi and probably jihadist militants among the protesters, images of the protests, with the carnival-like style—including *dabke* dancing and satirical songs—that developed in places such as Hama and Homs until late 2011, reveal that they did not follow the pattern of radicalized Salafi manifestations. Therefore, Salafis were taking part in the protests, but they did not have hegemonic control over the discourses or the political projects that circulated and emerged from them. Even among Salafis there are important differences, as could be seen in the harsh dispute that erupted in Homs regarding female participation in the protests.

The accusations of Sunni sectarianism and radicalism coming from the regime were refuted with irony by the protesters, who started to stress the participation of non-Sunnis and non-Muslims in their demonstrations. At a protest in the coastal city of Baniyas, one poster asked, "Hal al-shahid Hatim Hannam assihi salafi?" (Was the martyr Hatem Hanna a Salafi Christian?), in a reference to a Christian protester who had been killed by security forces (Al Jazeera 2011e). A banner at a demonstration in Zabadani, near Damascus, stated, "La salafiwa la ikhwani . . . ana ta'ifati al-huriyya" (Neither Salafi, nor [Muslim] Brother . . . my sect is freedom) (Al Jazeera 2011f). Similarly, in ethnically or religiously mixed areas, such as the Kurdish regions of northern Syria or the Sunni/Christian/Alawi cities of the coast, the chanting of "Wahid, wahid, wahid, al-sh'ab al-Suri wahid" (One, one, one, the Syrian people are one) became a common practice in the protests. The protesters thus tried to neutralize the regime's accusations by articulating discrete ethnic and religious identities within the framework of the Syrian nation-state.

However, the continuous investment of discrete political, religious, and national imaginaries in the cultural idiom of antigovernment protest led to a process of saturation in which the capacity of the protest to provide cultural equivalence to the discrete and sometimes divergent meanings that were being expressed through it reached its limits.[23] By saturation of a cultural idiom, such as anti-Baathist political protest in Syria, I mean the process in which it becomes overinvested with discrete social imaginaries to the point where it loses the capacity to articulate the various political projects that are generated by the various actors who are mobilizing it. This process leads to the precipitation of divergent and even incompatible political projects, fragmenting the movement that was created under a shared cultural idiom. This was clearly the case in the Syrian uprising, in which the shared cultural idiom of anti-Assad or anti-Baathist protest allowed the articulation of a vast gamut of social and political actors, ranging from defenders of a more liberal political system to Salafis, but, as the protests evolved, they became oversaturated with discrete understandings of society and politics, which, in turn, precipitated as political projects that were incompatible in the eyes of the protesters, fragmenting the opposition to the Baathist regime.

In the antigovernment protests in Syria, the political slogan demanding the downfall of the regime was articulated with religious vocabulary and symbols, echoing the religious nationalism that had become conspicuous in the public discourse under Bashar al-Assad. Initially, this religious nationalism was still inclusive enough for Alawis and Christians to share it with Sunnis in the antigovernment protests; however, it gradually became more and more invested with clear Sunni meanings, deepening the tension between inclusive and sectarian understandings of religious nationalism. This alienated the non-Sunni protesters, who became increasingly uncomfortable with the range of meanings that were encoded in the religious references mobilized in the protests, which they understood as expressions of Sunni sectarianism. For example, many Alawis saw the chanting of anti-Iranian and anti-Hezbollah slogans during the protests in Der'a (Pierret 2011d), which targeted the international allies of the Baathist regime, as anti-Shia Sunni sectarianism. Also, some Christians interpreted the role of mosques and the use of Islamic religious vocabulary in the protests as proof of Sunni militancy. Even in all-Sunni demonstrations, the discrete religious and social imaginaries invested in the idiom of anti-Baathist protest precipitated as incompatible social and political projects, as could be seen in the dispute over female participation in the protests in Homs.

This process of saturation of the cultural idiom of the protests and of precipitation of divergent political projects was accentuated by the competition between discrete political and religious forces to shape and control the diffuse political project that began to emerge from the protests. In addition to the already mentioned efforts of the established secular opposition and the opposition in exile, various Sunni religious figures, inside Syria and in exile, attempted to gain a leadership role in the protests. In August 2011, at the beginning of the holy month of Ramadan, the 'ulama of Damascus and Aleppo issued communiqués attributing the responsibility for the violence and deaths in Syria to the government and urging Assad to end repression, start political reforms, and free political prisoners.

The Aleppine document was signed by important figures of the religious establishment, including the two muftis of the city, Ibrahim al-Salqini, now deceased, and Mahmud ʿAkkam; their general secretary, Muhammad al-Shihabi; and Sheikh Nur al-Din Itr, a nationally recognized specialist on Hadith (traditions of the Prophet). The Damascene communiqué had no signatures from such high-ranking figures, but it was signed by Sheikh Krayyim Rajih, the chief reader of the Qur'an in the Umayyad mosque, and by well-known figures of the Islamic opposition to the regime — Moaz al-Khatib, former preacher of the Umayyad mosque, and Jawdat Saʿid, the theoretician of nonviolence — as well as by the Sufi sheikh Hisham al-Burhani.[24] Both documents had the signatures of ʿulama who had been exiled for their participation in the Islamic uprising of 1979–82 led by the Muslim Brothers and had returned to Syria after being pardoned by the regime. The document from Aleppo was signed by Abu al-Fath al-Bayanuni, brother of the former general secretary of the Muslim Brotherhood, and Nadim al-Shihabi, disciple of ʿAbd al-Qadir ʿIsa, a Sufi sheikh of the Shadhiliyya who played an important role in mobilizing his disciples to join the Islamic uprising. The document from Damascus included the signatures of Usama and Sariya al-Rifaʿi, leaders of the Jamaʿat Zayd movement (Pierret 2011e).

The ʿulama in exile also tried to claim leadership in the uprising, using satellite TV channels and the Internet to spread their discourses into Syria. Sheikh Adnan al-ʿArʿur, who lived exiled in Saudi Arabia for having taken part in the Islamic uprising in 1982, called for punishment of those responsible for the violence and for the downfall of the regime (Saud 2011). On a television program in June 2011, Sheikh ʿArʿur, who is known for his anti-Shia positions, commented on the situation in Syria:

> I am warning specifically the Alawi sect [al-taʾifa al-ʿAlawiyya]: those who don't take sides [in the conflict] will not be harmed. Anyone who supports us is on our side, and will be treated as any other citizen. But [he points his finger at the camera] those who violate what is sacred, by God [he stands] we will mince them in meat grinders and feed dogs with their flesh.[25]

Sheikh ʿArʿur's Sunni sectarian discourse, which he tried to downplay by supporting a declaration condemning sectarianism issued in Cairo by several groups of the Syrian opposition in exile (Pierret 2011b), helped the government in its efforts to portray the uprising as a Sunni militant revolt. It also frightened the members of non-Sunni communities, such as the Alawis and the Christians, who ended up seeing the continuity of the regime as a better option than the empowerment of Sunni sectarian figures.[26]

Although Sheikh 'Ar'ur achieved great visibility in the media and certainly gained supporters among the protesters, who chanted thanks to him in Homs, his message did not have the consensus of all the protesters, nor did he have any control over the discourse that emerged from the protests. Indeed, other exiled sheikhs competed with him for the role of external "moral voice" of the protests. Sheikh Muhammad 'Ali al-Sabuni posted a video on YouTube in which he urged the inhabitants of Aleppo, his hometown, to rise against the government. Similarly, Sheikh Muhammad Abu al-Huda al-Ya'qubi, who was teacher of theology at the Umayyad mosque in Damascus until he went into exile in Saudi Arabia after the start of the uprising, lambasted in a video the members of the Damascene bourgeoisie, who, according to him, had exchanged their honor and sense of justice for material affluence and consumerism (Pierret 2011c). In addition, the Syrian Muslim Brothers, based in London, had become the major political force in the Syrian National Council. They had been trying to re-create an internal base of operations through the organization of relief aid for the protesters, in preparation for a possible return to the political arena of a post-Assad Syria, but these efforts continued to have very limited success (Al-Hajj 2012, 7–8).

A large part of the Sunni religious establishment in Syria, such as many Sufi sheikhs in Aleppo who still remembered the repression directed against them in the 1980s, adopted a "wait and see" attitude in relation to the uprising. They condemned the regime's violence in their sermons but also discouraged their disciples from joining the protests. Nevertheless, some 'ulama started to organize and to vie for leadership in the political arena that emerged from the uprising. Some of them joined organizations such as the Syrian National Movement (al-Tayyar al-Watani al-Suri), where they associated with lay Islamic thinkers, Salafis, and secularists (Pierret 2012). This mobilization of a group of 'ulama happened in response to the growing internal demand for moral and political leadership from the religious establishment, as well as to the external challenges to their authority coming from the religious leaders and political organizations in exile.

The mobilization of some Sunni religious leaders inside Syria, to dispute a more active role in the protests or in the articulation of political movements, stands in contrast to the attitude of the non-Sunni religious elite, which rallied all its forces on behalf of the regime. While many Sunni clerics still supported the regime, the Christian clerics and Alawi sheikhs expressed their commitment to Assad's rule in a much more unified way. Furthermore, they were accompanied by many members of their communities, who viewed with growing anxiety the prospect that the uprising would turn into a Sunni Islamic revolution (Rosen 2011a; *Independent* 2011). Therefore, the participants in the protests were becoming more homogeneously Sunni Muslim, as many Christians and Alawis refrained from participating and identified less and less with them. Beyond that, the impact of state repression and the emergence of armed groups among the opposition were creating a context conducive to social and political fragmentation.

The Dynamics of Repression and Social Fragmentation

The saturated idiom of anti-Baathist protest was gradually precipitating through various social fault lines—sectarianism, class, rural/urban differences, regionalism—into discrete social and political projects for Syria. The dynamics of repression and the strategic and symbolic uses of violence by the regime are very important parts of this process. The repressive tactics deployed by the regime were in many ways a revival of those used in the time of the confrontation with the Islamic opposition in 1979–82; at that time the conflict between the Baathist regime and the Islamic groups led by the Muslim Brothers radicalized into armed confrontation, and the regime used its military force to crush the opposition. Military force—in particular the Fourth Armed Division under the command of Maher al-Assad—was used to conquer and occupy urban areas previously taken by the protesters.

The regime also used a selective distribution of violence in order to deepen sectarian fault lines among the protesters, and thus to divide and isolate them. Whenever the protests occurred in mixed Sunni/Alawi or

Sunni/Alawi/Christian cities, such as Latakiya and Baniyas, even when members of all communities took part in the protests, military and paramilitary violence was directed mainly at Sunni neighborhoods. A Syrian Brazilian who was in Latakiya in July 2011 told me that "during the day there would be protests in all neighborhoods, but at night only our [Sunni] streets were attacked by the army and the *shabiha*" (personal interview 2011a).

Not that the protesters from other religious communities were spared from violence; instead of using military and paramilitary forces, the regime used its intelligence and security apparatus to mobilize internal repressive mechanisms under the threat that the whole community would be targeted if the actions of certain individuals were not suppressed. Therefore, Alawi, Christian, or Druze protesters faced repression and violence coming from their own groups, sometimes even from their own families.[27] The Alawi actress Fadwa Sulayman described this pattern of mobilization of community or family mechanisms of repression and violence against non-Sunni protesters in an interview in 2011:

> Families from minority groups exert a lot of pressure on the individuals who dissent. Many splits within families are happening because of this. . . . People cannot voice their opposition because the government is even more brutal on dissidents belonging to minority groups than those from the majority Sunni Muslims. They threaten them and their families and children even before they decide to protest. (Atassi 2011b)

This policy of enhancing the visibility of the violence directed against Sunnis and reducing the visibility of the violence directed against non-Sunni groups fed into the government's discourse that the uprising was led by Sunni militants and that the Baathist regime was overwhelmingly supported by all the other religious groups as their "protector" against Sunni radicalism. The resulting resentment over the unequal distribution of violence among the various communities reinforced the possibility of sectarian strife, creating a self-fulfilling prophecy in which the violence that the state claimed was necessary to crush sectarianism became the very mechanism through which sectarian tensions were inscribed or enhanced in the social tissue.

The regime also aimed to reinstate fear as an instrument of governability, as happened after the massacre in Hama in 1982.[28] The para-military gangs known as *shabiha*, composed of youth recruited from impoverished regions and local mafias, were deployed to produce fear in the population. These gangs, together with regular security forces, were responsible for indiscriminate arrests, torture, executions, and mutilations in the areas that had held protests against the government. The joint action of the army and the *shabiha* produced several massacres throughout Syria. One of the largest of these happened in Hula, a village near Homs where 108 persons, including children and women, were slaughtered in May 2012. The account of an elderly woman who survived the massacre shows the indiscriminate violence unleashed by the *shabiha*, who apparently came from nearby Alawi villages, upon the residents of Hula:

> I was in the house with my three grandsons, three granddaughters, sister-in-law, daughter, daughter-in-law and cousin. [On May 25] around 6:30 p.m., before sunset, we heard gunshots. I was in a room by myself when I heard the sound of a man. He was shouting and yelling at my family. I hid behind the door. I saw another man standing outside by the entrance door and another one inside the house. They were wearing military clothes. I couldn't see their faces. I thought they wanted to search the house. They walked in the house; I didn't hear them break in because we never lock the doors. After three minutes, I heard all my family members screaming and yelling. The children, all aged between ten and fourteen, were crying. I went down on the floor and tried to crawl so I could see what was happening. As I approached the door, I heard several gunshots. I was so terrified I couldn't stand on my legs. I heard the soldiers leaving. I looked outside the room and saw all of my family members shot. They were shot in their bodies and their head. I was terrified to approach to see if they were alive. I kept crawling until I reached the back door. I went outside, and I ran away. I was in shock so I don't know what happened later. (quoted in Human Rights Watch 2012)

The brutality of repression and the high level of cruelty deployed in the torture and executions revealed the aim of the regime to use fear as a tool for political demobilization of the population. The paradigmatic symbol of this strategy—of restoring power through terror—was the tortured and mutilated body of Hamza al-Khatib, a thirteen-year-old boy who was killed after being arrested in Der'a in April 2011 (Macleod and Flamand 2011). The succession of massacres that could be attributed to the regime and its paramilitary forces, such as the one in Hula in May 2012, revealed the intensification of the regime's efforts to gain control and govern through fear and unrestrained violence, a political configuration that French sociologist Michel Seurat (1989) described as "the barbaric state" (l'état de barbarie) in his analysis of the repression of the 1982 Islamic uprising in Syria by the Baathist regime.

The symbolic use of violence sometimes took forms that could be described as a macabre parody of Franz Kafka's story "In the Penal Colony," where the "crime" against the regime is inscribed in the body of the perpetrator through the destruction of the "transgressive" organ. Thus 'Ali Farzat—an internationally known Syrian cartoonist who had published a cartoon showing Qaddafi running away in a car and Bashar al-Assad trying to hitch a lift with him—was kidnapped in August by masked gunmen who beat him brutally and broke his hands (Bakri 2011). Before that, in July, Ibrahim Qashush, a fireman from Hama who had become famous for singing the satirical song "Yallah irhalya Bashar" (Come on Bashar, leave!) at demonstrations, was killed, his throat sliced and his vocal cords ripped out (Shadid 2011).

However, this strategy of restoring governance through terror and fear had clear limitations, for the protests continued, even in cities and towns that were targeted by violent repression. This situation generated a spiral of violence that sharpened and deepened tensions and fault lines in both the opposition and the regime. Inside the regime, some fractures started to appear. During the repression in Der'a, in April 2011, two members of parliament linked to the Baath Party and the mufti of Der'a renounced their positions in protest against the indiscriminate violence directed against the inhabitants of the city. The Sunni religious establishment became deeply divided, with many high-ranking religious leaders—such as the mufti of Syria, Sheikh Ahmad Badr al-Din Hassun, and the "media sheikh," Sa'id Ramadan al-Buti—giving unconditional support to the regime while others distanced themselves from it or even passed to the opposition camp.[29]

Some sheikhs cut their ties to the regime and joined the opposition, as was the case with Sheikh Muhammad al-Ya'qubi, who was dismissed from his position as preacher in the al-Hassan mosque in Damascus after he criticized the violence of the regime in that Umayyad mosque. Sheikh Ya'qubi spoke to Al Jazeera in July 2007 about the situation:

> Dialogue is impossible now after the army and the secret service people just started killing the demonstrators in the streets. . . . The regime lost its legitimacy in the first moment when it started shooting its own people in the street, this has been confirmed with these mass demonstrations. . . . The regime should start thinking of a dialogue which aims at saving the country.[30]

In another interview given in 2012 to the same news channel, he expressed the radicalization of the struggle, saying that the Syrian people "will not accept any compromise; they are not making any concessions; the ultimate goal is to Asad to step down."[31] Also, as the cycle of violence continued, defections from the army became more frequent, even among high-ranking officials, such as Manaf Tlas, son of former minister of defense Mustafa Tlas and commander of the Republican Guard, who went into exile in Turkey in July 2012. Nevertheless, the military power of the regime was still unthreatened.

The opposition was also becoming more fragmented and polarized as divergent social and political projects were precipitating, under the impact of state violence, from the saturated idiom of anti-Baathist protest. Even among the Sunni Muslims, discrete social imaginaries were producing incompatible social and political projects. An incident that happened during a protest in Homs in October 2011 is quite revealing of this process. Speakers were taking turns addressing the protesters, always using religious vocabulary in their speeches, when one of them started saying that women should not take part in the demonstrations because this was un-Islamic. Soon a fight erupted between those against and those in favor of female presence in the protests; it ended with the speaker and his supporters being chased away by those who were outraged by their proposals.

Class and Regionalism

Other fault lines in Syrian society, such as class, regionalism, and the urban/rural divide, were also reinforced in this period. Aleppo, Syria's main economic center, was probably the best example of this trend. The relative calm of the city during the 2011 uprising came as a surprise to all, given the long history of opposition to the government in Damascus and the fact that Aleppo was a stronghold of the Islamic uprising of 1979–82. One of the reasons for the lack of mobilization in Aleppo, with the exception of some working-class neighborhoods, was the fact that the Aleppine commercial and industrial bourgeoisie benefited from the economic liberalization fostered by Bashar al-Assad, since the city is the main industrial and commercial hub of Syria. Other reasons included the class urban/rural divisions that separated the protesters from the Aleppine middle class. The Aleppine elite and middle classes reacted with indifference or rejection to what they perceived as a rural and poor people's revolt.

Regionalism also played a role, in particular the urban identity of the inhabitants of Aleppo, which included their self-representation as heirs of an urban civilization with a long history. This perspective made it very difficult for the Aleppines to identify with a political movement coming from what they perceived as less cultured and backward regions. This mixture of class prejudice and urban snobbery was well expressed by an Aleppine friend who had no sympathy for the Baathist regime, as he said to me during a meeting in Europe: "Do you really think that people in Der'a or in Baniyas understand what is democracy? Or that they care about freedom? No way! They are only protesting because some sheikh told them to do so" (personal interview 2011b).

The protesters viewed Aleppo's lack of mobilization with dismay, as they knew that the regime had a better chance to stand as long as it did not have to deal with a revolt in Aleppo. A banner displayed at an April 2011 demonstration in Baniyas asked, "Waynak, ya Halab?" (Where are you, Aleppo?), scolding the Aleppines for not staging massive protests against the government (Reuters 2011a). As time passed and the repression of the demonstrations became more violent, incredulity gave way to hostility against the metropolis of northern Syria. In October, banners at a demonstration in Homs bore angry slogans directed against Aleppo's passivity. Some read "Shame on the people of Aleppo" and "Aleppo the gray; Aleppo the coward" (Halab shahba'; Halab jubana'), while others called on Syrians to boycott goods from Aleppo (Al Jazeera 2011d). Even with the occupation of parts of the city by the Free Syrian

Army, the population of Aleppo did not join the rebels, who came mainly from the countryside or even other Arab countries.[32] The example of Aleppo shows how regional divisions were also becoming deeper and increasingly political.

This trend was also spreading in the countryside, where religious and local identities were becoming territorialized as villages and towns were organizing defense forces through sectarian lines. In religiously mixed regions, such as the Ghab, near Hama, killings and clashes between armed groups from different villages allowed sectarian and political stereotypes, such as Alawi-Christian/pro-government and Sunni/anti-Baathist opposition, to acquire social reality by resignifying and reorganizing a variety of social conflicts that were now recovered by and expressed through these categories. Arms smuggled from Lebanon fed this process of territorialization and militarization of locally produced combinations of regional, political, and sectarian identities (Rosen 2011b), which created a pattern of diffuse sectarian violence throughout central Syria.

Also, the continuous defection of soldiers and a few high-ranking officials—mostly Sunnis—from the Syrian army led to the militarization of the protests. In Homs and other places, such as Idlib, defected soldiers created brigades for defending the protesters against the army and the *shabiha*. Attacks on soldiers and members of the security forces were becoming recurring events throughout Syria. In July 2011, a group of defected soldiers and officers created the Free Syrian Army (al-Jaiysh al-Suri al-Hur), which gradually became an umbrella organization for defected military personnel throughout Syria, as well as for some foreign fighters who joined the struggle against Assad. In the beginning, the Free Syrian Army gathered a large number of soldiers in the city of Rastan, which had a powerful symbolic meaning as the hometown of Mustafa Tlas, the former minister of defense who was pushed into retreat by Assad. The defectors fought a fierce battle against the Syrian army in the beginning of October 2011. The Syrian army regained control of Rastan, but at the cost of an enormous amount of destruction and death (Al Jazeera 2011c). Nevertheless, the city continued to be a battleground in the ongoing confrontation between the Syrian army and the Free Syrian Army. The Free Syrian Army engaged in battles for the control of Homs, the suburbs of Damascus, and, after July 2012, Aleppo. While the rebels were not fully successful in any of these battles, they gained some urban bases and brought the fight into Syria's major cities.

The battle of Aleppo showed the tactical limitations of both the regime and the armed opposition. The regime deployed only a fraction of its military force, keeping most units at military bases out of fear of mass defections among regular soldiers. The Syrian army used the tactic of bombarding neighborhoods in order to prevent the Free Syrian Army from controlling significant parts of the city.[33] The army also tried to make the civilian population of Aleppo pay a high price for the presence of the Free Syrian Army in the city, bombarding bakeries to create shortages of bread, the main food staple still found at affordable prices in the city. On the other hand, the fighters of the Free Syrian Army, among whom there were very few Aleppines, were trying to trap the army into a war of attrition, occupying neighborhoods and moving out as the army attacked. The result was that Aleppo became a war zone, caught between two armed forces that treated its neighborhoods purely as military targets. This led to an enormous death toll among the civilian population as well as to the destruction of Aleppo's unique historic and architectural heritage.

On November 16, 2011, the Free Syrian Army launched an attack against an air force intelligence base in a suburb of Damascus, hitting the regime in its military structure (Atassi 2011a), a pattern that would become more common in the following months of confrontation between the regime and the armed rebels. Following December 2011 a series of bombings and suicide bombings hit Damascus, Aleppo, and Dayr al-Zor, raising fears that jihadist groups inspired by al-Qaeda might be coming from Iraq or Lebanon and could be acting in Syria. However, evidence also suggested that the security forces could have promoted these attacks or allowed them to happen so that the regime could capitalize on them, pointing to them as proof of the Islamist radicalism of the opposition (Pierret 2011a).

As the prospect of civil war loomed on the horizon, the Baathist regime, which many players in the international and regional scene viewed as a key element in regional stability, started to lose its political capital and was becoming increasingly isolated. It was constantly criticized, both by opponents such as the United States and by former allies such as Turkey and Qatar. The Baathist regime shifted from being seen as the main element in a political solution to the crisis to being treated as a factor that could cause further destabilization and violence.

Turkey, a former ally, decided to take a preeminent role in the transition to a post-Baathist political situation, pressuring the Syrian government to stop the violent repression of the protests, sponsoring meetings of the Syrian opposition, and even harboring the central command of the Free Syrian Army. On November 13, 2011, the Arab League decided to suspend Syria's membership if the violence did not stop. The international pressure on the Baathist regime was mounting, with Turkey, Saudi Arabia, Qatar, the United States, and France trying to isolate it while giving support and resources to the armed opposition. In June 2012, Turkish prime minister Recep Erdogan made it clear that he was working for Assad's removal from power and stated: "What Assad is doing is barbarism and persecution. . . . As a country sharing a border of 910 kilometers with Syria, we will not remain silent. I want to make it very clear that Assad will soon go away. He just cannot stay in power any longer. Bashar al-Assad is preparing his own end" (quoted in Turkish Weekly 2012). In a more laconic way, U.S. secretary of state Hillary Clinton, addressing the United Nations–backed Action Group on Syria when it convened in Geneva in July 2012, similarly stated, "Asad will still have to go."[34]

However, a direct intervention was unlikely to happen. Since the beginning of the conflict, the American government and some of its European and Arab allies had been reticent to remove Assad from power through military action or to supply the armed opposition with heavy weaponry.[35] Furthermore, the regime still had important allies in international and regional spheres, such as Russia, Iran, and China, who opposed the removal of Assad from power while continuing to support and arm the Syrian regime. In September 2012, Russian president Vladimir Putin warned the Western nations that their "dangerous" stand on Syria could come back to haunt them (RIA Novosti 2012). The lack of consensus in the U.N. Security Council meant that any U.N. resolutions and plans approved for Syria would be only watered-down calls for cease-fires or missions to monitor the conflict, with no effect in diminishing the violence.

By mid-2012, the Syrian protesters and opposition had not managed to produce a unified mobilization on a full national scale. The opposition did not have the unity, resources, or national support to topple the regime and was becoming more and more identified with the military insurrection led by the Free Syrian Army. The multiplication of direct sources of financing and arms supplies to the armed opposition—with France favoring former Baathist nationalists and Saudi Arabia and Qatar favoring Islamist factions of the opposition—led to splits within the Free Syrian Army and the creation of new armed groups, including one under the control of Sheikh Adnan al-'Ar'ur (Al Jazeera 2012). At the same time, Bashar's government could not enforce its control of large portions of Syrian territory without resorting to the continuous use of military and paramilitary forces. Nevertheless, the Baathist regime showed no sign that it was heading toward any kind of negotiated transition, albeit limited, to a more liberal political order. As result, the fault lines of Syrian society were becoming deeper, and a process of social fragmentation and polarization was firmly installed. The protests were increasingly militarized, centers of armed resistance became part of the landscape of the uprising, and the dynamics of civil war were present throughout the country. Therefore, while the slogans of the first protests in the Syrian uprising, which simply called for *hurriya* (freedom) and declared that "al-sh'ab al-Suri ma bihaf" (the Syrian people are not afraid), still summarized the hopes of the protesters, they were dismissed by a regime that saw them as the machinations of "terrorists." Moreover, the regime continued to insist that the only solution lay in illusory reforms that never gained any reality. Tragically, in this confrontation, the logic of violence and revenge continued to gain ground, destroying the very social fabric of the nation that both sides claimed they wanted to save.

Notes

1. On January 26, 2011, Hassan Ali Akleh, a young Kurdish man, poured gasoline over his body and set himself on fire in Hassaka, in northeastern Syria. He was

emulating the example of Mohamed Bouazizi, whose self-immolation unleashed the wave of protests that ended Ben Ali's dictatorship in Tunisia. Similar cases of self-immolation took place in Egypt, Algeria, Jordan, and Saudi Arabia.

2. The concept of the "moral insult" was developed by the Brazilian anthropologist Luís Roberto Cardoso de Oliveira (2006). It refers to violence or aspects of violence that cannot be measured by material damages, for such violence acts through the denial of the moral dimension of the subject.

3. See "Pro-Assad Rally Staged in Damascus," YouTube video, March 29, 2011, http://www.youtube.com/watch?v=xQAOQfIVCOM (accessed March 15, 2013).

4. The Fourth Armored Division was created when the special paramilitary unit known as the Defense Brigades (Saraiya al-Difa') merged into the Syrian army. The soldiers of this division are mainly recruited from Syria's religious and ethnic minorities, following the regime's strategy of forging alliances with these groups by exploiting the tensions between them and the Arab Sunni majority (see Van Dam 2011, 114–23).

5. No reliable estimates of the numbers of peopled detained and tortured since the beginning of the uprising are available. The numbers of political prisoners the Syrian regime periodically released to show its "goodwill" in engaging in dialogue with the opposition or its compliance with calls from the international community and the Arab League to end the repression were always in the hundreds or thousands. On November 5, 2011, the Syrian government released 553 prisoners as a gesture of goodwill before the 'Eid al-Adha, and on November 15, another 1,180 prisoners were released ahead of the meeting of Arab ministers in Rabat, Morocco, to discuss Syria's suspension by the Arab League (see Oweis 2011b; Reuters 2011b).

6. Sufism is the mystical tradition in Islam. It is organized into various esoteric traditions or "paths" (*tariqa*; plural *turuq*) that are transmitted through a process of mystical initiation of the disciples by their masters, who are those who have already been successfully initiated by other masters, becoming Sufi sheikhs. The social expression of Sufism involves communities, each of which is organized around a charismatic leader, the Sufi sheikh, who is the main religious authority for his followers and disciples. In Syria, Sufism is an integral part of Muslim religiosity, with a large proportion of the nation's religious leaders being initiated in Sufism and acting as Sufi sheikhs for their communities (Pinto 2007a).

7. Estimates of the number of deaths range from five thousand to twenty-five thousand (Van Dam 2011, 111).

8. Ironically, the rejection of this dynastic model of authoritarianism was one of the mobilizing factors in the revolutions and uprisings that took place in Tunisia, Egypt, Libya, and Yemen. The term *jumlukiyya* is a neologism created by the fusion of two Arabic words: *jumhuriyya* (republic) and *mamalukiyya* (kingdom).

9. A Kurdish political militant from Aleppo told me in 2006 that the Kurdish party Yekîtî tried to forge an alliance with the leaders of the Civil Society Move-

ment, but their refusal to incorporate Kurdish demands of cultural recognition into their political project led to the eventual failure of this initiative.

10. Makhlouf is the main shareholder of the mobile phone company Syriatel and had a large share of the other company that operated in Syria, Arreba/MTN. He is also a major shareholder in nine of the twelve private banks that operate in Syria, including two Islamic banks (Donati 2009, 231).

11. See "Syrians' Opposition Body Calls for Dialogue with Government," Press TV video, August 15, 2012, http://www.presstv.ir (accessed March 15, 2013).

12. The 1980 law to which he refers made affiliation with the Muslim Brotherhood a crime punishable by death. The fact that the Muslim Brothers did not manage to keep even clandestine cells in Syria shows how the Brotherhood's social basis, which never reached much beyond the traditional elites and the urban middle classes, became even narrower after 1982 (Abd-Allah 1983; Batatu 1988; Carré and Seurat [1983] 2001).

13. See "Talbeesa—Protesters Burn Syriatel SIM Cards Owned by Rami Makhlouf, Cousin of Assad," YouTube video, May 21, 2011, http://www.youtube.com/watch?v=r9Y5q2HnmaY (accessed March 15, 2013).

14. This slogan was answered in the pro-regime demonstrations organized in Damascus and Aleppo with chants of "Allah, Suriya, Bashar wa bas" (God, Syria, Bashar, and that's enough), restoring the position of the president in the Baathist national imaginary.

15. See, for example, "Syria—al-Assad Statue Burns," YouTube video, April 22, 2011, http://www.youtube.com/watch?v=tyMtuszY7k4 (accessed March 15, 2013); "Hama, 29th of June 2011," YouTube video, June 25, 2011, http://www.youtube.com/watch?v=ziUUtbXPVhw (accessed March 15, 2013); "People Want the Execution of the President—Free Syria," YouTube video, August 27, 2011, http://www.youtube.com/watch?v=H17AAosDxIs (accessed March 15, 2013).

16. When I was doing my first period of fieldwork research in Syria, from 1999 to 2001, a widespread cultural nostalgia for the 1950s already existed among the urban middle classes. The 1950s were constructed as a "golden age" of economic growth, liberal politics, and cultural effervescence, and this narrative came to be appropriated as a sort of anti-Baathist nationalism during the protests. A similar process of reclaiming the political past through the flag happened in Libya, where the pre-1969 monarchic flag was adopted by the opposition to Muammar Qaddafi.

17. Hariri was seen as a "modernizer" of Lebanon and had strong connections with the United States, France, and Saudi Arabia. It was widely suspected that Syrian agents had killed Hariri because of his opposition to the Syrian military presence in Lebanon. The assassination prompted an intense reaction from Hariri's allies, and as a result Syria was forced to remove its troops from Lebanon in 2005, ending an occupation that had provided Syria with many economic benefits.

18. Syrian historiography treats the Umayyad period (661–750) as a mythical reference point that gives historical depth to the fusion of Syrian nationalism, pan-Arabism, and Islam as cultural heritage made by the Baathist ideology (Valter 2002, 53–58).

19. For an example in Aleppo, see "25/March, Syrian Policemen Wear Civil Clothes Attack Protesters at Umayyad Mosque," YouTube video, March 26, 2011, http://www.youtube.com/watch?v=V3mh-StEuSA (accessed March 15, 2013). See also "A Protest at Umayyad Mosque in the Syrian Capital Damascus on Friday 18/March," YouTube video, http://www.youtube.com/watch?v=aOyPDonA30A (accessed March 15, 2013).

20. See the "Manifesto of the Islamic Revolution in Syria" and "The Programs of the Islamic Revolution" in Abd-Allah (1983, 201–67).

21. The Salafiyya is a reform movement in Islam that appeared in the nineteenth century, preaching a "return" to the sources of the Islamic tradition in order to "purify" Islam—that is, to rid it of the innovations and additions that it had received in various social and cultural settings throughout its history. Some Salafis criticized as "un-Islamic" many of the religious beliefs and practices connected to Sufism, such as the cult of saints. Despite its emphasis on re-creating the "original" Prophetic message, the Salafiyya was never a unified movement; it produced several trends that developed discrete understandings regarding which sources could give access to the Islam of the *salaf* (predecessors) and how to interpret them. In Syria the Salafiyya was met with fierce competition from the religious establishment, which was heavily influenced by Sufism, and it gained some ground only in rural areas and midsize towns, mainly because of the labor migration of residents of these areas to the Gulf countries and Saudi Arabia, where they were exposed to various forms of Salafi religiosity (Lenfant 2008).

22. Hizb al-Tahrir is a pan-Islamic political organization devoted to uniting all Muslim countries in a re-created caliphate. It was founded in 1953 in Jerusalem by the Palestinian sheikh Muhammad Taqi al-Din al-Nabhani. This organization rejects both liberal democracy and jihadist violence as ways to implement its political project; it has no connections to the Salafiyya or to the Muslim Brotherhood in Syria (Lenfant 2008).

23. The concepts of saturation and precipitation as discussed here come from Robert Weller's (1994) analysis of protest movements and revolts in China, such as the Taiping revolt and the protests in Tiananmen Square. Weller shows how cultural idioms can become saturated by the investment in them of divergent social imaginaries and how this leads to the precipitation of discrete social movements and political projects.

24. For excellent analysis of the role of the Syrian *'ulama* in the uprising, see the articles in Thomas Pierret's Mediapart blog, http://blogs.mediapart.fr.

25. See "Syrian Sunni Cleric Threatens," YouTube video, July 13, 2011, http://www.youtube.com/watch?v=Bwz8i3osHww (accessed March 15, 2013).

26. The Alawis are a branch of Shia Islam that developed an esoteric and sometimes allegorical understanding of Islamic doctrines and rituals. While among the Alawis religious knowledge traditionally was secretive and reserved to the sheikhs, a long process of convergence between the Alawis and mainstream Twelver Shiism has taken place, and the former have adopted doctrinal and ritual traditions of the latter. However, some Sunni Muslims, such as many Salafis, still see the Alawis as heretics. Bashar al-Assad and a large part of the inner circle of the Baathist regime belong to the Alawi community, but most members of the Alawi community do not benefit from the regime, which also has many non-Alawis. Further, the opposition includes some Alawis. The Baathist regime marketed itself as a promoter of secularism and a protector of the religious minorities against "Sunni radicalism," causing many Christians and Alawis to support it (Pinto 2007a; Van Dam 2011).

27. This information comes from interviews conducted with Alawi and Christian Syrian Brazilians who have family in Latakiya, Homs, and Tartus.

28. Summary executions were part of the "restoration of order" in Hama even after the uprising was crushed. Memories of this period were still alive when I did my first fieldwork in Syria in 1999–2001. However, I could see them fading away and losing political relevance in the subsequent years.

29. While cooperation with the regime is a widespread practice among Sunni religious leaders in Syria, it is often done within clear boundaries that prevent the religious authority of the sheikhs from being harmed in the eyes of their followers. Whenever the charismatic power of a sheikh is challenged or diminished because of his connection to the regime, the sheikh's ending the relationship or confronting the state becomes a possibility (see Pinto 2007b).

30. See "Interview with Mohamed al-Yaqoubi," YouTube video, July 16, 2011, http://www.youtube.com/watch?v=CH0Irzb_l6M (accessed March 15, 2013).

31. See "Syrian Uprising," YouTube video, August 4, 2012, http://www.youtube.com/watch?v=yVPtgLYMffM (accessed March 15, 2013).

32. See "Foreign Fighters Join the Battle of Aleppo," YouTube video, August 25, 2012, http://www.youtube.com/watch?v=C3b_G75ka54 (accessed March 15, 2013).

33. I thank Thomas Pierret for calling my attention to this fact.

34. See "Clinton—'Assad Will Still Have To Go,'" YouTube video, July 1, 2012, http://www.youtube.com/watch?v=AS8M4SySEbc (accessed March 15, 2013).

35. The Israeli government also had been reticent about the possibility of removing Assad from power. Nevertheless, it had engaged in declarations that could enhance the sectarian tensions in Syria, as was the case of the announcement by the chief of staff of the Israel Defense Forces that Israel was preparing to receive Alawi refugees from Syria in case of the downfall of Assad's government (Lis 2012).

References

Ababsa, Myriam. 2007. "Le Démantèlement des fermes d'état Syriennes: Une Contre-réforme agraire (2000–2005)." In *La Syrie au présent: Reflets d'une société,* edited by Baudoin Dupret, Zouhair Ghazzal, Yussef Courbage, and Mohammed al-Dbiyat, 739–45. Arles: Actes Sud.

Abbas, Hassan. 2011. "The Dynamics of the Uprising in Syria." Jadaliyya, October 19. http://www.jadaliyya.com (accessed November 18, 2011).

Abd-Allah, Umar. 1983. *The Islamic Struggle in Syria.* Berkeley, Calif.: Mizan Press.

Aita, Samir. 2007. "L'Économie de la Syrie peut-elle devenir sociale? Vous avez dit economie sociale de marché?" In *La Syrie au présent: Reflets d'une société,* edited by Baudoin Dupret, Zouhair Ghazzal, Yussef Courbage, and Mohammed al-Dbiyat, 541–88. Arles: Actes Sud.

Al Arabiya News. 2011. "Protests' Shockwave Hits Syria and Djibouti." February 28. http://www.alarabiya.net (accessed November 14, 2012).

Al-Hajj, 'Abd al-Rahman. 2012. *Al-Islam al-siyasi wa al-thawra fi Suriya.* Al Jazeera Center for Studies. http://studies.aljazeera.net (accessed June 12, 2012).

Al Jazeera. 2011a. "Assad Attempts to Appease Minority Kurds." April 8. http://www.aljazeera.com (accessed November 3, 2011).

——. 2011b. "Death Toll Rises as Syria Crackdown Continues." May 1. http://www.aljazeera.com (accessed November 3, 2011).

——. 2011c. "'Horrific Aftermath' of Syria Clashes." Video from YouTube, October 5. http://www.aljazeera.com (accessed November 4, 2011).

——. 2011d. "No Let-Up in Syria Unrest." October 22. http://www.aljazeera.com (accessed November 4, 2011).

——. 2011e. "Syria Live Blog." April 22. http://www.aljazeera.com (accessed November 3, 2011).

——. 2011f. "Syria Live Blog." April 23. http://www.aljazeera.com (accessed November 3, 2011).

——. 2012. "Syria's FSA 'Splintering into Factions.'" Video, October 12. http://www.aljazeera.com (accessed March 14, 2013).

All4Syria. 2011. "The Dynamics of the Uprising in Syria." October 29. http://all4syria.info/Archive/34022 (accessed March 14, 2013).

——. 2012. "Q&A: Aref Dalila, Former Dean of the Faculty of Economics at Damascus University." June 13. http://all4syria.info/Archive/45245 (accessed March 14, 2013).

Atassi, Basma. 2011a. "Free Syrian Army Grows in Influence." Al Jazeera, November 16. http://www.aljazeera.com (accessed November 20, 2011).

——. 2011b. "Q&A: Syria's Daring Actress." Al Jazeera, November 23. http://www.aljazeera.com (accessed November 15, 2012).

Bakri, Nada. 2011. "Political Cartoonist Whose Work Skewered Assad Is Brutally

Beaten in Syria." *New York Times,* August 25. http://www.nytimes.com (accessed November 4, 2011).

Batatu, Hanna. 1988. "Syria's Muslim Brethren." In *State and Ideology in the Middle East and Pakistan,* edited by Fred Halliday and Hamza Alavi, 112–32. New York: Monthly Review Press.

Bayoumy, Yara. 2011. "Syria Lifts Niqab Ban, Shuts Casino, in Nod to Sunnis." Reuters, April 6. http://in.reuters.com (accessed November 3, 2011).

BBC News. 2011a. "Syrian Opposition Meet in Damascus to Support Protests." September 17. http://www.bbc.co.uk (accessed November 3, 2011).

———. 2011b. "Syria Protests: Assad to Lift State of Emergency." April 20. http://www.bbc.co.uk (accessed November 3, 2011).

Cardoso de Oliveira, Luís Roberto. 2006. *Droit légal et insulte morale: Dilemmes de lacitoyennetéau Brésil, au Québec et aux Etats-Unis.* Quebec: Les Presses de l'Université Laval.

Carré, Olivier, and Michel Seurat. (1983) 2001. *Les Frères Musulmans: 1928–1982.* Paris: l'Harmattan.

Donati, Caroline. 2009. *L'Exception Syrienne: Entre modernisation et résistance.* Paris: La Découverte.

George, Alan. 2003. *Syria: Neither Bread nor Freedom.* London: Zed Books.

Human Rights Watch. 2012. "Syria: UN Inquiry Should Investigate Houla Killings." May 28. http://www.hrw.org (accessed November 15, 2012).

Independent. 2011. "Life after Assad Looks Ominous for Syria's Christian Minority." September 5. http://www.independent.co.uk (accessed November 4, 2011).

IRIN (Humanitarian News and Analysis, U.N. Office for the Coordination of Humanitarian Affairs). 2010. "Syria: Drought Pushing Millions into Poverty." September 9. http://www.irinnews.org (accessed November 3, 2011).

Le Gac, Daniel. 1991. *La Syrie du General Assad.* Brussels: Complexe.

Lenfant, Arnaud. 2008. "L'Évolution du salafisme en Syrie au XXe siècle." In *Qu'est-ce que le Safisme?,* edited by Bernard Rougier, 161–78. Paris: PUF.

Lis, Jonathan. 2012. "IDF Chief: Israel Ready To Absorb Some Syria Refugees Once Assad Falls." *Haaretz,* January 10. http://www.haaretz.com (accessed March 15, 2013).

Macleod, Hugh, and Annasofie Flamand. 2011. "Tortured and Killed: Hamza al-Khateeb, Age 13." Al Jazeera, May 31. http://www.aljazeera.com (accessed November 4, 2011).

Malas, Nour. 2011. "Opposition Meeting in Syria Shows Split among Activists." *Wall Street Journal,* June 28. http://online.wsj.com (accessed November 3, 2011).

McNaught, Anita. 2011. "Syria's Opposition Finds Its Voice." Al Jazeera, October 4. http://www.aljazeera.com (accessed November 15, 2012).

Oweis, Khaled Yacoub. 2011a. "Interview: Muslim Brotherhood Supports Anti-

Assad Protests." Reuters, April 11. http://www.reuters.com (accessed November 15, 2012).

———. 2011b. "Syria Crackdown Toll Rises Despite Arab Peace Deal: U.N." Reuters, November 8. http://www.reuters.com (accessed March 14, 2013).

Perthes, Volker. 1995. *The Political Economy of Syria under Asad.* London: I. B. Tauris.

Pierret, Thomas. 2011a. "Les Attentats de damas 'revendiqués' par un proche du Grand Mufti?" Mediapart blog, December 27. http://blogs.mediapart.fr (accessed May 22, 2012).

———. 2011b. "Des islamistes syriens tendent la main à la communaute alaouite." Mediapart blog, October 4. http://blogs.mediapart.fr (accessed November 3, 2011).

———. 2011c. "Des oulémas syriens exiles tentent de 'réveiller' la bourgeoisie pieuse via YouTube." Mediapart blog, October 21. http://blogs.mediapart.fr (accessed November 4, 2011).

———. 2011d. "Le Parcours du combattant des opposants syriens." *Le Monde,* April 7. http://www.lemonde.fr (accessed November 21, 2011).

———. 2011e. "Qui sont les oulémas contestataires en Syrie?" Mediapart blog, August 15. http://blogs.mediapart.fr (accessed November 3, 2011).

———. 2012. "Le Courant National Syrien, un concurrent pour les Frères Musulmans?" Mediapart blog, February 7. http://blogs.mediapart.fr (accessed June 21, 2012).

Pinto, Paulo. 2007a. "Religions et religiosité en Syrie." In *La Syrie au présent: Reflets d'une société,* edited by Baudoin Dupret, Zohair Ghazzal, Youssef Courbage, and Mohammed Dbiyat, 312–58. Arles: Actes Sud.

———. 2007b. "Sufism and the Political Economy of Morality in Syria." In *Sufism and Politics: The Power of Spirituality,* edited by Paul Heck, 103–36. Princeton, N.J.: Markus Wiener.

———. 2011. " 'Oh Syria, God Protects You': Islam as Cultural Idiom under Bashar al-Asad." *Middle East Critique* 20 (2): 189–205.

Reuters. 2011a. "Almost 90 Dead in Syria's Bloodiest Day of Unrest." Slide show, April 22. http://www.reuters.com (accessed March 15, 2013).

———. 2011b. "Syria Frees Dissident, Prisoners as Pressure Mounts." November 15. http://www.reuters.com (accessed March 14, 2013).

RIA Novosti. 2012. "Putin Warns West's Syria Policy Could Backfire." September 6. http://en.rian.ru (accessed November 15, 2012).

Rosen, Nir. 2011a. "Assad's Alawites: An Entrenched Community." Al Jazeera, October 12. http://www.aljazeera.com (accessed November 4, 2011).

———. 2011b. "Assad's Alawites: The Guardians of the Throne." Al Jazeera, October 10. http://www.aljazeera.com (accessed November 4, 2011).

Saud, Fahad. 2011. "Saudi-Based Syrian Cleric Urges Continued Protests against Assad's Regime." Al Arabiya News, August 6. http://www.alarabiya.net (accessed November 3, 2011).

Seurat, Michel. 1989. *Syrie: L'État de barbarie*. Paris: Seuil.

Shadid, Anthony. 2011. "Lyrical Message for Syrian Leader: 'Come on Bashar, Leave.'" *New York Times*, July 21. http://www.nytimes.com (accessed November 4, 2011).

Syrian Arab News Agency. 2012. "'Syria Will Remain Free'—President Bashar al-Assad Speech on January 10, 2012." Syrian Free Press, January 11. http://syrianfreepress.wordpress.com (accessed October 16, 2012).

Turkish Weekly. 2012. "Bashar Al-Assad Preparing His Own End, Says PM Erdogan." June 8. http://www.turkishweekly.net (accessed November 15, 2012).

Valter, Stéphane. 2002. *La Construction nationale Syrienne: Légitimation de la nature communautaire du pouvoir par le discours historique*. Paris: CNRS.

Van Dam, Nikolaos. 2011. *The Struggle for Power in Syria: Politics and Society under Asad and the Ba'th Party*. London: I. B. Tauris.

Wall Street Journal. 2011. "Interview with Syrian President Bashar al-Assad." January 31. http://online.wsj.com (accessed November 3, 2011).

Weller, Robert P. 1994. *Resistance, Chaos, and Control in China: Taiping Rebels, Taiwanese Ghosts, and Tiananmen*. Seattle: University of Washington Press.

Personal Interviews

Personal interview. 2011a. Anonymous. Latakiya, July.
Personal interview. 2011b. Anonymous. Strasbourg, May.

Jordan

JILLIAN SCHWEDLER

ON MARCH 24, 2011, hundreds of Jordanians calling themselves the March 24 Youth began what they intended as an indefinite sit-in outside the Ministry of the Interior in the capital city of Amman. As one member stated prior to the event:

> We are a mixture of free Jordanian young men and women, who are tired of delays and the promise of reform, who see the spread of corruption, the deterioration of the economic situation, the regression of political life, the erasure of freedoms, and the dissolution of the social fabric. (Jadaliyya 2011)

The police were mostly peaceful on the first day, blocking off the Dakhili traffic circle, watching and wandering among the demonstrators, and trying to defuse tensions. The Youth waved Jordanian flags and donned the red-and-white kaffiyehs that signify Jordanian national identity, hoping their expressed patriotism might deflate a repressive response from the regime.[1] Aside from the original protesters, the only group to gain access to the circle was a Loyalty March, the participants in which were allowed (with some cars) to enter the circle and position themselves facing the March 24 Youth.[2] This group chanted in praise of King Abdullah and launched insults at the March 24 Youth, but the first day of the sit-in was mostly calm, and the evening passed with little incident (Jadaliyya 2011). The police seemed to be primarily neutral, trying to prevent an escalation of tensions as the two sides seemed to compete for the title of "most patriotic" in their songs and slogans.[3] As one eyewitness described the scene:

> Underneath the bridge was a fairly well-organized group of young 20-something year olds. They had their posters in Arabic and English. They had a truck with a sound system. They had low-level organizers with bullhorns who would walk around making sure their group kept to the sidewalk. They had brooms and garbage bags, and people designated the task of keeping the area clean. They had tents, food, laptops, Internet connections, digital cameras, camcorders, a live feed going, as well as a fire roaring in near-freezing weather. At the tip of the sidewalk, their members were lined up facing the circle, where across from them was another group, and in between them both were about two dozen policemen. (Tarawnah 2011)

In the morning, as the Youth began their morning prayers, the Loyalty March began blaring music, a practice that is understood as unacceptable. The confrontation escalated as Loyalty Marchers, swelling in number, began throwing rocks at the March 24 Youth.

Most Jordanians viewed the general police with less animosity than they did the Darak riot police. As Darak troops began entering the square that second afternoon, the March 24 Youth realized that the situation was about to turn toward violence, that the Darak were not there to protect them from the stone-throwing counterprotesters. The Darak began charging toward the Youth to break up their camp. Dozens were arrested and more than a hundred were injured; videos documenting the aggressiveness with which the security and unarmed thugs (the by then infamous *baltajiyya*) chased demonstrators, beating them with clubs and other objects, were soon posted on YouTube.[4] Many protesters struggled to escape around barricades and over fences that had been rapidly assembled to constrain them. In the melee, one Jordanian was killed (Bouziane and Lenner 2011; Tobin 2012).

As millions of protesters throughout the Arab world took to the streets in 2011, and as tens of thousands lost their lives, what made this one death—and this one event—remarkable? It was the only protest-related death in Jordan the whole year, despite weekly gatherings throughout the country that sometimes reached into the thousands. By the end of the year, major roadblocks, bonfires fueled by tires, and increasingly bold expressions of dissent against the regime were commonplace, but injuries remained remarkably low.

For an authoritarian state, Jordan has had a surprisingly long and vibrant history of political protests with only limited incidents of violence. In contrast to the kingdom's northern neighbor, Syria—where before long the government had killed upward of ten thousand of the nation's own people in an attempt to put down the uprising that began in 2011—Jordan had a relationship with protesters that was largely civil and respectful. On many occasions, police distributed cases of water to protesters and chatted with them as they hovered casually around the margins of events. The repressive Darak troops always waited a short distance away, but the regime was relatively restrained in utilizing them. The March 24 Youth sit-in was an exception. Protests in all parts of Jordan were so common, in fact, that many Jordanians were more annoyed by them (and the traffic delays they caused) than worried that they would spark a heavy-handed response from the regime. Even the 1989 protests that began in the southern town of Ma'an, which famously spread across the kingdom and led King Hussein to initiate political liberalization, resulted in few injuries (Ryan 2002).

As the Arab uprisings spread across the Middle East more than two decades after tens of thousands protested in 1989, King Abdullah appeared to respond to some of the demands for political reforms. But unlike in Tunisia, Yemen, Egypt, and Syria, Jordan's reigning and ruling political regime did not appear to be in any danger of being overthrown (Bouziane and Lenner 2011; Ryan 2011; International Crisis Group 2012; Tobin 2012). The protests that began in January 2011 and continued into 2012 demanded constitutional reform, a reduction in the king's power, and a revised electoral system and law, but virtually no voices demanded an end to the monarchy itself. Unlike elsewhere in the region, many of these protests had, for the most part, been organized by the same groups that have always organized protests—political parties across the political spectrum, including the conservative Islamic Action Front and the leftist Widha party, the Muslim Brotherhood, the professional associations (organizations of groups such as doctors, lawyers, dentists, engineers, agricultural engineers, and pharmacists), and so on. Large numbers of Jordanians did not take to the streets as did citizens of Tunisia, Egypt, Libya, Syria, and Yemen. In Saudi Arabia and Bahrain, Shiite minorities and majorities launched protests to demand a greater voice and representation in those regimes, but Jordan's majority Palestinians did not mobilize, and they showed no signs of doing so despite their being significantly disadvantaged by the gerrymandering of electoral districting in Jordan.

The Hashemite Kingdom of Jordan was sparsely populated in its early days of the 1920s, home to Bedouin tribes and a few modest urban centers.[5] Many of the kingdom's most prominent families hailed from outside the new state's territory—including the ruling Hashemites, who originated in the Hijaz (in today's western Saudi Arabia) and were put on the throne by the British in recognition of their support of British aims in World War I (Alon 2007). Decades later, Palestinians flooded into Jordan in two massive refugee flows across the Jordan River, in 1948 and 1967. While they were granted full citizenship and eventually came to make up a majority of the kingdom's population—the king even annexed the West Bank as a permanent part of Jordan (between 1949 and 1988, although Jordan lost control of those lands in 1967)—the ruling family found its loyal base in East Bank families (as opposed to Palestinians, who came from the West Bank).[6] Jordanians of Palestinian origin (and their descendants) eventually grew to constitute a majority of the kingdom's population. But with that majority largely not participating in the protests against the monarchy, Jordan seemed to have evaded the instability of the Arab Spring, with its astute and modernizing King Abdullah leading the way for reforms.

But how *did* the Jordanian regime manage to contain weekly protests, which sometimes swelled into the tens of thousands? One conventional answer is that monarchies have been immune to pressure from below, largely because they do not have to demonstrate their legitimacy through periodic staged electoral contests. But monarchies from Morocco to the Gulf have indeed seen their share of protests, sometimes entailing large portions of the population, as in Bahrain. In any case, exceptional moments, such as revolutions and outbreaks of large-scale protests, need to be understood within the context of a nation's history of protest activities, with particular attention paid to the sorts of protests the regime tolerates (and why), as well as the types that are not permitted.

A Long(er) View of Protests

The state of Transjordan was created through a series of agreements between Great Britain and France following the dissolution of the Ottoman Empire. It gained independence from Great Britain in 1946 and was renamed shortly thereafter as the Hashemite Kingdom of Jordan. From almost the moment of independence, Jordan enjoyed a vibrant political sphere, with multiparty elections, independent newspapers, and near-free reign to discuss politics openly. Large- and small-scale demonstrations were common throughout most of the 1950s. In the 1956 election for the lower house of parliament, leftist parties won a plurality and selected the socialist Suleiman Nabulsi as prime minister (Aruri 1972, 134). Nabulsi pushed a bit too far in calling for a reduction of the monarch's powers. King Hussein—then twenty-three years old—dismissed Nabulsi in early 1957 and implemented martial law by royal decree a few months later (Pollack 2002). Dozens of leftist activists and parliamentarians were jailed, while others fled to the Egypt of Gamal Abdel Nasser. The king continued to call for parliamentary elections through 1967. Parliament was suspended following Jordan's defeat in the Six-Day War, and it was not called back into session until 1984.

What is remarkable about this period is that while protest activities declined when martial law was introduced in 1957, they never went away. More remarkable is that the regime was selective in its repression of public protests, even those critical of government policies. While leftists found little room for any expressions of dissent, the Muslim Brotherhood repeatedly mobilized rallies and criticized the regime for its policies. The Brotherhood had fashioned itself as a "loyal opposition" to the King's government, ergularly standing alongside the regime and assailing the secular Arab nationalist movement, for example. But even while embracing loyalty and moderation, the Brotherhood continued to critique the state, and it periodically organized protests, particularly in opposition to the regime's relations with Great Britain and later the United States (Boulby 1999). At times, its members were even arrested and jailed.

By the late 1960s, however, the regime was increasingly nervous. Palestinian militias, eventually under the umbrella of the Palestine Liberation Organization, controlled growing swaths of land east of the Jordan River. After three and a half years of conflicts with these militias, the regime was determined to either crush them or force them off Jordanian lands. Demonstrations broke out throughout the kingdom, with Palestinians demonstrating in support of the PLO militias while East Bankers expressed their support for the regime. Numerous international socialist groups called for solidarity with the pro-PLO supporters, but that attention led the king to further characterize those protests as sponsored by outside agitators and, thus, as a threat to Jordanian sovereignty. The regime escalated its campaign against the militias for a month in 1970, now known as Black September. The clashes led to thousands of deaths, mostly of militia members, until the remaining Palestinian resistance fighters were exiled to Lebanon in July 1971 (Pollack 2002). Since then, the legacy of the prime minister at the time, Wasfi al-Tal, has remained that of either a hero (to East Bankers) or a monster (to Palestinians).

During those months of bloody confrontation, the Muslim Brotherhood chose to support the regime rather than the Palestinian militias. This move seemed surprising, given that the Brotherhood had long been a strong advocate for a free Palestine, even naming the "full liberation of Muslim Palestine" as its second primary objective (after the full implementation of sharia in all spheres of life) in its first formal organizing document in the early 1950s. The Brotherhood was partly concerned with the leftist and Marxist orientation of most of the militias but also viewed their activities on Jordanian soil as a threat to the regime, which they supported.

The rest of the 1970s were relatively quiet in terms of protest activities, with the exception of labor protests, primarily small sit-ins and strikes at factories outside Amman, which averaged three to four per year. For the most part the regime did not move to crush these protests and on some occasions sent emissaries to facilitate talks between factory owners and workers. The 1980s brought renewed protest activities, however, as Jordan's economic conditions steadily deteriorated. In April 1989, a series of protests began in the south, notably in the town of Ma'an, where a major trucking depot was located. The initial protests were largely in opposition to economic reforms that had been undertaken by the regime as part of a structural adjustment program mandated by its agreement with the International Monetary Fund. In addition to devaluing the Jordanian dinar by half in late 1988, the IMF program required that the regime begin lifting subsidies on certain products, including gasoline. Those reforms were begun in spring 1989, and the gasoline-reliant trucking industry based in the south was the first to revolt (Lucas 2005). But what began as isolated demonstrations quickly spread throughout the kingdom. By the summer, the king convened a meeting of advisers and decided, against the advice of some of the members of that group, to introduce political liberalization quickly as a means to defuse domestic tensions and channel dissent into debates about political reforms and away from economic grievances (Mufti 1999). Competitive parliamentary elections were held in November 1989, the first full elections in more than twenty years and the first since the kingdom had relinquished its claims over the West Bank in 1988. Islamist candidates, most of whom were affiliated with the Muslim Brotherhood, won 40 percent of the seats, while leftist and liberal parties won another 20 percent; the remainder went to independents, including members of many of the prominent families who make up the regime's traditional base of support.

Over the next few years, Jordan saw the lifting of martial law, the liberalization of the media, and the introduction of constitutional amendments (Robinson 1998). Along with these developments, the kingdom witnessed an evolution in the field of political contestation. Most notably, Islamists and leftist groups that had previously refused to speak to each other, let alone cooperate, began to co-organize highly public events, including press conferences (such as one in 1993 that opposed a new elections law) and a range of protests (Ryan 2002; Schwedler 2006). A new provision to the public gathering law introduced in 1992 now required that event organizers notify the governor of their intention to hold *any* public gathering, whether a protest, a march, an assembly to watch a documentary, a commemoration of an event, or another kind of meeting. Political activists made little comment on this particular provision, as most were actively engaged in organizing new political parties, which were legalized the same year in preparation for the next round of parliamentary elections in November 1993.

Over the next decade, the regime gradually reversed many of these impressive political openings, in large part because it set out to sign a peace treaty with Israel. King Hussein understood that such a move would be wildly popular. Given that the elected lower house of parliament (the Council of Deputies) would need to approve such a treaty, he initiated a series of additional reforms to the electoral law that disadvantaged the majority Palestinian population, which was based around Amman, to the benefit of the "loyalist" East Bank towns and rural areas. Parliamentary seats held greater weight in East Bank–dominated areas: some southern towns had one seat for every three thousand citizens, while districts in Amman where Palestinians were concentrated had one seat for every thirty thousand citizens. The electoral reforms had the desired effect of producing a compliant, loyalist-dominated assembly, and the peace treaty was signed in October 1994 and ratified soon thereafter. The Islamic Action Front—now the political wing of the Muslim Brotherhood—saw its numbers in parliament diminish. The party continued to describe itself as loyal opposition to the regime, stressing that its complaints had to do with the manipulation of the electoral system. Even as political freedoms continued to erode, Jordan's Islamists consistently stressed that they did not challenge the legitimacy of the regime or call for its overthrow.

Other freedoms were also gradually reversed during the mid-1990s, including, notably, freedom of the press. A major boycott of the 1997 elections by all political parties and several prominent former government officials was organized in large part in reaction to the manipulation of the elections law and of the press and publications law (Kilani 1997). The new assembly of 1997 therefore contained virtually no opposition figures, and the regime continued its backsliding away from political freedoms and its advance of IMF structural adjustment reforms to the economy.

The death of King Hussein and the ascent of King Abdullah II to the throne in 1999 did not usher in a new era of reform. On the contrary, in spring 2001, King Abdullah dismissed the parliament in anticipation of elections scheduled for November. Those elections were never held, and the country remained without a parliament for nearly two years. In the interim, the prime minister, who is appointed by the king, exercised a provision of the constitution that allows his office to introduce "temporary" laws when the parliament is not in session. More than 210 such laws were introduced, including significant revisions to the public gatherings law (Ryan and Schwedler 2004) that served as the primary legal reference point for political protests.

Under the new provisions, the organizers of public gatherings now had to receive permission—by obtaining a permit from the governor—prior to holding an event. An application could not be submitted more than seventy-two hours prior to the planned event; the governor, however, was required to provide an answer only twenty-four hours before the event. While these changes were highly restrictive, the most controversial provision was the clause indicating that the individual organizers would be held personally responsible for the cost of any damages to property that occurred during an event. Activists and political parties were outraged, as they recognized that the new law was a ploy to rein in protests, which had escalated in recent years in response to the outbreak of the second Palestinian Intifada in October 2000. As activist (and dentist) Hisham Bustani said at the time:

> This is a tactic to stop us from protesting. The regime will send in thugs [baltajiyya], or sometimes even young kids who had been arrested for petty theft, and tell them to break some car headlights and they will drop the charges against them. Then the police step in to supposedly restore order, arresting us peaceful protesters and holding us responsible for the damage. (personal interview 2002a)

Another major wave of protests in March and April 2002 shut down large portions of Amman for more than a month (Schwedler and Fayyaz 2010). The temporary law requiring protesters to obtain permits became permanent when the new assembly convened following elections in June 2003 and passed the new provisions into law.

So what effect did the new law have? Perhaps surprisingly, Jordan did not see fewer protests. In fact, the law seemed to have little effect at all on the frequency and type of protests. However, the regime began pressuring groups to hold events only in certain locations, to limit their size, and to hold stationary events rather than marches (Schwedler and Fayyaz 2010). Also, of the many groups that routinely organized protests, some of them consistently sought to obtain permits for their events while others did not. The Islamic Action Front, for example, applied for permits with such regularity that independent activists accused the party of having been co-opted by the regime. For example, it would routinely organize or join anti-Israel events and boycotts of U.S. and Israeli products. The party organized a boycott of Danish projects during the cartoon scandal (when a Danish newspaper published cartoons that depicted images Islamists felt were blasphemous), burning a large pile of Danish products and a lot of cheese. Numerous other protests expressed opposition to the U.S.-led invasion of Iraq in 2003. But these protests were relatively small and contained, never pushing the boundaries of what the regime found acceptable. Public security officers (the regular police) typically stood around casually and chatted with participants at these events, which seldom, if ever, resulted in escalated tensions with any of the security services. Aida Dabbas, an independent liberal activist and frequent protester, was typical in her critique of the Islamists. She pointed out that Muslim Brotherhood leaders and members would frequently show up for protests that were likely to attract media attention. "But just watch," she said, "if it starts to get contentious with the police they will disappear; all their green banners you see now will be gone, and only the red [leftist] flags will remain. They are afraid of really confronting the regime" (personal interview 2002b). Indeed, this dynamic was readily visible at many of the protests that were initially co-organized between Islamists and leftists.

The professional associations, in contrast, largely refused to apply for permits for more contentious events—that is, events that were critical of government policies—but they did seek permits for most less controversial events, such as the rally to honor the fifty Jordanians who were aboard the flotilla that sailed from Turkey to Gaza in June 2010. At that event, hundreds filled the parking lot of the Professional Associations Complex in Amman. The crowd was visibly dominated by Islamists, with many green Muslim Brotherhood flags and women seated in a section separate from the men. But a vocal leftist contingent of several dozen was also present, waving the flags of Jordan's several communist and socialist parties. Police stood across the street and later delivered cases of water to those present, who were mostly seated on chairs facing a stage and listening to a series of speeches. Tensions flared hours into the event when young Muslim Brotherhood supporters lost patience with the leftists' endless chanting, which reached its highest volume when religious prayers were given from the stage. A shoving match ensued until elder Islamist leaders defused the situation, demanding that their own followers withdraw.

In this context of tensions, certain groups worked hard to carve out spaces for protest, but without pushing too hard at the regime. The regime sought to permit protests while attempting to control the specific locations and dynamics as much as possible, favoring stationary and contained events over open-ended marches. For their part, the political parties and some activists worked with the regime, not always reaching agreement but typically working to come to a compromise. These patterns related to negotiations between state and nonstate actors supply a rich background against which we can view how, in more tumultuous periods such as the time of the Arab uprisings that began in 2011, protests began to deviate from known "scripts" of acceptable behavior, former "cooperators" with the regime began to refuse to cooperate, and the regime responded to this variety of transgressions.

The Political Geography of Protests

In much of the Muslim world, protests frequently have been organized to begin following the noon prayer on Friday. This is typically the largest gathering of the week, and few need to return directly to work. There is nothing surprising about this strategy for mobilization: the civil rights movement in the United States gained momentum in southern black churches for the same reasons, and the Iranian revolution was framed as "Islamic" only after the regime made it impossible for people to mobilize anywhere other than in mosques. In Jordan, campuses, refugee camps, and the Professional Associations Complex also became common sites of protest, largely for similar practical reasons: each had a ready constituency for mobilization. Marches from these locations were often organized to conclude at the sites of power being critiqued—that is, at the locations associated with the individuals responsible for specific policies or actions. Common symbolic sites of protest, for example, included foreign embassies and the Prime Ministry.

To give a concrete example of symbolic geography in protests, in March and April 2002, Amman was virtually shut down for weeks as Jordanians protested Israel's invasion of Jenin, Nablus, and a few other towns in the West Bank. Thousands of protesters filled numerous public spaces, with Friday crowds stretching into the tens of thousands. They chanted primarily for the dissolution of the peace treaty with Israel, accusing the government of caring more about its relations with Israel and the United States than about the humanitarian needs of the Palestinian people. When the regime failed to stop the protests after nearly a month of trying, the Jordan River Foundation, a nongovernmental organization (NGO) with close ties to the royal family, announced that Queen Rania would lead a Palestinian solidarity march marking the beginning of a state-run telethon to raise money for aid to the Palestinians. Protesters had been demanding that Jordan sever its peace treaty with Israel or, at the very least, withdraw its ambassador. The regime ignored these demands; instead, the queen held a luncheon and then led a march (Schwedler and Fayyaz 2010).

The event attracted a few hundred people, many of them government officials and parliamentarians, but other protesting groups considered it a farce, not because it was led by the queen but because of its route—beginning at a traffic circle where the Sheraton and Four Seasons hotels are located and ending at a minor U.N. relief office a half kilometer away. For six weeks, demonstrations had criticized Israel, the United States for its support of Israel, and the Jordanian regime for its peace treaty with Israel. Central sites of protest included the Israeli embassy, the U.S. embassy, and the Jordanian prime ministry. And here was the queen, wearing jeans and a sweater, surrounded by members of the royal court, parliamentary deputies, and other members of the political establishment. They were expressing solidarity with Palestinians and advocating humanitarian aid, but they were also carefully avoiding criticisms of the United States and Israel and physically avoiding the locations that the protesters viewed as saturated with symbolic importance.

The political geography of protest in Jordan was not only about symbolic locations; it also had to do with physical changes to the urban fabric of Amman and how those changes open and close possibilities for protests. At the end of an interview with activist Ibrahim Alloush following the widespread protests of March and April 2002, I asked if there was anything I had overlooked. He responded, "The laws are a problem, sure, but the real issue is that we are losing places to hold demonstrations" (personal interview 2002c). It was not that previously permissible spaces were now prohibited, but rather that many of them simply no longer existed. Others were still there, but they had become irrelevant, sometimes almost invisible.

Political protests in Jordan were not limited to the capital city, but the rapidly changing space of Amman illustrates well how patterns of protest and repression can be structured by space. Jordanians have described Amman as being divided between East and West Amman, in one sense drawing a distinction between dusty, crowded, poorer, and less developed East Amman and gleaming, vibrant, and modern West Amman. West Amman is what most tourists and other visitors to the city experience, with its top-end restaurants, bars, hotels, government offices, foreign embassies, parliament, and universities (Schwedler 2010; Tobin 2012). But the area that counts as West Amman is not simply geographical. The label "West Amman" is used to refer only to a particular part of western Amman, the part that is predominantly wealthy, cosmopolitan, and the center of foreign finance. Some literature would call this part of Amman "neoliberal." In the decade leading up to 2011–12, the Jordanian regime had advanced economic reforms that prioritized foreign investment and free trade, which in turn required an infrastructure to sustain those interactions—that is, roads, office space, electricity, water, telephone, and high-speed Internet, along with other basic services. With the increased presence of foreign firms, there also came the need for the services demanded by the foreign employees of these firms: five-star hotels, sushi bars, Irish pubs, and so on. As one government official told me in 2004, the government's goal in restructuring West Amman was to create an experience whereby the foreign visitor "doesn't feel like he is in the Third World from the moment he steps off the airplane" (personal interview 2004).

Among the infrastructure projects connected to this economic vision were widened arteries to move people and goods around the city more efficiently. For example, Zahran Street—a major artery that leads from the airport road in West Amman directly into the downtown area—was entirely repaved, with five major underpasses added to facilitate rapid flow of traffic in and out of downtown. These new projects to widen roads, speed traffic, and improve other basic infrastructures were disproportionately located in certain parts of West Amman.

The headquarters of the General Intelligence Directorate, the notorious *mukhabarat*, or secret police, was originally located at the outskirts of town. As the city expanded, it was eventually moved farther out, and the building—since located at the geographic center of the city—was finally razed in 2002. In its place, an elaborate multiuse project called Abdali Boulevard is being constructed. The project has been described as "A New Downtown for Amman"—including high-end housing, a shopping mall, business suites, sidewalk cafés, and many gleaming glass towers.[7] Of course, a number of infrastructure projects were also launched in East Amman, but overall the physical landscape of the eastern portion of the city, with its narrow winding streets and crumbling stairways, remains little changed.

What did the changing geography of Amman have to do with protests? First, the tactics for policing and repressing protests were in large part a function of space, visibility, and the potential for disruption. On campuses and in refugee camps—which are located in all parts of Amman—the typical strategy for policing protests had been containment, so that people even just outside the area would probably be unaware of the demonstrations nearby. As a student activist at the University of Jordan told me in 2006, "We can do anything we want, as long as we don't try to leave campus and march [down University Road] toward downtown" (personal interview 2006). In the major commercial parts of West Amman, in the posh neighborhoods where foreign diplomats and the economic elite reside, protests are often prevented from happening in the first place, or else they are shut down as quickly as possible. Heavy weaponry is seldom used, although on occasion tanks have been deployed to prevent protesters from reaching rallying sites, particularly foreign embassies. In terms of geography, it is important to note that in most parts of East Amman the use of tanks would be virtually impossible because of the narrow streets; West Amman—much like Haussmann's Paris—has numerous wide streets, overpasses, and bridges designed specifically to facilitate the movement of tanks by both the Darak riot police and the army.

The second way in which the changing geography of Amman has affected protests concerns the symbolic targets of protests. Protest organizers typically choose the locations for their protests either to facilitate mobilization or because of the locations' symbolic importance. Government officials carefully regulate the spaces in which protests are permitted, so that real tensions between state and nonstate actors over protest events often begin well before the events themselves, when organizers seek to gain permission to hold the demonstrations they desire or when they refuse to seek permission but the government is aware that events are being planned.

In this manner, changes in the spatial layout of the most internationally visible parts of Amman equate to a changing geography for protest. As public spaces have become privatized, as is the case with the Abdali project, protesters have no right to access them. Protesters used to shut down the intersection in front of the Prime Ministry, but the intersection's new high-speed underpasses mean that protesters can still crowd around the circle and obstruct turning traffic, but the traffic on the underpasses will have no idea that a protest is even taking place. Protest activities in these certain spaces have become not only less disruptive but also far less visible. Similarly, protests in the narrow streets of the neighborhood of Shmeisani have already been highly disruptive to traffic and to locals for five to six years and continue to be so. But given that the most powerful corporations and investment firms have moved from Shmeisani and into new gleaming complexes surrounded by guarded parking lots and wide, easy-access roads, protesters clogging the streets of Shmeisani create an inconvenience for the middle-class citizens who work and relax there, but they no longer disrupt commerce as they once did.

The restructuring of the financial spaces of West Amman has also rendered other locales nearly invisible (Schwedler 2010). The regime used to be very concerned about protests by the Muslim Brotherhood in the old downtown or city center, which was the country's main commercial district some twenty years ago. As Amman's business district moved first to Shmeisani and then dispersed throughout West Amman, the downtown protests were no longer visible or disruptive to anyone outside the immediate area. The Muslim Brotherhood continued to hold protests in the area on a wide range of issues. Many of them expressed opposition to Jordan's peace treaty with Israel or to particular reforms that further excluded the Islamic Action Front from the political scene. In 2007, for example, the outcome of the parliamentary elections was widely viewed as illegitimate, with the Islamists winning only six seats and losing in districts where they clearly had strong support. Downtown protests continued to attract Brotherhood followers in the hundreds, but these events seemed to accomplish little more than to demonstrate the group's power for an audience made of its own constituency; the protests simply put little pressure on the regime. In fact, the governor routinely issued permits to the Muslim Brotherhood and the Islamic Action Front for Friday events in this area while refusing their requests for permits to hold events in other locations.

This, however, is likely to change in the next few years. Beginning in 2012, rental property law reforms went into effect, allowing owners to raise rents and evict working-class residents. The area's many merchants of low-end goods, used clothing, and refurbished appliances are likely to be forced out. In their place, the regime is imagining a new "old Amman," hoping to create a romantic, old-style souk environment that will attract tourists and affluent Jordanians, providing Amman with the much-sought combination of a gleaming cosmopolitan city paired with a romantic, exotic old city.

The 2011 Protests

In 2011, Jordanians protested weekly, although they received only limited international attention, and the size of their demonstrations paled in comparison to the massive and often bloody protests in Egypt, Yemen, and Syria. Jordanians demanded specific changes to the constitution, primarily to limit the power of the monarchy and to reintroduce a process by which the prime minister is elected by the lower house of parliament rather than appointed by the king. But unlike in Egypt, Tunisia, Yemen, or Syria, virtually none of the weekly protests, which took place in all major urban areas as well as numerous towns in more remote locations, called for the overthrow of the regime (Bouziane and Lenner 2011; Ryan 2011; International Crisis Group 2012; Tobin 2012). King Abdullah responded in a manner familiar to Jordanians: by dismissing the prime minister (twice), calling for a national dialogue, and forming a committee to consider constitutional reforms. Most of those proposed changes had yet to take effect, but the public gatherings law was revised in mid-2011 to eliminate the requirement that event organizers obtain permits for gatherings in advance.

Unquestionably, compared to Tunisia, Libya, Syria, and even Egypt, Jordan was far more liberal and tolerant of political dissent and far less prone to excessive use of force in repressing such dissent. The simple description of Jordan as "more liberal," however, is inadequate as an explanation, because it fails to account for the variation in regime responses to protests, in which some are tolerated and contained whereas others are quickly repressed. For example, on March 25, 2011, the police and Darak violently dispersed the few hundred March 24 Youth protesters who had gathered at the Dakhili traffic circle, but not the Loyalist March that was also occupying the same space. Why was this protest different from other Friday protests? Three issues were in play: the kind of protest, who organized it, and where it was located.

First, the kind of protest: the organizers of the March 24 Youth demonstration had called for an indefinite sit-in, Tahrir-style. When rumors spread that the event had been canceled, its organizers issued a statement that said (in part):

> O free Jordanians, our sit-in is peaceful and civilized and holds an esteemed value (dignity, freedom, and democracy). Our demands are legitimate and do not bear postponement. We will confront violence, thuggery, persecution, and threats with the strength of freedom. We will repel procrastination, delay, and attempts to fool Jordanians through sacrificing our time, efforts, and self-interests for the sake of the Jordanians, who deserve a system of good governance. (quoted in Jadaliyya 2011)

The regime sought to disperse the protesters violently on the second day in part because of its fear that an ongoing protest would represent a reclaiming of public space that the regime could not control. In short, the March 24 Youth refused to adopt what the regime viewed as an acceptable protest script—that is, one limited in scope and duration. Protests may be permitted, but protesters (and policing agencies) understand what kinds of protests will invite greater repression than others. The March 24 Youth fully understood that they were pushing this boundary and clearly hoped to shake up the tame protests that had been taking place weekly.

Second, who organized the protest: the Jordanian regime appeared to have a strong preference for protests organized by known groups— the Muslim Brotherhood, political parties, professional associations, NGOs, and so on. The March 24 Youth departed from the acceptable protest script not only by calling for an indefinite occupation of a major traffic circle but also by being activists who were hardly the usual suspects and thus largely unfamiliar to the security services. Naseem Tarawnah (2011), author of the Black Iris blog on Jordanian politics and society, participated in the protests and wrote of the event:

> They were not associated with political parties. There were some leftists, communists, socialists, and yes, even some Islamists—but for the most part this seemed to be a group of people who represented "the other." Many of those I spoke to came only because they did not feel represented by other mainstream political parties, and saw March 24 as an alternative they could get on board with. . . . Most of the organizers were unknown individuals and some were from university youth groups and/or students councils, et cetera, so there's really no history to go on. This may have been what helped create an "Islamist" propaganda around them, but in my book, they were anything but Islamists.

The regime's security agencies had no ongoing dialogue with these protesters, no personal connections or experience, and no knowledge of what they were likely to do. One protester later suggested that it was precisely because they were unknown that the Darak troops were willing to be so brutal: "Most well-known activists have family connections and lawyers, and they know their rights. Average Jordanians don't have any of these things, so [the Darak] are not afraid to act brutally" (personal interview 2012).

Third, where the protest was held: the Ministry of the Interior was not a common site for political protest, so by holding an event there the March 24 Youth certainly caught the regime by surprise. Particularly because the Tunisian Ministry of the Interior had been a central site of protest during the toppling of that regime just two months earlier, a shift in Jordan from other locations to this site was viewed as an extreme provocation. When the protest entered its second day and the possibility of a long-term occupation began to emerge, the Darak riot police moved in quickly, circling the protesters so that they had little opportunity to escape. When the usual groups organized in the usual locations in the usual ways, the regime responded also in the usual ways, because it knew that it could contain them, and the protesters understood well the limits of what the regime would tolerate. When part of that script changed, as it did in this case, the regime did not hesitate to move in to end the demonstration.

This one protest—and the death that resulted—can be set in contrast with the ongoing and sometimes large-scale protests that continued to be organized by the Muslim Brotherhood and Islamic Action Front. Jordan's Islamists had joined many protests and organized others since the beginning of the Arab uprisings. But in every case, they were careful to direct their critiques toward particular policies rather than at the regime itself. They were demanding—along with a wide spectrum of the Jordanian political scene—that the regime implement substantive reforms that would allow for real political contestation in elections and grant the parliament more power in legislating. They also routinely protested in opposition to Jordan's peace treaty with Israel and called for the permanent closure of the Israeli embassy in Amman (Schwedler 2012). Thus while the small group of peaceful protesters who called themselves the March 24 Youth were harshly repressed, Jordan's Islamists continued to protest weekly with little interference. They adhered to a well-established protest script, whereby the legitimacy of the regime was never challenged. One could not know if this pattern would continue indefinitely, but it was clear that the uprisings around the region had not shaken Jordan's Islamists from their role as the regime's quiescent and loyal opposition.

New and Old Alliances

Without a doubt, the character and boundaries of protest activities in the Middle East underwent a sea change in 2011. While Jordan's relatively calm protests received little international attention, they captured several critical dynamics that were playing out globally. A close look at the history of protests in Jordan reveals that many familiar groups — notably the Muslim Brotherhood and various leftist parties — have long histories of protest activities (Boulby 1999; Schwedler 2006). Beginning in the mid-1990s, however, these groups began to organize together, holding rallies against normalization with Israel (Schwedler 2005) as well as large protests against the presence of U.S. troops in the Middle East. In the Arab uprisings of 2011, many of these groups continued to coordinate some events while also holding many separate events — just as they had in the previous two decades. As the March 24 Youth illustrated, however, other Jordanians had also begun to protest, although not in the mass numbers seen in other parts of the region. Palestinians, who by most counts made up at least half of Jordan's population of seven million, had not mobilized in large numbers.

In fact, most of the nonparty mobilizations had been among East Bank Jordanians — those of non-Palestinian origin. These included highly educated urban intellectuals who were otherwise not active in party politics, as well as tribal and clan-based mobilizations, particularly in the southern regions of Jordan. In these areas, extremely poor economic conditions had led many to shut down roads with piles of burning tires, or to shout outside courthouses when locals were being prosecuted for cursing the king. These activities — shutting down major roads with bonfires, holding indefinite sit-ins, and directly and personally critiquing the king — all violated the conventional protest script that had dominated the kingdom since reliberalization in 1989, and they marked a significant shift that the monarchy did not fail to notice. As of this writing, the prospects for a massive movement calling for the overthrow of the monarchy appear unlikely. The possibility of massive mobilizations should not be underestimated, however, and in the new revolutionary context of the Middle East, even the most stable regimes are feeling more than a bit nervous.

Notes

1. Many video clips of the first day of the sit-in are available on YouTube. For example, video showing the Youth and participants in a concurrent Loyalty March chanting at each other, with the police monitoring the space between them, is available at http://www.youtube.com/watch?v=uq-FTL4oRWA (accessed March 24, 2013).

2. See "Dakhliyyeh Circle—March 24 Protests," YouTube video, March 25, 2011, http://www.youtube.com/watch?feature=player_embedded&v=7-LrPnQK VHE (accessed March 18, 2013).

3. This practice of protesters framing their events as "pro-Jordanian" and nationalist in an effort to deflate repression from the regime dates at least to 1997. That January, a protest against an Israeli trade fair outside Amman adopted this tactic, distributing Jordanian flags and chanting pro-Jordan slogans. The Bedouin-dominated riot police at the event responded by singing nationalist tribal songs, which in effect aimed to prove their own loyalty to the state (see Schwedler 2005).

4. See, for example, "The Darak Beat Traitors at the Dhakhili Circle," You-Tube video, March 25, 2011, http://www.youtube.com/watch?v=ieGqRd8pbOQ&f eature=related (accessed March 18, 2013).

5. Transjordan was created as a British mandate, or overseership, in 1921 and gained its formal independence as a state in 1946 as the Hashemite Kingdom of Jordan; British officers continued to lead the Jordanian army until 1958.

6. Jordan ruled the West Bank from 1948 until 1967, when it lost control to Israel during the Six-Day War. The kingdom did not formally relinquish its claim on the territory until 1988, when Yasser Arafat, chairman of the Palestine Liberation Organization (PLO), declared an independent state of Palestine. Today the regime refuses to conduct a census or to acknowledge that Palestinians constitute a majority in the country, although virtually every demographic study and analysis conducted to date has recognized that this is the case. Jordanians also widely acknowledge the fact.

7. See the Web site devoted to the project, http://www.abdali.jo (accessed March 18, 2013).

References

Alon, Yoav. 2007. *The Making of Jordan: Tribes, Colonialism, and the Modern State.* London: I. B. Tauris.

Aruri, Naseer H. 1972. *Jordan: A Study in Political Development (1921–1965).* The Hague: Nijhoff.

Boulby, Marion. 1999. *The Muslim Brotherhood and the Kings of Jordan, 1945–1993.* Tampa: University of South Florida.

Bouziane, Malika, and Katharina Lenner. 2011. "Protests in Jordan: Rumblings in the Kingdom of Dialogue." In *Protests, Revolutions and Transformations: The Arab World in a Period of Upheaval,* Working Paper No. 1, edited by Center for Middle Eastern and North African Politics, 148–65. Berlin: Free University of Berlin.

International Crisis Group. 2012. *Political Protest in the Middle East: Dallying with Reform in a Divided Jordan.* Middle East/North Africa Report No. 118, March 12. Brussels: International Crisis Group. http://www.crisisgroup.org/en (accessed May 7, 2012).

Jadaliyya. 2011. "Jordan's March 24 Youth Sit-In Violently Dispersed." March 26. http://www.jadaliyya.com (accessed March 18, 2012).

Kilani, Sa'eda. 1997. *Blaming the Press: Jordan's Retreat from Democracy.* London: Article 19.

Lucas, Russell E. 2005. *Institutions and the Politics of Survival in Jordan: Domestic Responses to External Challenges, 1988–2001.* Albany: State University of New York Press.

Mufti, Malik. 1999. "Elite Bargains and the Onset of Political Liberalization in Jordan." *Comparative Political Studies* 32 (1): 100–129.

Pollack, Kenneth. 2002. *Arabs at War: Military Effectiveness, 1948–1991.* Lincoln: University of Nebraska Press.

Robinson, Glenn. 1998. "Defensive Democratization in Jordan." *International Journal of Middle East Studies* 30 (3): 387–410.

Ryan, Curtis R. 2002. *Jordan in Transition: From Hussein to Abdullah.* Boulder, Colo.: Lynn Rienner.

———. 2011. "Identity Politics, Protest, and Reform in Jordan." *Studies in Ethnicity and Nationalism* 11 (3): 564–78.

Ryan, Curtis R., and Jillian Schwedler. 2004. "Return to Democratization or New Hybrid Regime? The 2003 Elections in Jordan." *Middle East Policy* 11 (2): 138–51.

Schwedler, Jillian. 2005. "Cop Rock: Protest, Identity, and Dancing Riot Police in Jordan." *Social Movement Studies* 4 (2): 155–75.

———. 2006. *Faith in Moderation: Islamist Parties in Jordan and Yemen.* New York: Cambridge University Press.

———. 2010. "Amman Cosmopolitan: Spaces and Practices of Aspiration and Consumption." *Comparative Studies in South Asia, Africa, and the Middle East* 30 (3): 547–62.

———. 2012. "Jordan: The Quiescent Opposition." In *The Islamists Are Coming: Who They Really Are,* edited by Robin Wright, 99–108. Washington, D.C.: Woodrow Wilson Center.

Schwedler, Jillian, and Sam Fayyaz. 2010. "Locating Dissent: Space, Law, and Protest in Jordan." In *Policing and Prisons in the Middle East,* edited by Laleh Khalili and Jillian Schwedler, 275–94. New York: Columbia University Press/Hurst.

Tarawnah, Naseem. 2011. "The Quick Death of Shabab March 24 and What It Means for Jordan." Black Iris (blog), March 26. http://www.black-iris.com (accessed March 18, 2012).

Tobin, Sarah A. 2012. "Jordan's Arab Spring: The Middle Class and Anti-revolution." *Middle East Policy* 19 (1): 96–109.

Personal Interviews

Personal interview. 2002a. Hisham Bustani. Amman, June 13.

Personal interview. 2002b. Aida Dabbas. Amman, February 9.

Personal interview. 2002c. Ibrahim Alloush. Amman, June 6.

Personal interview. 2004. Marwan Muasher. Amman, June 5.

Personal interview. 2006. Name withheld by request. Amman, August 23.

Personal interview. 2012. Name withheld by request. Via telephone, Amman, April 10.

Lebanon

MAYA MIKDASHI

ON FEBRUARY 27, 2011, a group of Lebanese citizens working toward
changing the Lebanese political system came together under the slogan "For the fall of the sectarian regime in Lebanon: toward a secular,
civil, and democratic regime." Soon their enthusiasm spilled over the
movement's Facebook page and onto the streets of Beirut. Thousands
of people walked through the city demanding an overhaul of political
sectarianism in Lebanon and its replacement with a meritocratic and
civil state (Ya Libnan 2011). Convinced that the system of political
sectarianism breeds corruption, sexism, and weak state institutions,
activists conflated civil reforms with secularization in their desire for
change. Inspired by popular uprisings that were happening across the
Arab world, Lebanese of all ages, genders, classes, and regions came
together to try to force a debate on their nation's political system. They
chanted words that had become famous in Cairo, in Tunis, and across
the Arab world: "Al-sha'b yurid isqat al-nizam" (The people want the
downfall of the regime). Hundreds of citizens walked through the rain
stating their desire for a new and different Lebanon. Unlike in Tunis or
in Cairo, the protesters met no resistance, and no army or police personnel were dispatched to stop them (Meguerditchian and Monzer 2011).

Many activists hoped that this uprising for a civil/secular state was the beginning of Lebanon's Arab Spring. But was it?

The movement to overthrow the sectarian regime in Lebanon was inspired by the Arab uprisings of 2011, but the protesters could not emulate the popular uprisings in Tunis and Cairo because their movement had a fatal flaw: in order to preserve a broad coalition, the group decided to ban any discussion of the two most salient and controversial political issues in Lebanon today. With this decision, a group that was dedicated to highlighting and changing the political and economic injustices endemic to the system of political sectarianism censored debate on the topic of the United Nations Special Tribunal for Lebanon's investigations into the 2005 assassination of Prime Minister Rafik al-Hariri, and on the topic of whether or not Hezbollah, an armed resistance group that effectively controls South Lebanon, should disarm.[1]

Any discussion of these subjects, it was said, might splinter the group into the polarized and overtly sectarian camps of the March 14 political movement, led by Rafik al-Hariri's son, and its Hezbollah-led counterpart, the March 8 movement. In addition to imposing this crippling self-censorship, many would-be revolutionaries ignored what is perhaps the biggest lesson of Lebanese history: the individual does not create her or his own identity. Instead, political identities are forged through interactions among complex political, social, and economic forces. One cannot be outside history, nor can one deny the role that social and political institutions play in the construction of identity. While activists have dreamed of being able to shrug off the legacies of sectarianism and violence like dirty clothes, in reality both have been constitutive and unavoidable aspects of citizen subjectivity in Lebanon.

Historical Legacies

Lebanon has been characterized as the Switzerland of the Middle East. This cliché highlights how Lebanon, a country of four million citizen residents, four hundred thousand Palestinian refugees, and more than one million foreign migrant laborers, has been considered an exception in the Arab world because of its multiconfessional "consociational" democracy whereby minorities share political power in a country with no majority (Lijphart 1968). While Lebanon is often regarded as more "secular" than many other Arab states, Lebanese secularism is different from its North Atlantic counterpart; in Lebanon secularism is riddled with religious identity structures, legal subsystems, and sociopolitical classifications. To be a Lebanese citizen one must be a member of one of eighteen legally recognized religious sects, the minorities (officially only minorities exist) that form the basis of power sharing in the Lebanese state (Picard 2002). Inheriting the jurisdiction of fifteen sets of personal status laws (three sects do not have "their own" personal status laws), with just as many court systems, marriage registries, schooling systems, and so on, affects the life course of citizens in terms of their personal affairs and in terms of their political possibilities. In the domain of politics, for instance, only a member of the Sunni personal status community can be prime minister, and only a Maronite Christian can be the president of the republic or president of the army. At the level of personal status, the religious/sectarian laws differently adjudicate marriage, divorce, child custody, and inheritance (Joseph 1997). Thus to characterize Lebanon as being more or less secular than other Middle Eastern nations is to miss the complexity of the relationship between the Lebanese state and its religion(s).

In the minds of many early Lebanese nationalists, Lebanon was supposed to be created as a Christian state. In the decades leading up to and immediately preceding World War I, the Ottoman Empire was being torn apart by internal strife and European wars, and in the resulting fragmented map of the Middle East there was an opportunity to create an independent state where Christians would constitute the majority—though barely. In the minds of the advocates of this project, Christians would have one place in the Middle East where they would be secure and sovereign (Thompson 2000). This project never came to be, and ultimately the borders of greater Lebanon were drawn in 1920 to embrace a demography that made the idea of a Christian Lebanon all but impossible.[2] In Mandate Syria, the French set up what they determined to be ethnically differentiated "ministates" such as the Alawi state, the Druze state, and the state of Aleppo. The aim of this policy was to weaken the ability of resistance movements to centralize, unite, and rebel against French rule (Khalidi 2004). The French government had lobbied hard and long for a colonial presence in the Middle East and was not about to let the anti-imperial sentiments of the peoples residing in historic Syria get in its way. In fact, in the eyes of many historians "Lebanon" was one of these ministates that was carved out of historic Syria. The French experiment in ministates failed in what became the nation-state of Syria, and it inspired much resistance in what became the nation-state of Lebanon (Khoury 1987).

In Lebanon, French imperialists saw political sectarianism as a win-win situation; it would make a widespread revolt less likely given the institutionalization and politicization of sectarian difference, and it would benefit their "historic allies," Maronite Catholic Christians, who claimed a slight demographic majority in the territory of Lebanon. This slight demographic majority and overall demographic competitiveness was essential to making two claims: (1) that Lebanon is a country of minorities, and (2) that as the largest minority, the Maronites should be the political community in the Lebanese state with the greatest representation in the government (Salibi 1988). This sectarian demography was produced through a flawed census undertaken in 1932, under French mandate. The information gathered during this census project identified eighteen different sectarian communities, enumerated them, and established them as ethnicized categories of identification in the state census registry. Power sharing among these communities supposedly mirrored the demographic facts revealed or created by the census. As Rania Maktabi (1999) suggests, the census was one technology among many used to "buttress Christian supremacy." Moreover, there had been no census since 1932 because the subject of Lebanon's sectarian demography was considered too controversial (ibid.).

Beginning with the French mandate–era 1926 Lebanese constitution and the independence-era "national pact" between the country's Sunni Muslim and Maronite Christian elite, the state has been organized through the logic of sectarian power sharing. The Ta'if Accord, which ended the Lebanese civil war of 1975–90, made amendments to the power-sharing agreement but in doing so further entrenched political sectarianism as the only "solution" to the presence of multiple confessional communities (Hanf 1993). Sectarianism has occupied a hegemonic position in Lebanese political discourse and in political discourse about Lebanon. Widely recognized to be a "problem" that stands in the way of national unity, political sectarianism has also been considered to be the only way to maintain Lebanon's "diversity." Thus words such as *tolerance, plurality,* and *coexistence*—always deployed in relation to sect—saturate both the language of political power and the language of political opposition in Lebanon (Mikdashi 2011). Sectarianism is seen as something that is innate, primordial, and something that must be overcome if Lebanon is to achieve modernity and *true* citizenship. In this logic, only when sectarianism no longer exists can political sectarianism be removed in a responsible and peaceful manner. Many of the activists who marched in the protest "for the fall of the sectarian regime in Lebanon" agreed with this point, arguing that the immediate removal of political sectarianism would lead to a tyranny of the (Muslim) majority at the expense of Lebanon's Christians. As one activist said, "A government made up of one color is not safe" (personal interview 2011a). In fact, this has been the ideological basis of the Lebanese state itself, which claims that "political sectarianism" is only a temporary system and that it is the state's job to prepare citizens for "true democracy" by weaning them away from primordial attachments and toward national ones. Thus the modernity of sectarianism is elided, as is the state's role in producing difference as a mode of politics, thus producing its own legitimacy as a state that "arbitrates difference" (Mikdashi 2011).

To summarize, the Lebanese state has a short but dense history. French imperialists implanted its legal and institutional skeleton in 1920; it then was slowly extended and fleshed out until the French imperial government was driven out by a Lebanese independence movement and its international and regional allies in 1943. The First Republic was, as postcolonial states tend to be, the heir to the colonial state, its institutions, and its ideological practices of free market economics and political sectarianism as a secular mode of political pluralism (Traboulsi 2007). Since independence, the Lebanese state has been the site of violent power struggles. Three of those struggles became civil wars. In fact, after gaining independence in 1943 the Lebanese state was either embroiled in a civil war or at war with Israel for thirty-seven years.

Throughout these wars Lebanese territory was, time and time again, converted into a battlefield.

In 1948, the nascent Lebanese army fought in the Arab–Israeli War. The resulting Palestinian Nakba—the catastrophe of ethnic cleansing during which Arab residents were expelled from their homes, lands, and communities in historic Palestine—changed Lebanon irrevocably, as Palestinians fled north into Lebanon. Into the second decade of the next century more than four hundred thousand Palestinian refugees (the vast majority of them Sunni Muslims) were living in camps spread throughout the country. Their presence—and their politicization—had a radicalizing effect on Lebanese political factions of all persuasions. It also created a demographic reality that continued to polarize political discourse in Lebanon. In 1958, a civil war was fought between Arab nationalists and the U.S.-allied Lebanese president. Ultimately the United States sent marines to enforce stability and ensure Lebanon's Westward-leaning foreign policy (Gendzier 1993). Beginning in 1975, for fifteen years the Lebanese civil war pitted Israelis and their Lebanese allies against Palestinians and *their* Lebanese allies—capitalists against communists, conservatives struggling to preserve the status quo against Arab revolutionaries, Islamists against secular Muslim militias, Syrian-allied parties split against each other, and, finally, overtly religious and sectarian militias pitted against the other. At least 150,000 Lebanese citizens died during this war, more than 300,000 emigrated, and more than one million people were internally displaced. Massacres were conducted in refugee camps and in Lebanese villages, and large swaths of the country were destroyed (Hirst 2011; Picard 2002; Traboulsi 2007).

The Specter of War

The landscape of political identities and state formations that had been the legacies of these wars radically circumscribed memories of the past and fears of the possible futures for Lebanon. This impossibility of disentangling the history of the Lebanese nation-state from a history of violence was precisely what inspired many activists in 2011 to try to change the sectarian system. As one leader of the movement told me, "If we do not act, there will be another war. A Sunni-Shiite war. A catastrophe" (personal interview 2011b). However, it is important to remember that wars are fought for many reasons, and many discourses and ideologies undergirded much of the fighting in 1958 Lebanon and in 1975–90 Lebanon. In this analysis, the Ta'if Accord was only the latest example of how the inscription of the terms of peace could be used to script the politics of conflict retroactively (Johnson 2002). In 1861 Ottoman rulers adopted a sectarian power-sharing formula to assuage what was to a large extent class conflict between peasants and landlords in Mount Lebanon (Makdisi 2000). In 1943 the nation readopted a sectarian formula to address the competing nationalisms of Arabism and Lebanonism (Maktabi 1999). In 1958 a civil war fought over ideology was "solved" by foreign interference and retrenchment (and gerrymandering) of the same sectarian formula (Gendzier 1993). In 1975 another civil war began, this time over several pressing issues: solidarity with the Arab–Israeli conflict; growing dissatisfaction with uneven sectarian delegation of power under the sectarian system, as well as with the sectarian system itself; and economic disparities that had been stretched to a breaking point (Salibi 1976).

In 1989 a peace was proposed that effectively "evened out" the lopsided state and promised, as the constitution of 1927 and the national pact of 1943 had promised, that the sectarian nature of the state was a necessary but temporary evil (Picard 2002). The Ta'if Accord, which ended the Lebanese civil war of 1975–90, ushered in the era of the Second Republic of Lebanon with the promise of reforms that were meant to eventually de-sectarianize the state, a goal that was yet to be realized by the time of this writing. Again, the early transformative antisectarian possibilities of war were channeled into constitutional amendments. By using this discourse, the Ta'if Accord effectively neutralized alternative analysis of both the causes of war and its sociality. The function of this type of "preemptive" peacemaking is to ensure that violence that has transformative goals (such as class struggle or rejections of sectarianism) is always articulated into law in ways that ensure that *peace* means the redistribution of power according to sectarian lines; this in turn functions to perpetuate class domination as well as to protect elites' economic and political interests. For example, rather than replace the system of political sectarianism with one of direct democracy, the Ta'if Accord merely rebalanced the sectarian makeup of parliament. In this way, the accord could be understood as the perpetuation of the omnipresent *threat* of sectarian violence, which the system needed to generate in order to reinforce the "necessity" of protecting vulnerable minority identities. It was a self-fulfilling prophecy.

Lebanese Stability in a Revolutionary Arab World

Despite this fractious history, Lebanon remained, surprisingly, a status quo state in a revolutionary Arab world. The apparent stability of the Lebanese state was particularly surprising given the fact that the country had long been a topic of interest in the international discourse of the "war on terror" and the bloody manifestations of this discourse on the ground. In fact, it became more possible to imagine a new civil war erupting in Lebanon than it was to imagine a popular uprising against Beirut's political regime and/or economic system. There were structural reasons Lebanon would not be the site of an Egypt- or Tunisia-style revolution. In fact, in an odd twist of fate, much of what made Lebanon perennially unstable is also what shielded it from the possibility of revolution.

Given that Lebanese citizens have had more civil and political rights than most other Arab citizens in the region (Ayubi 1995), one might have expected Lebanese citizens to stand up and demand responsible and effective leadership from politicians who had contributed to a political statement that began with a wave of political assassinations in 2005. Faced with a paralyzed government, high unemployment (and higher underemployment), eroding infrastructure and public works, and crippling underfunding of national institutions such as the public school system and national health care, one would expect Lebanese citizens to demand an end to the six-year stalemate, during which successive governments failed at basic tasks and corruption continued to be business as usual for political elites. Despite these factors, however, what happened in Egypt, Tunisia, or Libya could not be repeated in Lebanon. The factors contributing to the unlikelihood of a popular revolution in Lebanon can be loosely grouped under three headings: the nature of the state and its institutions, the domestic political environment, and the nation's geopolitical position. One must understand these factors in order to understand the nonrevolutionary fervor gripping Lebanon in the environment of the "Arab Spring." However, I also suggest that any analysis of Lebanon that does not consider the effects that contending memories and experiences of war had on the Lebanese body public(s) is insufficient. First, however, I offer an explanation of those three unavoidable macropolitical factors.

Nature of the State and Its Institutions

Lebanon is not an authoritarian state. It is a parliamentary democracy that functions through a system of political sectarianism in which political power and positions are distributed among sectarian communities according to predetermined quotas (Traboulsi 2007). It has a functional constitution, universal suffrage, a system of checks and balances, and an active judiciary, and it holds regular parliamentary elections that witness fierce competition between political rivals. By 2012, the main political division for the previous six years was between the Iranian–Syrian–allied and Hezbollah-led "March 8" coalition on one hand and the opposing U.S.–Saudi Arabia–allied "March 14" coalition, which was led by the son of the assassinated former prime minister Rafik al-Hariri. While the system of political sectarianism defines much (and erodes much) of political life in Lebanon, the fact that Lebanon has fairly functional democratic institutions cannot be denied. Lebanon also enjoys a relatively free press. In fact, Lebanon's status as a relatively liberal parliamentary democracy may have been be a factor in the dampening of revolutionary fervor among its citizens, who were generally less oppressed (although they may have been just as powerless vis-à-vis any government once it was elected) than their Arab neighbors (Ayubi 1995).

The Lebanese state does not enjoy hegemony over the use of violence in Lebanon, and its coercive capacities have been weak. While there were attempts to bulk up both the army and the internal security services in a bid to counter Hezbollah's military strength, the institutions of the army, the police, and the security services play very different roles in Lebanon than in most of the Arab world. They are relatively small institutions with little influence on state policy, but recently they played an important and impartial role during times of civil strife. Lebanon is *not* an authoritarian state that must rely on force to sustain an unpopular regime. Furthermore, Hezbollah's militia is better trained and better equipped than the Lebanese army and has been *much* more effective than the army at defending Lebanon's southern border against Israeli encroachment and occupation. Hezbollah's ability to protect South Lebanon is the main reason for what many in the Western mainstream media have refused to recognize as the group's wide popular support. Still, the Lebanese army, not Hezbollah, was perhaps the most respected national institution in the country, particularly as it began to de-sectarianize following the Lebanese civil war of 1975–90 (Picard 2002). However, by 2012 de-sectarianization had not been implemented in the higher ranks of the military, membership in which was still allocated on a sectarian basis.

Domestic Political Environment

Both the March 14 and March 8 political coalitions are mass-based popular movements. The strong support enjoyed by both political camps was evident in the 2009 parliamentary elections, when Hezbollah-leaning March 8 won the overall popular vote but U.S.-leaning March 14 won the most parliamentary seats. This split electoral result came about because of the way elections are held in Lebanon: all Lebanese citizens vote, but they vote only in (and for) their districts. Each district has a set number of candidates who are supposed to reflect the "sectarian makeup" of that district. Therefore, while a simple majority of Lebanese citizens voted for March 8 candidates, March 14 won the election because the number of seats allocated to districts does not always correspond to demography, and because there was higher voter turnout in pro–March 8 districts.[3] Simply put, more March 8 supporters voted in the 2009 elections, demonstrating their desire to participate in democratic elections. In 2005, the year that witnessed the assassination of Rafik al-Hariri and the birth of the subsequent political impasse in Lebanon, both the March 14 and March 8 camps were able to mobilize hundreds of thousands of people (in a country of four million citizens) who protested for "their [political] teams." After the assassination of Prime Minister Hariri, civilians occupied Martyrs' Square, a public park facing the parliament building. They demanded accountability for a history of political assassinations that had plagued Lebanon since the civil war of 1975–90 (*Economist* 2005). BBC News (2005) quoted a protester as saying that "it is my civic duty as a Lebanese to take part in this uprising. . . . Enough bloodshed and disasters. It is the 21st Century, and people should be able to govern themselves. The situation has become unbearable and we have to regain our country." Hassan Nasrallah, the secretary general of Hezbollah, spoke to Israel directly at the opposing rally: "Forget about your dreams about Lebanon. . . . What you did not win in war, I swear, you will not win with politics" (quoted in Fattah 2005).

This gesture was repeated after the 2006 war with Israel, which destroyed much of the country and displaced more than a quarter of the country's population. In the wake of this devastating war, supporters of the March 8 alliance took to the streets and "occupied" that same public space facing the parliament. They pitched their tents and demanded accountability for how their government had performed, or not performed, during the war with Israel. The protesters called for an investigation into the government's conduct during the war, a demand that proved prescient when, years later, the Arabic daily *Al-Akhbar* published WikiLeaks cables implicating the Lebanese government in Israel's war planning (see In the Middle of the East 2011). In doing so, they were engaging with a form of politics that became familiar not only across the Arab world but across the world more generally through the Occupy movement. In fact, many journalists and activists cited the mass protests of 2005 as having played an important role in inspiring them to, in the words of one would-be regime changer, "be out there on the streets" (personal interview 2011c).

Geopolitical Position

A third reason Lebanon was not on the way to becoming another Egypt or Tunisia was that, despite what many Lebanese nationalists might have thought, Lebanon was not a very geopolitically important state in the Arab world, and it was not considered a regional power broker. Instead, the Lebanese state has relied on regional brokers to maintain it throughout its history. Lebanon has no natural resources (save water), its economy is not large, and it has a very small population. Its total population at that time, four million, represented roughly one-fifth of the population of Greater Cairo. Furthermore, the investment by international powers in Lebanon has been much more varied than it has been in Egypt, where the United States underwrote the Mubarak regime for thirty years. In Lebanon, different power configurations have come into play, different international powers have exerted varying pressures, and the interests of nations such as the United States, France, Saudi Arabia, Syria, and Iran have waxed and waned according to the political winds (Ayubi 1995). In fact, it may be that in Lebanon different regional and international powers have funded different factions of Lebanese politics, such as the Saudi Arabian government's bankrolling of the March 14 alliance and Iran's similar funding of the March 8 alliance (Hirst 2011). Unlike Egypt, Lebanon has not been the recipient of consistent foreign aid; it never has been, in part because Lebanon has been in a state of war with Israel since 1948, and it remains the only non-Palestinian "hot border" in the ongoing Arab–Israeli conflict.

Despite the fact that the Lebanese state itself is not geopolitically important, Lebanon has always been a site for geopolitical struggles that have regional importance (ibid.). In this way, Lebanon's positioning within the Arab world has been ambiguous. It is not a powerful state, but the state's weakness magnifies the role that Lebanon has played in regional struggles. Its weakness and enclaved nature have allowed it to be used as a site for proxy wars between patrons of different sects. In this way Lebanon has operated as a site for the articulation of international politics and conflict. Thus the well-founded fear that any power struggle in Syria would not be complete until it has also been fought in the cities and mountains of Lebanon. This fear became a reality when armed clashes erupted in May 2012 between supporters of the Syrian regime in Lebanon and opponents of that same regime. In one month, twelve people were killed and more than one hundred were wounded.

TAKEN TOGETHER, these three factors explain how, unlike in Egypt, Tunisia, Libya, or Syria, in Lebanon there was no one, monolithic symbol of oppression that a majority of the population could coalesce against. The majority of Lebanese citizens did not see the army, the security forces, the state, Hezbollah, or even the system of political sectarianism as a single complex of oppressive rule that needed to be overthrown. In the case of political sectarianism, even if large numbers of citizens did desire change, they wanted to achieve that change through reform, not revolution. But to explain why it is difficult to imagine a popular, broad-based revolution taking place in Lebanon, rational academic analysis of these macropolitical factors does not suffice. This big picture only re-reveals what has become commonsense knowledge (and a perhaps overly confident discourse) on Lebanon: that it is a machine composed of many parts that are supposed to, but do not always, interlock. This machine sputters along precariously and often breaks down. When it does, both local and foreign mechanics rush to provide maintenance to, but not to redesign, a political system that is most successful at protecting and promoting the interests of those same mechanics — the local and regional political and economic elites. Tweak, tighten, loosen, grease, update, increase, decrease, charge, replace this with that, and abracadabra: a Lebanon that can sputter along for another decade or two.

Beyond Macropolitics: The Gravity of History

At the micropolitical level, things are not as clear as this engineered analogy would have us think. Away from the "big picture," the messiness of life and the messiness of history saturate the field of possibility for collective action against a political and economic system of political sectarianism. Lebanese citizens do not stand outside this system that oppresses them from above. In fact, Lebanese citizenship is constituted *through* this system *and its periodic breakdown*. The legacy of these breakdowns, in 1958, 1975, 1982, 2006, and 2008, has been not only an increasingly sectarian political and geographic terrain, the slow and painful eradication of the middle class, or the polarization of the population into rival political camps that have successfully paralyzed the country since 2005. More than a fractured political body, the legacy of these multiple breakdowns of the Lebanese machine has been a fragmented memoryscape within which Lebanese citizens have found themselves differently positioned. As we know, the future is always made possible by the past, and in Egypt and in Tunis a shared past of oppression emanating from a particular center of power sparked revolution. In Lebanon, the past is a minefield of injuries, deaths, fears, and vulnerability radiating from multiple centers of power that citizens experience differently depending on sect, social class, and place of residence. It is important to read the history of Lebanon as a history of violence because such a reading begins to explain that to be a Lebanese citizen is to be implicated in the system of political sectarianism and the ever-present threat of its violent breakdown. Each citizen is not only produced bureaucratically and legally through the stitching together of sectarianism and nationalism but also refracted through a historical narrative that emphasizes sectarian violence and difference. Furthermore, often these memories split the country into shifting terrains of perpetrators and victims of different incidents of violence wrought upon each other at different times and under different circumstances. Thus generations of Lebanese citizens have found themselves differently positioned within shared memories of 1958, 1975, 1982, 2006, and 2008. Fears of a future civil war spurred some activists, inspired by the Arab uprisings of 2011, to try to remove the sectarian regime in Lebanon. But the contesting memories of past wars, and the fact that Lebanese citizens had yet to accept their roles as both perpetrators and victims (whether passive or active) within this history of violence, were precisely what made such an uprising unlikely. These memories were partially articulated in the political emotions of Lebanese citizens and in the different, sometimes conflicting, futures they imagined out of their different pasts.

Ultimately, would-be Lebanese revolutionaries of 2011 could not build a mass movement. In addition to the fact that Lebanon has not been an authoritarian state, the Lebanese population was either apathetic or politically polarized, and in the relatively shifting geopolitical significance of the state, Lebanon's silenced history continued to form a barrier to broad-based popular consensus. In seeking to circumvent this history by focusing solely on the vision of a shared future, the protesters made the fatal mistake of assuming the past, present, and future to be segregated units of time that do not interpenetrate one another. They believed that institutional, historical, and social difference could be transcended by shared political desire alone. In the words of one twenty-something female protester, "I am here to choose a different future for myself and my country" (personal interview 2011d). While this desire for a new political horizon was perhaps revolutionary in the context of Lebanon, the reality was that the citizens could not ignore the roles played by other people, institutions, and histories in the formation of who they were. They could not autonomously "choose" to un-become these classes, genders, and sectarian identities that had been forged through law, life, and the liminal space between perpetrator and victim saturating the warscape of Lebanese history. At the least, they could not expect to succeed at this un-becoming or begin to change the system of political sectarianism if they refused to explore and understand how Lebanese citizens have fought, lived, and remembered Lebanese history in many different ways.

Notes

1. The political discussions of the evolution of the movement known as Al-sha'b yurid isqat al-nizam were captured on the movement's Facebook page. Facebook was the primary "meeting place" for activists dedicated to this cause.

2. For more on modern Lebanese history, see Salibi (1988), Picard (2002), and Traboulsi (2007).

3. For more on the 2009 election, see coverage in the Lebanese daily newspaper *Al-Akhbar.*

References

Ayubi, Nizar. 1995. *Over-stating the Arab State: Politics and Society in the Middle East.* London: I. B. Tauris.

BBC News. 2005. "Beirut Protesters Denounce Syria." February 21. http://news.bbc.co.uk (accessed October 6, 2012).

Economist. 2005. "Democracy Stirs in the Middle East." March 3. http://www.economist.com (accessed October 6, 2012).

Fattah, Hassan M. 2005. "Hezbollah Leads Huge Pro-Syrian Protest in Central Beirut." *New York Times,* March 8. http://www.nytimes.com (accessed October 6, 2012).

Gendzier, Irene. 1993. *Notes from the Minefield: United States Intervention in Lebanon, 1945–1958.* Boulder, Colo.: Westview Press.

Hanf, Theodor. 1993. *Coexistence in Wartime Lebanon: Decline of a State and Rise of a Nation.* London: I. B. Taurus.

Hirst, David. 2011. *Beware of Small States: Lebanon, Battleground of the Middle East.* New York: Nation Books.

In the Middle of the East (blog). 2011. "Lebanon 2006 WikiLeaks on Al-Akhbar Website." March 19. http://middeno.wordpress.com (accessed March 19, 2013).

Johnson, Michael. 2002. *All Honourable Men: The Social Origins of War in Lebanon.* London: I. B. Tauris.

Joseph, Suad. 1997. "The Public/Private—The Imagined Boundary in the Imagined Nation/State/Community: The Lebanese Case." *Feminist Review* 57: 73–92.

Khalidi, Rashid. 2004. *Resurrecting Empire: Western Footprints and America's Perilous Path in the Middle East.* Boston: Beacon Press.

Khoury, Philip S. 1987. *Syria and the French Mandate: The Politics of Arab Nationalism, 1920–1945.* London: I. B. Tauris.

Lijphart, Arend. 1968. *The Politics of Accommodation: Pluralism and Democracy in the Netherlands.* Berkeley: University of California Press.

Makdisi, Ussama. 2000. *The Culture of Sectarianism: Community, History, and Violence in Nineteenth-Century Ottoman Lebanon.* Berkeley: University of California Press.

Maktabi, Rania. 1999. "The Lebanese Census of 1932 Revisited. Who Are the Lebanese?" *British Journal of Middle Eastern Studies* 26 (2): 219–41.

Meguerditchian, Van, and Ashraf Monzer. 2011. "Hundreds of Lebanese Rally against Sectarian Regime." *Daily Star,* February 28. http://www.dailystar.com.lb (accessed June 4, 2012).

Mikdashi, Maya. 2011. "What Is Political Sectarianism?" Jadaliyya, March 25. http://www.jadaliyya.com (accessed June 5, 2012).

Picard, Elizabeth. 2002. *Lebanon: A Shattered Country.* Teaneck, N.J.: Holmes & Meier.

Salibi, Kamal S. 1976. *Crossroads to Civil War: Lebanon, 1958–1976.* Ann Arbor, Mich.: Caravan Books.

———. 1988. *A House of Many Mansions: The History of Lebanon Reconsidered.* Berkeley: University of California Press.

Thompson, Elizabeth. 2000. *Colonial Citizens: Republican Rights, Paternal Privilege, and Gender in French Syria and Lebanon.* New York: Cambridge University Press.

Traboulsi, Fawwaz. 2007. *A History of Modern Lebanon.* London: Pluto Press.

Ya Libnan. 2011. "Lebanese Youth Protest to Overthrow the Sectarian Regime." February 27. http://www.yalibnan.com (accessed June 4, 2012).

Personal Interviews

Personal interview. 2011a. Rana, protester and activist (name has been altered). Beirut, January.

Personal interview. 2011b. Tarik, leader of antisectarian civil society group (name has been altered). Beirut, January.

Personal interview. 2011c. Jean, university student and protester (name has been altered). Beirut, January.

Personal interview. 2011d. Leila, schoolteacher and protester (name has been altered). Beirut, January.

Palestine

TOUFIC HADDAD

MAY 15 IS A SPECIAL DAY for Palestinians because it commemorates
the displacement of eight hundred thousand fellow countrymen at
the hands of Zionist militias during the 1948 War and the declaration
of Israeli independence. One might expect that these events, known
throughout the Arab world as the Nakba (Arabic for "catastrophe"),
would have faded in importance after more than sixty years. In fact,
Israel's first prime minister, David Ben-Gurion, explicitly noted such
an expectation when he infamously stated, "The old [generation of
refugees] will die, and the young will forget." But history has proven
otherwise. Generation after generation of Palestinians have kept the
memory of their dispossession alive while continuing to demand the
implementation of their "right of return," articulated in United Nations
Resolution 194, passed more than 110 times in the General Assembly.
Not only does the United Nations continue to administer fifty-eight
refugee camps scattered throughout the Palestinian diaspora, but the
historical memory of the Nakba has been transferred across the years
as more recent experiences of oppression, dispossession, statelessness,
and discrimination at the hands of Israel tie the younger generations of
Palestinians to the old.

This underlying sense of identity and consciousness, largely invisible to non-Arabic speakers, has consistently spilled over throughout the decades of the Palestinian struggle for self-determination and return. Over the years, Nakba Day demonstrations have become a routine staple of nationalist organizing, with Israel regularly beefing up its security force numbers at the known "points of friction" throughout the West Bank and Gaza. Yet in the context of the revolutionary processes taking place throughout the Arab world, commemoration of the Nakba in 2011 was something qualitatively different and will be remembered for its particularly daring nature. While Israel concentrated its forces within the Occupied Palestinian Territories (OPT), it was the Palestinian diaspora that was really on the move. Galvanized by the "people power" manifested in the Egyptian Revolution's unseating of Hosni Mubarak less than two months previous, Palestinian refugee communities in four different countries organized "marches of return" to the borders of Palestine, attempting to translate their symbolic and legal rights into practice.

In one of these events' most dramatic expressions, thousands of demonstrators descended a mountainous landscape on the Syrian–Israeli-occupied Golan Heights border, approaching an active minefield separating the two. Cell phone footage shot by members of the local Syrian Druze community from the "Israeli" side captured the cordon of demonstrators approaching the fence, carrying Palestinian flags and defiantly chanting, "The people demand the liberation of Palestine." As demonstrators approached the fence, those around the cameramen attempted to plead desperately with demonstrators not to advance any farther, fearing the triggering of mines. But to no avail. The demonstrators eventually reached the fence, continued their chanting, and, after reaching a critical mass, began climbing over and dismantling it. The demonstrators were warmly welcomed by the local Syrian population on the other side, who embraced and kissed them, with the sound of women ululating in the background. One of the cameramen spontaneously interviewed a returnee, who identified himself as a Syrian refugee from the Golan Heights who was also a member of the Popular Front for the Liberation of Palestine. Dozens of demonstrators would traverse the "border," with one (Hassan Hijazi) even finding his way to his grandfather's home city of Jaffa. Interviewed by a Palestinian journalist in Jaffa before his deportation back to Syria, Hijazi noted, "It has always been my dream to come to Jaffa because it is my hometown, and I had assumed that if I were able to do it, I would be with millions of others, as was said on Facebook. . . . I don't recognize Israeli law, or what they call the state of Israel. . . . I consider [my return] a symbolic victory, however the real victory will come with armies."

The poignant sequence of events of Nakba Day 2011 captures a great deal regarding the ideas, bonds, and vision underlying contemporary Palestinian and Arab consciousness, particularly that of the youth. Yet an explanation of the fission between a reified national commemorative practice and an invigorated sense of empowerment is not so self-evident. The classical analytical paradigm that sees the "Palestinian theater" agitated and influenced by the "Arab revolution," as though both are hermetic categories, is problematic for reasons I will address. Explaining these problems, however, in addition to explaining an alternative conceptualization of Arab revolution–Palestinian dynamics, entails having a degree of patience to allow for complicated ideas and histories to have their say. These are, after all, aspects that traditionally get bumped to footnotes or fail to be mentioned at all, but that nonetheless are significant historically, while also showing expression in the unfolding of events throughout the region. All the inconvenient truths systematically elided in the vacuity of so much contemporary Western political discourse on the Arab world need to be reinserted if we are to have a hope of understanding that world's dynamics.

This chapter will attempt to begin this work, illustrating how a suppressed history and narrative of the Arab quest for self-determination, identity, and "modernity" dialectically and symbiotically relate to the Palestinian cause. Moreover, in a world where advances in political and organizational communication collide in real time with socioeconomic factors, a contagion of radical transformation is unleashed, the wave of which will not only reach the shores of Palestine but also eventually redraw the political map and balance of regional forces vis-à-vis the West and beyond.

Palestine as Exception

Attempts to read the Palestinian context and dynamics as a theater similar to other Arab state theaters in light of the Arab revolutions will be disappointed. Still in pursuit of national self-determination, Palestinians do not have a state with a recognized sovereign territory, governed by a national leadership, with a clear social and political contract between the governing and the governed. Although traces of these elements can be said to exist, the dynamics of mass popular revolt against an autocratic, corrupt leader, as witnessed in other Arab theaters following the winter of 2010, was not reproducible for the Palestinian movement at that stage in its struggle.

The predominant condition of the Palestinian people and their movement has been marked by a state of dispersion as a result of the 1948 Nakba, the 1967 Israeli occupation, and the apartheid reality created in the wake of the 1993 Oslo Accords. Of roughly ten million Palestinians worldwide, four and a half million have lived under Israeli military occupation (since 1967) and another million and a half have been second-class citizens in the state of Israel. Two-thirds of Palestinians overall have been refugees from what is today Israel; the majority of these live in Jordan, the Gaza Strip, the West Bank, Syria, and Lebanon. This ontological predicament means that there has been no one definitive condition or leadership that Palestinians could revolt against or otherwise engage with in any form of support or reform.

Even the political contract between the Palestinians and their national leadership, embodied in the Palestine Liberation Organization (PLO), has been nonbinding and has witnessed the development of a significant competing framework outside its purview—the Islamic Resistance Movement, or Hamas. In most settings where Palestinians have resided, the PLO, the Palestinian Authority (PA), and Hamas have had no official jurisdiction or enforceable powers. In the areas where they have had margins of governance (but not sovereignty)—essentially the Areas A and B in the West Bank and the Gaza Strip—the continued effective presence and domination of the Israeli occupation army has meant that the Palestinian leadership could not be held fully responsible for the ultimate condition of the Palestinian people and their movement. Although this has not absolved the Palestinian political leadership of its shortcomings, it is a legitimate argument that most Palestinians have acknowledged.

Such has been the state of limbo for the largest and longest-lasting refugee population in the world today.[1] Palestinians have yet to be granted the right to be fully governed by their own true dictator, let alone a democratic system.

In any case, Palestinians have always been cautious in addressing "the internal [Palestinian] front" because Israel has been constantly engaged in its own tinkering and psychological conditioning vis-à-vis Palestinians to weaken them and foment internal schisms. Israel has commonly used historic policies of assassinating, imprisoning, exiling, and humiliating the Palestinian national movement's leadership to manipulate and undermine the organizational potential, morale, and unity of the Palestinian people. While rejecting this conditioning has also bred an unhealthy, undemocratic tendency within the national movement, scripted democratic practice has been equally impossible in the variegated conditions under which Palestinians have resided—be it under the boot of the Israeli occupier, as "non-Jews" in the "Jewish state," or within the repressive conditions of the Arab states.

A Suppressed Narrative and History

In order to grasp the manner in which the question of Palestine interacted with the "Arab Spring," it is essential first to gain a command of the embedded historical processes and narratives that operated beneath the surface. That is to say, the manner in which Palestine and the Arab Spring interacted did not emerge from a vacuum; rather, it was part of a continuity of ideas whose historical roots and contemporary practices we must grasp if we are to understand where they were heading.

Two main poles structured the determination of the Palestinian question in its various formulations and practices. On one hand was the Western imperial pole, led by the United States and the European Union, whose geostrategic and economic interests formed the basis of external intervention in the region—and Palestine in particular.

A dependent subactor within this pole was the state of Israel, as the expression of political Zionism and its settler-colonial achievements on the ground in historical Palestine. The fierce alliance of interests within this pole, despite minor contradictions between these actors, allowed for their unity around the common objective of subverting the coalescence of the region on the basis of its preexisting linguistic, national, cultural, historical, and economic bonds.

The second pole was composed of the region's states and people, who formed a loose pan-Arab/Muslim bloc with significant ethnic minorities and religious faiths and denominations within it. Although this bloc encapsulated the ingredients that would allow for forms of its unity, primarily within national or religious expressions, internal political differences together with the legacy of colonial division had prevented this from taking form. The entrenching of domestic political elites within regional states, as well as the alliance of many of these to the Western bloc in the modern period, further undermined the potential for this pole to find unified expression. Nonetheless, the potential for unity remained, and such unity had been a consistent political demand raised by different groups throughout the post–World War II history of the region. For this reason "radical nationalism," as the United States called it, was to be prevented at all cost, with the state of Israel playing a frontline role to this end, historically and into the future.

Territorial Palestine formed the locus where the confluence of competing interests between these poles met. It was not by accident that the British Empire facilitated the Zionist movement's creation of the state of Israel at the geostrategic juncture that cleaved the Levantine and Arabian Gulf peninsula (al-Mashriq al-Arabi) from Egypt and North Africa (al-Maghreb al-Arabi), and that also happened to be in immediate proximity to the Suez Canal. Israel was the embodiment of this cleavage in its historical, economic, and cultural dimensions and remained an unfulfilled project in its settler-colonial dimension and its political role. This explains the continuation of Israel's settlement construction in the West Bank: its repeated historical attempts to prevent or defeat Arab attempts at unity or at steering an independent politics and economy and, specifically, the smashing of Palestinian nationalism as the indigenous movement of resistance to these processes.

With this understanding of what shaped the structure of the competing forces at play, we can begin to grasp the relation between the Palestinian cause and its Arab periphery in light of the outpouring of revolutionary energy in the Arab Spring.

Palestine at the Heart of Arab Collective Consciousness

"Palestine" is an organic part of the Arab people's history, consciousness, and identity. It is at once the goal of the national movement of the Palestinian people and a cause that has embodied and shape-shifted the collective Arab aspiration for self-determination in its struggle for freedom from Western colonialism and Zionism. There is hence a dual nature to "Palestine"—one formed by the Palestinians themselves and the second formed by its Arab and Islamic periphery, which looks to Palestine in a distinct way. Because Palestine has failed to exist as a sovereign state, however, both sides have the capacity to influence what the Arab Spring meant for "Palestine" and, conversely, what "Palestine" meant for the Arab Spring. Palestine's very immateriality gave impetus to the fluid nature of the movement's significance and goals, making it subject to evolution over time and context while it varies according to who engages and signifies these ideas into praxis.

Needless to say, many well-established and historically overlapping cultural, social, religious, and economic ties connect Palestine, its people, and its Arab periphery, which is unsurprising considering Palestine's location, history, and religious significance. But beyond this, Palestine pervades a great deal of the common intellectual, cultural, and political productions of the Arab world in its post-Ottoman history—productions whose price has been paid for in time, resources, and struggle. These productions were kept alive by the new generation of Arab youth and had already taken expression in the Arab revolution, as evidenced by the 2011 Nakba demonstrations.

It is helpful to understand that many of the critical historical junctures of Arab history in the past century have had the Palestine cause as a central or related element. It is a history of thousands of Arab volunteers who mobilized (outside their governments) to stop the fall of Palestine to the Zionist armies in 1948; it is the story of thousands of others who joined the ranks of the fedayeen with the launch of the

Palestinian revolution after the defeat of 1967. It is the story of the six major wars that Israel engaged in against the people of the region over six decades, of the eight Arab countries Israel bombed (Jordan, Egypt, Tunisia, Syria, Lebanon, Sudan, Iraq, OPT/Palestine), of the hundreds of thousands Israel killed and injured, and of the direct intervention Israel undertook in internal battles between social forces within Arab states for the purpose of bolstering one side over another in the service of strategic Zionist and/or Western goals (Lebanon, Algeria, Jordan, Morocco, Yemen).

This bloody and dirty history is part of the material evidence affirming the trope that Israel, after all, has acted as the watchdog of Western imperial interests in the region, determined to ensure that the Arab world remains divided, submissive, and exploited. In this logic, the continued existence of Israel as the territorial base of the Zionist project, and the usurped homeland of the Palestinian people, became the symbol of continued Arab defeat, weakness, and submissiveness. In contrast, "Palestinian liberation" represented the end of Palestinian dispersion and oppression at the hands of Israel, as well as collective Arab self-realization. The relational and dialectical nature of Palestine, Palestinian nationalism, and pan-Arab nationalism prevented the isolation of each categorical trajectory from the others. It also meant there was a unique relationship between Palestine and the Arab revolution that did not exist for other revolutionary theaters.

History and Strategy

All major political trajectories of modern Arab thought have shared some variation of these understandings as the conceptual launching point of their worldview vis-à-vis the Palestinian question—from Arab leftist currents to Nasserists, Baathists, Islamists, and even among the few liberal tendencies. The major debates surrounding these questions have had less to do with contesting the nature of Israel and its role in the region and more to do with what to do about it. How to end the Nakba and bring about Palestinian liberation for the Palestinian people and, by extension, the broader cause of self-determination of the larger Arab-Muslim bloc behind them?

Two predominant historical trajectories have attempted to take up this cause: the Nasserist project and the Palestinian-led track. The early period of Palestinian displacement (1948–73) witnessed the dominance of Nasserist ideals, which held that Arab unity was necessary to the achievement of Palestinian liberation. Since 1967, and particularly since 1974, a distinct Palestinian national movement has asserted itself more independently from the Arab regimes and has argued instead for the Palestinians to go it alone. This strategy, promoted by the Palestinian National Liberation Movement, or Fateh, is influenced by the belief that the idea of Arab unity is too threatening to the regional order (in terms of Arab state allies and how the West would view such a transformation), thus focus needs to remain on the "practical" and "achievable." From 1974, Fateh and the "moderate Arab states" that supported it interpreted this as the establishment of a Palestinian state on the 1967 Occupied Palestinian Territories, with other Palestinian rights left open for achieving in the future based on existing United Nations resolutions and international law.

By 2011, of course, neither strategy had succeeded in bringing an end to Palestinian dispossession. Although there are many reasons for this failure, it is fair to assess these factors along two lines: their *external* defeat at the hands of the Western/Zionist bloc and their *internal* politics, dynamics, and structures, which played a part in their weakness and inability to resist their own defeats.

The first trajectory—led by the Nasserist project—was externally devastated by the premeditated Israeli attack in June 1967 (Tolan 2007). This defeat led to a cascading series of defeats for pan-Arabist movements across the region, which ultimately led to Egyptian president Anwar Sadat swinging his allegiance in 1977 and adopting neoliberalism, peace with Israel, and leadership of the camp of pro-U.S. countries in the region. Aside from this external factor, however, the internal practices of Nasserism, and particularly its inability to resolve the question of democratic citizenship, undermined the project and its legacy, weakening it and its ability to revive.

The Palestinian-led track would also fail. Its pinnacle was reached in the Oslo "peace process," which, rather than leading to a peaceful resolution to the conflict, enabled Israel to restructure and entrench its occupation while further fragmenting the Palestinians. Efforts by the

Palestinian movement to reverse the negative impact of the Oslo process, represented in the Second Intifada, were also militarily defeated at great cost to the national movement. Israel used the Intifada to launch a war against the Palestinian national movement and to delineate the boundaries of its theft of Palestinian land by expanding settlements, constructing a planned 810-kilometer "separation barrier," and consolidating a veritable apartheid regime on both sides of the Green Line. Palestinian communities in the OPT were devastated and left in conditions of extreme asymmetry between themselves and Israel, whereby a Palestinian could not even grow, harvest, or move a box of tomatoes between one town and another without approval from the Israeli occupiers. Palestinian citizens of Israel became the subjects of plans for transfer, and new laws demanding their loyalty and legitimating discrimination against them were passed (see Adalah 2010).

Internally, the Palestinian-led track was also hamstrung by its failure to resolve its own "democratic question," even given the limited margins within which it could operate. The historical corruption and undemocratic practices of the PLO ultimately sapped that organization's credibility among many Palestinians, leading in part to the rise of Hamas as a parallel and competing structure. Hamas's rise in popularity can be traced to Palestinians' demands for organizational and political reform within the national movement at the same time the notion of resistance remained an important part of the movement's program of action—a notion many Palestinians felt Fateh had abandoned in favor of its strategic 1974 turn to negotiations (see Hroub 2006).

The legacy of these processes was a situation in which the national movement stood miserably divided in the "self-governed" regions of the OPT, with a Hamas-governed Gaza Strip and a Fateh-governed West Bank. This split also reflected a conflict of political power over the issue of governance and the strategic trajectory of the Palestinians in the OPT, with the diaspora and Palestinians in Israel alienated from influencing this strategic debate due to the de facto deactivation of the PLO, replaced by the activities of the PA.

Aside from dividing the potential of the Palestinian people, however, both strategic trajectories had weak political traction in terms of achieving Palestinian goals, even if united: Gaza was on total lockdown by Israel and the international community. Hamas's tactics and discourse had little serious leverage potential over Israel in terms of achieving Palestinian rights, either militarily or diplomatically. Fateh's approach in the West Bank was equally ineffective, revolving primarily around a policy of nonconfrontation vis-à-vis Israel. Focus was placed on developing Palestinian capitalism and on diplomatic jockeying. The net effect was an ugly neoliberal reality on the West Bank as Fateh failed to amass the diplomatic weight necessary to break the alliances between Israel and the United States and the European Union, all of which were more or less united in rejection of even Fateh's minimalist approach.

What the world had witnessed, then, was a significant ideological, political, and organizational failure on the Palestinian front for the previous sixty years, and particularly for the previous twenty years of the "peace process." The failure was both Arab and Palestinian, as the bankruptcy of the main strategies employed for the purpose of winning Palestinian liberation had proven insufficient and weak in the face of U.S. and Israeli power.

Acknowledging all this, however, must not come at the expense of avoiding the very real agenda-setting practices of Israeli settler-colonial designs, which consistently worked to deepen and permanently integrate the West Bank into pre-1967 Israel while cutting off Gaza not only from the rest of the OPT but also from the world. Palestinians were either to accept Israeli colonialism and hegemony over the new Palestinian "reservations"/"Bantustans" (Gaza, Area A in the West Bank, and even Palestinian localities within Israel) or, quite simply, to leave. The gross asymmetry of power exposed quite clearly how Palestinians in and of themselves did not have the means to counter this reality, given that they had no effective counterbalance to the Israeli–Western axis. In the foreseeable future, that counterbalance would not exist in any meaningful form. The reason such a counterbalance did not exist can largely be traced to the fact that the "natural" sources of political, economic, and moral support that could sustain Palestinian steadfastness and resistance (the Arab and Muslim world, together with strong solidarity forces internationally) had been depleted in the context of external defeat, totalitarianism, and the weakness of left forces internationally.

Ever since the 1979 Camp David Accords between Israel and Egypt, the Palestinian front had witnessed a sustained retreat in support from its Arab periphery. The 1991 Gulf War and the 2003 invasion and occupation of Iraq accelerated U.S. domination throughout the region and witnessed the widening of the number of regimes that were part of the pro-U.S. axis. The reversal of course emptied the Arab world of any pan-Arabist agenda, ripening the conditions for tribal, religious, and sectarian subidentities to surface. This process grew worse with the creeping assumption of neoliberal economic policies in many individual states, which began to infect what had generally been protectionist, state-welfare societies. The retreat on Palestine and pan-Arabist ideals at official governmental levels was so far-reaching in recent years that the non-Arab states of Iran and Turkey competed in scavenging for opportunities to profit politically from the Palestinian cause and its appeal among the Arab and Muslim masses. While the cause remained alive within the popular imagination and consciousness, activism around Palestine within the Arab world was restricted and relegated to the purpose of acting as a regime-sanctioned safety valve for the release of accumulating pressure within Arab states.

The Run-Up to the Arab Spring

The preceding lengthy, although admittedly cursory, summary of the relationship between Palestine and its Arab periphery has been a necessary prelude to the following discussion of Palestine in the context of the emergence of the so-called Arab Spring. The latent tendencies, processes, and histories described above formed the bedrock of consciousness and practice throughout the region that accounts for how Palestine was addressed exogenously and endogenously by Arab and Palestinian actors in that new historical period.

First, the exogenous, Arab dimension: The poor performance of Arab states on both a collective level and an individual level, together with the many economic, political, social, and citizenship questions each country embodies domestically, played a part in the toxic cocktail that began exploding in the wake of Mohamed Bouazizi's now mythical act of self-immolation. The Arab youth so central to the Arab revolution experienced the worsening tides of history closing in around them in a particular manner, which, as we shall see, also saw Palestine playing a central role in the run-up to the revolts.

Here it is not necessary to dwell on the known socioeconomic and developmental indicators that made this demographic a tinderbox— unemployment, food prices, inequality, and so on. These factors certainly played a large part in radicalizing the masses and fueling their struggle. At the same time, Arab youth were not the mere guinea pigs of social science indicators. That is to say, these youth were equally political agents who demonstrated a consciousness about themselves and others (including Palestinians), as well as a capacity to learn, mobilize in large numbers, and adapt. This political consciousness translated itself in many ways, playing a central role in the success of the revolutions up to that point. It was this dynamism and its ability to find competent organizational expression that could truly challenge the forces of political and economic subjugation in which the Arab world found itself. It was also what would determine how far the revolutionary processes in the region would ultimately go.

It is impossible to overstate the significance of the role that Al Jazeera, the Arabic satellite television news channel, played in this process, providing a catalyst and crystalizing force for the public genesis of this consciousness across the Arab world. Starting in 1996, Al Jazeera broke the monopoly that Arab states had held over information and discourse, offering a comparatively free space in which the Arab and broader Islamic world could air and gestate its deepest political and social contests. On Al Jazeera, "radical" nationalist and Islamist movements were given relatively unfiltered expression, while the Palestinian cause was featured front and center. The outburst of the Second Intifada in September 2000 marked the beginning of an epic period of cutting-edge journalism for Al Jazeera. Images of Palestinian youth were broadcast into millions of Arab living rooms as these youth played a dramatic role in leading a failed counterinsurgency against Israeli colonialism. Israel's scorched-earth campaigns were extensively covered as well. Every Palestinian political dynamic was covered in depth, including Hamas's taking of power in Gaza; the "Palestine papers"; and "Cast Lead," Israel's 2008–9 ruthless preplanned assault on Gaza (Haddad 2009; see also Finkelstein 2010).[2] Palestinian affairs consistently received disproportionate airtime, and the inner debates of the movement became topics of popular interest and debate across the Arab world. Each of these events added to the collective consciousness of Palestinians and Arabs, contributing to its evolution of ideas about Israel, resistance, and the Palestinian cause in general.

Al Jazeera, together with other copycat stations, also contributed to other influential processes through its broadcasts. The U.S. invasion and occupation of Iraq inflamed anti-American sentiment across the region, but it also sounded the death knell of the empty bombastic regimes that had traditionally claimed to be defenders of everything Arab and Palestinian while causing their own populations to live in police states and doing little to help bring about Arab unity or Palestinian liberation. Al Jazeera's coverage of the Hezbollah movement was extensive, from the movement's success in leading the resistance against Israel's occupation of the south of Lebanon in 2000 to its steadfastness during the 2006 Israeli assault. Hezbollah's disciplined resistance stance served to expose the flatulent nature of the Arab order, which could exhibit nothing similar in terms of defiance and liberation of national territory from Israeli occupation. Al Jazeera also covered the emergence of the international solidarity movement as an increasingly significant player in dynamics concerning Palestine; its coverage of the *Mavi Marmara* incident, which shocked, inflamed, and impressed Arab audiences, was especially important.[3]

Each of these experiences brought with it an accumulation of experiments in Arab resistance to American and Israeli aggression in the region. Arab audiences were equally exposed to countercurrents in the West, which had somewhat left-leaning political orientations, through coverage of antiwar movements and "antiglobalization" rallies. Although Al Jazeera's role would begin to shift with the outbreak of the Arab Spring, demonstrating the network's caution particularly around the revolution's emergence in and around the Arabian Gulf, the "genie" that Al Jazeera helped create was already out of the bottle.

The Revolution Unfolds

This is the potent cocktail of political ideas that informed the Arab Spring's larger political vision. When the revolutions erupted, we began to see their unfolding in visible ways on the ground, be this in symbolic or very real challenges to the prerevolutionary status quo.

Here it is important to note that because Palestine activism was moderately tolerated—largely as a pressure valve—under Arab regimes before the revolutions broke out, the infrastructure of Palestinian activist organizing played a part in the early organization of revolutionary protests that emerged and quickly mushroomed in Tunisia as well as Egypt. Pro-Palestine chants were a part of the very first demonstrations in Sidi Bouzid, where the Tunisian revolution began, while the Palestinian flag and the subject of Egyptian–Israeli ties quickly became lightning-rod issues that revolutionary forces in Egypt could rely upon to encourage mobilization. The symbolic potency of the Palestinian cause was stunningly exemplified in the aftermath of Mubarak's toppling, when a rally of three million persons in Tahrir Square witnessed the roaring chant "Lil Quds, rayheen, shuhada' bilmalayeen" (To Jerusalem, we are going, martyrs by the millions).

The issue of Palestine as a galvanizing collective force had already moved well beyond the symbolic or romantic in the Arab revolutions. The September 10, 2011, sacking of the Israeli embassy in Cairo by a crowd some five thousand strong and the narrowly missed lynching of the Israeli embassy staff there gave indication of the seriousness with which revolutionary forces take the goal of annulling the 1979 Camp David Accords—an anchoring fixture of U.S. policy in the region. Moreover, the repeated targeting of the Egyptian–Israeli gas pipeline in the Sinai Peninsula by unknown assailants (at least seven attacks had occurred by November 2011) functionally blocked a crucial element of the economic agendas of this accord. While Egypt was particularly vulnerable to this kind of mobilization as one of only two countries with official diplomatic relations with Israel, the message was clear for all: normalization with Israel will not be tolerated under any circumstances; diplomatic and economic relations must be cut, while popular mobilization must move in the direction of helping the Palestinian cause, in practice and not only in rhetoric.

This found most prominent expression in a loosening of the economic stranglehold upon the siege on the Gaza Strip, imposed by Israel but formerly upheld by Mubarak's regime to Gaza's south. "Post"-revolutionary Egypt witnessed a substantial loosening of this siege, facilitating the flow of goods and weapons—many allegedly from revolutionary Libya (Pfeffer 2011)—into Gaza, functionally breaking the isolation of the strip and the Hamas government there and annulling an important bulwark of Western/Israeli policy vis-à-vis the Palestinians.

The Diaspora

As a natural component of the revolutionary forces unleashed across the Arab world stood the Palestinian diaspora, located and activated within various Arab state and revolutionary theaters, with particular relevance to Egypt, Syria, Jordan, and Lebanon, which ring historical Palestine. Although the different theaters witnessed various levels of these communities' ability to engage with the domestic revolutionary processes against the existent regimes, a broader tendency could be delineated—that of this constituency using some of the very same means of mobilization used by domestic revolutionary forces to advance their particular Palestinian demands as refugees. The early revolutionary period witnessed social media being used as sites where political organizing and political imagining could take place, beyond the real boundaries and security apparatuses that prevent such organizing and discourse in the "real" world. For instance, simple Photoshopped images of masses of prayer-goers from the Arab world descending on and praying in Al-Aqsa Mosque in Jerusalem began making the rounds on pro-revolutionary Facebook pages. The idea behind such graphics was to try to get audiences to imagine scenarios that were once thought to be impossible but were now possible thanks to the power and collective action of the Arab/Muslim masses.

The most dramatic expression of this phenomenon of imagining an alternative future came in the "Third Intifada" Facebook page, which garnered a quarter million members in a few days, before eventually being shut down under pressure from the Israeli government. The Third Intifada was a grassroots Internet campaign that spread like wildfire across Palestinian refugee communities and Arab youth movements in the diaspora. It was responsible for the Nakba Day demonstrations in May 2011, which eventually resulted in Israel scrambling to ruthlessly contain and suppress the phenomenon, killing fifteen protesters and injuring hundreds of others. The Third Intifada was also successful in organizing a follow-up mass-coordinated demonstration on June 5, 2011, Naksa Day, the day commemorating Israel's occupation of Arab lands in 1967. Twenty-three more protesters, mostly refugees from Syria and Lebanon, were killed in those demonstrations. The message of these initiatives to Israel and the world was unquestionable: the question of Palestinian refugee rights to their homeland remained; indeed, *the* most sensitive of issues of discrepancy between Israel, the Palestinians, and the Arab world remained alive, defiant, and continually seeking means to actualize itself within the historical balance of forces.

The Internal Palestinian Front

Now to the "internal front"—Palestinians who still lived in historical Palestine in the OPT, as well as in Palestinian communities in Israel. The tide of emotion unleashed by the Tunisian and Egyptian revolutions, together with the dramatic footage from Nakba Day on the historic borders of Palestine, quickly penetrated the circuits of political consciousness and activism throughout these communities, although it affected their ability to mobilize in different ways.

As in all other Arab theaters, the first whiff of the events in Tunisia and Tahrir Square catalyzed the domestic demands of each given locality. Whereas in most Arab states this was quickly translated into demands for mass reform, if not full-on revolution, in the particular context of the OPT, and for the reasons explained previously, the pressing domestic demands took expression in the form of unrepentant calls for political unity between the main two political streams, Fateh and Hamas. Instead of "Asha'b yureed isqat annitham!" (The people demand the downfall of the regime!)—the battle cry of Tunisia, Egypt, Yemen, and others—the cry heard across the OPT was "Asha'b yureed inha' al-inqisam!" (The people demand the end of the division!).

The push for unity was led by groups of disaffected youth who consciously modeled their organizations on the youth formations of Egypt and Tunisia and even replicated those groups' technique of occupying public spaces for extended periods of time to get their demands across.[4] This demand for unity, however, emerged from previous periods and was based upon the perceived heavy price Palestinian society and politics were paying for the division between Hamas and Fateh, as well as the lack of respect for democratic norms under both. This came in the wake of Palestinian society feeling that it had suffered greatly during the Second Intifada, with these sacrifices translated into a costly division that transgressed all Palestinian red lines regarding internal political praxis. A popular consensus existed that the division could lead only to destruction, nationally and vis-à-vis the Palestinian cause's allies internationally.[5] How could Palestinians demand solidarity from world forces if they had no one representative leadership structure to state these claims to the world?

Although the authorities in both the West Bank and Gaza initially felt threatened by the mobilizations and took repressive action against them, they realized that the movements were hardly threatening their own grip on power. Moreover, both authorities tacitly understood that they would not overcome the dead ends reached in their own strategies by cracking down on Palestinian youth calling for unity. Both leaderships hence opportunistically gave in to the demand for unity and signed a cold unity government deal on April 27, 2011.

Although on the ground little had changed, with the deal unlikely to advance politically to any serious degree given the divergent worldviews of the two groups, the initiative was welcomed by the Palestinian masses and was a wise maneuver by the political leaderships of both groups. Hamas and Fateh could agree that there was a need to safeguard the collective interests of the Palestinian people beneath one banner in the turbulence of the Arab arenas around them. A prevalent fear also existed that the division could threaten to expose and divide Palestinian communities in diaspora, where revolutionary processes were/are taking place, and no one was interested in seeing a repeat of the disastrous experience of Palestinians in Iraq after the fall of Saddam Hussein (Human Rights Watch 2006). In general, however, it could be stated that there was a political consensus around the Arab revolutions from the Palestinian political leadership, which agreed that the Palestinian front needed to be patient and weather the turbulent tides in one boat. The leadership hoped that by taking this course, Palestinians would be able to reap some important political gains from the historical shifts taking place.

Of the two authorities, Hamas was probably better poised to benefit from the upsurge throughout the Arab region. In a speech delivered on the occasion of the 2011 Eid festivities after the passing of the Islamic holy month of Ramadan, deposed Hamas prime minister Ismail Haniyeh described the Palestinian people as the biggest benefactors of what was taking place in the Arab world "because the Palestinian people are loved by the Arab people and do not recognize the Zionist entity. Today we celebrate two occasions — Eid El Fitr, and Eid of the Arab revolutionaries who are bringing down tyrants. There is nothing greater than to have the people as decision makers and raise the banner of unity in their capitals!" (quoted in *Al Mustaqbal* 2011). Hamas had always espoused a pan-Arabist/pan-Islamist tendency as part of the movement's strategic outlook. The influential power of Islamic movements, as the oppositional current in many of the Arab revolutionary theaters, would also mean that Hamas would benefit from any democratic shift taking place in countries such as Tunisia, Egypt, Libya, Syria, and Yemen.

Given its alliances with the traditional Arab order (Egypt, Saudi Arabia, and Jordan), Fateh, which for many years had dissuaded engaging the masses as part of its strategy, was certainly more cautious about the Arab revolutions. The loss of Mubarak's regime as Fateh's strategic ally weakened PA president Mahmoud Abbas's hand, although the general tide across the region buoyed the overall Arab hand vis-à-vis Israel and the West. Fateh was likely to attempt to co-opt the tide of revolutionary potential among Palestinians, steering it toward Fateh's diplomatic efforts for statehood through the United Nations. Moreover, it was not unlikely that Fateh could tolerate and support a limited grassroots campaign to target specific campaign issues such as Israeli settlements and the Wall, which remained Israeli "sticking points," simply because the PA's own track of negotiations had led to a serious dead end. West Bank PA prime minister delegate Salam Fayyad, for example, launched his own campaign to encourage consumers to boycott settlement products, distinct from the Boycott, Divestment and Sanctions Movement, which began with a statement issued by 170 Palestinian organizations in 2005.[6] This kind of corralling maneuver is likely to be seen repeated in different contexts as the political leadership looks for ways to harvest popular sentiment and activism without attracting attention to itself that would make it a target of Israel or the West.

Popular forces shared a cautious optimism about the rising regional tides for their cause, with some sectors (particularly youth) no doubt willing to struggle for it. At the same time, it would be dishonest to ignore the heavy sense of precaution, mixed with fatigue, that also existed. Palestinian communities, especially Gaza, were under serious states of siege, with Israel's violence and power ever present and at unprecedented levels. Those in the West Bank, only slowly emerging from the traumatic experience of life under the Second Intifada, had little appetite for receiving that kind of treatment again and could basically be described as hunkering down in positions of self-preservation, thanks in part to eight billion dollars in international donor aid from 2006 to the present, forty projects of the World Bank, and the fact that a third of the families of the West Bank were linked to the public sector and the international aid that pays for it. There was an acknowledgment in this sense that a great many issues were out of their hands, and that with Israel's designs on West Bank land clear, the best they could do would be to organize themselves and their communities so they could remain steadfast, or *samed,* for the challenges ahead.

In any case, an outstanding question for the Palestinian arena remained one of tactics and strategy. That is to say, even if the people had the political energy to engage in struggle, how they should do so was not self-evident, considering the arc of tactical experiences the Palestinian movement had undergone in recent years.

The experience of the Second Intifada left Palestinians aware of the limits of militarization as a tactic in struggle, but it did not pose an alternative. Experiments in nonviolent resistance had gained increased currency as legitimate and effective, based on the struggles of the villages of Bil'in and Budrus to push back the path of the Israeli apartheid wall, but these were drops in the sea considering the enormity of the issues Palestinians had to contend with under occupation: from house demolition to identity card confiscation, from land appropriation to political detention, and from questions of freedom of movement to the right of return of refugees and their property restitution. Also, no one can deny the enormously effective matrix of control that had been imposed on the lives of Palestinians in both Gaza and the West Bank, which incorporated cutting-edge military, bureaucratic, and economic technologies of domination.

Palestinians in Israel

A similar hunkering down appeared to be taking place among the Palestinians living inside Israel. On one hand, the uprising lifted their spirits with the prospect that broader sets of powers were emerging that would buoy the Palestinian cause in general. On the other hand, they still lived in Israel, where the government was the most right-wing in the state's history and had become openly intolerant, targeting the minimal civil rights that Palestinians enjoyed. The members of the Palestinian community rightly perceived that to "rise up" and consciously identify themselves as part of the swarming Arab masses seen burning Israeli flags across the Arab world would be to invite the Israeli government and its paramilitary settler formations to forcefully accelerate plans to carry out their declared intentions of expelling the Palestinians. Caution and patience, hence, remained the imperative of the Palestinian community's political leadership and base.

At the same time, the ironic development of a Jewish Israeli struggle for social justice tangentially inspired by the Arab Spring created a new actor of potential relevance. It was too early to tell what the political direction of the social movement would be, or even if it would remain a movement at all. However, it was clear that resolution of the large questions the demonstrators raised—concerning "social justice," citizenship, discrimination, inequality, poverty, and security—would entail definitive choices within Israeli politics regarding some of the fundamental elements of Zionism and Israel's preferential priorities as a "Jewish state."

Here Palestinian citizens in Israel would be strategically positioned as the test of any real reforms the movement raised and might or might not win. Since 2007, virtually the entire political leadership and civil society of Palestinians inside Israel had coalesced around basic political principles that would lead to equality between Jews and Arabs. That is to say, the Palestinian leadership had already written the blueprint for the deconstruction of Israeli apartheid, through which Israel would become a state of its citizens and not the state of the Jews worldwide.[7] The ability of Israel's Jewish protesters to mature politically remained to be seen. A Palestinian fear surrounding the Israeli protests, of course, was that the crisis could be resolved at the expense of the Palestinians—through an accelerated Zionism and a more brutal capitalism to boot. The hesitant approach that Palestinians in Israel had taken toward the Israeli Jewish protests was understandable considering the fact that the intentionality behind the protests was yet to be determined. The character of the demonstrations at that point seemed to affirm that the majority of the Jewish participants were demanding a stake in and a larger portion of the "pie," seeking to revert to the social democratic norms enjoyed by the collectivist Zionist project before its hard-right turn to neoliberalism in the mid-1980s that accelerated during the first decade of the twenty-first century. Very little about this movement, however, indicated that it was willing to question whether the pie itself needed to be shared with the Palestinians, not just those in Israel, but also Palestinian refugees, whose property and livelihoods were essentially stolen and privatized by the major Zionist organizations and the Israeli state after the ethnic cleansing of Palestine in 1948. It seemed unlikely such a "radical" turn could become possible in the context of the prevalent ideas circulating throughout the Israeli political establishment and in the context of an unstable Arab political periphery.

Conclusion

Where and how these various political tendencies will unfold is impossible to know. Nonetheless, various conclusions can be drawn from the developments at hand that are important to note.

To begin with, the Arab revolutions demonstrate certain dynamics that have important ramifications for the Palestinian cause in the future. At their heart is a fundamental demand for the redefinition of Arab national citizenship based on antitotalitarian, democratic norms and a fair distribution of wealth within each country. This means that the thrust of the revolutionary process is likely to revolve around the *internal* demand for civil rights, respect for democracy, an end to corruption and nepotism, and an end to state abuses of power domestically. Such processes take years to congeal, but they are essential to the resolution of a core historical weakness of modern Arab political projects. If these processes are successful, the core base of Arab states will be greatly strengthened and will have cascading effects on the *external* expressions of the new political constituencies and orders being formed and created. If the popular will of the Arab masses can be respected in governing institutions on socioeconomic and civil rights issues, that will necessarily entail the airing of this constituency's political outlook vis-à-vis Palestine and other foreign policy matters, while freeing up the resources at its disposal for backing up that political outlook with more practical action.

Without question, the issue of Arab unity has remained far off, as it takes years to break down the old entrenched orders that have profited from their alliances with Western channels of rent seeking, first in each individual state, let alone operating on a collective level. Nonetheless, the possibility for increased experimentation in individual and collective Arab state action vis-à-vis Palestine—the creation of a possible counterweight to the Western/Israeli bloc—for the benefit of Palestinian rights seems inevitable from this historical process overall. Here it is worth noting that the Fateh/Hamas divide within Palestinian politics is largely a product of and structured by the *previous* alignment of regional powers and the weakness of the Arab order overall. But if this were to change—which the Arab revolutions promise—new political imaginings would become possible, whether in the transformation of the old party structures or in the emergence of new ones.

The mass shift in the political composition of the regional order has already borne fruit for the Palestinian theater. The Israeli government has already acknowledged that the October 2011 prisoner deal between Hamas and Israel was influenced by the understanding that the regional winds of change could only bear negatively on the fate of the captured Israeli prisoner of war Gilad Shalit.[8] The mass concessions offered by Israel in the Shalit deal were made with the understanding that Israel needed to cut its losses now, before deeper losses took place in an unknown future.

An ironic counterdynamic to the prisoner deal also existed, however, whereby the reactionary military council that still ran Egypt—and was linked to the old regime—used the prisoner deal (through its mediation of the Hamas–Israel talks) to contain and diffuse the rising domestic pressure against the council. The deal bought the council a modicum of time and probably indicated that the United States pressured Israel to finally cut the Shalit deal in the end, for this purpose. This attested to how the Palestinian issue remained a chess piece of manipulation for the old Arab order as well, not merely the domain of action for the revolutionary forces newly emerging.

All this said, the unleashing of revolutionary spirit and consciousness has already taken place and cannot be reversed so easily. As the reverberations of this process ripple throughout the Arab world, and subsequently influence even the West in movements such as the "Occupy" phenomenon, unpredictable new horizons open up for consciousness and political action. As these dynamics unfold, it is crucial for the new social and political actors to steep themselves in an understanding of the historical processes and dynamics at play and of the valuable lessons previous struggles provide. Such knowledge could help them to avoid repeating the mistakes of previous struggles, so that the revolutionary processes in effect would not lead to co-optation or chaos but to a genuine new and just social and political order for Palestine, the Arab region, and the world at large.

Notes

1. For a comprehensive survey of the refugee situation, see Gassner (2009).

2. The so-called Palestine papers were a set of sixteen hundred leaked documents that revealed the inner workings of Israeli–Palestinian negotiations and discussions among the members of the Palestinian negotiating team (see Swisher 2011).

3. The *Mavi Marmara* incident involved an attack by Israel on a humanitarian aid flotilla that had been organized by Palestinian solidarity activists; the flotilla was attacked while attempting to bring supplies into the Gaza Strip on May 31, 2010. For more information on the incident, see Bayoumi (2010).

4. These groups included the Manara group; Al Herak Al Shababiy; We Are All Gaza, We Are All Palestine; Gaza on Our Mind; Nuwwat; and 15 April.

5. Recall that the division arose after the 2006 victory of Hamas in the elections, which Fateh refused to recognize. Instead, the latter's most corrupt sections, in alliance with the U.S. Central Intelligence Agency, attempted to prevent Hamas from exercising its authority by instigating a coup. Privy to these plans, Hamas preemptively attacked the security headquarters occupied by the Fateh coup backers, killing them or forcing them to flee to the West Bank (see Rose 2008).

6. For the text of this statement, see Palestinian BDS National Committee (2005).

7. This document, titled *The Future Vision of the Palestinian Arabs in Israel* (National Committee for the Heads of the Arab Local Authorities in Israel 2006) was formulated by the unofficial heads of the Palestinian Arab sector in Israel. Three similar documents were issued around the time by various coalitions of civil society organizations.

8. As the *Washington Post* reported: "Israeli Prime Minister Benjamin Netanyahu had previously warned that a swap for Shalit would free dangerous militants and put Israel's security at risk. But amid a relentless campaign by Shalit's family that won the hearts of the Israeli public, Netanyahu ultimately bowed. In remarks Tuesday night, he acknowledged that Israel, which has become increasingly isolated amid the regional tumult, was faced with the stark choice of winning Shalit's freedom now or seeing the chance disappear forever" (Greenberg 2011).

References

Adalah (Legal Center for Arab Minority Rights in Israel). 2010. "New Discriminatory Laws and Bills in Israel." November 29. http://adalah.org/eng (accessed March 19, 2013).

Al Mustaqbal. 2011. "Haniyeh in the Eid Sermon: Palestine Is the Largest Benefactor of the Arab Muslim Revolutions" [in Arabic]. August 31.

Bayoumi, Moustafa, ed. 2010. *Midnight on the Mavi Marmara: The Attack on the Gaza Freedom Flotilla and How It Changed the Course of the Israel/Palestine Conflict.* New York: OR Books.

Finkelstein, Norman G. 2010. *"This Time We Went Too Far": Truth and Consequences of the Gaza Invasion.* New York: OR Books.

Gassner, Ingrid J., ed. 2009. *Survey of Palestinian Refugees and Internally Displaced Persons, 2008–2009.* Bethlehem: BADIL Resource Center for Palestinian Residency & Refugee Rights.

Greenberg, Joel. 2011. "Gilad Shalit, Israeli Soldier Held by Hamas, to Be Released

as Part of Deal, Netanyahu Announces." *Washington Post,* October 11. http://
www.washingtonpost.com (accessed October 28, 2011).

Haddad, Toufic. 2009. "The Road to Gaza's Killing Fields." *International Socialist
Review* 64 (March–April), online edition. http://www.isreview.org (accessed
November 11, 2011).

Hroub, K. 2006. "'New Hamas' through Its New Documents." *Journal of Palestine
Studies* 35 (4): 6–27.

Human Rights Watch. 2006. *Nowhere to Flee: The Perilous Situation of Palestinians
in Iraq.* September 10. E1804. http://www.unhcr.org (accessed October 28, 2011).

National Committee for the Heads of the Arab Local Authorities in Israel. 2006.
The Future Vision of the Palestinian Arabs in Israel. http://www.adalah.org/news
letter/eng/dec06/tasawor-mostaqbali.pdf (accessed October 28, 2011).

Palestinian BDS National Committee. 2005. "Palestinian Civil Society Call for
BDS." July 9. http://www.bdsmovement.net (accessed March 19, 2013).

Pfeffer, Anshel. 2011. "Libyan Arms Expected to Continue Flowing into Sinai for
Months." *Haaretz,* August 23. http://www.haaretz.com (accessed November 11,
2011).

Rose, David. 2008. "Gaza Bombshell." *Vanity Fair,* April.

Swisher, Clayton E. 2011. *The Palestine Papers: The End of the Road?* Chicago: Hes-
perus Press.

Tolan, Sandy. 2007. "Rethinking Israel's David-and-Goliath Past." Salon, June 4.
http://www.salon.com (accessed October 28, 2011).

Iraq

HAIFA ZANGANA

AT THE HEART of most Arab capital cities there is a Tahrir Square. Baghdad is no exception. Following February 25, 2011, demonstrations and vigils were taking place in Baghdad's Tahrir Square as well as in similar squares in other Iraqi cities—Basra, Kut, and Karbala in the south, Mosul in the north, and Ramadi in the west. Those taking place in Erbil and Sulaimaniya in the Kurdistan region extended the definition of the Arab Spring, since Kurds as well as Arabs were taking part. The question was whether the characteristics of the protests in Egypt, Libya, Bahrain, Yemen, and Syria applied to Iraq, a country that has certain unique features among Arab countries. Iraq, during the Arab Spring period, was emerging from military invasion and occupation, leaving behind a mixed parliamentary-presidential system that drew upon and exacerbated sectarian and ethnic fractures.

In this chapter, I shall examine the specific characteristics of the Iraqi protests. I will look at the symbolic importance of Baghdad's Tahrir Square, the social makeup and political claims of the demonstrators, the obstacles they faced, and the relationship between these nonviolent protests and the forms of armed resistance and insurgency. I will also examine what the protesters achieved and their prospects for their future.

Why Tahrir Square?

Sahat al-Tahrir, or Tahrir Square, known also as Liberation Square, is the central square in Baghdad, which used to be called Bab al-Sharqi, or Eastern Gate.[1] It was named for the famous Nusb al-Huriyya (Liberty Monument), one of Baghdad's most recognizable landmarks produced by the renowned Iraqi painter and sculptor Jawad Salim (1920–61). Erected after the July 14 Revolution in 1958, it depicts scenes of the Iraqi people's struggle for liberation from British colonial rule and commemorates the establishment of the Republic. The monument (fifty meters by ten meters by six meters in height) consists of fourteen bronze reliefs depicting the historical continuity of Iraq as a country emerging from Sumerian, Babylonian, and Assyrian roots into the Islamic era. The reliefs are mounted on a background designed by architect Rifa'at al-Chadirchi and are inspired by the banners of the people's protests and demonstrations demanding an end to British colonialism—famously in the 1920 Revolution and in the 1941 and 1948 demonstrations that brought down the Portsmouth Treaty and the government. Liberty Monument has become part of the Iraqi collective memory and an expression of national identity. It is a national symbol of unity and inherited culture in struggles against foreign hegemony. Its "Iraqiness" has defied attempts by successive regimes to redefine national symbols according to their own ideologies.

In addition to its representation of ordinary people (a woman hugging a martyr, a political prisoner, workers and soldiers, a child pointing to the future), names of the places surrounding the square contribute to shaping perceptions of the monument's significance. Sahat al-Tahrir is the square linking Jumhuriyya (Republic) Bridge, Kifah (Struggle) Street, and Nasr (Victory) Square. The monument itself overlooks Umma (Nation) Gardens, where, in the 1970s, young Baghdadis strolled in the evenings to enjoy the cool breeze sustained by the gardens' fountain. Tahrir Square has been a place of celebrations, demonstrations, festivals, and peace parades. The area is also the heart of Baghdad cultural life, with cinemas and theaters. The back streets have been contested spaces among marginalized people, drunks, prostitutes, and the police. The square has also hosted horrendous events such as the 1969 public hanging by the Baath regime of fourteen people, nine of them

Jews, who had been convicted of spying for Israel. Political changes and deterioration in the economy have touched the square as much as they have affected the people. During the sanctions years (1990–2003), which Denis Halliday (2000), U.N. humanitarian coordinator in Iraq in 1997–98, described as "genocide," the square was crowded with vendors selling secondhand clothes and bric-a-brac; it was where poverty-stricken Iraqis sold everything they had. After the U.S. invasion, the square was the place to buy pornographic videos and magazines, Viagra, drugs, weapons, stolen goods, U.S. soldiers' combat meals, uniforms, and—in contrast—CDs of resistance songs.

The U.S. invasion of Iraq in 2003 and the ensuing occupation broke open the heart of a city already fragile from decades of Baath rule and brutal sanctions. Massive bombardment of the city in the early phase of the invasion was followed by its reconstruction as a garrison town. Checkpoints and bomb blasts interrupted the flow of daily life. It carved the city into neighborhoods and strengthened existing sectarian divides through ethnic cleansing and armed conflict, against the occupation and equally against different Iraqi communities. In the midst of the firefights and the enforced segregation, the Liberty Monument sustained bombardment from the occupiers and from the resistance. The latter focused much of their attack on the Green Zone, the gated area for the occupation. One mile away from the square, it now houses the biggest U.S. embassy in the world.[2] Described by the late Iraqi sculptor Khalid al Rahal (1926–87) as the second most important "epic" in Iraq's history after *Gilgamesh* (Mohammed 2007), Tahrir Square is, not surprisingly, the setting for numerous Iraqi novels and poems.[3] Saadi Youssef's 2003 poem "A Personal Song," written on the eve of the invasion, is one example:

Palm trees will collapse under the bombing;
The shores will be crowded
With floating corpses.
We will seldom see Al-Tahrir Square.[4]

Fallujah's Peaceful Protest

On February 25, 2011, six thousand Iraqis gathered in Tahrir Square (as well as thousands in the centers of other Iraqi cities) in response to a call for a "Day of Rage" by activists using social networks and by some Iraqi TV channels abroad, mainly the Cairo-based channels Al-Rafidain and Al-Baghdadiya and the London-based channel Al-Sharqiya. The aim was to express public anger with Nouri al-Maliki's regime, which had failed to provide the services, jobs, and security promised during the elections. There were also calls for the full withdrawal of occupation forces at a time when al-Maliki's regime seemed willing to extend the presence of the U.S. forces in Iraq beyond December 2011 (in compliance with the status of forces agreement made with the Bush administration in November 2008). Most mainstream media news coverage barely mentioned the latter demand, feeding the notion that the protests were ignoring the importance of the occupation.

It was not the first time Iraqis had demonstrated peacefully. A week earlier hundreds of lawyers had demonstrated across Iraq to protest widespread corruption and unemployment, and to demand that the government open up so-called secret prisons to scrutiny and give detainees access to legal counsel. They held up signs that said, "Lawyers call for the government to abide by the law, and provide jobs for the people," and "The government must provide jobs and fight the corrupt" (Abdul-Jabbar 2011). Following the practice of football (soccer) referees, the protesters carried yellow cards (signals of warning) for the government. "Today we are carrying yellow cards," said Rabia al-Masaudi, head of the Karbala lawyers' guild, "but if services are not improved we will return with red cards" (quoted in ibid.). Intellectuals had also protested against the lack of freedom of expression and the raids on the writers' union. Journalists had taken to the streets against laws restricting their movement, which prevented them from reporting. A prominent Iraqi trade union leader said it was a "matter of shame for the new Iraq that its new and democratic trade unions are under such attacks from a government that should adhere to the rule of law and democratic pluralism, as enshrined and guaranteed by Iraq's constitution" (quoted in General Federation of Iraqi Workers 2011; see also International Trade Union Confederation 2011).

Despite the violent response of the occupation and its proxy regimes, demonstrations, vigils, and strikes had taken place since the start of the occupation. The General Union of Oil Employees in Basra staged a strike at the Basra Oil Refinery in Sheiba in June 2003 (see

International Viewpoint 2005). The workers had not been paid their wages since the invasion and occupation in March. Angry that they had to report to KBR (the U.S. engineering firm) rather than to an Iraqi concern, one hundred workers blockaded the road to the refinery and confronted British troops for five hours. Negotiations went in favor of the workers, who won their wages that very day. The Basra strike was the first action that culminated in the Southern Oil Company Union winning a raise from 69,000 Iraqi dinars to 102,000 Iraqi dinars per month.[5] Iraqi trade unions, teachers' associations, and medical staffs have organized protests. Groups of women have often gathered or lined up in front of prisons, detention centers, military camps, and the Ministry of Human Rights to seek information about missing loved ones. They have often faced harsh treatment and been subjected to sexual harassment or demands for bribes.

One of the first and most significant protests took place in Fallujah (city of a thousand mosques), west of Baghdad, on April 28, 2003. Approximately two hundred people gathered outside al-Qaaed primary school after the U.S. forces declared a curfew, demanding that the occupation troops vacate the building to allow their children to return to school. Supposedly enforcing the curfew, U.S. troops from the Eighty-Second Airborne Division fired at the demonstrators, killing seventeen and wounding more than seventy. Even local paramedics were shot. Among the dead were three children.[6] The killings in April did not stop. A few days later more civilians died at the hands of the Third Armored Cavalry Regiment in front of the Baath Party headquarters and mayor's office (Human Rights Watch 2003).

Reporting from Fallujah, the *Daily Mirror*'s Chris Hughes (2003) described the demonstration and the Occupation troops' response:

> I watched in horror as American troops opened fire on a crowd of 1,000 unarmed people here yesterday. . . . Many, including children, were cut down by a 20-second burst of automatic gunfire. . . . *Mirror* photographer Julian Andrews and I were standing about six feet from the vehicle when the first shots rang out, without warning. Apache helicopters circled above. . . . We heard no warning to disperse and saw no guns or knives among the Iraqis whose religious and tribal leaders kept shouting through loud hailers to remain peaceful. . . . We ran towards the compound to get away from the crowd as dozens of troops started taking aim at them, others peering at

them through binoculars. . . . Then came the gunfire—and the death and the agony. . . . Those left standing—now apparently insane with anger—ran at the fortress battering its walls with their fists. Many had tears pouring down their faces. . . . Still no shots from the Iraqis and still no sign of the man with the AK47 who the US later claimed had let off a shot at the convoy.

What followed was the destruction of 70 percent of the city and the killing of eight hundred people, a figure disputed by many as an underestimate. According to the organization Iraq Body Count (2004), "Between 572 and 616 of the approximately 800 reported deaths were civilians, with over 300 of these being women and children."

For Iraqis who may have believed in Western democracy, Fallujah became an epitaph on its tombstone, soon to be followed by many others. The photos of the abuse perpetrated at Abu Ghraib prison, as well as "the Haditha, Ishaqi and Qaiem massacres have been seen by most Iraqis as part of a pattern serving a strategic function beyond indiscriminate revenge: to couple collective humiliation with intimidation and terror" (Zangana 2006). Numerous images had been cut razor sharp into people's minds: a detainee hooded and wired with electrodes; a pyramid of naked prisoners piled on top of each other; a cowering naked detainee in front of barking dogs; male and female U.S. soldiers smiling and giving the thumbs-up in front of Manadel al-Jamadi's "battered corpse, iced to keep it from decomposing in order to hide the true circumstances of his dying" (Zagorin 2005). These racist images entered Iraqi art and literature, indicating how deeply they touched the collective consciousness of the Iraqi people. Abdul Karim Khalil's hooded prisoner of Abu Ghraib, as a marble statue in classical style, became the symbol of Abu Ghraib. Khalil's works and those of other artists are not just depictions of horror; on a deeper level, they constitute an attempt to understand the inhumanity of the "liberators."

In Tahrir Square

The atmosphere in Tahrir Square on February 25, 2011, was one of defiance and unity. Approximately six thousand people of all ages and backgrounds were gathered there. They chanted, "Il ma ezour al tahrir omrahkhasara" (Whoever is not visiting the square has wasted his life) and "Kathab Nouri al-Maliki kathab" (Liar Nouri al-Maliki liar) (Juhi 2011).[7] The concerns of the protesters included opposition to U.S. occupation. Banners conveyed their feelings of anger and disappointment at the lack of services, such as electricity, clean water, and access to food rations, and they denounced al-Maliki's corrupt sectarian regime. Women and children carried photos of their detained or missing relatives. Some banners questioned the fate of Iraq's oil revenues. "I'm a laborer. I work one day and stay at home for a month," said Oday Kareem to Jane Arraf (2011) of the *Christian Science Monitor*. Kareem was with a group who called al-Maliki a liar. "He said people will do better than they did under Saddam Hussein—where is it?" Those who took part in elections held up posters depicting how they should have chopped off the finger that had been dipped in indelible ink to show they had voted. Many carried Iraqi flags to emphasize Iraq's unity.

The demonstrators tried to cross al-Jumhuriyah Bridge to get to the Green Zone. The government had posted riot police along blast walls to seal off the area. Protesters broke through two of the blast walls, at which point the riot police pushed the crowd back toward Tahrir Square as two army helicopters buzzed the crowd. As a fire truck hosed the crowd, the riot police fired on them and killed at least three people. It was the end of the Day of Rage (McDermid 2011).

Who Were They?

They came from many walks of life: members of grassroots organizations, groups of women, independent writers, journalists, artists, heads of tribes, and religious figures. They were not well organized and in general bypassed the ideology of political parties, whether Islamist, communist, Arab nationalist, or neoliberal. Among them was the Popular Movement to Save Iraq, an alliance of several groups including the Movement to Liberate the South of Iraq, the Organization of Students of a Free Iraq, the Coalition to Support the Iraqi Revolution, and the Movement of Iraqi Youth. Their statement was signed by all these groups, followed by their location, "Occupied Baghdad." Members included Uday al-Zaidi and his brother Muntadher, the journalist who threw his shoe at the former U.S. president George W. Bush during his last visit to Iraq in 2008. The Popular Movement was joined by other human rights groups, such as Where Are My Rights, Iraqi Women's Freedom, Union of the Unemployed, the Iraqi Women's League, and members of the Communist Party (the party itself having been an early supporter of the occupation).

What was significant about the gathering in Tahrir Square was the absence of the al-Sadr current. U.S. officials and the media often portray Muqtada al-Sadr, its leader, as a "fierce opponent of the United States" (for example, see Abdul-Zahra and Santana 2011). He used to present himself as the leader of the "honorable" armed resistance. In August 2005, however, he announced that he would join the political process and instructed his followers to hand over their weapons to the U.S. military in exchange for money.

Since then, al-Sadr had become an active part of the occupation's political process and was responsible for tilting the balance in favor of al-Maliki's remaining in office after the March 2010 elections. Al-Sadr militias roamed Sadr city in cars, calling on residents not to take part in demonstrations but to give al-Maliki's regime six months to carry out its promises, thereby upstaging al-Maliki himself, who asked only for one hundred days! Meanwhile, the Popular Movement to Save Iraq had a clear message: government officials and parties within the political process should not be in Tahrir Square unless they were willing to apologize for their involvement in government.

Challenges and Responses

The protesters of Tahrir Square faced serious difficulties (and continue to do so). Two days before the Day of Rage, al-Maliki and other officials issued statements insinuating that demonstrators were planning to do "everything possible to create chaos, disturb public order, and endanger the state institutions," as al-Maliki said on television network Al Iraqiya on February 23, 2011. He accused them of being "Baathist—terrorists—al-Qaeda." This legalized their arrest and detention under Article 4 of the Antiterrorist Act. A curfew was imposed across Baghdad, preventing thousands from reaching the square. Al-Jumhuriyah Bridge, which led to the Green Zone, was closed. Some participants had to walk miles to reach the square. People from other cities were banned from entering Baghdad. Security forces, police, and U.S.-trained special forces surrounded the square, and snipers were located on the rooftops of buildings overlooking the square. Water hoses, truncheons, tear gas, and live ammunition were used to disperse the demonstrators. U.S. helicopters hovered a few meters above the protesters in an attempt to intimidate them. Barriers were erected on the roads leading to the square, which protesters tried to remove, together with some concrete walls (in Baghdad there are fifty-five walled-in areas and fourteen hundred checkpoints). Al-Marjiaya (Shiites' highest religious authority) issued warnings "to protect the people" while the al-Sadr current instructed followers not to participate.

The regime issued arrest warrants against several journalists, including Muntadher al-Zaidi. Live broadcasting was prohibited, and broadcasting and recording equipment was confiscated from journalists at security checkpoints. In 2004, the Iraqi regime and U.S. intelligence officials claimed that Al Jazeera was inflaming the situation because the channel had broadcast images of beheaded victims of insurgents. The channel was prohibited, ostensibly for that reason. In fact, the real reason Al Jazeera was proscribed was its daily coverage of the second U.S. attack on Fallujah. This coverage provided comparisons to the Palestinian Intifada. Al Jazeera correspondent Ahmed Mansour was in Fallujah and offered spirited reports that angered the regime and the U.S. government. Most transnational Arab television offices in Iraq were closed. There was no Arab or Iraqi media coverage of the 2011 protest events in Iraq. This is in marked contrast to what was seen in Egypt and Tunisia. In Cairo, Al Jazeera turned Tahrir Square into a virtual twenty-four-hour studio that provided the demonstrators with support and protection. In the Baghdad protests, a number of journalists were physically attacked, and five journalists were arrested. At a press conference, one of those journalists, Hadi al-Mahdi, said that the arrested reporters had been blindfolded and made to sign papers without being allowed to read what was written on them. According to Haider Najm (2011), "The other journalists spoke of physical abuse and beatings with rifle butts and threats of rape." Internet communication was limited because computers were not widely available; in any case, reliance on computers was limited because of the lack of electricity (on average, the national grid supplied electricity only three hours per day).

Twenty-nine protesters were killed across Iraq on that day. Three days later, al-Maliki held a press conference to announce that he would enact reforms within one hundred days, adding, "Is there any country in the region, or the world, which enjoys such levels of freedoms as Iraq?" He added in wonderment, "I doubt it" (quoted in ibid.).

One Hundred Days On

Despite these obstacles, protests continued for the entire year of 2011 and into 2012. Certainly there were protests every Friday. The Day of Rage was followed by a "Day of Salvation," a "Friday of the Imprisoned," a "Day of Freedom," a "Day of Dignity," and, on September 9, the "Meeting of the Revolutionaries." Earlier in the year, on April 9, thousands of protesters took part in a twenty-day sit-in in the northern city of Mosul, demanding the immediate withdrawal of the U.S. occupation forces, the termination of all agreements with the occupation, an end to a political process based on sectarian quotas, and a sectarian constitution. On April 13, officials barred street protests in Baghdad. Any protests that were allowed were required to be held at one of three soccer stadiums.[8]

The protesters called for June 6 to be the "Day of Retribution," to coincide with the end of the hundred-day deadline set by al-Maliki for his reforms. On that day, coaches full of al-Maliki's Da'wa Party members arrived at Tahrir Square. Armed with sticks and clubs, they attacked peaceful protesters, including women, as the security forces stood by. The Da'wa members chanted, "We're with Maliki. You're Baathists." Similar attacks took place on Friday, June 17. Women protesters of the Organization of Women's Freedom were molested, beaten, and called "prostitutes" and "communists" by regime-sponsored thugs (Stites 2011).

What Was Achieved?

The square itself had become a unifying space where protesters could unite and organize. Under the freedom monument old and young, men and women, gathered every Friday to protest against an *al-naqisa* (flawed) government that had concentrated power in the hands of the prime minister and his sectarian Da'wa Party. The resilience of the demonstrators had shaken al-Malaki, forcing him to promise reforms within one hundred days and to dismiss three governors accused by the protesters of incompetence and corruption. As described at the time, the governor of the northern city of Mosul, Atheel al-Najifi, openly defied al-Maliki's forces to defend the right of Iraqis to demonstrate. In response to al-Maliki's threats of a clampdown—backed by live ammunition—nearly the entire city (Iraq's second largest) went on a general strike on May 25, chanting the words of the Arab Spring, "The people want the downfall of the regime!" (Issa 2011b).

The Iraqi government's claims to be supporting "freedom of assembly and peaceful demonstration" had been challenged once again. Human Rights Watch (2011a) warned: "Authorities in Baghdad and in Iraqi-Kurdistan are keeping their citizens from demonstrating peacefully. . . . Iraq needs to make sure that security forces and pro-government gangs stop targeting protest organizers, activists, and journalists." Social networks were set up to exchange information, photos, videos, and statements. Web sites and blogs had already been established, such as the Media Office of the Great Iraqi Revolution and the February 25th Revolution Coalition. Direct contact was established between protesters and international human rights organizations such as Human Rights Watch and Amnesty International, and this led to the release of reports and press releases on the protests. One of the better reports available, featuring direct testimony from protesters, is Amnesty International's "Days of Rage: Protests and Repression in Iraq" (2011). It includes eyewitness accounts from several participants, including the following two illustrative cases.

Activist Uday al-Zaidi (whose name is transliterated in the Amnesty International report as Oday Alzaidy) said that on February 13 he and other protesters had gathered on the street in Baghdad when armed forces came to disperse them. Uday agreed to go to an alternative place of protest in an army vehicle. After being transferred into another vehicle by men in plain clothes, he was blindfolded and beaten. He was then held for five days in an unknown location, where he was tortured. "Every day they beat me and gave me electric shocks. They told me to confess that I was sent by the Ba'ath party. When I denied this, they beat me even harder with batons and they shocked me with electric prods." Uday was hospitalized for two days after he was released. This did not stop him from participating in the Day of Rage on February 25.

Fatima Ahmed (pseudonym), a forty-two-year-old activist, joined with other women in Erbil on the morning of February 25 to hold a demonstration. That night, after the demonstration, three armed men in plain clothes came to her home. She told Amnesty International, "I asked them what they wanted from me. . . . He started threatening me. He said if you don't stop your political opposition activities we will kidnap you, rape you and videotape the rape." Fearing for her safety, Fatima left her two children with their father and moved in with a friend. She also stopped going to work. She did not go to the courts because she believed they would do nothing about the threats made against her. Although she feared retribution, she did protest on February 25.

Oday, Fatima, and thousands of others carried banners, chanted slogans, sang songs, and recited poems at the protest. The banners were adorned with slogans and collages. Later, video clips of the protest and short animation films depicting the activities of that day were shared with the world via the Internet. These artistic and political productions both expressed and enriched the outcome of the protest and provided its memory.

Prospects

Because of the extreme measures taken by al-Maliki's regime, especially prohibiting vehicles and increasing checkpoints, the number of protesters in Tahrir Square dwindled in the weeks following February 25 to a few hundred. However, protests grew in size and intensity all over Iraq after the assassination of journalist, theater director, and activist Hadi al-Mahdi on Thursday September 8, 2011. Al-Mahdi was helping to organize the Meeting of the Revolutionaries on the first Friday after the end of the Eid (the three-day feast following the monthlong fasting of Ramadan). Al-Mahdi was shot twice in the head in his home in the Al-Karada district in the heart of Baghdad. Witnesses at the crime scene told Human Rights Watch (2011b) that they saw no evidence of a struggle or theft, suggesting that the killing was deliberate. On al-Mahdi's Facebook page there was an announcement for the demonstration, and he posted the following message describing threats against him in the hours before his death:

Enough. . . . I have lived the last three days in a state of terror. There are some who call me and warn me of raids and arrests of protesters. There is someone saying that the government will do this and that. There is someone with a fake name coming on to Facebook to threaten me. I will take part in the demonstrations, for I am one of its supporters. I firmly believe that the political process embodies a national, economic, and political failure. It deserves to change, and we deserve a better government. In short, I do not represent any political party or any other side, but rather the miserable reality in which we live. . . . I am sick of seeing our mothers beg in the streets and I am sick of news of politicians' gluttony and of their looting of Iraq's riches. (quoted in ibid.)

The assassination of al-Mahdi sent an unmistakable message to the activists, journalists, and protesters: a bullet is waiting for anyone who dares protest the regime's policy, corruption, and servitude to the U.S. occupation. Given the government's widespread corruption and the absence of independent investigation, Iraqis knew that there was almost no hope the perpetrators of the crime would be held responsible. This dire situation raised an important question: Would this point-blank execution deter protesters? Certainly not, said Uday al-Zaidi on behalf of the Popular Movement to Save Iraq, which had been one of the main organizing forces behind the protests in Baghdad and Mosul. The Popular Movement was clear in its commitment to continued peaceful protests, to not returning home "until al-Maliki steps down, the occupation leaves, corrupt politicians are held accountable, face trial, and the parliament is disbanded. . . . We call for the formation of a transitional government of technocrats that can run the country for a temporary period, and after a period of no more than 6 months, they will set up transparent elections without regional or outside interference" (quoted in Issa 2011b).[9]

Various factions of the armed resistance saluted the peaceful protests, recognizing the protest movement in Iraqi cities as another strand of resistance against the occupation to be added to the political, civil, community, and cultural strands. They acknowledged the movement as a complementary aspect that was extremely important in an organic process that drew a wider range of frustrated Iraqis into the long-term resistance, seeking liberation and peace based on justice and equality.

Meanwhile, the governments of the United States and the United Kingdom, outspoken champions of Iraqi human rights before the invasion, remained silent on the scale of death, destruction, systematic human rights violations, and oppression enveloping Iraqis' daily lives and destroying their aspirations for genuine democracy.

To follow the trajectory of goals set up by the resistance, of which the protests were but one phase, we need to examine the three main intermingling stages of resistance goals. The first of these was to neutralize an overwhelming military machine, the greatest in the world, with effectively unlimited funds and arms. This goal had been accomplished at a great cost in lives lost and the threat of the destruction of much of the Iraqi social fabric. It was pressure from the activists and the broader liberation movement in Iraq that forced al-Maliki's government to call for an end to the extraterritorial protection of the U.S. occupation forces; it was this call that effectively ended the formal period of the U.S. occupation, with the troops departing in late 2011.

The second goal was to expose and neutralize the neocolonial political setup represented by the so-called political process while dealing at the same time with an unholy de facto alliance between the U.S. and Iran and the sectarian establishment on one hand and, on the other, the new unscrupulous and self-serving class of politicians at national and local levels recruited by the occupation. The resistance had managed to totally emasculate this setup and proved over nine years that it had no future in Iraq. With the continuity of the peaceful protest movement, which included families, independent nongovernmental organizations (NGOs), cultural and neighborhood associations, religious organizations, and unions, among many others, the resistance aimed to challenge the al-Maliki regime's move to label anyone who opposed it or demanded reforms as either Baathist or al-Qaeda.

The resistance's third goal was to break the religious, sectarian, and ideological barriers that were enforced by the occupation and nurtured by some international and national NGOs, which used various ways of subverting mass movements, involving promises of money and positions as much as they made use of street thugs and infiltration.

The prospect of development in Tahrir Square, at that point in time, was not yet clear. However, the relatively small-scale gathering of protesters compared to demonstrations in Egypt, Libya, Yemen, and Syria should not have been underestimated, since the participants were determined to persist as the U.S. occupation morphed into a new stage (as the U.S. policing presence, its army of NGOs and contractors, and its commercial and financial hegemony continued). Furthermore, resilient protesters, in the square and elsewhere, had to handle the negative if not damaging declarations of some high clergy who maintained their authority through political parties within the regime.

The demands of the protesters were depicted in the media as sheer calls for employment and the improvement of daily services, but they were more conclusive than that. As Uday al-Zaidi of the Popular Movement to Save Iraq stated: "We are a country that has lost its dignity and freedom. That is why our central demand is and will continue to be an end to the occupation, and an end to this political process which is built on a sectarian quota system" (quoted in Issa 2011b). This yearning for freedom, dignity, and justice is what linked Iraqi protesters to their fellow protesters in other Arab countries. And it was this deeply shared spirit that led the youth of the Great Iraqi Revolution to send a message of solidarity in an "open letter to the Heroic Syrian Revolution" on August 22, 2011, saluting the Syrian people's struggle against tyranny and saying, "Be assured that your coming victory will strengthen us to resist our tyrants and the occupiers that sponsor them" (quoted in War Resisters League Blog 2011).

Notes

1. When Abu Ja'far al-Mansour built Baghdad in 762 c.e., it was a fortified round city, with walls and four gates at an angle of 90 degrees.

2. A delegation of Italian experts visited the square in June 2011 and recommended the immediate restoration and rehabilitation of the monument.

3. The *Epic of Gilgamesh,* a masterpiece of Mesopotamian literature, is the oldest written story. Written in Sumer, south of Iraq, between 2750 and 2500 b.c.e., it relates the adventures of the king of Uruk and his quest for immortality.

4. Youssef wrote the poem in London on March 15, 2003.

5. This information comes from a one-page document titled "Iraq's New Trade Unions," available at http://www.dlandmj.pwp.blueyonder.co.uk/docs/iusbriefing1 .pdf (accessed March 21, 2013).

6. See "Second Battle of Fallujah," World News Network video, http://wn.com (accessed March 21, 2013).

7. "Il ma ezour al tahrir omrahkhasara" played on a popular chant encouraging people to visit Salman al-Farisi's burial place in Ctesiphon, al-Mada'in, in Iraq. Salman was one of the Prophet's companions.

8. For further discussion of the twenty-day sit-in, see Freedom Socialist Party (2011).

9. See also Issa's (2011a) important interview with Uday al-Zaidi on June 9, 2011.

References

Abdul-Jabbar, Nafia. 2011. "Lawyers Protest against Iraq Government." Middle East Online, February 10. http://www.middle-east-online.com/english/?id=44251 (accessed May 9, 2012).

Abdul-Zahra, Qassim, and Rebecca Santana. 2011. "Muqtada al-Sadr Iraq Return, Anti-U.S. Cleric Ends Exile." Huffington Post, January 5. http://www.huffingtonpost.com (accessed May 9, 2012).

Amnesty International. 2011. "Days of Rage: Protests and Repression in Iraq—Testimonies/Case Studies." April 12. http://www.amnesty.org (accessed May 15, 2012).

Arraf, Jane. 2011. "Iraqis Stage 'Day of Rage' Despite Government Lockdown." Christian Science Monitor, February 25. http://www.csmonitor.com (accessed May 11, 2012).

Freedom Socialist Party. 2011. "Iraqis Continue Protests against the US Occupation and Maliki's Government." June 7. http://www.socialism.com (accessed March 21, 2013).

General Federation of Iraqi Workers. 2011. "Iraqi Writers Union Raided Again." January 20. http://www.iraqitradeunions.org (accessed March 21, 2013).

Halliday, Denis J. 2000. "The Deadly and Illegal Consequences of Economic Sanctions on the People of Iraq." Brown Journal of World Affairs 7 (1): 229–33. http://www.watsoninstitute.org (accessed March 21, 2013).

Hughes, Chris. 2003. "Two Killed in New Iraq Demo Shooting." Daily Mirror, May 1. http://www.informationclearinghouse.info/article3183.htm (accessed May 9, 2012).

Human Rights Watch. 2003. Violent Response: The U.S. Army in al-Falluja. June. Washington, D.C.: Human Rights Watch. http://www.hrw.org (accessed March 25, 2013).

———. 2011a. "Iraq: Protest Organizers Beaten, Detained." June 2. http://www.hrw.org (accessed March 21, 2013).

———. 2011b. "Iraq: Radio Personality Shot Dead." September 9. http://www.hrw.org (accessed March 21, 2013).

International Trade Union Confederation. 2011. "Annual Survey of Violations of Trade Union Rights—Iraq." http://survey.ituc-csi.org (accessed March 21, 2013).

International Viewpoint. 2005. "Oil Workers' Union Confronts Occupation and Privatization." September 17. http://www.internationalviewpoint.org (accessed March 21, 2013).

Iraq Body Count. 2004. "No Longer Knowable: Falluja's April Civilian Toll Is 600." Press release, October 26. http://www.iraqbodycount.org/analysis/reference/press-releases/9 (accessed March 21, 2013).

Issa, Ali. 2011a. "Iraq after Maliki's '100 Days': An Interview with Iraqi Organizer Uday al-Zaidi." Jadaliyya, June 9. http://jadaliyya.com (accessed March 21, 2013).

———. 2011b. "'We Weren't Really Waiting': A Fuse 100 Days Long." War Resisters League Blog, June 7. http://warresisters.wordpress.com (accessed May 9, 2012).

Juhi, Bushra. 2011. "Iraq Protesters Accuse Security Troops of Beatings." *Washington Post,* March 11. http://www.washingtonpost.com (accessed March 21, 2013).

McDermid, Charles, with Karim Lami. 2011. "The Missing Ingredient in Iraq's Day of Rage." *Time,* February 25. http://www.time.com (accessed May 16, 2012).

Mohammed, Maha. 2007. "Artists Remember Celebrated Sculptor." Iraq Slogger, April 2. http://iraqslogger.powweb.com/index.php/post/2194/Artists_Remember_Celebrated_Sculptor (accessed May 10, 2012).

Najm, Haider. 2011. "Demonstrations in Baghdad Gather Pace." Niqash, March 2. http://www.niqash.org (accessed May 16, 2012).

Stites, Jessica. 2011. "Iraqi Feminists Sexually Assaulted during Pro-Democracy Protests." Ms. Magazine Blog, June 13. http://msmagazine.com (accessed May 9, 2012).

War Resisters League Blog. 2011. "'Stands Against Its Oppressor': Iraqi–Syrian Solidarity." September 16. http://warresisters.wordpress.com/2011/09 (accessed March 21, 2013).

Youssef, Saadi. 2003. "A Personal Song." Translated by Sinan Antoon. Al-Ahram Weekly On-Line, April 17–23. http://weekly.ahram.org.eg/2003/634/bsc13.htm (accessed March 21, 2013).

Zagorin, Adam. 2005. "Haunted by The Iceman." *Time,* November 14. http://www.time.com (accessed May 9, 2012).

Zangana, Haifa. 2006. "All Iraq Is Abu Ghraib." *Guardian,* July 5. http://www.guardian.co.uk (accessed May 9, 2012).

Sudan

KHALID MUSTAFA MEDANI

THE PROTESTS in the Middle East and North Africa that began in late 2010 highlighted a number of issues that had been obscured by long-standing ahistorical understandings of Middle Eastern and Islamic societies and Western-centered fallacies. Specifically, they demonstrated the crucial importance of bringing both political economy and identity-based politics "back in" as parts of a key framework of analysis. The conventional thesis privileging the idea of a "durable authoritarianism" (Schlumberger 2007) in the region had been undermined by a transregional civil society confronting the power of the combined forces of international capital, domestic commercial interests, and the formidable security apparatus of the state. Those events also helped set the stage for a new analytical agenda in important ways. In the social sciences, scholarship that has long focused on grassroots political mobilization centered on the analysis of social and economic grievances has often been relegated to the sidelines across the disciplines. What these protests indicated, however, is that local-level resistance is in fact the site of grand and revolutionary politics. More specifically, they demonstrated that social networks and class- and ethnicity-based mobilization can indeed produce state-level outcomes of revolutionary potential, including democratization and secession, both of which can undermine the political monopoly of so-called persistent authoritarian regimes in the Middle East and North Africa.

These revolutionary movements also reaffirmed that the locus of study and intellectual attention must include the local as well as the international level. The notion that critics of economic globalization and of the scramble over oil wealth on the part of external powers represent a small and elite-centered ideological community rather than a broad-based political alliance in the region was discredited by the thousands who took to the streets articulating their own "lived" experience with decades of economic austerity measures. In Tunisia, young men and women rallied against an economic model that was geared exclusively toward European markets and dependent on regionally based low-skilled labor in manufacturing; in Egypt, both service-sector informal workers and formal labor organized against excessive austerity measures; and in Yemen and Sudan, protesters revolted against the misuse of antiterrorism campaigns that had been responsible for undermining the life chances and political aspirations of a cross section of social groups.

Far from a "marginal" case, Sudan stood at the very center and not at the periphery of these historic protests. In the context of the partition of the country and the unprecedented protests among its neighbors, the failure of both North and South Sudanese governments to reform their respective ruling parties and include opposition groups had been aggravating divisions and conflict and alienating marginal areas such as Darfur in North Sudan and regions such as the Blue Nile and the oil-rich South Kordofan states bordering the new country of South Sudan. Taken together these developments threatened to fragment both North and South Sudan. The ruling National Congress Party (NCP) of President Omar Beshir and South Sudan's Sudan People's Liberation Movement (SPLM) led by Salva Kir had not addressed the root causes of conflicts in their respective countries. Instead, they stifled debate about Sudan's diversity and identity and tightened their grip on power, resulting in factionalization and the persistence not of an authoritarian monolith but of two weak states threatened by civil unrest and conflict. In the case of Sudan, any analysis of future political developments had to address both the country's similarities and its contrasts with other Arab countries that were concurrently undergoing profound political transitions. Moreover, in order to understand the challenges and prospects for a democratic transition similar to those witnessed in Tunisia and Egypt at that time, it is crucially important to examine the roots and consequences of the country's historic partition.

Sudan in the Context of the Arab Uprisings

At a time when the attention of the Western and Arab media focused on the historic victory of the Muslim Brotherhood's presidential candidate in Egypt, in the summer of 2012 street protests of a scale not witnessed for two decades erupted in Khartoum and other major Sudanese cities. Antigovernment protests, initially led by students from the University of Khartoum, inspired nationwide demonstrations in al-Obeid, Kosti, al-Gadaref, Port Sudan, Wad Medani, and Atbara. They began on June 16, 2012, with female students at the University of Khartoum's downtown campus taking to the streets chanting "No, no to higher prices" and "Freedom, freedom." The students initially protested the announcement of a 35 percent hike in public transportation fees and called for the "liberation" of the campus from the presence of the ubiquitous National Intelligence and Security Services (NISS). Subsequently, Khartoum and other cities witnessed daily protests driven by a widening political agenda. Echoing calls heard in the uprisings in Tunisia, Egypt, and Syria, protesters chanted "The people want the fall of the regime," "We will not be ruled by a dictator," and "Revolution, revolution until victory." Clearly mindful (and no doubt apprehensive) of the protesters' slogans referencing the Arab uprisings as well as two previous popular intifadas that had removed military regimes, President Beshir quickly insisted that this is "no Arab Spring" (Medani 2012).

However, throughout the summer of 2012, street protests expanded in both their geographic reach and their social profile. Moving beyond the middle-class campus of the University of Khartoum, protests included more lower-class students from other universities, supporters and activists belonging to the major opposition parties, civil servants, the unemployed, and workers in the informal sector. Moreover, despite the use of tear gas, batons, and sweeping arrests on the part of the NISS, the protests expanded to include residents in the populous informal settlements and working-class neighborhoods of Buri, al-Ilafoon, al-Gereif, al-Sahafa, al-Abbassiya, and Mayo south of the capital of Khartoum.

The government's decision to abolish fuel subsidies and the imposition of a wider austerity package that resulted in a spiraling inflation rate that peaked at more than 30 percent in May 2012 sparked the wave of demonstrations. These developments came on the heels of smaller, albeit persistent, protests that began in early 2011 in response to pre-existing economic policies linked to the secession of South Sudan in the summer of 2011. The secession of South Sudan resulted in the loss of two-thirds of Sudan's oil reserves, leaving Khartoum with a widening budget deficit, a weakened currency, and rising costs for food and other imports. To make matters worse for Khartoum, landlocked South Sudan shut down its oil production in January 2012 after accusing Khartoum of charging exorbitant transit fees for transporting the South's oil through Khartoum's pipeline. Following years of unprecedented oil exports, which fueled economic growth, the financial basis that helped maintain the patronage networks of the regime dwindled overnight. In response, and immediately following the South's secession, the Beshir regime placed restrictions on the outflow of foreign currency, banned certain imports, and reduced state subsidies on vital commodities such as sugar and fuel. With a budget deficit estimated at the time at $2.4 billion, on June 18, 2012, Beshir imposed yet another round of more drastic austerity measures, lifted fuel subsides, and announced the stringent enforcement of higher taxes on capital, consumer goods, telecommunications, and a wide range of imports.

While the protests in the summer of 2012 were partially inspired by the Arab uprisings, the grievances fueling the protests were decidedly Sudanese. The students and largely unemployed activists confronting the security forces in the streets of Khartoum, members of the professional syndicates, and the leaders of the National Consensus Forces (NCF), a coalition of opposition parties, argued against the government's claim that the deep economic crisis was beyond the government's control and the result of "malicious" traders, operating in the informal economy, who were smuggling fuel and hard currency at the expense of the Sudanese people. They noted that these macroeconomic initiatives were indefensible and persuasively cited widely covered corruption scandals involving members of the ruling National Congress Party. The NCF had also marshaled and publicized overwhelming evidence showing that the bulk of the national budget was allocated to the escalating military campaigns in Darfur as well as to the clashes along the borders with South Sudan that began in earnest in April 2011. Moreover, as the local media noted, at the same time the regime imposed deep austerity measures, the NCP announced greater investments in government apparatuses, concerned as it was with sustaining its patronage networks and security apparatus in the context of wide-scale protests calling for the removal of the regime. Ironically, influential Vice President Ali Osman Taha blamed the economic crisis on the Sudanese themselves, who, as he put it, had been "living beyond their means." In a country where the majority of families rely on funds from labor remittances sent by expatriate relatives (Sudanese workers abroad) for their livelihoods, Taha angered the protesters further by publicly stating that the tendency of Sudanese to maintain extended families in which one individual works and ten others rely on his income was the real reason that local production and incomes were at such low levels (El Gizouli 2012). For its part, the NCF, comprising the major opposition groups, including the Popular Congress Party of Islamist Hassan Turabi and the National Umma Party of former prime minister Sadiq al-Mahdi, declared that they would continue to mobilize street protests to oppose the government's austerity measures and to seek a democratic transition to authoritarian rule. On July 4, in the midst of the street protests against the Beshir regime under the umbrella of the NCF, the opposition groups signed the Democratic Alternative Charter. The text of the charter, which was officially released in September 2012, outlines a blueprint for a transition to democracy for the country. This would involve the establishment of a parliament and an interim government that would subsequently draft a permanent constitution for the country. More specifically, the charter proposes that representatives from the country's historically marginalized regions be included in any interim government, and that a presidential council of six members be established to represent six regions. Most significant, in the context of insurgencies in Darfur and the border regions of South

Sudan, the Democratic Alternative Charter calls for the recognition of the demands of armed groups in the country's peripheral regions for development and equal distribution of power and wealth.

Authoritarianism in Sudan: How Durable?

While the secession of the South had immediate and profound consequences for both countries, it was the imposition of macroeconomic policies inspired and rationalized by neoliberal principles that sparked the 2012 protests. However, the magnitude of the protests and organizational strategies utilized therein were clearly inspired by the protests and transitions taking place in the larger Arab world. Nevertheless, in the wake of the Arab uprisings, scholars of Sudan were near unanimous in declaring that the Sudanese government would "not buckle" to popular protests anytime soon. Interestingly, while the Arab region has long been viewed as immune to democratization, in the context of the Arab protests of 2010–12, Arab "exceptionalism" was replaced by "Sudanese exceptionalism" in much of the analysis on Sudan. Following in the lines of scholars of Arab authoritarianism, these analysts insisted, with little evidence, that Sudan's military establishment was beholden to the government just as it had been since Beshir first took power through a military coup in 1989. That is, the upper ranks of the military and the security forces were still loyal to his rule, the political opposition was weak and discredited, and Sudanese civil society was even more divided than that of Tunisia and Egypt. These were the very same factors that compelled scholars to predict the durability of authoritarian rule in the Arab world. As one Sudan analyst put it: "There is certainly discontent with the regime, but it's unclear if enough of the right factors are present to complete the equation in Khartoum [because] protests undertaken thus far have not taken root with a broad section of the population" (Thurston 2011). The influential International Crisis Group similarly argued that "years of subjugation at the hands of the ruling National Congress Party (NCP) have yielded both political apathy and a weak opposition" (Gettleman 2011).

In reality, in recent years, deep divisions had emerged within the state security forces and the National Congress Party: over the potential pitfalls for Khartoum associated with South Sudan's secession, over the ongoing negotiations with the Sudan People's Liberation Movement in the South concerning the oil-rich border regions, and over the conduct of the ongoing military campaigns in South Kordofan. Indeed, far from presenting a unified front as in the early years of the Beshir regime, the ranks of the security establishment exhibited increasing dissension, leading Beshir to sack several high-ranking officials for the sake of his self-preservation. These divisions were in clear evidence when Beshir removed Salah Gosh, the long-standing director general of Sudan's National Intelligence and Security Services, from his post in April 2011. Gosh fell out with Nafie Ali Nafie, the powerful presidential adviser of Beshir's National Congress Party, after the former initiated a dialogue with opposition parties leading to fears on the part of Beshir and Nafie that he was in the process of plotting a coup against the regime.[1] One year later, on June 24, 2012, in response to the continued spate of protests throughout the country, Beshir issued a decree removing nine of his top-ranking advisers, including six from the NCP, from their positions. The move, part of a countrywide reshuffle designed to revive waning legitimacy for the regime, saw entire regional governments tendering their resignations, with the exception of South Darfur state, whose government simply refused to step down.

In the case of Sudan, this analysis, like analyses of Tunisia and Egypt in the past, presented only a partial picture with respect to the prospects of a Sudanese democratic "spring." The question of whether Sudan would remain resistant to a significant uprising, if not a democratic opening, required an analysis that would take seriously the insights of scholars who focused on the durability of Arab authoritarianism, as well as the pitfalls of their approach. Would Sudan remain resistant to democratization? The answer to this question hinged on an understanding of factors long associated, albeit mistakenly, with the durability of authoritarian regimes in the Arab world. These included the fact that Arab countries possessed weak civil societies, middle classes beholden to state patronage for their survival, and opposition political parties that were either weak (as in Egypt and Sudan) or simply nonexistent (as in Tunisia). However, as the events in Tunisia and Egypt had shown, none of these conditions necessarily precluded the move toward the difficult struggle to dismantle the long-standing political, economic, and social institutions of authoritarian rule. Indeed, what they had demonstrated was that a weakly organized opposition does not necessarily prevent effective mass mobilization.

What, then, explained the divergence of Sudan's experience from that of its northern neighbors? And how can we evaluate the potential for a similar popular intifada leading to another period of democracy in Sudan? For Sudan, the answer is relatively straightforward: it was in the Beshir regime's capacity to maintain a monopoly on the means of coercion. As analysts of Arab authoritarianism have usefully demonstrated across the region, when the state's coercive apparatus remains coherent and effective, it can face down popular disaffection and survive significant illegitimacy (Bellin 2005). Conversely, where the state has a weak capacity for coercion or lacks the will to crush popular protests, the unraveling of authoritarian rule—in the Arab world and elsewhere—may begin to occur. In the case of Sudan, while the protests in the summer of 2012 petered out by the beginning of the holy month of Ramadan, they clearly demonstrated that after twenty-three years in power the Beshir regime's capacity for coercion was weak and increasingly disconnected from the Sudanese people. The Sudanese Armed Forces, demoralized and weakened from fighting armed insurgencies in Darfur and in the two southern border states of South Kordofan and Blue Nile, chose not to step in against the protesters. There were clear signs of discontent between the NISS and police forces in the way the security agents handled the detentions of Sudanese citizens. The protesters were well aware of the political and social divisions between the NISS and the police forces and were clearly banking on persuading elements in the police to sympathize with their shared grievances against the state. In one of the largest and most significant protests outside the Imam Abdel Rahman Mosque in Omdurman that followed Friday prayers in the summer of 2012, protesters attempted to enlist the support of the police, chanting, "Oh police, oh police, how much is your salary and how much is a pound of sugar?" in a clear strategy to persuade the police, the military, and members of the government to join the protests, as was the case with previous successful intifadas in 1964 and 1985 known as the October and April Revolutions. Like their counterparts in Tunisia and Egypt before them, the protesters and the opposition political parties in Sudan were well aware that the dismantling of a long-standing authoritarian regime required sustained protests and popular street mobilization that would potentially enlist the support of significant elements in the military establishment and incorporate the demands of insurgent groups in the country.

Consequently, in the case of Sudan, the key question in the context of the aborted protests of summer 2012 was not whether they were of the same scale as those in Egypt and Tunisia, but rather what was the relative strength of the Beshir regime's capacity for coercion vis-à-vis what was clearly a resurgent and emboldened civil society opposition in the country. What the examples of Tunisia and Egypt had demonstrated was that the answer to this question depended on the state's fiscal health, the level of international support, and the degree to which the state security sector was entrenched in civil society. As in other Arab countries, taken together, these factors were likely to determine whether the level of popular mobilization and protests outweighed the capacity of the coercive apparatus of the Beshir regime. In this regard, it would be likely that the authoritarian regime in Khartoum would be less durable than most analysts had argued, for a number of reasons.

First, the level of international support was extremely low. Indeed, only a few months after the South's secession, the United States reimposed economic sanctions on Sudan. In combination with the standing International Criminal Court's indictment of Beshir issued in July 2010, this increased the Beshir regime's pariah status and resulted in important divisions within the ruling party. It also diminished the hopes among some members of the NCP that they could generate much-needed foreign direct investment.

Second, following almost a decade of remarkable growth in real gross domestic product (GDP) averaging 7.7 percent annually thanks to oil exports, after 2010 growth sharply declined to 3 percent even before the secession of the oil-rich South (Ahmed 2010). Sudan's already depleted oil revenues shrank by a further 20 percent after its main Heglig oil field was damaged and shut down in fighting with South Sudanese troops in April 2012. Consequently, the Beshir regime suffered from an enormous scarcity of foreign currency with which to finance spending to shore up its support base. It was this grave financial crisis that led to the imposition of economic austerity measures, which in turn led to the cost-of-living protests. Perhaps more important in political terms, it also weakened Khartoum's capacity to suppress dissent, since more than 70 percent of oil export revenue prior to South Sudan's secession had been funneled to support for the military and popular defense forces in the country.

Third, as the protests in Khartoum and throughout the north demonstrated, a wide cross section of Sudanese had already mobilized in a process parallel to that seen among their northern neighbors. In addition, protests that spread to central and northern Sudan had been accompanied by cyberactivism spearheaded by the group Girifna (the name translates as "We are fed up"). In a pattern similar to that playing out in Egypt and Tunisia, such actions maintained the link between Sudanese in the country and the hundreds of thousands of Sudanese citizens in the diaspora. Taken together, these factors continued to weaken the capacity of the Beshir regime to forestall the call for democratization indefinitely.

The most telling and important reason for the Beshir regime's diminishing durability was the fact that the previously institutionalized security sector was increasingly fragmented, and the top leadership was gravely divided. Following the country's partition, political power became increasingly centered on Beshir and a close network of loyalists. Moreover, concerned about a coup from within the military establishment, Beshir had purposely fragmented the security services, relying on personal and tribal loyalties. The formerly strong NCP no longer had a significant base of social support even among hard-line Islamists (International Crisis Group 2011). This division was clearly illustrated in 2011 following a much publicized dispute between two of the most influential figures in Beshir's government, Nafie Ali Nafie and Ali Osman Taha. Nafie (presidential adviser and head of state security), along with Beshir, represented the hard-liner faction in the regime, and both had vehemently opposed constitutional reforms. In contrast, Taha (the second vice president) had come into bitter political conflict with the hard-liners by calling for the inclusion of some opposition parties in the drafting of a new constitution.

Secession and the Recurrence of Civil Conflict

In contrast to the uprisings in Egypt, which were characterized by the mobilization of social groups across class coalescing around a wide range of informal social networks (El-Ghobashy 2011), political developments in the *upper* Nile valley can be fully understood only in the context of the impact of the intervention of external forces and political mobilization embedded in ethnic as well as religious networks. These no less revolutionary protests and insurgencies resulted from the formation of identity-based politics of resistance; they were evident in the resurgence of cost-of-living protests in the summer of 2012 and in the ethnicity-based insurgencies not only in Darfur but also in the Red Sea region in the north as well as in the southern provinces of the Nuba Mountains, Blue Nile, and Unity state.

Also, in contrast to Egypt, where the focus at that time was on the prospects for democratic consolidation, the most important question in the case of Sudan was one that has been posed in other secession-based conflicts. That is, would the recent partition prevent the recurrence of ethnic civil conflict? There were two general views on this subject in the scholarly literature. Proponents of partition (that is, the formation of one or more states out of the lands of an existing state) maintained that secession can prevent future conflict if it manages to separate warring factions and create homogeneous units where ethnic groups' security fears are reduced (Kaufmann 1998). Other scholars insisted that partition often leads to future conflict, mainly because identifying new borders does not prevent the recurrence of war or low levels of violence (Horowitz, Weisiger, and Johnson 2009; Etzioni 1992–93). This is primarily because secession requires population transfers and a level of ethnic homogeneity that is nearly impossible to achieve (Sambanis 2000). Moreover, the potential for continued violent interethnic antagonism and a recurrence of civil conflict between the secession state and the rump (original) state is more likely within the context of continued disputes over territory and natural resources (Johnson 2008). Indeed, not only does the presence of natural resources increase the prospects of war and prolong conflict by providing funds to rebels and state actors alike, it may create a new political community organized around ethnic lines (Humphreys 2005; Collier and Hoeffler 2004; Weinstein 2006). For Sudan what was at stake was whether, at that juncture in the country's history, secession would lead to peace or conflict, and what aspect of the dispute would prove more difficult to resolve: the disagreement over the demarcation of new borders, or the economically based territorial dispute over oil resources located along the North–South border.

Answering these crucial questions requires an examination of the record of secessions and violence. While there is no scholarly consensus on either the potential benefits or the pitfalls of division within the context of secessionist-based conflicts (Mearsheimer 1993; Kaldor 1996), the literature on the subject of the aftermath of secessions provides some important lessons for North and South Sudan. In particular, there is broad agreement on some of the factors that may determine whether secessions are followed by peace or conflict. Most notably, these include whether separation produces ethnically homogeneous states, the extent to which the process is managed peacefully to limit the leaders' ability to use force "to revisit the secession-created boundaries" (Tir 2005), and whether the two parties agree on political and economic divisions prior to the secession (Choudhry and Basher 2002). Moreover, while the historical record demonstrates that secessions are no better or worse in ending civil wars than other political solutions (Sambanis 2000), lessons from other countries have shown that ethnically based territorial disputes are more likely to lead to armed conflict, whereas democracies are less prone to a recurrence of violence in the aftermath of separation (Tir 2005).

In the case of the two Sudans, determining the likelihood of future conflict necessitated posing four interlinked questions: What role had political elites played in shaping the conflict between the North and the South? To what extent would the persistence of ethnicity-based grievances, particularly in the disputed regions, represent a challenge to the prospects for sustainable peace? What was the role of external actors in overseeing a peaceful process of secession? And what were the prospects of further political divisions within the North and the South following secession? More specifically, to what extent would the continued concentration of power in the hands of the NCP and the SPLM affect further fragmentation in the outlying regions of the country, including Darfur?

One of the most important lessons that can be drawn from past secessions is that partition is most effective where populations are already separated in ethnic terms at the time of secession, and where the international community is willing to separate groups using mass population transfers if necessary (Johnson 2008). In this respect, in the case of Sudan, the probability of conflict recurrence was quite strong because of a number of factors that have not been present in cases of more peaceful partition. First, Sudan was not divided neatly into homogeneous regions along the lines of an "Arab" North and an "African" South. The ethnic, religious, and linguistic heterogeneity of both parts of the country made the demarcation of homogeneous entities difficult to determine in political terms. Second, there were multiethnic regions in the center of the country. An estimated 1.5 million southern Sudanese resided in the greater capital area of Khartoum. Finally, and most important, oil resources were located in the South and along the disputed North–South borders. In this context, the likelihood of economically based territorial disputes (that is, disputes over oil revenue) was quite high, and these disagreements promised to be far more difficult to resolve than those concerning ethnically demarcated borders.

"Greed," and specifically oil, was certainly a driving force behind the escalation of the conflict between the Beshir regime and the South (Collier and Hoeffler 2004). That is, while the primary cause of Sudan's civil war could not be attributed to natural resources alone, Sudan's increasing natural resource dependence had determined both the conduct of the civil war and the content of the negotiations that ended the military confrontation between the warring parties.[2] Following the discovery of oil, Khartoum was keen to ensure that there would be no opposition to its plans to develop the oil economy. In a strategy used later in Darfur to devastating effect, the Sudanese Armed Forces, along with armed militias, conducted devastating aerial bombardments against civilians in the oil-rich areas of the South. In addition, since the regime was unable to find willing recruits to join in what it termed a "jihad" in the South, Khartoum encouraged ethnic tensions, using local communities in its proxy war. By the early 1990s, the Beshir regime had expanded its military campaigns against civilian populations in the South and the Nuba Mountains, a campaign that became more deadly as Khartoum began to profit from increasing oil revenues (Patey 2007).

Sudan's Antidemocratic Islamists

Across the wide swath of the "Arab Spring" countries such as Tunisia, Egypt, and even Syria, Islamist social movements had emerged as driving forces of democratization. In a historical irony, in Sudan—where the first politically successful Islamist movement emerged—these movements had consistently demonstrated an antipathy toward democratic forces in civil society. More specifically, while the recent discovery and development of oil resources had exacerbated the territorial and economic dispute between Khartoum and the South, by the late 1980s Islamist politics emerged, sharpening the cultural and religious conflict between the two regions in ways that had been difficult to resolve. Historically in Sudan, Islam was promoted by Sufi orders reflecting a more tolerant and accommodating version of the religion distinguished by the extent to which it incorporated pre-Islamic rituals and traditional African religious beliefs with Muslim rituals. In contrast, the rise of Islamic fundamentalism (or Islamism) sharpened conflicting identities in the country and set the stage for a stronger call for self-determination and secession on the part of southern Sudanese. Political Islam emerged as a strong force in Sudanese civil society as early as the 1970s, but in the following decades, its chief legacy in terms of Sudan's civil conflict had been the obstruction of the forces of democracy in ways that undermined national unity. This was clearly evidenced in the origins of the Islamist-backed military coup of 1989 that overturned Sudan's last democratic experiment. Indeed, contrary to recent scholarship arguing that democracy does not promote internal peace because electoral competition in poor multiethnic countries is rarely able to produce accountable and legitimate government, the short-lived experience of democratization in Sudan pointed to its "peace-promoting" possibilities (Collier 2009, 19).

To be sure, democratic consolidation had a poor record in Sudan. No multiparty election had produced an enduring democratic transition, and elected governments had been overthrown three times by military coups. As in many African countries, in Sudan successive multiparty elections faced shortcomings of leadership, a divisive legacy of colonial rule, and ethnic, sectarian, and regional politics. Moreover, a range of corrupt practices—ranging from ballot stuffing and intimidation to the use of government resources and state-controlled media—had long characterized Sudan's three failed experiments in parliamentary democracy (1956–58, 1964–69, and 1985–89) (Willis, el-Battahani, and Woodward 2009). What is noteworthy, however, is that in terms of resolving the North–South conflict, democratic contestation had the potential to broker peace within a national unity framework—that is, to forge peace with unity rather than peace with secession.

While Sudan's third, and last, multiparty period (1985–89) did not represent the wide spectrum of Sudanese (the southern parties, for example, boycotted the elections because of the war in the South), multiparty competition opened avenues for a resurgent civil society that placed pressure on the civilian government to resolve the civil war. In December 1988, widespread demonstrations erupted in Khartoum, led by a newly revitalized coalition of farmers, professional syndicates, and civil servants, as well as senior military officers. Their actions stemmed from the frustration caused by the squabbling among the traditional Umma and Democratic Unionist Parties and by the alliance of the Islamist party the National Islamic Front with the Umma Party to form a majority in parliament (Bechtold 1990). The declining legitimacy of the parliamentary regime, increasing criticism of corruption on the part of elected state officials, and the government's lack of accountability to the electorate placed pressure on the democratic regime to meet the demands of Sudanese civil society, foremost of which was the call for peace. The demonstrators' primary demands were a peaceful solution to the civil war between the government and the SPLM's armed wing, the Sudan People's Liberation Army (SPLA), and the repeal of the sharia-based laws of September 1983. The possibility of democracy resulting in a peace dividend seemed likely. In mid-June 1989, Prime Minister Sadiq al-Mahdi's government announced that a cabinet meeting on July 1 would formally repeal the September laws, contingent upon the laws' review by a legal committee comprising representatives from all political parties. On July 4, a government delegation and the SPLA were to meet to propose a permanent resolution to the civil war (ibid.). Twenty-four hours before the meeting, a group of midlevel officers took over the Republican Palace (the presidential residence), the parliament, and the national broadcasting station; they also rounded up top party and civil society leaders throughout the North and announced the establishment of the Revolutionary Command Council under the leadership of Lieutenant General Omar Hassan Beshir. It quickly became evident that Islamists had mounted the coup.

The Islamists had been marginalized by widespread popular support for a swift resolution to the country's political crisis by way of ending the civil war. Their twofold aim was to preempt any peace agreement that would repeal the imposition of Islamic law and to reverse the influence of pro-democracy forces, many of which had been incorporated into the government following growing protests. Beshir and the leaders of the National Islamic Front immediately canceled the North–South cease-fire, imposed a stricter "Islamic" legal system, and outlawed all political parties and other "nonreligious institutions" (*Al-Hayat* 1989). Consequently, the war in the South took an abrupt turn for the worse. The national army bombed camps of southern war refugees, and paramilitary militia expelled southerners from displaced camps around the capital. In the mid-1990s, the Beshir regime called for "jihad" and armed proxy militias in the Nuba Mountains and South Kordofan to execute scorched-earth tactics that included attacking refugee camps as far afield as the Sudan–Uganda border.

By the time of the cease-fire brokered in 2003, more than two million southerners—most of them civilians—had been killed. The sheer magnitude of human suffering led to stronger calls for self-determination in the South and increasing support for an orderly "separation" of the two regions by the international community. It was because of the devastating humanitarian cost of the war and instability in the South that the Chevron Corporation and later the Canadian oil company Talisman sold their interests in the oil fields (Idahosa 2002). However, while by the late 1990s Canada and the United States barred their oil companies from doing business with Khartoum because of the Islamist-backed regime's war against southern rebels, this left the door open for China, Malaysia, and India to expand their oil operations in the country. They came to dominate the oil sector in Sudan, with the Sudanese government owning only 5 percent of the oil consortium, the Greater Nile Petroleum Company (Helly 2009, 44). Beijing at that time derived 5 percent of its oil from Sudan, and Chinese officials countered accusations that their policies toward Sudan had undermined security and fueled civil conflict in Darfur by arguing that those were concerns internal to Sudanese affairs and that Beijing was "not in a position to impose upon them."[3]

The Role of External Actors in Sudan's Partition

By the late 1990s, the two warring sides were at a military stalemate, both believing victory was at hand and neither willing to concede to the other's demands. Talks led by the East African initiative the Intergovernmental Authority for Drought and Development achieved agreements in principle that collapsed as the prospect of implementation loomed. The Beshir regime, by this point, had distanced itself from the National Islamic Front's radical ideologues because of increasing infighting between Islamist leader Hassan Turabi and the more politically pragmatic-minded Beshir. At this juncture, external actors played an important role in brokering the Comprehensive Peace Agreement (CPA) and ending the civil war. The Bush administration's Sudan envoy, former senator John Danforth, in particular played an influential role. One of the reasons for the success of the peace talks was that the United States did not immediately insist that hostilities cease before it would begin to mediate talks between the two combatants. Danforth accomplished a key confidence-building step by brokering an agreement on the protection of civilians that did not explicitly require Khartoum to cease its military campaign in the South. After the extended mutually destructive stalemate, external actors—representatives of the United States, Britain, and Norway—were thus able to broker a peace agreement focused on resolving the issues of the separation of state and religion, and self-determination for the South. The door was now open for the signing of the CPA.

Like other postconflict peace accords in Africa, the Sudanese Comprehensive Peace Agreement represented what Donald Rothchild (1999, 328) has termed a "minimalist route to implementation" between two formerly warring parties, neither of which had been able to achieve a military victory against its rival. It was, in other words, a negotiated agreement among ethnic and military elites who accepted a minimal form of elite participation designed to achieve political stability while avoiding opposition from other forces in society. While these elite power-sharing systems are not as participatory as democratic regimes, they do resemble democracies in that they are characterized by an ongoing process of bargaining among elites with the objective of achieving a transition to stable social relations (ibid.). This is what the CPA was designed to accomplish. It consisted of a series of protocols on power sharing, wealth sharing, border territories, the status of Khartoum, self-determination, state and religion, and security arrangements. Notably, in addition to re-creating an autonomous region of South Sudan, the CPA brought southerners into the central government in coalition with the Beshir regime. John Garang was made president of South Sudan and first vice president of Sudan, and, perhaps more important, oil revenues were to be divided evenly between the central and southern governments. There was, among many, an atmosphere of hope that the CPA could usher in a new era for a united Sudan, whose political factions would no longer exploit ethnic and religious differences in accordance with zero-sum power calculations. This optimism, however, was dependent on two aspirations that would not be realized. The first was that the CPA would eventually extend to incorporate the legitimate grievances of other outlying regions, including Darfur and the East, and the second was that the central government would implement one of the CPA's most important stipulations: the convening of free and fair elections prior to holding the referendum.

The first harbinger of pessimism with regard to the unity option was, of course, the Darfur conflict that erupted in 2003. The conflict itself was sparked by the ongoing peace talks between the North and the South. When the forces of Darfur's Sudan Liberation Army (SLA) took up arms against Khartoum, it was in the hope of acquiring similar concessions along the lines of the resource- and power-sharing formula granted to the South. Instead, Khartoum ordered the brutal bombing of Darfur and utilized the now notorious paramilitary forces of the *janjaweed* against the rebels. Five years later, the International Criminal

Court in The Hague indicted Beshir for "crimes against humanity and war crimes" in Darfur, the first time in history that a sitting president had been so charged.

The conflict in Darfur highlighted some key shortcomings of the CPA and its implementation in a number of respects. First, it signaled the problem associated with viewing the crisis in Sudan as one between the North and the South, irrespective of the fact that long-term peace in the country would require a more comprehensive solution to the problem of an authoritarian regime at the center and disaffected populations in other outlying regions beyond the South. Second, by assuming that a North–South peace was the primary component of a resolution to the civil conflict, the CPA underestimated the fact that neither northern nor southern Sudan was homogeneous in population. There were millions of African southerners residing in the North and scores of Arabs in the South. This was made apparent by the riots that broke out in the Sudanese capital and in the southern capital of Juba in 2005, when the SPLA's leader, Garang, was killed in a helicopter crash. Millions of southerners were angered by the "lack of respect" the state accorded to their leader upon his death. The ensuing riots took on an ethnic dimension, as the shops of Arabs were attacked while those of "Africans" were spared. On October 10, 2010, less than three months prior to the scheduled referendum vote of January 9, 2011, supporters of the two sides clashed violently again in the capital of Khartoum. Several thousand demonstrating in favor of unity turned on about forty southern Sudanese who arrived at the rally calling for southern secession (BBC News 2010).

In September 2010, Beshir's minister of information, Kamal Obeid, announced that southern Sudanese would not be granted rights of citizenship in the North "if they vote to secede." Moreover, he threatened to expel southern residents, stating that they would not enjoy the right to employment or to being treated in hospitals in the North. On October 3, 2010, presidential adviser Mustafa Osman Ismail went further, calling on the country's youth and students to prepare for war to defend the country against the challenges it would face in the event of South Sudan's secession (*Al-Tayaar* 2010). While Beshir later criticized these statements, claiming that they did not reflect official government policy, it was clear that influential members of the NCP supported the expulsion of southerners in the North and even war if the South voted to become an independent country (*Sudan Tribune* 2010). The fact that there was no indication that southern secession would produce two ethnically homogeneous states (of the type that could engender a sustainable peace following the referendum) suggests that there was a high possibility of ethnic conflict in both the South and the North. There were estimated to be more than 1.5 million southerners settled in the North, and it was unclear whether they would be afforded the rights to work, reside, and move freely between the two countries after separation. Moreover, while the SPLA at that time held the greatest political influence in the South, the organization continued to be dominated by the Dinka tribe. Less known was the fact that the Equatorian ethnic groups of the far south had long experienced economic and political marginalization and land dispossession at the hands of the SPLA (personal interview 2010a).

Given the fact that Sudan's last experiment with electoral democracy (1986–89) put pressure on the country's political parties to bridge the divide between North and South within the framework of unity, many supporters of a united Sudan placed their hopes on the CPA's stipulation that elections be held prior to the southern plebiscite for independence in early 2011. Ultimately, however, the lack of credibility associated with the elections of April 20 undermined any hopes for a peaceful, democratic transition that would usher in the possibility of greater political participation in the North and help to make, in the words of the CPA, "unity more attractive" to southern Sudanese prior to the plebiscite for self-determination.

The NCP's manipulation of the elections and vote rigging were clear from the start. In 2008, the SPLM leadership rejected the census figures reported by the central government; the purpose of the census had been to determine the number of eligible registered voters in the run-up to the elections of April 2010. The Beshir regime announced that the census had determined that 8.26 million people resided in the southern provinces, or 22 percent of the total population. SPLM leaders claimed that the South held a third of Sudan's population, and they viewed the census figures as the regime's attempt to backtrack on the fifty-fifty oil revenue–sharing agreement brokered by the CPA. Ultimately, the NCP and SPLM forged a strategic alliance to ensure that both parties remained in power, albeit for different objectives. The NCP wanted to preserve the status quo in the North and ensure that other political parties remain excluded from decision making at the center. For its part, the SPLM's primary objective was to preside over a successful referendum that culminated in independence for the South (personal interview 2010b).

Consequently, the elections of April 2010 were not only unrepresentative of Sudanese civil society; their ultimate purpose was to pave the way for the referendum the following year. This is not to say that dissent from the regime did not remain endemic. This was clearly in evidence in the April 2010 elections, when all the major opposition parties (including SPLM candidates running in the North) boycotted the national elections amid widespread allegations of fraud. Nevertheless, both parties achieved their primary political objectives: the SPLM won reelection to office in the autonomous South with 93 percent of the vote, while the NCP, running in a largely uncontested field in northern Sudan, held on to power by "winning" 68 percent of the vote.

In retrospect, the flaws associated with the implementation of the compromise agreement between essentially two elite factions in northern and southern Sudan played an important role in preventing the reorganization of a unified Sudanese state. These shortcomings also set the stage for the obstacles to a peaceful secessionist process. The "brittleness" of the elite pact was thus primarily a result of the motivation on the part of two nonrepresentative factions that benefited from the promotion of a minimal form of elite participation.

The record of peace agreements in Africa has shown that externally induced pacts have proven far less durable and effective in forging sustainable peace than internally negotiated power-sharing agreements. In this regard, the CPA suffered from three important weaknesses: the reluctance of the government of Sudan and the SPLM to incorporate new political parties and regional opposition movements into negotiations, the concentration of power in the hands of two belligerents to the exclusion of the political aspirations and human rights concerns of other groups, and the prioritization of narrowly defined security concerns rather than a commitment to national reconciliation and democratic transformation. Taken together, these factors not only led to the CPA's failure to alleviate the dilemma of ethnic security in the disputed North–South border regions but also stood in the way of the resolution of the biggest threat to peace and stability in Sudan: the conflict in Darfur. It has since been widely acknowledged that the Sudan Liberation Army, which initiated the insurgency in Darfur, timed its insurrection in response to its exclusion from the power- and resource-sharing agreements brokered at the Naivasha peace talks. In other words, the potential to resolve the conflict in Darfur, as well as conflicts in other marginalized regions in the East and far North, continued to be dependent on the SLA's inclusion in the peace process. The absence of wider participation of other forces in negotiations of power and wealth sharing in particular had undermined democratization and the resolution of the Darfur conflict. Doubtless, it would also prove to be the biggest challenge to a sustained peace between Khartoum and the South over an extended period following the southern vote for self-determination and the secession of the South.

Political Exclusion, Civil Conflict, and Struggle over Oil Wealth

While it was difficult to ascertain with certainty whether Sudan would experience widespread recurrence of civil war or low-level violence, there was little question that the tensions between North and South Sudan would continue unabated. Moreover, given the history and nature of Sudan's civil war and the failure of genuine democratic reform, there was a strong likelihood of more violence, especially in the disputed border regions. The question that remained had to do with the probability of a widespread recurrence of conflict—that is, whether southern secession would generate war or peace. These two scenarios were in turn dependent on whether negotiations involving disputes over water, debt, wealth sharing, citizenship, and, most important, the North–South border, including the oil-rich region of Abyei, would be concluded peacefully prior to the southern plebiscite. At that time of regional conflict, however, the likelihood of a credible popular consultation process in

South Kordofan and Blue Nile was remote. Failure to generate popular legitimacy among the Arab and African ethnic groups in these disputed territories would most likely result in a cycle of border clashes between the government of Sudan and the SPLM/A-supporting local militias. This would serve as a tinderbox capable of sparking a new round of civil war. Consequently, the probability of a peaceful secession process in the short term hinged on whether or not an agreement could be reached regarding who was eligible to vote in the referendum and on the crucial issue of the demarcation of boundaries.

However, in the longer term, the state of governance in the North beyond 2011 was the single most important criterion that would determine whether Sudan moved toward long-term peace and stability or increased conflict. A grievance shared by Sudanese in the South, in the East, and in Darfur was that political and economic power was concentrated in Khartoum and its immediate environs. This was the root cause of Sudan's multiple regional conflicts. Consequently, while the South might well vote for independence at that time, the state of Sudan's governance would be a crucial issue in any future attempts to resolve the Darfur crisis and maintain peace and stability in the border regions of South Kordofan and Blue Nile. How these issues would be resolved, and whether resolution would be pursued within a national or narrowly focused reform agenda, would determine whether Sudan moved toward a sustainable peace or plunged further into conflict.

The main problem had to do with the fact that the implementation, albeit not the spirit, of the CPA had been flawed. Under U.S. auspices, the CPA was intended to facilitate a national reform agenda that included decentralization of power and resources, a more inclusive and representative national civil service, and the reform of national laws culminating in free and fair national elections. Little of this agenda had been implemented. The Beshir regime had resisted, perceiving it as a threat to its survival, and the SPLM was focused exclusively on holding a referendum vote for self-determination and gaining international recognition for a new South Sudan. Moreover, even if the impending secession of the South proceeded peacefully, this would not necessarily engender a sustainable peace in the country. The failure to make progress on the question of national reform would mean that insurgents in

Darfur and the East would continue to resort to violence in order to gain rights from the center similar to those granted to southern Sudanese (personal interview 2010c). As other cases of secession have demonstrated, under a more open, democratic, and transparent government at the center, there is a greater likelihood of a sustainable and durable peace. In the case of Sudan, democratization remained the best option for peaceful North–South coexistence and for the resolution of regional conflicts such as the one in Darfur. Moreover, the reform of political institutions in both Khartoum and Juba would help increase the possibility of cross-border links between the two independent states and encourage peaceful coexistence based on a durable commitment over postreferendum arrangements.

Finally, of the many implications of southern secession, oil revenue sharing was the most contentious, with a high risk of a return to war if mutually beneficial arrangements were not brokered peacefully prior to southern independence. The significance of oil production in Sudan began immediately following the signing of the CPA in 2005. Over the subsequent decade Sudan's rapid economic growth, averaging 7 percent annually in aggregate terms, had been the result of the development of the oil industry. As late as 2008, oil revenue accounted for 15 percent of Sudan's GDP ($10 billion in oil exports and $60 billion in GDP) and more than 75 percent of the government budget (International Monetary Fund 2009). But while Sudan was predicted to continue producing increasing levels of oil over the next decade, the oil boom had been concentrated narrowly in the service sector and had not improved the deteriorating livelihoods of the majority of Sudanese. Not surprisingly, the regime in Khartoum had been reluctant to give up oil revenues, and while southern Sudan had received 50 percent of its share from oil revenues at that point, tensions between Khartoum and the SPLM/A had risen sharply over the lack of transparency associated with these transfers. In the run-up to the referendum, there remained an absence of an agreement ensuring transparency in the sharing of oil revenue after 2011. Moreover, with no agreement on border demarcation and the fact that the bulk of Sudan's oil is in the South, although the pipeline runs through the North, the recurrence of armed conflict over this coveted resource remained a grave threat in the aftermath of secession.

The potential for resolving this contentious issue would depend on the involvement of foreign stakeholders in Sudan's oil industry and on the fact that both parties understood that cooperation would be the only way to secure a stable flow of oil revenue to both sides.

Conflict or Democratization in Sudan: What Is at Stake for the Middle East and Africa?

While the fact is rarely emphasized in the scholarly literature, Sudan is very central to the politics of the Arab world. Indeed, as Francis Deng (1995) has noted, Sudan (both North and South) is a microcosm of the people of Africa and a bridge between the Arab world and sub-Saharan Africa. As a consequence, the stability of North and South Sudan has had important consequences for both regions. The spillover effect of renewed large-scale conflict would threaten peace and security for the rest of the Horn of Africa, Kenya, Uganda, and the eastern Democratic Republic of the Congo. These neighboring countries risk being affected by forced migration, displacement, humanitarian crises, and cross-border armed groups and militias (Lewis 2009). In addition, a recurrence of conflict in Sudan would undermine international agreements on the use of the Nile waters (two-thirds of which are within Sudan's borders) and, in so doing, would embroil Egypt and Ethiopia in protracted involvement in any potential conflict between Khartoum and the newly independent South Sudan. Moreover, failure to resolve the conflict in Darfur peacefully would continue to impact the domestic stability of Chad and the Central African Republic.

The emergence of two new nation-states in what is Africa's largest country raised new challenges for the continent and the international community. As part of the Middle East, Sudan was a matter of concern for Arab states that had been undergoing the most significant moments of political transition they had experienced in more than three decades. Sudan was also important to emerging regional powers such as India and China, which have invested substantially in the country's oil sector. Moreover, connections between the Beshir regime and global Islamist movements made the country an important player for the United States and other global powers and, perhaps most significant, for the prospects of Islamist movements in countries such as Tunisia and Egypt, which have had very close connections to the Islamist movement in North Sudan. After four decades of civil war, the probability of southern secession was not surprising. What remained to be examined, and what remained of significance worldwide, was how postsecessionist arrangements would be managed to help promote stability rather than exacerbate the country's multiple conflicts, which had so far resulted in the death and displacement of millions. In Sudan, this would depend on how deals were negotiated on wealth transfers (oil revenues, debts, Nile water management) and on power and sovereignty issues (citizenship, border security, and more inclusive and transparent southern governing institutions). The international and regional implications of secession in Sudan, therefore, were of paramount significance for both Africa and the international community.

In this regard, the political consequences of Sudan's partition and the continued oppositional protests and insurgencies in Khartoum and in Sudan's peripheries held the potential to effect profound political change in Sudan. More specifically, the significant division in the ruling National Congress Party in combination with the country's international isolation, the deep economic crisis following the South's secession along with the loss of oil revenue, and persistent levels of popular discontent and mobilization (even if low) were strong indications that Sudan could find itself drawing important inspiration from its Arab neighbors, even as it continued to follow its own path and distinctive "Sudanese" trajectory.

Notes

1. In November 2012, the Beshir regime imprisoned Salah Gosh, along with Brigadier General Mohamed Ibrahim Abdel-Galil of the Sudanese Armed Forces and thirteen other army officers, on suspicion of plotting a coup d'état.

2. Humphreys (2005) makes this important distinction in his discussion of "permissive" versus "root" causes linking natural resources, civil conflict, and the nature of conflict resolution agreements such as Sudan's Comprehensive Peace Agreement.

3. In 2004, China's deputy foreign minister Zhou Wenzhong explained China's Sudan policy succinctly: "Business is business. We try to separate politics from business" (quoted in Zweg and Bi 2005, 32).

References

Ahmed, Medani M. 2010. *Global Financial Crisis Discussion Series, Paper 19: Sudan Phase 2*. London: Overseas Development Institute. http://www.odi.org.uk (accessed September 27, 2012).

Al-Hayat. 1989. Interview with former Sudanese minister of the interior Mubarak al-Fadl [in Arabic]. September 2–3.

Al-Tayaar. 2010. "The SPLM Warns NCP against Delaying the Referendum" [in Arabic]. October 4, 1.

BBC News. 2010. "South Sudan 'Reneging on Peace Deal'—President Bashir." October 10. http://www.bbc.co.uk (accessed November 8, 2011).

Bechtold, Peter K. 1990. "More Turbulence in Sudan: A New Politics This Time?" *Middle East Journal* 44 (4): 579–95.

Bellin, Eva. 2005. "The Robustness of Authoritarianism in the Middle East: Exceptionalism in Comparative Perspective." *Comparative Politics* 36 (2): 139–57.

Choudhry, Saud, and Syed Basher. 2002. "The Enduring Significance of Bangladesh's War of Independence: An Analysis of Economic Costs and Consequences." *Journal of Developing Areas* 36 (1): 41–55.

Collier, Paul. 2009. *Wars, Guns, and Votes: Democracy in Dangerous Places*. New York: HarperCollins.

Collier, Paul, and Anke Hoeffler. 2004. "Greed and Grievance in Civil Wars." *Oxford Economic Papers* 56 (4): 563–95.

Deng, Francis. 1995. *War of Visions: Conflict of Identities in the Sudan*. Washington, D.C.: Brookings Institution Press.

El-Ghobashy, Mona. 2011. "The Praxis of the Egyptian Revolution." *Middle East Report* 258. http://www.merip.org (accessed November 8, 2011).

El Gizouli, Magdi. 2012. "Khartoum: The Political Economy of Bankruptcy." *SudanTribune*, June 24. http://www.sudantribune.com (accessed September 27, 2012).

Etzioni, Amitai. 1992–93. "The Evils of Self-Determination." *Foreign Policy* 89: 21–35.

Gettleman, Jeffrey. 2011. "Young Sudanese Start Movement." *New York Times*, February 2. http://www.nytimes.com (accessed September 27, 2012).

Helly, Damien, ed. 2009. *Post-2011 Scenarios in Sudan: What Role for the EU?* ISS Report No. 6. Paris: European Union Institute for Security Studies.

Horowitz, Michael C., Alex Weisiger, and Carter Johnson. 2009. "The Limits to Partition." *International Security* 33 (4): 203–10.

Humphreys, Macartan. 2005. "Natural Resources, Conflict, and Conflict Resolution: Uncovering the Mechanisms." *Journal of Conflict Resolution* 49 (4): 508–37.

Idahosa, Pablo. 2002. "Ethics and Development in Conflict (Zones): The Case of Talisman Oil." *Journal of Business Ethics* 39 (3): 227–46.

International Crisis Group. 2011. *Divisions in Sudan's Ruling Party and the Threat to the Country's Future Stability.* Africa Report No. 174, May 4. Brussels: International Crisis Group. http://www.crisisgroup.org/en (accessed September 27, 2012).

International Monetary Fund. 2009. *Sudan: Staff-Monitored Program for 2009–10.* Country Report No. 09/218, July. Washington, D.C.: International Monetary Fund.

Johnson, Carter. 2008. "Partitioning to Peace: Sovereignty, Demography, and Ethnic Civil Wars." *International Security* 32 (4): 140–70.

Kaldor, Mary. 1996. "Balkan Carve-Up." *New Statesman and Society* 9: 24–25.

Kaufmann, Chaim D. 1998. "When All Else Fails: Ethnic Population Transfers and Partitions in the Twentieth Century." *International Security* 23 (2): 120–56.

Lewis, Mike. 2009. *Skirting the Law: Sudan's Post-CPA Flows.* Geneva: Small Arms Survey.

Mearsheimer, John J. 1993. "Shrink Bosnia to Save It." *New York Times,* March 31. http://www.nytimes.com (accessed November 8, 2011).

Medani, Khalid Mustafa. 2012. "Understanding the Challenges and Prospects of Another Intifada in Sudan." Jadaliyya, June 27. http://www.jadaliyya.com (accessed September 27, 2012).

Patey, Luke A. 2007. "State Rules: Oil Companies and Armed Conflict in Sudan." *Third World Quarterly* 28 (5): 997–1016.

Rothchild, Donald. 1999. "Ethnic Insecurity, Peace Agreements, and State Building." In *State, Conflict, and Democracy in Africa,* edited by Richard Joseph. Boulder, Colo.: Lynne Rienner.

Sambanis, Nicholas. 2000. "Partition as a Solution to Ethnic War: An Empirical Critique of the Theoretical Literature." *World Politics* 52: 437–83.

Schlumberger, Oliver, ed. 2007. *Debating Arab Authoritarianism: Dynamics and Durability in Nondemocratic Regimes.* Stanford, Calif.: Stanford University Press.

Sudan Tribune. 2010. "Sudanese President Pledges to Protect Southerners Living in the North." October 3. http://www.sudantribune.com (accessed September 27, 2012).

Thurston, Alex. 2011. "Northern Sudan's Protests Sparked by Egypt and Tunisia, but Will They Have the Same Effect?" *Christian Science Monitor,* January 31. http://www.csmonitor.com (accessed September 27, 2012).

Tir, Jaroslow. 2005. "Keeping the Peace after Secession: Territorial Conflicts between Rump and Secessionist States." *Journal of Conflict Resolution* 49 (5): 713–41.

Weinstein, Jeremy M. 2006. *Inside Rebellion: The Politics of Insurgent Violence.* Cambridge: Cambridge University Press.

Willis, Justin, Atta el-Battahani, and Peter Woodward. 2009. *Elections in Sudan: Learning from Experience.* Report commissioned by the U.K. Department of International Development. London: Rift Valley Institute, 2009.

Zweg, David, and Bi Jianhai. 2005. "China's Global Hunt for Energy." *Foreign Affairs,* September–October, 25–38.

Personal Interviews

Personal interview. 2010a. Members of the Equatoria Defense Force. Khartoum, July 14.

Personal interview. 2010b. Yasser Arman, SPLM deputy secretary for North Sudan. Khartoum, July 14.

Personal interview. 2010c. Amina Hamad, chairwoman of the Eastern Front. Khartoum, July 22.

Acknowledgments

IT HAS BEEN a tremendously exciting and illuminating time, gathering together this superb team of engaged scholars and political analysts and collaborating in the publication of such a comprehensive collection. First, we thank Lisa Duggan at New York University for bringing us, the two editors, together at the 2010 American Studies Association meeting and for suggesting in 2011, when the wave of Arab uprisings began, that we "absolutely must" do a book together. We thank the many readers and reviewers who, anonymously, gave their time to read chapters or the entire manuscript and made crucial suggestions that improved this book significantly. We are indebted to other nonanonymous readers, including Fawwaz Trabulsi, Haider Abdul, Amr Abdelrahman, Mozn Hassan, Ahmed Shukr, Hesham Sallam, Bassam Haddad, Omar Dahi, and Mayssun Sukarieh, who combed through certain chapters in great detail and offered crucial input.

We give special thanks to Tess Popper, who, as she wrote her delightful and insightful dissertation on the social history of music and nationalism in Egypt, served valiantly as copy editor, formatter, and reference fixer and offered expert research assistance. Finally, we acknowledge with profound gratitude the friendliness, brilliance, and efficiency of the work of our publishers, Sudhanva Deshpande at LeftWord Books (Delhi) and Richard Morrison at the University of Minnesota Press (Minneapolis).

Contributors

Paul Amar is associate professor in the Global and International Studies Program at the University of California, Santa Barbara. He specializes in comparative politics, international security studies, American studies, human geography, political sociology, global ethnography, theories of the state, and theories of gender, race, and postcolonial politics. He focuses on democratic transitions in the Middle East and Latin America, and traces the origins and intersections of new patterns of police militarization, security governance, humanitarian intervention, and state restructuring in the megacities of the Global South. He has been interviewed regularly on radio and television and has contributed to Jadaliyya e-zine, Al Jazeera Online, *Courrier International, Cairo Times, Frankfurter Allgemeine Zeitung,* and other international news publications. His books include *The Security Archipelago: Human-Security States, Sexuality Politics, and the End of Neoliberalism*; *Cairo Cosmopolitan: Politics, Culture, and Urban Space in the New Globalized Middle East* (edited with Diane Singerman); *New Racial Missions of Policing: International Perspectives on Evolving Law-Enforcement Politics*; and *Global South to the Rescue: Emerging Humanitarian Superpowers and Globalizing Rescue Industries.*

Sheila Carapico is professor of political science and international studies at the University of Richmond and visiting professor at the American University in Cairo. She is a contributing editor to *Middle East Report* and author of *Political Aid: Paradoxes of Democracy Promotion in the Middle East* and *Civil Society in*

Yemen: The Political Economy of Activism in Modern Arabia. A former Fulbright Scholar in Yemen and president of the American Institute for Yemeni Studies, she has written extensively on Yemeni politics and society, Arab activism, and Middle East politics.

Nouri Gana holds a joint appointment in comparative literature and Near Eastern languages and cultures at the University of California, Los Angeles. He has received several awards, including a Social Sciences Humanities Research Council of Canada Postdoctoral Fellowship and a Rackham Faculty Research Grant from the Rackham Graduate School at the University of Michigan, Ann Arbor. He is writing a book on the affective politics of Arab contemporaneity and editing a collection of essays on the intellectual history and contemporary significance of the Arab novel in English.

Toufic Haddad is coeditor of *Between the Lines: Readings in Israel, the Palestinians, and the U.S. "War on Terror"* and *Towards a New Internationalism: Readings in Globalization, the Global Justice Movement, and Palestinian Liberation.* His writings on the Israeli–Palestinian conflict have been featured in print publications and online news sites, including *The National,* Al Jazeera English, *Journal of Palestine Studies,* Monthly Review Zine, Znet, *CounterPunch,* Jadaliyya, *Al Akhbar, International Socialist Review,* and *Socialist Worker.* He is a PhD candidate in development studies at the School for Oriental and African Studies, University of London.

Adam Hanieh is a lecturer in development studies, School of Oriental and African Studies, University of London. His research focuses on the political economy of the Middle East and processes of state and class formation in the region. He is author of *Capitalism and Class in the Gulf Arab States* and *Lineages of Revolt: Issues of Contemporary Capitalism in the Middle East.* His research and commentary on the Middle East have been published in *Journal of Palestine Studies, Capital & Class, Studies in Political Economy, Monthly Review, Middle East Report,* Jadaliyya, and Znet. He is an editorial board member of the journal *Historical Materialism.*

Toby C. Jones is associate professor of history at Rutgers University. He has lived and worked extensively in the Middle East, including several years in Saudi Arabia and Bahrain. During 2008–9 he was a fellow at Princeton University's Oil, Energy, and the Middle East project. From 2004 to early 2006 he worked as the Persian Gulf political analyst for the International Crisis Group. His research interests focus on the environment, energy, and the history of science and technology. He is author of *Desert Kingdom: How Oil and Water Forged*

Modern Saudi Arabia and is currently working on a book, *America's Oil Wars.* He has written for *International Journal of Middle East Studies, Journal of American History, Middle East Report, Raritan Quarterly Review, The Nation, The Atlantic, Arab Reform Bulletin,* and the *New York Times.* He is a member of the editorial committee for *Middle East Report.*

Anjali Kamat is a producer/correspondent with *Fault Lines,* a current-affairs documentary show that airs on Al Jazeera English. Her films include *Punishment and Profits: Immigration Detention* and *Battle for the Sinai.* From 2007 to 2011, she was a producer/correspondent for the independent television and radio show *Democracy Now!* and traveled to Libya several times during the uprising. Her writings have appeared in the Huffington Post, Jadaliyya, *The Progressive, OPEN Magazine, The Hindu,* and *Economic and Political Weekly.*

Khalid Mustafa Medani is associate professor of political science and Islamic studies at McGill University. He has recently published in *Journal of North African Studies, Journal of Democracy,* and *UCLA Journal of Islamic and Near Eastern Law.* He serves on the editorial committee of *Middle East Report,* and in 2007 he was named a Carnegie Scholar on Islam. He is author of the forthcoming book *Joining Jihad: Black Markets, Militants, and Clans.*

Merouan Mekouar is assistant professor in the department of social sciences at York University. He has written for *Foreign Policy, Open Democracy,* and *Les Cahiers du Cérium* (Université de Montréal) and is coauthor of a chapter, with Pr. Rex Brynen, in *Beyond the Arab Spring: Authoritarianism and Democratization in the Arab World.*

Maya Mikdashi is a faculty fellow and director of graduate studies at New York University's Hagop Kevorkian Center for Near Eastern Studies. She is codirector of the documentary film *About Baghdad* and a coeditor of Jadaliyya e-zine. Her forthcoming publications include essays in *International Journal of Middle East Studies* and *American Indian Culture and Research Journal,* as well as a book, *Da'wa Secularism and Religious Conversion: Practicing Citizenship in Contemporary Lebanon.*

Paulo Gabriel Hilu Pinto is professor of anthropology at the Universidade Federal Fluminense, Brazil, where he is also director of the Center for Middle East Studies. He has conducted fieldwork in Syria since 1999 and with the Muslim communities in Brazil since 2003. He is author of articles and books on Sufism and other forms of Islam in contemporary Syria, as well as on Arab ethnicity and Muslim communities in Brazil. His recent publications include *Árabes no Rio de Janeiro: Uma identidade plural* and *Islã: Religião e civilização, uma abordagem antropológica.* He coedited, with Baudoin Dupret, Thomas Pierret, and Kathryn Spelman-Poots, *Ethnographies of Islam: Ritual Performances and Everyday Practices,* and, with John Karam and Maria del-Mar Logroño-Narbona, *Crescent of Another Horizon: Islam in Latin America, the Caribbean, and Latino USA.*

Vijay Prashad is professor of international studies and George and Martha Kellner Chair in South Asian History at Trinity College. He is the author of eleven books, most recently *The Darker Nations: A People's History of the Third World,* which received the 2009 Muzaffar Ahmad Book Prize and was chosen as best nonfiction book of 2008 by the Asian American Writers' Workshop. He is a columnist for *Frontline* magazine (Chennai, India), a contributing editor for *Himal South Asia* (Kathmandu, Nepal), a contributing editor for *Bol* (Lahore, Pakistan), a contributor to *Asia Times,* and a contributor to *CounterPunch.*

Jillian Schwedler is professor of political science at Hunter College at the City University of New York. She is author of *Faith in Moderation: Islamist Parties in Jordan and Yemen* and the forthcoming book *Protesting Jordan: Space, Law, Dissent,* and editor (with Laleh Khalili) of *Policing and Prisons in the Middle East.* Her writing has been published in *World Politics, Comparative Politics, Middle East Policy, Middle East Report, Journal of Democracy,* and *Social Movement Studies,* and she is a regular contributor online to *Middle East Report,* Jadaliyya, Al Jazeera English, and Middle East Channel. She was formerly a member of the editorial committee and chair of the board of directors of the Middle East Research and Information Project (MERIP), publishers of *Middle East Report*; she has conducted research in Jordan, Yemen, and Egypt.

Ahmad Shokr is a doctoral candidate in Middle Eastern history at New York University. He is a book review editor for *Arab Studies Journal* and a former senior editor at *Egypt Independent.* His writings have appeared in *Middle East Report,* Jadaliyya, and *Economic and Political Weekly.* He traveled to Libya several times during the 2011 uprising.

Susan Slyomovics is professor of anthropology and Near Eastern languages and cultures at the University of California, Los Angeles. Among her books are *The Object of Memory: Arab and Jew Narrate the Palestinian Village*; *The Performance of Human Rights in Morocco*; *Waging War and Making Peace: The Anthropology of "Reparations"*; and *Clifford Geertz in Morocco.*

Haifa Zangana is an Iraqi author and activist. She is a founding member of International Association of Contemporary Iraqi Studies (IACIS) and cofounder of Iraqi Women Solidarity. She is a consultant at the U.N. Economic and Social Commission for Western Asia on gender and social affairs. She writes a weekly column for the newspaper *Al-Quds al-Arabi* and lectures on Iraqi literature and women's issues. She has published three novels and four collections of short stories and is the author of essays, articles, and book reviews on subjects ranging from Iraqi studies to Arab literature, cinema, and art. Her publications include *Torturer in the Mirror*; *Women on a Journey: Between Baghdad and London*; *City of Widows: An Iraqi Woman's Account of War and Resistance*; and *Dreaming of Baghdad*. For information on Women Solidarity for Independent and Unified Iraq, visit http://solidarityiraq.blogspot.com.

Index

215; Umayyad mosques in, as sites of antigovernment protests, 219
Alexandria, Egypt: presidential elections of 2012 in, 47
Algeria, 3, 122–34; "Berber Spring" movement (1980s), 123; economy of, 125–26; as French colony, 122, 128, 129; internal wars of 1990s, 123; Libyan uprising and, 131; military's hidden power in, 127–33; network of oppositional movements, 123–27, 133; participants in unrest, 125; "state of emergency" laws in, 132; war of independence (1954–62), 122, 129
Algérie Telecom, 124
Algiers: protests in, 124, 125
Al-Hayat, 340
Al Jazeera coverage: of Algeria, 124, 133n1; in Bahrain, 79; of Iraq, 316; role in run-up to Arab Spring and, 294–95; in Syria, 208, 219, 221, 229, 230, 231; in Tunisia, 6, 7, 8, 10, 22n2; in Yemen, 103, 120
All4Syria, 205, 217
Alloush, Ibrahim, 255
Al-Marjiaya, 316
Al-Masry Al-Youm (newspaper), 49–50
Al Menbar National Islamic Society, 73
Al Mustaqbal, 300
Al-Nahda (Tunisian political party), 19, 20
al-Qaeda: in Islamic Maghreb, 130–31; Libyan uprising and, 176–78, 194n30–31; in Yemen, 115–16, 119
Al-Tawati, Ghaidaa, 185, 189
Al-Wasat (newspaper), 64, 82
Al Wefaq National Islamic Society (Bahrain), 73, 77, 79, 80, 83

Amazigh community in Libya, 174, 182, 194n24
Amin, Hassan al-, 165, 183
Amman, Jordan: Abdali Boulevard, 256, 257; business district, 257–58; changing geography of, 255–58; changing geography of, protest visibility and, 257–58; divided between East and West Amman, 255–58; protests in 2002 in, 251, 252–53, 254–55; protests in 2011 in, 243; Shmeisani neighborhood, 257; Zahran Street, 256
Amnesty International, 70, 180, 181, 318, 319; fact-finding visit to Libya (2011), 193n19
Amnesty USA, 80
Andrews, Julian, 312
antifundamentalist religious movements in Egypt during 2011 uprisings, 29–30
Antiterrorist Act (Iraq), 315
apartheid, Israeli, 285, 291, 301, 303
Arab collective consciousness: Palestine at heart of, 288–89, 295
Arab exceptionalism, viii
Arab–Israeli conflict: June 1967 war, 290; Lebanon in, 271, 277; Oslo "peace process," 285, 290–91, 292
Arab League, 233, 235n5
Arab Resurgence, xi–xii
Arab Revolt (al-Thawra al-Arabiyya), new, viii–ix
Arab Spring: context of changing global landscape, 190; counterrevolution, reassertion of, ix–x; demonstrations in Kurdistan region and extension of definition of, 308; Egypt as fulcrum of, 24; fundamental demand for redefinition of Arab national citizenship

at heart of, 303–4; Islamist social movements as driving forces of democratization in, 338; moments in larger arc of, x–xii; Morocco and, 143–49; naming of, viii–ix; Palestine and, 288, 293–95; regional actors, insertion of, x; revolutionizing the Middle East, vii–xiii; revolutions referenced by, ix; spread of revolt, viii; as stage in long-term struggle, xiii; Sudan in context of, 327–30. *See also specific countries*
Arab unity issue, 304
Arab Winter, xi
Arafat, Suha, 7
Arafat, Yasser, 263
artists: in Morocco, defense of "king's constitution" in 2011, 148–49; revolutionary graffiti and public murals in Egypt, 53; tradition of cultural critique in Tunisia, 11–16, 18. *See also* intellectuals
'Ar'ur, Adnan al-, 223–24, 234
Asharq al-Awsat, 178
Assad, Bashar al-, 89, 99, 119; as Alawi, 238n26; attempt to identify protesters with September 11, 2001, 219–20; concessions and repression in response to uprising, 208–9; non-Sunnis supporting, 224, 225, 238n26; political and economic reforms under, 212–13, 215; popularity in Damascus and Aleppo, 206–7; protests against, 204, 205–6; reconfiguration of Baathist authoritarianism under, 209–15; rhetoric of confident calm, 204–5; rise to Syrian presidency, 211, 212; symbolic destruction of statues/posters/murals of, 218
Assad, Basil al-, 218

Assad, Hafiz al-, 210, 211, 212, 218
Assad, Maher al-, 208, 225
Assad, Rifa'at al-, 211–12
Assange, Julian, 7
Associated Press, 79
Atlantic world, imperial power bloc from: counterrevolution and reassertion of, ix–x, xi; retreat of, ix. *See also* Britain; International Monetary Fund; United States
ATTAC in Germany, 28
authoritarianism: durable, 325; dynastic model of, 211, 235n8; in Sudan, durability of, 330–34
authoritarianism studies, vii
Awlaqi, Anwar al-, 116, 119
Aziz, Naif bin Abd al- (Prince Naif), 91, 95, 97–98

Baathist regime in Syria: history of resistance and opposition to, 209–10; international allies, 233; loss of political capital, 232–33; performative destruction or subversion of symbols of, 218; reconfiguration of Baathist authoritarianism under Assad, 209–15; religious nationalism promoted by, 219, 222; uprising against, 204–6, 207–8. *See also* Syria
Baath regime in Iraq, 309–10
Bab al-Aziziya: assault on Qaddafi's compound, 178
Baccar, Jalila, 14
Baghdad, Iraq: demonstrations in Tahrir Square, 308, 309–10, 313–19; Green Zone, 310, 314; Liberty Monument in, 309, 310; al-Mansour's original building of, 322n1; U.S. invasion and, 310
Bahrain, 63–88; colonial imprint on, 65–67; constitution (1973), 68, 72;

Blair, Tony, 54
blogs, role of: in Algeria, 124, 133n1; in
    Bahrain, 77, 78, 85n7; in Iraq, 318,
    322; in Jordan, 260; in Libya, 185,
    189, 193n15, 194n26; in Morocco,
    135, 147, 148; in Syria, 233n7n24; in
    Tunisia, 9; in Yemen uprising, 102,
    103
blue bra scandal (Egypt), 32, 53
Blue Nile (Sudan), 326, 332, 347
Bouazizi, Mohamed: self-immolation
    of, viii, 2, 8, 9–10, 13–14, 143, 235n1,
    293–94
Boughedir, Férid, 13
Boumediene, Houari, 129
bourgeoisie: in Morocco, 144–45, 148,
    150; in Syria, 206–7, 213–14, 224,
    230. See also middle class
Bourguiba, Habib, 2–4, 5, 12, 13, 16, 17.
    See also Tunisia
Bouteflika, President Abdelaziz,
    124, 126, 132, 133; as American ally
    against al-Qaeda, 130–31. See also
    Algeria
Bouzayen, Chadli, 14
Bouzid, Nouri, 12–13, 14
Boycott, Divestment and Sanctions
    Movement, 300–301
bread riots, 17, 47, 125
Britain: Bahrain and, 83; colonialism,
    and control over Gulf, 66–68;
    colonialism, in Iraq, 309; Jordan
    and, 247
Bulleid, Al-Hadi, 20
Buqnah, Firas, 90
Burhani, Hisham al-, 223
Bush, George H. W., 71
Bush, George W., 162, 177, 311, 314
Bustani, Hisham, 251
Buti, Sa'id Ramadan al-, 228

Cairo, Egypt: Obama's speech in
    (2009), xiii; sacking of Israeli
    embassy in (September 10, 2011),
    296; Tahrir Square (Liberation
    Square, or Midan al-Tahrir), 25–26,
    28, 28–29, 41, 41–44, 51–52, 103. See
    also Egypt
Camp David Accords (1979), 293;
    revolutionary goal of annulling,
    296
capitalism: the Gulf's impact on
    overall development of contempo-
    rary, 74; neoliberalism in Bahrain
    and uneven development of, 75–76;
    Palestinian, 292, 303; social market
    economy in Syria and, 213. See also
    International Monetary Fund;
    neoliberalism; oil and gas; United
    States
cartels, religionized commercial, 39,
    55, 56
Carter, Jimmy, 161
Carthage International School, 16
census: sectarian demography of
    Lebanon produced through 1932,
    269; Sudanese (2008), elections of
    2010 and, 344–45
CENTCOM (U.S. Central Com-
    mand), 74
Central Informatics Organisation, 74
Central Intelligence Agency, U.S., 131,
    306n5; evacuation from Benghazi
    after armed attack on U.S. diplo-
    matic mission, 183; extraordinary
    rendition program, 162, 177
Central Security Forces (Egypt), 25, 31
Chadirchi, Rifa'at al-, 309
Chamber of Deputies (Bahrain), 72
"Change Square" (Midan Al-Taghayr
    in Sanaa, Yemen), 103, 112–13, 115

Charter for Peace and National Reconciliation (Algeria), 127
Chevron Corporation, 340
China: oil operations in Sudan, 340–41, 351n3
Christians: in Egypt, Maspero Massacre (2011) of, 32; in Lebanon, 268–70; Syrian 2011 uprising and, 221, 224, 225, 226
Christian Science Monitor, 314
CIA. *See* Central Intelligence Agency, U.S.
cinema: critique in Tunisia disseminated through, 12–14
citizenship: Arab revolutions and fundamental demand for redefinition of Arab national, 303–4; Jordanian, given to Palestinian refugees, 246; Lebanese, 268, 270, 278; Palestine and issue of, 290, 302; in Sudan, partition and, 343, 346, 350; Syrian, conceded to Kurds in Jazira, 208
civic revolution: defined, 38; in Egypt, 40–54
civil disobedience in Yemen, 114
civil society(ies), 105–6; civic activism in Yemen and, 106, 107; confronting power of international capital, domestic commercial interests, and security apparatus of state, 325; in Libya, building, 189; Qaddafi on, 164; Saudi manipulation of clergy and, 94–97; in Sudan, 333, 338; weakness of Arab, 331
Civil Society Movement (Harakat al-Mujtama' al-Madani [Syria]), 212–13, 235n9
civil state: in Egypt, goal of, 30, 32; in Lebanon, 2011 protest movement for, 266–67, 270, 271–72, 279
civil war: Lebanese (1958), 271, 272;

Lebanese (1975–90), 269, 271, 272, 275; Libyan uprising as, 174–75; in Sudan, 335–38, 339–40; in Sudan, Comprehensive Peace Agreement and, 341–46; in Syria, prospect of, 232–33, 234; in Syria, uprising portrayed as prelude to, 207
class: expansion of protests in Sudan and, 327–28; gender and class mergings in Egypt, 51–54; Moroccan middle, state mobilization of, 148; in Syria, Islamic struggle against Baathist regime and, 209–10; in Syria, state bourgeoisie and, 213–14; in Syria, uprising and, 229–34. *See also* bourgeoisie; middle class; working class
clientelism in Morocco, 140, 153n6
Clinton, Bill, 54, 71
Clinton, Hillary, 233
Coalition of the Republic (Bahrain), 80, 81
Coalition to Support the Iraqi Revolution, 314
coercion: state capacity for, 332, 333. *See also* police; violence
Cold War: Algeria's alignments with Soviet bloc countries during, 130
collective consciousness: of Iraqi people, 313; Palestine at heart of Arab, 288–89, 295
colonialism: in Bahrain, 65–67; British, control over Gulf and, 66–68; British, in Iraq, 309; French, in Algeria, 122, 128, 129; French, in Lebanon, 268–69, 270; French, in Morocco, 137; Palestine as cause in Arab struggle for freedom from Western, 288
Combating Terrorism Center at West Point, 194n29

Communist Party in Iraq, 315
Comprehensive Peace Agreement
(CPA), Sudanese, 341–46; flawed
implementation of, 347–48;
national reform agenda of, 347;
shortcomings of, 342–43, 345–46
Congress for Republic (CPR) party
(Tunisia), 19
Congressional Research Service, 182
consciousness, revolution in: defined,
38–39; in Egypt, 40–54
Constitutional Court (Egypt), 36
constitutional maneuvering strategy for power consolidation in
Morocco, 136, 139–40, 145–46,
153n10
Constitutional Movement (CM), or
al-Haraka al-Disturiyya (Bahrain),
70
cooperative movement in North
Yemen, 107–8
coordination committees in Syrian
uprising, 215
Coptic Christians, 27, 29–30
corruption: in Iraq, 320; in Lebanon,
273; of PLO, 291; in Sudan, 329, 339;
in Syria, 206, 207, 213–14; in Tunisia,
7, 8, 17, 21; in Yemen, 104
counterrevolution, ix–x, xi; in
Morocco, 147; Saudi, 90–99; in
Tunisia, 21; in Yemen, 115–18, 119.
See also police; violence
Cretz, Gene A., 186
cronyism, structures of, 39, 55. See also
corruption
cultural idioms of protest: saturation
of, 221–22, 225, 229, 237n23

Dabbas, Aida, 252
Daily Mirror, 312
Dalila, Aref, 216–17

Damascus, Syria: communiqué about
2011 uprising issued by ʿulama
of, 222–23; relative calm during
anti-Baathist protests, 206–7, 215;
Umayyad mosques in, as sites of
antigovernment protests, 219
Damascus Spring, 212–13, 216
Danforth, John, 341
Danish cartoon scandal, 252
Darak riot police (Jordan), 244, 245,
257, 259, 260–61
Darfur (Sudan), 326, 329, 332, 335, 337,
341; conflict in, 342–43, 346, 347,
349
Daʿwa Party (Iraq): attacks on
protesters by, 317
Day of Rage: in Bahrain, 78; in Egypt,
41; in Iraq, 311, 313–14, 315, 317, 318;
in Libya, 166–67; in Saudi Arabia,
92; in Yemen, 113
"Days of Rage: Protests and Repression in Iraq" (Amnesty International), 318
Defense Brigades, 235n4
democracy: in Algeria, demands for,
124; in Bahrain, calls for, 79–81, 83;
civic associational network and
lively public intellectual sphere of
civility and development of, 105;
in Egypt, alternative movements
for local self-rule and, 40, 41–44; in
Egypt, innovative electoral mobilizations and, 41, 44–49; Egypt as
fulcrum of future transitions to,
24; Islamist social movements as
driving forces of democratization
across "Arab Spring" countries, 338;
in Lebanon, 268, 270, 274; in Libya,
challenge of building, 188–90; in
Morocco, demands for, 143–45; in
Morocco, international pressure

infrastructure and organization of protest in, 296; political economic history of development, 26–28; population in 2010, 27; repressors and reactionaries, 31–37, 41; revolution as "third way," metaphor of, 54–55; revolution in question, 37–41; revolution of consciousness in, 40–54; Tahrir and emancipation, 1, 25–30, 41, 51–52, 103

Egyptian Democratic Labor Congress, 50

Egyptian Federation of Independent Trade Unions (EFITU), 56n2

Egyptian Initiative for Personal Rights, 35

Egyptian–Israeli gas pipeline in Sinai Peninsula: targeting of, 296

El-Banna, Hassan, 57n3

ElBaradei, Mohamed, 48

elections: in Algeria, 123, 130, 132, 133; in Bahrain, 68–69, 73, 77, 83; in Egypt, 33, 36–37, 41, 44–49; in Iraq, 314, 315; in Jordan, 247, 249–51, 258; in Lebanon, 274, 275; in Libya, 179, 182, 186, 188; in Morocco, 140, 150–52; Palestinian, 306n5; in Saudi Arabia, 91–92; in Sudan, 338–39, 344–45; in Tunisia, 5, 18–20; in Yemen, 107, 108, 109

electoral mobilizations in Egypt, innovative, 41, 44–49

El-Gallal, Hana, 189

El Général (rapper), 15–16

el-Haked (rapper), 148

El Himma, Fouad Ali, 144–45, 150

elite power-sharing system, Sudanese Comprehensive Peace Agreement as, 342, 345

El Naja, Mohammad Abu, 189

emigration from Morocco: revenues from, 152–53

entrepreneurial class: in Morocco, 140; in Syria, 213–14; in Tunisia, 16–17

Epic of Gilgamesh, 310, 322n3

Equity and Reconciliation Commission (Morocco), 141

Erdogan, Recep, 233

Essaïda (film), 13–14

Essebsi, Béji Caïd, 4, 5, 19

ethnic civil conflict, secession and, 335–38; factors determining, 336, 348

Ettakatol (Democratic Forum for Labour and Liberties) party (Tunisia), 19

exceptionalism, Arab, viii

exile, opposition in: from Bahrain, 70; Libyan, 160, 165, 187; Syrian, 217, 222, 223–24; from Yemen, 109, 113

export and production sharing agreements (EPSAs), 163

"extraordinary rendition" program, U.S., 162, 177

Facebook, role of: in Algeria, 124; in Egypt, 42, 103; in Lebanon, 266, 280n1; in Libya, 166; for Palestinians, 297; in Saudi Arabia, 92; "Third Intifada" page, 297–98; in Tunisian revolution, 1, 6–7, 9; in Yemen, 103

Fakhrawi, Karim, 64

Fallujah, Iraq: peaceful protests at, 312–13, 316

Farzat, Ali, 228

Fateh (Palestinian National Liberation Movement), 290, 291, 292, 306n5; calls for political unity

Henderson, Ian, 70–71

Heritage Foundation, 76, 196n45

Hezbollah, 267, 274, 276; ability to protect South Lebanon, 275; Al Jazeera coverage of, 295

Hicham, Moulay, 148

Higher Council of Ulama, 95

Higher Executive Committee (Bahrain), 67

Hijazi, Hassan, 284

hip-hop and rap music: critique in Tunisia disseminated through, 14–16

al-Hirak (South Yemeni movement for secession), 104, 110–11, 113

Hizb al-Tahrir, 220, 237n22

Homs, Syria: protests in, 215, 216, 220, 221, 222, 229, 230, 231

housing in Bahrain: problems with inequality, 76–77

Hudayda, Yemen: protest in, 114, 115

Hula, Syria: massacre in (2012), 227, 228

humanitarianism: NATO intervention in Libya and, 172–74

human rights: in Egypt, 35–37; in Iraq, U.S. and U.K. silence on, 321; in Morocco, 141. See also torture; violence

human rights groups: in Iraq, 315

Human Rights Watch: on Bahrain protests, 70, 71, 82; on Iraq uprising, 312, 318, 319; on Libyan uprising and violence, 170, 177, 180, 181, 182, 183, 191n1, 191n4, 193n12–13, 195n38; on Palestinians in Iraq, 299; on Syrian uprising, 227

Hussein (king, Jordan), 245, 247; electoral system, manipulation of, 250; peace treaty with Israel (1994), 250, 254, 258

Hussein, Saddam: fall of, 299

Ibb, Yemen: protest in, 113

Ibrahim, Moussa, 169, 175, 181

identity: forces constructing political, 267; Palestine at heart of Arab collective consciousness, 288–89, 295

identity-based politics of resistance, 335

Idris, King (Libya), 159

IFLB (Islamic Front for Liberation of Bahrain), 70, 73

al-Ikhwan al-Muslimun fi Suriya (Muslim Brothers in Syria), 210, 217, 224

Imam Abdel Rahman Mosque (Omdurman, Sudan): protest outside, 332

Imazighen/Amazigh people, ix, 174, 182, 194n24

IMED, 142

IMF. See International Monetary Fund

immigration control: Qaddafi's cooperation in, 162–63. See also diaspora

imperialism: imperial power bloc from Atlantic world, ix–x, xi; Israel as watchdog for Western imperial interests in region, 287, 289; NATO intervention in Libya and, 172–74. See also Britain; International Monetary Fund; United States

Independent Republic of Greater Mahalla, 50–51, 54

Independent Trade Union Federation (Egypt), 50

Independent Workers' Republic of Mahalla, 41

Index of Economic Freedom (2011), 196n45

Indignados in Spain, 28
infrastructure: Jordanian projects prioritizing foreign investment and free trade, 255–58
intellectuals: in Iraq, protests by, 311; in Morocco, state mobilization of, 147–49; in Syrian uprising, 212, 216–17
Intergovernmental Authority for Drought and Development, 341
internal Palestinian front, 286, 298–302
International Criminal Court (The Hague): indictment of Beshir, 333, 342–43
International Crisis Group, 76, 195n37, 245, 259, 330, 334
International Monetary Fund, ix, x, 138, 348; Morsi's accord with (2012), 34–35; Mubarak's accord with (1991), 34; pressure for neoliberal policies, xi, xiii; structural adjustment programs, 138, 249, 250
international solidarity movement: Al Jazeera coverage of, 295
International Trade Union Confederation, 311
International Viewpoint, 312
Internet, role of: in Algeria, 124; cyberactivism in Sudan, 334; in Iraq, 318, 319; in Libya, 165; in Syrian uprising, 216, 223; "Third Intifada" campaign, 297–98; in Yemen, 103. *See also* social media, role of
"In the Penal Colony" (Kafka), 228
intifada: in Bahrain in 1990s, 69–71; popular, in Sudan, 332; popular, in Yemen, 101–2, 110, 113–14; Second Palestinian Intifada (2000), 56n1, 251, 291, 294, 299, 301; Third Intifada, 297–98

"'Irā'dit al-hayā't" [The Will to Life] (poem, al-Shabbi), 11–12
Iran: aspirations of, x; Bahrain and, 65; March 8 alliance in Lebanon and, 277; Revolutionary Guard, U.S. indictment for al-Jubeir assassination plot, 98; Saudi anti-Shiism and, 98–99
Iraq, 308–24; achievements of protest in, 317–19; Baath regime in, 309–10; Baghdad's Tahrir Square, 308, 309–10, 313–19; calls for full withdrawal of occupation forces, 311, 317, 321, 322; continuation of protest into 2012, 317, 319–21; demonstrations throughout all of, 310–13; economy of, 310; Fallujah's peaceful protest, 312–13, 316; features unique to, during Arab Spring, 308; July 14 Revolution in 1958, 309; prospects for future in, 319–22; sanctions years (1990–2003), 310; suicide bombers in, 194n29; trajectory of goals set up by resistance in, 321; U.S. invasion and occupation of (2003), 56n1, 293, 295, 310, 312–13
Iraq Body Count, 313
IRIN, 214
'Isa, 'Abd al-Qadir, 223
al-Islah (Yemeni political party), 108, 109, 113
Islam. *See* Salafism; Shia Muslims; Sunni Muslims
Islam, Saif al-, 163, 175, 177, 179
Islamic Action Front (Jordan), 245, 250, 252, 258, 261
Islamic Action Society (Bahrain), 73
Islamic Front for Liberation of Bahrain (IFLB), 70, 73
Islamic Resistance Movement. *See* Hamas

Islamic Salvation Front party (Algeria), 123

Islamism (Islamic fundamentalism) and Islamists, 338; in Algeria, 130, 131; in Egypt, 28, 45, 47–48; in Egypt, Morsi's Brotherhood-led presidency, 32–37; Islamist social movements as driving forces of democratization across Arab Spring countries, 338; in Jordan, 245, 247–48, 249, 250, 252–53, 258, 260, 261–62; in Libya, 157, 161, 162, 165, 166, 177–78, 184, 185, 187, 188; in Morocco, 138, 138–39, 139, 142, 151; in Palestine, 294, 300; political, xi–xii, xiii; Saudi manipulation of clergy, 94–97, 99; in Sudan, significance to global Islamist movements of, 349–50; Sudan's antidemocratic, 338–41; Syrian uprising and, 209–10, 218–25; in Tunisia, 5, 20, 22n5; in Yemen, 116. *See also* Muslim Brotherhood

Israel: agenda-setting practices of settler-colonial designs in West Bank, 287, 292; Al Jazeera coverage of, 294–95; apartheid in, 285, 291, 301, 303; bombardment of Gaza, xi; Camp David Accords (1979) between Egypt and, 293, 296; as embodiment of cleavage of Levantine and Arabian Gulf peninsula from Egypt and North Africa, 287; internal Palestinian front and, 298–302; invasion of West Bank (2002), protests against, 254–55; Jewish Israeli struggle for social justice, 302–3; Morsi's presidency in Egypt and, 33–34; Nakba Day demonstrations and, 283–84, 298;

1948 War, 282; occupation of Palestinian territories, 285–86; October 2011 prisoner deal between Hamas and, 304–5; Palestinians living inside, 285, 291, 302–3; peace treaty with Jordan (1994), 250, 254, 258; "separation barrier" constructed by, 291; Syrian uprising and, 238n35; war with Lebanon (2006), 276; as watchdog for Western imperial interests in region, 287, 289

Issawi, Ali, 184, 187

Istiqlal party (Morocco), 137, 138

Itr, Sheikh Nur al-Din, 223

Ittihadiya, Battles of (2012), 35–37, 54

Jadaliyya, 46, 93, 243, 244, 259

Jalil, Abdel, 193n12

Jama'at Zayd movement, 223

Jamadi, Manadel al-, 313

Jamal2ofev, 145

Jamri, Mansour al-, 82

janjaweed (paramilitary forces), 342

Jastaina, Shaima, 92

Jebali, Hamadi, 5

Jewish Israeli struggle for social justice, 302–3

Jibril, Mahmoud, 163, 179, 184, 187, 188, 194n28, 195n41

Joint Meeting Parties (JMP) in Yemen, 109, 116

Jordan, 243–65; annexation of West Bank, 246, 263n6; economy of, 249, 250, 255–56; Hashemite Kingdom of, 246, 247, 263n5; history of protests in, 245, 247–53, 262; independence of, 247, 263n5; new and old alliances in, 262–63; Palestinians in, 246, 248, 250, 262, 263n6; parliamentary elections in, 247, 249, 250;

peace treaty with Israel (1994), 250, 254, 258; political geography of protests in, 253–58; protests framed as "pro-Jordanian" and nationalist in, 244, 263n3; protests of 1989 in, 245, 249; protests of 2011 in, 243–47, 258–62; public gatherings law in, 249–53, 259

Jordan River Foundation, 254

journalists: freedom of the press, 250, 274, 311, 316, 319–20; in Iraq, arrest warrants and abuse of, 316, 319–20. *See also* media coverage

Jubeir, Adel al-, 98

judiciary in Egypt, 34

jumlukiyya, 211, 235n8

Justice and Development Party (PJD, Morocco), 138, 143

Kafka, Franz, 228

Kareem, Oday, 314

Karman, Tawakkol, 101, 112, 113, 117; Nobel Peace Prize (2011), 102, 118–19

KBR, 312

Khaddam, Abd al-Halim, 212

Khalifa, Khalid al-, 79

al-Khalifa rule in Bahrain, 65–67, 68; King Hamad bin Isa al-Khalifa, 71–72; Sheikh Isa bin Salman bin Hamad al-Khalifa, 68, 70

Khalil, Abdul Karim, 313

Khamsoun (aka *Captive Bodies*) (Baccar), 14

Khartoum, Sudan: protests in, 327, 328, 334; secession of South Sudan and, 328; southern Sudanese residing in, 337

Khatib, Hamza al-, 227–28

Khatib, Moaz al-, 223

Khawaja, Abdulhadi al-, 64

Khawaja, Zainab al-, 64

Koussa, Moussa, 177

Kurds: demonstrations in Erbil and Sulaimaniya, 308; in Syria, 208, 235n9

labor: imaginative labor actions in Egypt, 41, 49–51, 56n2; national independent workers' federation in Egypt, 29; protests in Bahrain during oil era, 68, 69; protests in Jordan, 248; strikes in Iraq, 311–12; Tunisian revolution and workers' movements, 17–18. *See also* migrant labor

labor unions: in Egypt, 43, 50; in Iraq, 311–12; labor protest in Bahrain for, 68, 69; in Morocco, 137, 138–39; Qaddafi on, 164; in Tunisia, 18

Lacoste, Robert, 129

Laroui, Fouad, 147

Law of Public Security (1965, Bahrain), 68, 69

Lebanon, 266–81; domestic political environment in, 275–76; economy of, 273; geopolitical position of, 276–77, 279; historical legacies of, 267–71, 278–80; independence of, 270; at micropolitical level, 278–80; nature of state and its institutions, 274–75; Palestinians in, 267, 271; population of, 267, 276–77; specter of war in, 271–73; stability in revolutionary Arab world, 273–78; as the Switzerland of Middle East, 267–68; Syria and, 236n17, 277; 2011 protest movement for civil/secular state, 266–67, 270, 271–72, 279; unlikelihood of popular revolution

media coverage: of Bahrain uprising and, 64, 79, 82, 84n2; of Iraqi protests, 311, 316, 318, 322; of Syrian uprising, 207; of Yemen uprising, 103. *See also* Al Jazeera coverage; social media, role of; *specific media*

Media Office of Great Iraqi Revolution, 318

Menoufiya, Egypt, 37, 57n4

Messadi, Mahmoud al-, 11, 12

middle class, 331–32; in Egypt, 27–28, 43, 44, 49, 51, 52; in Jordan, 257; in Lebanon, 278; in Libya, 164; Moroccan, 148; in Sudan, 327; in Syria, 209, 210, 212, 216, 230–31, 236n12, 236n16

Middle East: Arab Spring revolutionizing, vii–xiii; breakup of Ottoman Empire and, 268–69; revolutionary movement of 2011 forming single thread tying North Africa to the Gulf, 84; significance of Bahrain for patterns of foreign domination in, 65, 73–77, 83–84

migrant labor: in Bahrain, 74, 77, 79; in Lebanon, 267; in Libya, 162–63, 169, 181, 191n3–4, 193n14

militarization: limits of, as tactic in struggle, 301; in post-Qaddafi Libya, 158–59, 179–83, 195n35; of Syrian protests, 207, 231–32, 234

military political economies, 39, 55

military rule: in Algeria, 122, 123, 127–33; in Egypt, 25, 31–33, 37, 55; Qaddafi's security state in Libya, 160–61, 163

ministates: French Mandate Syria policy, 268–69

Ministère Français des Affaires Étrangères, 146

Ministry of Interior (Egypt), 31, 32

Misrata, Libya: divide between Tawergha and, 181–82

Misr Spinning and Weaving Company, 50

mobile phones, role of, 103, 213, 214, 218, 236n10. *See also* social media, role of

Mogherbi, Zahi, 180

Mohammad Mahmoud Street, battles of (2011), 53

Mohammed V (king, Morocco), 136–37, 147, 153n3–4

Mohammed VI (king, Morocco), 136, 139, 140, 153n3; constitution of 2011, 145–46, 148, 153n10; Palace's strategy of diverting accountability to elected government, 150–52; symbolic dissociation from Hassan II, 141–43; wealth of, popular disgruntlement over, 150

moral economy of protest, 125

"moral insult," 206, 235n2

moralism: hypocritical Brotherhood, 39, 55, 56

Morgan, Piers, 1, 6

Moroccan Association of Human Rights, 143

Moroccan Workers' Union (Union Marocaine du Travail, or UMT), 138

Morocco, 135–56; Arab Spring and, 143–49; challenges for future in, 149–53; colonial rule in, 137; discontent in, 149–50; economy of, 136, 138, 142–43, 149–50, 151–53; February 20 movement, 135–36, 143–45, 147–49; new strategies of power consolidation in, 140–43; traditional strategies of power consolidation in, 136–40, 153n5–6; urban/rural rift in, 137

Morsi, Mohammad: Battles of

Ittihadiya (2012) and, 35–37; Brotherhood-led presidency, 25, 33–37; cooperative security profile, 33–34; election of, 33, 47–48; labor law decree, 50–51

mosques: as sites of antigovernment protests in Syria, 219

Moudawana (Morocco's family code): reforms to, 141–42

Moussa, Amr, 48

Movement of Iraqi Youth, 314

Movement to Liberate the South of Iraq, 314

Mubarak, Mohammad Hosni, x, 1, 33, 132; aftermath of ousting of, 296; economic policy under, 34; gender segregation under, 52; Muslim Brotherhood's parliamentary participation under, 45; overthrow of, ix, xi, 2, 25, 28, 31, 42, 56n2, 114, 131, 143, 283; regime, 26, 43, 44, 52, 55; reverse development under, 27

Muhsin, General Ali, 110, 113, 115, 119

mukhabarat (secret police) of Jordan, 256

music: critique in Tunisia disseminated through, 14–16. *See also* artists

Muslim Brotherhood, 29, 30, 38; Battles of Ittihadiya (2012) and, 36–37; charity initiatives, 44; in Egypt, 25, 32–37, 45–49, 327; free Palestine, advocacy of, 248; history of, 57n3; in Jordan, 245, 247–48, 249, 252, 253, 258, 261, 262; in Libya, 188; in Syria, 209–10, 217, 219, 224, 236n12

Nabulsi, Suleiman, 247

Nafie, Nafie Ali, 331, 334

Naif (prince, Saudi Arabia), 91, 95; anti-Shiism of, 97–98; destruction of nascent reform, 97

Najifi, Atheel al-, 318

Nakba (1948), 271; historical memory of, 282–83; strategies to end, 289–93; 2011 commemoration of, 283–84, 288, 298

Naksa Day (June 5, 2011), 298

Nasrallah, Hassan, 276

Nasser, Gamal Abdel, 57n3, 247; socioeconomic advances and political repression under, 26–27

Nasserist project for Palestinian liberation, 290

National Action Charter (Bahrain), 71–73, 78

National Congress Party (NCP, Sudan), 326, 329, 336–37; divisions in, 330–31, 334, 350; manipulation of elections and vote rigging in 2010, 344–45

National Consensus Forces (NCF, Sudan), 328–29

National Constituent Assembly (Tunisia), 5, 21; elections (2011), 5, 18, 19–20

National Coordination for Change and Democracy (Algeria), 123–24

National Democratic Action Society (Bahrain), 73

National Dialogue of Political Forces (Yemen), 108

National Forces Alliance (Libya), 188

National Front for the Salvation of Libya (NFSL), 160

National Intelligence and Security Services (Sudan), 327, 331, 332

National Islamic Front (Sudan), 339, 340, 341

nationalism: radical, 287; religious, in Syria, 218–19, 222

Council and, 73–74, 75; in Libya, 160, 163, 164–66, 186–87; Saudi Arabia revenues from, 90, 94; in Sudan, 333, 336, 337, 338, 340–41, 342; in Sudan, revenues from, 348; in Sudan, secession of South Sudan and, 328; in Sudan, struggle over wealth from, 346–49

online forums, use of, 78, 85n8. *See also* Internet, role of

L'Opinion, 146

Oran, Algeria: protest in, 124

Organization of Students of Free Iraq, 314

Organization of Women's Freedom (Iraq), 317

Oslo "peace process" (Oslo Accords), 285, 290–91, 292

Ottoman Empire, 268; sectarian power-sharing formula (1861), 272

Ouadie, Salah El, 147–48

Palestine, 282–307; diaspora, 282, 283, 291, 297–98, 299; as exception, 285–86; at heart of Arab collective consciousness, 288–89, 295; history and strategy for, 289–93; internal front, 286, 298–302; liberation, strategies for, 289–93; marginal role in Arab affairs, 3; Nakba, 271, 282–84, 288, 298; refugees from, 282–86, 297–98; revolution in 2011, 296–97; run-up to Arab Spring and, 288, 293–95; suppressed narrative and history of, 286–88; United Nations partition plan for (1947), 3; UN Resolution 194 and right to return to, 282, 283, 298, 302

Palestine Liberation Organization (PLO), 3, 248, 263n6, 285, 291

Palestinian Authority (PA), 285, 291, 300

Palestinian Intifada (2000), 56n1, 251, 291, 294, 299, 301

Palestinian-led track for liberation, 290–91

Palestinian National Liberation Movement. *See* Fateh

Palestinians: in Israel, 285, 291, 302–3; in Jordan, 246, 248, 250, 262, 263n6; in Lebanon, 267, 271

pan-Africanist policy of Qaddafi, 162–63, 164, 192n8

Pan-Am bombing over Lockerbie, Scotland (1988), 161, 162

pan-Arab/Muslim bloc: Palestine and, 287

Parti de la Justice et du Développement (PJD, Morocco), 138, 143

patronage. *See* corruption

peacemaking, "preemptive," 272–73

peace talks in Sudan: external actors and, 341–46

Pearl Roundabout occupation (Bahrain, 2011), 78, 79–81

Pelletreau, Robert, 71

Peninsula Shield Command, 81

People's Bloc (Bahrain), 69

People's Democratic Republic of Yemen (PDRY), 104, 107, 111; civil war for secession (1994), 110; peaceful intifada starting 2007 in, 110; unification between North Yemen and, 108, 110

People's National Army (Algeria), 129

peripheralization of Egypt, 26

"Personal Song, A" (Youssef), 310

petrodollars, 73–74, 75. *See also* oil and gas

PFLB (Popular Front for Liberation of Bahrain), 69, 73, 80

Physicians for Human Rights, 82
Piers Morgan Tonight (TV), 1
PLO (Palestine Liberation Organization), 3, 248, 263n6, 285, 291
police: in Algeria, 124, 127, 130, 132; in Bahrain, 79; in Egypt, 31, 35, 41–43, 52; in Iraq, 314, 315; in Jordan, 243, 244, 245, 252, 253, 256, 257, 259–61; in Lebanon, 274–75; in Morocco, 137; in Saudi Arabia, religious police, 96, 97; Saudi security state and, 93; in Sudan, 332; in Syria, 205, 206
Polisario (Sahrawi independence movement), 146–47
political dissociation strategy for power consolidation in Morocco, 141–42
political instrumentation of feminism, 141–42
political Islam in Syria: as mobilizing force, 210; shift to moral reform of individuals, 210–11
political revolution, 38
political sociology of the Arab Street, vii–viii
Popular Front for Liberation of Bahrain (PFLB), 69, 73, 80
Popular Movement to Save Iraq, 314–15, 320, 322
popular sovereignty movements in Egypt, 30
Port Said massacre (2012), 33
Portsmouth Treaty (1948), 309
power: invisible substructures in Egypt of, 39–40, 41, 55–56
power consolidation strategies in Morocco, 136–43; clientelism, 140, 153n6; constitutional maneuvering, 136, 139–40, 145–46, 153n10; economic dissociation, 142–43; fragmentation, 136, 137–39; new,

140–43; political dissociation, 141–42; traditional, 136–40, 145–46, 153n5–6
precipitation of political projects: saturation of cultural idioms leading to, 221–22, 225, 229, 237n23
privatization: in Bahrain, 75, 76; in Egypt, 34, 39, 55; in Jordan, of public spaces, 257; in Libya, 187, 192n10; in Morocco, 152; in Syria, 213, 214; in Tunisia, 16, 16–17
Professional Associations Complex (Amman, Jordan), 252, 253
professionals, demonstrations by: lawyers in Iraq, 311; professional associations in Jordan, 252–53; professional syndicates in Egypt, 49–50
Progressive Democratic Tribune (Bahrain), 73
protest(s): patterns of, structured by space, 255, 256–58; strategy for mobilization, 253–54; symbolic targets of, location of, 257. *See also specific countries*
Prowler, The, 195n31
Putin, Vladimir, 233

Qaddafi, Muammar, ix, x, 89, 114, 159–66, 236n16; Abu Salim as symbol of terror under, 157–58; defections from, 187; fall of regime, xi, 131, 159; LIFG attempt to assassinate (1996), 161; pan-Africanist policy, 162–63, 164, 192n8; rapprochement with the West, 161–64, 172, 177; response to revolt of 2011, 158–59, 167–68, 170, 171, 193n19; state of repression under, 160–61; uneven treatment of different parts of country, 176

state bourgeoisie in Syria, 213–14

State Security Law (1974, Bahrain), 69, 72

Stavridis, James, 177

stereotypes in Syria, 231

Stevens, Christopher, 182, 195n40

St. John, Ronald Bruce, 160, 161

strikes: in Algeria, 123, 127; in Bahrain, 68, 69, 79; in Egypt, 29, 35, 50; in Iraq, 311–12, 318; in Jordan, 248; in Libya, 189; in Tunisia, 18; in Yemen, 106. *See also* labor; labor unions

student groups. *See* youth movements

sub-Saharan Africa: migration from, 162–63, 169, 181, 191n3; Sudan as bridge between the Arab world and, 349

Sudan, 325–53; antidemocratic Islamists of, 338–41; authoritarianism in, durability of, 330–34; centrality to politics of Arab world, 326, 349–50; in context of Arab uprisings, 327–30; Darfur conflict, 342–43, 346, 347, 349; economy of, 328–29, 333–34; ethnic, religious, and linguistic heterogeneity of both parts of, 337, 343, 344; Islamist-backed military coup of 1989, 338, 340; partition of, 326, 341–46; political exclusion, civil conflict, and struggle over oil wealth in, 346–49; root cause of multiple regional conflicts in, 347; secession and recurrence of civil conflict, 328, 335–38; three failed experiments in parliamentary democracy, 339–40, 344

Sudanese Armed Forces, 332, 337

"Sudanese exceptionalism," 330

Sudan Liberation Army: conflict in Darfur and, 342–43, 346

Sudan People's Liberation Army (SPLA), 339–40, 344

Sudan People's Liberation Movement (SPLM), 326, 331, 336–37, 339, 344–45, 347

Sudan Tribune, 344

Sufism and Sufis: description of, 235n6; Islamization of Syrian society and Sufi sheikhs, 210, 211; in Morocco, Mohammed VI and, 146; Salafi criticism of, 237n21; in Sudan, Islam promoted by Sufi, 338

suicide bombers: in Iraq, 194n29; in Syria, 232

Sulayman, Fadwa, 226

Sultan, Crown Prince, 91, 97

Sunni Muslims: in Bahrain, 66, 70, 71, 73, 74, 77, 80, 81, 83, 98; in Lebanon, 268, 269, 271; in Saudi Arabia, 93; in Syria, 208, 210, 217, 223–24, 231; in Syria, Assad's attempt to present protesters as militant, 219–21, 224, 226; in Syria, divisions within religious establishment, 228–29, 238n29; in Syria, religious nationalism and, 222; in Syria, uprising and, 222–25. *See also* Salafism; Sufism and Sufis

Supreme Constitutional Court (Egypt), 49

Supreme Council of Armed Forces (SCAF, Egypt), 31–35

Syria, 204–42; bloodletting in, xi; class and regionalism in, 229–34; contextualizing uprising in, 204–9; cultural nostalgia for 1950s in, 218, 236n16; defection from army in, 229, 231; dynamics of repression

of, 2–4, 5, 12, 13, 16, 17; challenge for postrevolutionary, 20–22; economic reform program, 16–17; educational system and literacy rate in, 12, 16; as French protectorate, 3; genealogical and polydirectional approach to revolution in, 10; National Constituent Assembly elections (2011), 5, 18, 19–20; origins of revolution in, 2–3, 6–18; Palestinian activist infrastructure and organization of protest in, 296; protests in, 326; protests in, in mining area of Gafsa in 2008, 17–18; protests in, sit-ins after revolution, 18–19; tradition of cultural critique in, 11–16, 18

Tunisia: A Journey through a Country That Works (Geyer), 16

Turabi, Hassan, 329, 341

Turkey: aspirations of, x; Syrian uprising and, 233

TV channels: Iraqi activists' use of, 311

TV's Coming, The (film), 13

Twelver Shiism, 238n26

Twitter, role of, 1, 6, 124, 133n1

UGTM (General Union of Moroccan Workers), 138

UGTT (General Union of Tunisian Workers), 18

UK Uncut movement, 28. *See also* Britain

'ulama (religious specialists), 222–25, 237n24; of Damascus and Aleppo, communiqués about 2011 uprising issued by, 222–23; in exile, Syrian uprising and, 223–24, 225; Islamization of Syrian society and, 210, 211; mobilization within Syria, 224–25

Ultras (Egyptian sports-fan clubs), 52–53

Umayyad period (661–750) in Syrian history, 219, 237n18

Umma Party (Sudan), 339

unemployment: in Algeria, 125, 126; in Bahrain, 70, 76, 77, 78, 82, 83; in Egypt, 44; in Libya, 162, 164, 192n11; in Morocco, 149; in Syria, 205; in Tunisia, 3, 17; in Yemen, 104

Unified Socialist Party (Morocco), 143

Union Feminist Action, 142

Union Nationale des Forces Populaires (UNFP, Morocco), 137

unions. *See* labor unions

Union Socialiste des Forces Populaires (USFP, Morocco), 138–39

United Nations, 209; Development Programme and Institute of National Planning, Egypt, 28; Fateh's diplomatic efforts for statehood through, 300; Human Development Index, 28; plan for post-Qaddafi Libya, 195n39; Resolution 194, 282, 283; sanctions on Libya, 161, 162; Special Tribunal for Lebanon, 267

United Nations Security Council, 193n19; lack of consensus on Syria, 233–34; no-fly zone resolution in Libya, 171; Resolution 2014 on Yemen, 117

United Press International, 184

United States: Bahrain and, 67, 71, 74, 83; Camp David Accords (1979), 293, 296; counterterrorism operations targeting al-Qaeda figures inside Yemen, 116, 119; diplomatic mission in Benghazi, September 2012 attack on, 182–83; dominance in Middle East, Arab revolts as most serious challenge to, 190; domination throughout Arab

women: Battles of Ittihadiya (2012) and, 36; in Egypt, 30; in Egypt, blue bra scandal, 32, 53; in Egypt, boundary-challenging gender solidarities, 41, 51–54; in Egypt, financing collectives led by, 43–44; in Egypt, graffiti images of martyrs, 53; in Egypt, rights under Morsi, 51; in Egypt, "virginity tests" of, 30, 31; Iraqi protest and, 312, 314, 317, 319; in Libya, future of, 189; in Morocco, political instrumentation of feminism, 141–42; Nobel Peace Prize (2011) awarded to, 102, 118–19; in Saudi Arabia, 90, 91–92; *sharshaf* worn by, 112, 117; Syrian uprising and, 229; Yemeni, protest by, 101, 112, 114, 117; Yemeni, under People's Democratic Republic of Yemen (PDRY), 107, 110

Women Journalists without Chains, 112

workers. *See* labor

working class: in Egypt, 29, 30, 42–44, 47, 49–50, 54; in Jordan, 258; in Sudan, 328; in Syria, 206

World Bank, 16, 192n7, 192n11, 194n27

World Trade Organization, 75

Ya Libnan, 266

Ya'qubi, Muhammad Abu al-Huda al-, 224, 228–29

Yehia, Karem, 20

Yekîtî (Kurdish party), 235n9

Yemen, 101–21; activist surges and public spheres in, 101–3, 105–10,
326; civic activism in, 106–10; civic consciousness in, 118–20; civil disobedience in, 114; counter-revolutionary forces in, 115–18, 119; discontent in, 104, 111; geographies of protest in, 104, 110–15; legacy of 2011 uprising, 118–20; transformative power of mobilization in, 102

Yemeni Socialist Party (YSP), 107, 108, 109, 110

Younes, Abdel Fattah, 167, 176, 178, 195n32

Youssef, Saadi, 310, 322n4

Youssoufi, Abderrahman, 138

Youth Congress of Sufi Guilds, 30

youth movements: in Algeria, 125; in Egypt, 29, 30; in Egypt, feminist groups allied with, 41, 51–54; in Iraq, 322; in Jordan, 243–47, 259–61; in Morocco, 143, 148; Palestinian, 297–98, 298–99; run-up to Arab Spring and, 294; in Sudan, protests led by students, 327, 328; in Syrian uprising, 216; in Yemen, 101, 102–3, 112, 119–20

YouTube, role of, 9, 103, 114, 124, 147, 224, 263n1

Zaidi, Muntadher al-, 314, 316

Zaidi, Uday al-, 314, 318, 320, 322, 323n9

Zionism, 287, 289, 302, 303. *See also* Israel

Ziu, Mahdi, 167

Zran, Mohamed, 12–13